SMOKE AND MIRRORS

SPECIAL VISUAL EFFECTS B.C.
(BEFORE COMPUTERS)

BY
MARK D. WOLF

SMOKE AND MIRRORS
Special Visual Effects B.C. (Before Computers)

Copyright © 2021 by Mark D. Wolf

All pictorial matter reproduced herein derives from the voluntary, non-compensated contributions of pictorial or other memorabilia from the private collections of the author and from the select private archives of individual contributors.

All rights reserved. No part of this work may be reproduced or used in any form or by any means—graphic, electronic, or mechanical, including photocopying or information storage and retrieval systems—without written permission from the publisher.

The scanning, uploading, and distribution of this book or any part thereof via the Internet or any other means without the permission of the publisher is illegal and punishable by law. Please purchase only authorized editions and do not participate in or encourage the electronic piracy of copyrighted materials.

"BearManor Media" and the bear logo are registered trademarks of BearManor Media.

Layout and graphic design by Ernest Farino

Text set in Lucida Sans and Gill Sans

ISBN: 978-1-62933-653-4

Published by BearManor Media
P.O. Box 71426
Albany, GA 31708
E-mail: orders@benohmart.com
Phone: 580-252-3547
Fax: 800-332-8092

See our 900+ books at:
www.bearmanormedia.com

Join our Newsletter for coupons, freebies & news!
http://eepurl.com/MNDT5

Join our Facebook page too!
https://www.facebook.com/BearManor-Media-153720364638943/

We are always looking for people to write books on new and related subjects. If you have an idea for a book, please contact Ben Ohmart: books@benohmart.com

Smoke and Mirrors
Special Visual Effects B.C.
(Before Computers)

Preface	4
Chapter One Little Things, Big Results	7
Chapter Two Spectacle—On Glass	39
Chapter Three Men In Suits	83
Chapter Four Prop It Up	133
Chapter Five Reel Scenes with Real People	197
Chapter Six It's All A Matter of Optics	223
Chapter Seven After the Good: The Bad and The Ugly	253
Footnotes	267
Acknowledgements	269
Bibliography	270

DEDICATION

I dedicate this book to my older brother, **Richard C. Wolf, Jr.**, who introduced me to a life-long love of science-fiction, starting by reading the novels of Jules Verne to me when I was a small child. In 1955 he took me along on a road trip to see a new movie called *Conquest of Space* (1955), and years later drove us to see *Minotaur, The Wild Beast of Crete* (*Teseo contro il minotauro*, 1960), which we soon discovered was an awful Italian import. In the 1960s, while visiting him in Madison, Wisconsin, he made sure I got to revel in the fantastic sights and sounds of my first Saturday matinee marathon, consisting of *It Conquered the World* (1956), *War of the Satellites*, (1958), and *Night of the Blood Beast* (1958) because he knew I was frothing at the mouth to see them. I was in B-movie and special effects heaven!

PREFACE

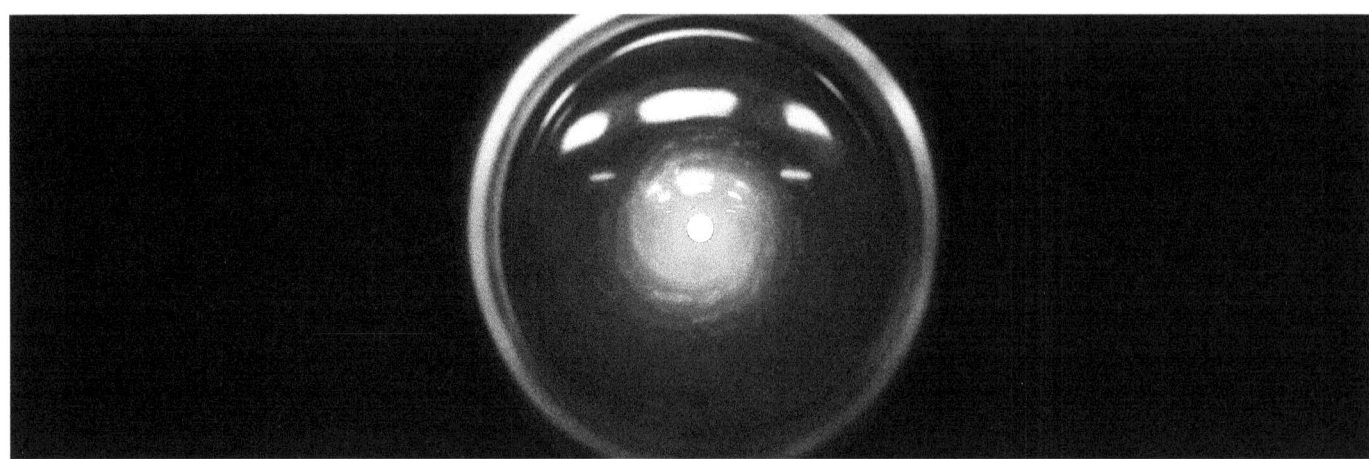

"I'm sorry, Dave. I'm afraid I can't do that."

Oh, yes they could!

It may come as a shock to those under thirty that, prior to today's "digital" reality, producers relied on clever artists and resourceful technicians who, by trial-and-error, learned photochemical processes, mechanical systems, and mastered new materials— all with the goal of realizing a Director's vision.

My purpose with this book is to acknowledge with the deepest respect those hearty souls who, through sheer force of will and abundant talent, overcame considerable limitations to deliver iconic moments of the cinema, such as a giant ape atop the Empire State Building in *King Kong* (1933). These passionate cinematic magicians, modern Renaissance Artists, were responsible for delivering what those of us in the industry call "money shots"—those spectacular moments that give producers—and the audience—the most visual bang for their buck.

Remember, there were no classes, no books, no manuals, no YouTube videos instructing them on how-to-do-it. From within they found the inspiration to apply themselves to literally inventing and perfecting the nuts and bolts of hand-making motion picture special effects. Their proficiency devising solutions provided filmmakers with options to produce stories that would have otherwise been prohibitively expensive, dangerous or flat-out impossible to make.

While a college student in the early 1970s I wrote a number of groundbreaking articles on special visual effects for *Cinefantastique* magazine, the first time anyone had tried to do scholarly articles discussing these processes while also giving credit to the mostly-unknown, unsung heroes who created the wonders. With a particular interest in the work of stop-motion maestro Ray Harryhausen, I was proud to make contributions to the legendary fanzine *FXRH*, which was dedicated to his films and career. Articles I wrote for numerous publications led me to meet many legendary filmmakers who became my mentors when I made them aware I was doing my own home experiments in an attempt to follow in their footsteps. This book is a culmination of my early passion about special effects enhanced by my own experiences in Hollywood.

In the spirit of my original articles, I have tried to acknowledge many of the pioneers, especially those who rightly deserve to be included in any historical overview. That being said, some deserving people unavoidably have been left out, simply because it is beyond the scope of this volume to include every person who built a miniature, painted a matte, glued on a rubber appliance, or pushed an animation puppet.

There may be instances where something or someone isn't covered in the text but will appear in the photos accompanying the main text or in the "Scrapbook" section at the end of each chapter. Companies and individuals who have received in-depth coverage elsewhere will not receive similar attention in my limited space here.

In motion pictures, nowhere has the reality of the technological leap into digital been more obvious than in the creation of special visual effects. Philosophically-speaking, CGI (Computer Generated Imagery) is the latest evolution of techniques which can be traced back to a parade of advances such as matte paintings, miniatures, rear projection and blue screen traveling mattes. Today, armies of "digital gypsies" equipped with the latest hardware, software and vast budgets comparable to the Gross National Product of some nations, can do literally anything—without the need for mold-makers, sculptors, or modelers. Scale miniatures, for instance, now seem to be the province of select filmmakers like Christopher Nolan and Wes Anderson.

My time frame covers the earliest days up until the bombshell of **Jurassic Park** (1993), the motion picture that truly ushered in the transition away from traditional special visual effects to CGI, usually just called CG these days. Some may criticize that my disenchantment with digital technologies is based on the negative impact that the transition to digital had on my own career. While it is true I made a living using traditional techniques like stop-motion, matte paintings, miniatures, motion control, and makeup effects, in 2008, Hollywood was decimated by a perfect trifecta of devastating events: a general financial meltdown, increasing runaway production from Los Angeles, and the accelerating transition away from celluloid-based filmmaking. My disappointment with CG is a combination of things relating to overall industry practices, and, as movie production has shifted to other venues here and abroad, I am wistful as the proud slogan, "Made in Hollywood" fades away.

The use of CG brought an unforeseen issue: films no longer had a distinctive "look." Consider that in the original **Raiders of the Lost Ark** (1981), Industrial Light and Magic's world-class miniatures, matte paintings, and cel animation swept audiences along on an eye-popping adventure unlike anything seen before—not counting Republic serials. ILM had methodically found its own style over numerous productions, but by the time of **Indiana Jones and the Kingdom of the Crystal Skull** (2008) the facility had transitioned largely to CG software that was essentially the same as what was being used by companies in India, China, Africa or Cedar Rapids, Iowa. Their work no longer had the distinctive "ILM" personality.

Even before the global pandemic of 2020 brought a seismic upheaval to motion picture exhibition around the world, executives did not understand that the biggest threat to the industry was that only immense-budgeted feature franchises were being made that relied on CG eye-candy to attract audiences. Unfortunately, these same people put special visual effects into the unenviable position of being the "tail that wags the dog," as story, plot and characterization were largely ignored.

Thankfully, there was a response to this as cable networks like AMC and FX punched above their weight to produce compelling entertainment such as **Breaking Bad** (2008-2013) and **The Shield** (2002-2008). Cable outlets became a refuge for filmmakers who wanted to tell stories that grabbed audiences, not just parade special effects across a screen. They used CG appropriately—often in conjunction with traditional effects—to help tell the story, not *be* the story.

In the era of the pandemic, streamers like HBO Max, Netflix, Amazon Prime and Apple+ have enjoyed significant subscriber growth and are willing to spend billions taking risks on new, unproven concepts that have racked up critical acclaim, audience loyalty and Emmys. Disney has announced it will be focusing on streaming instead of theatrical releases, in part because of their tremendous success with their **Star Wars** and **Marvel** franchise series.

In all fairness, credit should be given where due, and the digital arsenal has made it possible for dynamic regional filmmakers like Brett Piper to do more with less.

I have been privileged to receive generous contributions from the world's foremost film historians and in many cases, the filmmakers themselves, with many of whom I have had the great pleasure of working. They have filled in the gaps in my own collection of photos to share rare behind-the-scenes pictures. I am eternally grateful for their participation!

In 1966 it was a writer's gimmick for **The Man From U.N.C.L.E.**, the popular MGM TV series, when super-spy Napoleon Solo would call his boss, Mr. Waverly, at headquarters in New York City from anywhere in the world on a handheld mobile communications device. Now, when I see my grandkids using their iPhones, it reinforces to this baby-boomer that what **Popular Mechanics** magazine visualized fifty years ago as science-fiction predictions have indeed come to pass.

In this Brave New World of special visual effects, I hope this illustrated history will inspire filmmakers to adapt these tried-and-true techniques to modern productions like **The Mandalorian** (2019-2020).

As you experience the evolution of motion picture special effects, I'm sure you will have a new appreciation of the people and art forms that delighted, dazzled, and even terrified audiences!

And if you feel like applauding the artists who made it all possible, I'll join you...

— **Mark D. Wolf**
Grass Valley, California
June, 2021

For **Custer of the West** (1967), the crew of acclaimed Spanish craftsman Francisco Prosper built this highly-detailed civil war-era locomotive and sent it across miniature landscapes that duplicated the American west, including this dramatic trestle. Eugene Lourié—who had directed **The Beast from 20,000 Fathoms** (1953), **The Giant Behemoth** (1959), and **Gorgo** (1961)—was the production designer/special effects director and Fernando Gonzalez was the art director. In this photo, camera operator Eduardo Noe sits on the crane while Lourié observes from the ladder at right.

Chapter 1
Little Things, Big Results

On the stage at Paramount, technicians prep the miniature ark for George Pal's **When Worlds Collide** (1953), which won an Oscar® for special visual effects. The spaceship currently resides in the collection of Bob Burns.

Almost as soon as the cinema was born, films exploited motion picture-specific techniques to tell their stories. Thomas A. Edison's **The Execution of Mary, Queen of Scots** (1895), often mentioned as the first film with a narrative, had an additional first: the earliest use of a special effect to enable showing startled audiences the "actual" decapitation of the Queen (Mrs. Robert L. Thomas). The actors stood still in their positions while a dummy was substituted for the victim, and then the "execution" action proceeded. When the moments before and after the substitution of the dummy were edited together, the illusion was of a continuous event—and the use of visual effects grew exponentially afterwards. The film was also the beginning of an endless stream of exploitation films in the cinema that continues to this day, where producers use violence, sex or other gimmicks—like 3D—to sell box-office tickets.

Thomas A. Edison's Edison Manufacturing Company had a division called The Kinetograph Department which manufactured and sold Kinetoscopes, as well as also filming and distributing content—primarily comedies and documentaries. As soon as 1900, a growing number of titles such as **The Magician**, **An Artist's Dream**, **Uncle Josh in a Spooky Hotel** and **Uncle Josh's Nightmare** used the simple pop-on/pop-off technique to entertain audiences. The **Uncle Josh** films were possibly the earliest examples of franchise filmmaking.

For **A Railway Collision** (1900) director W.R. Booth and producer Robert W. Paul (of Paul's Animatograph Works) made this short 22-second film, which is one of the earliest attempts to realistically

Little Things, Big Results • 7

*This 1910 French card was part of a series, **Tricks of the Cinema** by Liebig beef gravy. It shows the behind-the-scenes filming of a model train on a tabletop landscape in front of a painted backdrop.*

re-create a railroad disaster by using miniatures; the film depicted two trains speeding toward each other on the same track, and colliding on a tabletop landscape.

In 1901, documentaries like **The Pan-American Exposition at Night** and **President McKinley's Funeral Cortege at Buffalo, NY** were still the most numerous titles in the Edison catalog, but filmmakers working under Edison's umbrella were moving beyond simple pop-on/pop-off effects to satisfy audiences that were becoming increasingly more sophisticated and demanding.

The film **Sampson-Schley Controversy** (1901) shows how inventive they were becoming by utilizing a forced perspective set for two angles; for one shot, an actor is positioned in the left foreground while a miniature dreadnaught (battleship) "sails" out from behind a nearby cliff, fires its guns at a fortress atop the cliff, turns around, and, as it departs, a second ship steams out.

In a second angle, using the same background set with a new foreground set piece representing a coastal gun emplacement, several actors load and fire at the distant ship, eventually sinking it with a second shot but not before one of the crew members servicing the gun is killed! It shows an astonishingly sophisticated understanding of how to incorporate the set and models with live performers and pyrotechnics.

Edison's release of **Jack and the Beanstalk** (1902) was made under the watchful eye of Edwin S. Porter, who had joined Edison's company in 1899; it features two sets with perspectivized backdrops ala **Sampson-Schley Controversy**. One features a relatively complex design that includes an artificial waterfall in the background while a water wheel in the foreground is turned by real water. Jack uses multiple camera tricks, such as pop-on/pop-off, dissolves (which Porter invented), a wire to raise a prop beanstalk, a flock of prop birds, a stand-in dummy for the falling giant and even a cow costume.

By the time of **The Great Train Robbery** (1903) Porter was comfortable using in-camera static mattes to add a view outside the ticket office window and from within a train car watching the outside zoom past. Porter's cross-cutting editing was another breakthrough that helped account for the film's tremendous success.

Porter's **The Night Before Christmas** (1905) stars live performers on sets and an outdoor location—appearing with live reindeer—following the Clement Clarke Moore poem from 1823. The highlight of the film is the ending: a continuous shot that goes on and on and on as the camera follows Santa's sleigh, pulled by his magical reindeer, as they journey from his North Pole mansion across a snowy landscape, up into the night sky, and race through falling snow before touching down on a rooftop. This was accomplished by rotating a tabletop landscape with slots that allowed a sleigh and mechanically-activated reindeer to pass though the settings, even into the "night sky!" Considering when this was made, it is mind-boggling in complexity and remains charming today; it must have thoroughly captivated audiences at the time. In fact, I would defy any professionals today to duplicate this on something comparable to Porter's budget!

While some of Edison's releases utilized assorted effects, and his Mannikin Films with special effects pioneer Willis H. O'Brien explored a new form of animation (stop-motion), it was a contemporary rival of Edison's who deserves to be honored as the true "Father of Special Effects": Frenchman Georges Méliès.

Méliès specialized in making fantastic films that were highlighted by enthralling special effects, and his library of titles required extensive use of miniatures, custom props, carefully painted sets, animatronics, and more. Acclaimed Director D.W. (David Wark) Griffith praised Méliès with the compliment, "I owe him everything." [1]

After the USS *Maine* sank in Havana harbor in February, 1898, Edison released documentaries **Burial of the Maine Victims** and

The Wreck of the Battleship Maine, while Méliès released a cleverly staged short, ***Divers at Work on the Wreck of the Maine*** (1898). Méliès film used a carefully painted set of the wrecked ship, actors wearing diving suits, and special effects such as a prop sailor's body to heighten the believability. The picture appears to have been filmed through an aquarium with live fish and bubbles to enhance the illusion of being underwater (though it is possible the fish were added as a double-exposure) and should be regarded as one of the earliest examples of recreating events "torn from the headlines" in the era before radio and television.

While some might dismiss this as the original "fake news" we hear so much about today, it clearly shows the philosophical difference in their approaches to making films. Edison was an inventor and businessman, not a creative-type, whereas Méliès was a showman dedicated to giving viewers bigger and better value for their patronage.

Méliès was in that first audience watching the Lumière brothers' Cinematographe on December 28, 1895, and it was an electrifying, life-changing event for the theatre owner/stage performer/magician. He became so enthused that he tried to buy a camera from the brothers. They refused to sell one to him, but, undeterred, he soon purchased a projector from Englishman Robert W. Paul, a machine based on an Edison Kinetoscope that Paul had purchased after he had discovered Edison had not patented his device in England. Inspired by Méliès' films, Paul would make many trick films himself, such as ***The "?" Motorist*** (1906).

After buying a Bioscope camera, Méliès started out as a documentarian like the Lumières, content to simply film day-to-day events. He presented these at his Théâtre Robert-Houdin, which he had founded in 1896. Later, he expanded his content, performing some of his magic tricks on-camera, quickly understanding the unique storytelling power of the medium.

Méliès improved upon the equipment of others, building improved versions of projectors and

*Georges Méliès' concept art for **Voyage to the Moon** (1902). His stage background made him the ideal person to embrace and refine trick films, which became the "Marvel movies" of the era.*

lab printers. But soon his need for better gear prompted him to hire two engineers to help him custom-design a camera, which reportedly weighed 75 pounds. Thanks to a camera jam, when viewing the processed footage, Meliés was startled to witness a bus seemingly transform into a hearse—by stopping and starting his camera he had accidentally discovered a simple editorial device: the pop-on/pop-off substitution (later used by Edison). The technique became one of Méliès' most consistently-used tools.

Some researchers incorrectly refer to the technique as "stop-motion." True stop-motion animation, however, is the sequential choreography of models photographed one frame at a time so, when projected, the animated characters move on their own, "performing" as though they were alive.

To make his films, Méliès built the first movie studio in Europe in 1897, made of glass to admit plenty of sunlight and incorporating trapdoors, overhead winches, and more devices that facilitated his growing catalog of effects. He was the first to use production sketches and storyboards, many of which were captioned in French *and* English. He recognized the importance of the American market and opened an office in New York City in 1903, run by his brother, Gaston, who had assisted Georges' writing and producing films in Paris. Méliès would shoot two negatives of each of his films, one of which would be sent to the U.S. for laboratory use in making release prints.

His stage background provided the training for him to paint imaginative backdrops and fabricate set pieces so he could fearlessly tackle ambitious fantasies few of his contemporaries could even contemplate. During his career, he produced over 500 films, many of which survive and have been

restored, especially **Voyage to the Moon** (1902), which many consider the first science-fiction movie, or the incredible **Conquest of the Pole** (1912) starring the first giant movie-monster. These epic productions showcased an assured craftsman/performer who was exercising his creative muscles to their fullest.

Charles Chaplin called him the "alchemist of light" (2) and acclaimed director Martin Scorsese summed up Méliès in this way: "Meliés actually was a magician. And so he understood the possibilities of the motion picture camera. He invented everything. Basically, he invented it all." (3)

Soon the new industry saw an increasing demand for longer films, which helped push the emergence of quality visual effects methods. After World War One, gifted craftsmen/technicians made it possible for silent-era audiences to be staggered by the parting of the Red Sea in **The 10 Commandments** (1923) and gasp at the ferocious dinosaurs of **The Lost World** (1925). The gamut of special effects, from water tank storms to exploding buildings to making creatures, appeared in all genres, from westerns to musicals, from war films to comedies. Special effects show up in films where you wouldn't normally expect to see something requiring visual effects. For instance, for the silent western **Black Cyclone** (1926), Joseph L. Roop animated a thrilling combat between a heroic horse and a ferocious mountain lion using stop-motion puppet "stunt animals," on a detailed tabletop landscape.

As cinema matured, assorted processes showed varying degrees of improvements over what Edison's producers and Méliès had done, and refinements in miniatures made them one of the foremost "tools of the trade." That is, craftsmen perfected the fabricating of smaller-scale versions of buildings, aircraft, automobiles, ships—and more—with sufficient detail so that, when properly lit and photographed, they would appear life-sized. Miniatures were made from

*Above: The miniature at UFA for Fritz Lang's **The Woman in the Moon** (1929).*

*Below: Two unidentified men on the London street miniature for **The Lost World** (1925). Willis O'Brien's marauding brontosaurus set the pattern for decades to come.*

wood, plaster, paper, metal, and other materials, and the larger the models could be made, the more effective ships, especially, would be. This applied especially to ship in water: Experience determined that 1/16 scale full-sized ships were the smallest size that could look realistic in water, which was always troublesome because water cannot be miniaturized. Wetting agents such as detergent or thickeners like Du Pont's food grade CMC controlled surface tension which reduced the size of droplets and splashes.

Photographing miniatures became an art in itself and followed the basic rule that the camera speed should be the square root of the scale. For example, a 1/4-inch-to-the-foot model is 1/16 full-size and will thus require shooting at four times normal camera speed, which would mean 96 frames-per-second (i.e., four times 24 fps). Shooting at high speed honors the laws of physics, giving smaller objects a more believable mass to size ratio, making them more realistic, such as the exploding big rig tanker truck in *The Terminator* (1984).

The studios developed departments that focused on the visual effects challenges for their in-house slate of movies. With miniatures, it became convenient, economically feasible, and safe to provide catastrophes on demand to enhance the drama of the stories and encourage better box-office. In most cases, miniatures were used as part of a mix of techniques depending on what the story demanded. For instance, life-sized set elements populated with stunt performers were combined with miniatures to dramatically recreate historic events like the 1906 earthquake in *San Francisco* (1936), the raging conflagration of *In Old Chicago* (1938), the sinking of the *Titanic* (in several films), the recreation of the massive volcanic eruption of 1883 in *Krakatoa East of Java* (1968), and more.

They were all following in the traditions of Edison and Méliès...

Director John Ford's *The Hurricane* (1937), based on a novel by Charles Nordhoff and James Norman Hall, is highlighted by the main title "star's" massive destruction created by visual effects veteran James Basevi (and his assistant, Robert Layton), who had departed from MGM in September, 1936, after supervising the earthquake simulations for the studio's successful *San Francisco*. According to an article in *LIFE* magazine, November 22, 1937:

"Sam Goldwyn allocated a budget of $400,000, of which $150,000 was spent to build a native village, complete with a 200 yard lagoon and the remaining $250,000 was spent destroying it."

The U.S. pressbook claims the native village set built for the talent to perform on—and be destroyed—took up two-and-a-half acres of the United Artists studio backlot. Staging the hurricane required several twelve-cylinder Liberty motor wind machines, paddle-mounted wave generators, high-pressure fire hoses and piping that fed chutes and dump tanks that could release thousands of gallons of water on cue.

In her 1959 autobiography *My Story*, actress Mary Astor described the rigors the performers went through during the storm:

"Huge propellers kept us fighting for every step, with sand and water whipping our faces, sometimes leaving little pinpricks of blood on our cheeks from the stinging sand." **(5)**

Because natural disasters were inherently dramatic, they were key elements of many stories that kept special effects technicians busy—and earning Oscar® nominations for *The Rains Came* (1939), *Typhoon* (1940), *The Rains of Ranchipur* (1955)—a re-make of *The Rains Came*—*Hawaii* (1966) and the Oscar®-winning *Earthquake* (1974). However, the most memorable weather-related scenes from any film are those with the tornado in the beloved classic, *The Wizard of*

Oz (1939), which was created by A. Arnold Gillespie and his crew at Metro-Goldwyn-Mayer.

Gillespie had a budget of $8,000 and shot a test with a water vortex, which he rejected, and then tried using an inverted thirty-five foot tall rubber cone, which was too rigid. As an aviator, he recalled that airport wind socks resembled the basic configuration of a tornado, which prompted him to design a muslin cloth "tornado" built over chicken wire that was sufficiently flexible so it could weave and react to stresses on it when maneuvered through the scene.

The top of the thirty-five foot tapered muslin tornado was rotated by a motor connected to a steel gantry that was purpose-built for the sequence by Bethlehem Steel (at a cost of more than $12,000) and could travel the length of the stage. The bottom of the tornado fed into a slot in the stage floor attached to a car below the miniature that the crew could pull along while a control rod came up through the base of the tornado to pull it from side to side; by simultaneously moving the gantry and rod in opposite directions, the tornado would energetically move around.

Unfortunately, the action was too strenuous and the muslin tore loose at the bottom; the fabric was then laced with thin, metallic music wire to reinforce it, which was a tedious undertaking as some poor crew member had to be inside the tornado to poke the needle with the wire back out after each stitch.

To enhance the illusion of debris flying around the tornado, fullers earth—a brown powder made from clay—was blown into the base and the top of the muslin by compressed air. Because the muslin was porous some of the fuller's earth migrated through the sides of the fabric, further contributing to the realistic flotsam and jetsam.

Several feet in front of the cameras, two large panels of glass were positioned with grey balls of cotton affixed so that when the panels were moved in opposite directions the illusion of churning detritus was enhanced while also conveniently hiding the gantry and top of the tornado. Dorothy's house and barn were scaled at 3/4" to 1'; the house was not more than three feet high and adjacent cornfields were about three inches tall.

It has been reported that dense clouds of yellow-black smoke made from sulfur and carbon were added to the scenes from a catwalk above the gantry to simulate rainfall. In those days, no one had respirators and some of the stage hands became ill, coughing up black-yellow mucous days later. I can understand what they went through, having used bee smokers, which burned small discs made of pine needles, paper egg cartons, and rotten wood, to "fog up" sets (commonly seen, for example, in Universal's Sherlock Holmes films), and that smoke was unpleasant in enclosed spaces. The *Oz* crew's experience sounds similar to health hazards encountered today by those using fiberglass, polyester resins, and polyurethanes.

Shots of the tornado were used as rear-projected backgrounds behind performers like Judy Garland while wind machines blew the performers hair and clothing and the crew tossed dried leaves at them. The tornado was the costliest special effect in **The Wizard of Oz**, but it was money well-spent to earn itself a place as one of the most unforgettable moments

Willis O'Brien holds a scale model ship from **The Last Days of Pompeii** *(1935). This was an unsatisfying show for OBie because most of his pre-production concepts were abandoned.*

in movie history. Incidentally, for *Poltergeist* (1982), the sound effects team created a sound for the tornado in that film and Spielberg rejected it, asking for something to sound more like the one in *Oz*. So they used the MGM sound effect!

Krakatoa East of Java (1969)—which is actually *west* of Java—reminds me that volcanic eruptions have always been grand opportunities for using a combination of mechanical effects, miniatures and opticals. *The Last Days of Pompeii* (1935) was a Merian C. Cooper production with visuals designed and supervised by Willis H. O'Brien, who had worked with Cooper on *King Kong* (1933).

OBie, as he was affectionately known, had previous experience creating an erupting volcano for his kandmark *The Lost World* (1925). For *Pompeii*, he spectacularly delivered the goods, demolishing Roman temples and statuary—and crushing fleeing crowds! The high speed miniatures were filmed as he called out directions to his crew—which included many *Kong* alumni like Byron Crabbe—during filming via a microphone and loudspeaker. Remember that models are filmed at high frame rates to better simulate real-world physics when the final film is projected but the action must be staged rapidly on the tabletop, requiring much planning to properly execute. The film should have had an Oscar® nomination but the category did not exist until 1938.

Volcanic pyrotechnics and lava are vividly displayed in Hal Roach's Oscar®-nominated *One Million B.C.* (1940) which was supervised by Roy Seawright; the most memorable shot shows a cave woman engulfed by a rapidly advancing "river of lava," accomplished by a flawless hand-rotoscoped traveling matte that composited a live actress with a well-designed and photographed miniature. Hammer Films' re-make, *One Million Years B.C.* (1966), with visual effects supervised by Ray Harryhausen, also clearly shows that cave people were no match for the fury of mother nature's miniatures!

Lava—made of colored oatmeal—appears in George Pal's outstanding version of H.G. Wells'

*Top, left: "Lava" (oatmeal) flows down a miniature street in **The Time Machine** (1960), which won an Oscar® for Project Unlimited's Wah Chang, Gene Warren, Sr., and Tim Barr.*

*Top, right: Scale vessels and a storm at sea in **Plymouth Adventure** (1952) earned A. A. Gillespie an Oscar®.*

*Left: L.B.Abbott and crew film the attack on Pearl Harbor for **Tora! Tora! Tora!** (1970).*

*Above: Natural sunlight made the fifty-foot volcano for **The Devil at 4 O'Clock** (1961) more realistic, and its size allowed for detonations of huge fireballs.*

The Time Machine (1960), with Oscar®-winning visual effects supervised by Gene Warren, Sr., Wah Chang and Tim Barr at their special effects shop, Project Unlimited. The crew spent the day prepping the scene where lava flows down a street after an "atomic satellite" strikes nearby and then broke for the evening. Returning the next morning, they were ready to shoot and as the cameras rolled, the lava was released from a storage tank... unfortunately, the mixture had soured overnight and poor cinematographer Wah Chang was splashed with the slimy, stinky mess! He and the miniature had to be cleaned up and prepared for Take 2—which came off without a hitch.

On other productions, colored bentonite (oil well drilling mud) or Methocel mixed with vermiculite achieved the same look. For scenes

Using Spanish technicians, Eugene Lourié (above) designed this hanging miniature for ***Crack in the World*** (1965).

*Above: The original **Ben-Hur** (1925) has an exciting introduction to the colosseum where the chariot race will he held, with the camera moving forward into the arena where hundreds of spectators can be seen. The bottom section of the live action arena was populated with Hollywood stars who were invited to participate in the fun. The top section was a beautifully detailed hanging miniature (also called a "foreground miniature" or, as Vincent Korda called them, a "front miniature"), so named because they were placed in front of the camera supported by scaffolding. There is a slight bump as the camera was slid into a mount that ensured the miniature and live action area were properly registered to each other, but overall the effect is quite convincing. The "crowd" of small-scale people could rise on cue and wave their arms, to help give the scene more life!*

Mark Wolf's special effects company, Wizard Works, based at Roger Corman's studio in Venice, California, provided motion control, makeup effects, special props, and stop-motion, but was best-known for hanging miniature "money shots" created for budget-challenged films such as Fred Olen Ray's **Phantom Empire** (1988) (above and middle). Wolf's production **Slave Girls from Beyond Infinity** (1987) made use of his whole bag of tricks. In its September 29, 1987 review, **Variety** marveled how a low-budget production managed "a large set," not realizing this castle interior was done with a hanging miniature (above).

showing the bubbling caldera, thinned Cream-of-Wheat with fluorescent-orange clumps was used.

A menacing volcano is the main title "star," that shares the screen with Frank Sinatra and Spencer Tracy in **The Devil at 4 O'Clock** (1961). For **Devil**, an eighteen foot diameter steel tube was positioned on a hill located at the Larry Butler Ranch in Fallbrook, California, and the built-up ground around it was "sculpted" with high pressure hoses to simulate natural-looking terrain. Steel mortars inside the fifty-foot volcano were loaded with carbon black and chunks of cork while gasoline bombs were also positioned and rigged with electrically-fired squibs (also known as bullet hits) for detonation. When fired, the action was shot at 96 frames-per-second to help give the flames and smoke more mass when viewed at normal 24 fps.

Magnificent ocean liners, heavily-armed war ships, paddlewheel river boats, and all-manner of sailing ships have frequently been represented via miniatures; in some cases they have been fanciful such as those seen in **The Big Broadcast of 1938** (1938) starring W.C. Fields and Bob Hope and the Oscar®-winning **20,000 Leagues Under the Sea** (1954) which featured the unforgettable *Nautilus* submarine. In other cases, they have represented earlier historical times such as Errol Flynn's pirate vessel in the Oscar®-nominated **The Sea Hawk** (1940) or the Oscar®-winning schooners—and giant squid—of **Reap the Wild Wind** (1942). **Plymouth Adventure** (1952) featured the Puritan's *Mayflower* on its dangerous voyage to America, and won an Oscar® for MGM's visual effects department. Throughout World War Two, battleships, aircraft carriers, and submarines were all convincingly staged in films, like Oscar®-winner **Crash Dive** (1942), and for nominees **The Navy Comes Through** (1942), **Stand By for Ac-**

Little Things, Big Results • 15

tion (1943) and John Ford's *They Were Expendable* (1945).

That tradition carried on with Oscar®-winners *The Enemy Below* (1957) and *Tora! Tora! Tora!* (1970), both featuring work by L.B. Abbott and Howard Lydecker.

Miniatures achieved the same illusion as a glass shot or matte painting but eliminated concerns about glass reflections or breakage, and also were not constrained to matching the *painted* direction of the sun and time of day. *The Thief of Bagdad* (1940) and *The Jungle Book* (1942) feature superb hanging miniature shots.

During the silent era the Germans used hanging miniatures to good effect in *Scheherazade* (*ca.* 1920) and other films, while they appear in U.S. productions such as Douglas Fairbanks' *The Black Pirate* (1926). Europeans continued to use them after the transition to sound production. Art director-turned-director Eugene Lourié supervised some convincing hanging miniatures for Errol Flynn's *The Adventures of Captain Fabian* (1951) and in 1965 for *Crack in the World*.

One of the foremost specialists of building and staging hanging miniatures was Spanish craftsman Emilio Ruiz del Rio, who did shots for Dino de Laurentiis' *Conan the Barbarian* (1982), *Dune* (1984), and many others. *(More about del Rio in the matte painting chapter.)*

In fact, hanging miniatures offered a very economical solution if properly designed and set-up. In the U.S., art director Mike Minor used a foreground miniature in *Star Trek: The Wrath of Khan* (1982) to enhance a scene in which McCoy and Kirk have a conversation in a hallway. Steve Koch Studio offered hanging miniatures, special props and tabletops as part of their production solutions for clients in the 1980s. In the 1990s, Steve expanded his horizons and became very well-respected for his special makeup effects, working with Rick Baker and others. Terry Huud produced foreground miniatures for *Spaced Invaders* (1990) while also providing miniatures and custom props for a host of projects, including the groundbreaking interactive series *Captain Power and the Soldiers of the Future* (1988), James Cameron's *The Abyss* (1989), and others.

Les Bowie, who seems to have contributed miniatures, matte paintings and/or special props to almost every Hammer film, came up with some highly effective foreground miniatures for Hammer's early foray into science fiction, *X the Unknown* (1956). The effects required Bowie-Margutti Ltd. to reach deep into their bag of tricks. Les Bowie and Vic Margutti's uncredited team included Roy Field (opticals), Ray Caple (matte artist) and Brian Johncock (later to win an Oscar® as Brian Johnson for *Alien* in 1979 and *The Empire Strikes Back* in 1980). I admire the excellence of their miniature shots in spite of minuscule budgets.

It has been claimed that to create the creature in *X*, Bowie pasted small fishing worms onto a basic form and shot the prop in a 6'x6' water tank. I cannot say for certain, but I don't detect any squirming

or writhing as if there are small worms in it, not to mention that shooting in such tanks is extremely time-consuming, requires extra lighting units, and generally just eats up budgets. Rather, it seems more likely that they often chose to do things more simply, sometimes as small scale tabletops and in some cases literally rolling the creature over a photographic enlargement of a background—a technique used liberally in *The Blob* (1958).

The Blob was the brainchild of Jack H. Harris, a distributor who had released over 500 films by the time he decided to make his first feature, which was produced through the auspices of Valley Forge Film Studios in Pennsylvania, which had previously only made 150 short, religious-themed films. The studio was headed by Methodist minister Irvin S. 'Shorty' Yeaworth, Jr., who had previously directed and co-produced *The Flaming Teenage* (1956) and who would direct *The Blob* over a 31-day shoot. He and Harris would later team-up on *The 4D Man* (1959) and *Dinosaurus!* (1960).

The visual effects needed nine months to finish and required a combination of verve and creative skill to overcome the budget limitations. These films defied tight budgets with enthusiasm and ingenuity. In an interview with Tom Weaver in *B-Movie Makers*, Jack H. Harris said, "The Blob was made of silicone, which was kind of a new thing at that time. We discovered that we could achieve varying degrees of consistency, from that of running water to hard glue, and we varied our consistencies to meet the requirements of each scene. There were a couple of scenes in which we used a barrage balloon, covered with goop and pulled along on a fishing line. And there were times when the Blob was airbrushed and animated—it all depended on the situation. Vegetable coloring gave it the red color; it got redder and redder as it grew and consumed more people. One thing we never resolved was: How do you keep the color in there? We just had to keep mixing it, like cake batter, otherwise it would all settle to the bottom.

"The most we worked with was about a washtub full. Naturally we couldn't afford to cover a *[full-size]* diner with The Blob, so what we did there was photograph the diner through a bent bellows to give it dimension. To correct any minute flaws we enhanced the photograph with touch-up and air-brushing. We then mounted it on plywood, set it up on an eight-foot-square gyroscope-operated table and tied cameras to the table, rock-steady. Then we were able to move the table in any direction we wanted; the Blob, of course, would always follow gravity. When we wanted he Blob to jump on the 'diner,' we put it on there and got it to jump off with a quick movement of the table. That footage shown in reverse, gave us our effect." **(6)**

Harris was referring to using an old-style large format negative camera on which an expandable bellows permitted the lens to be

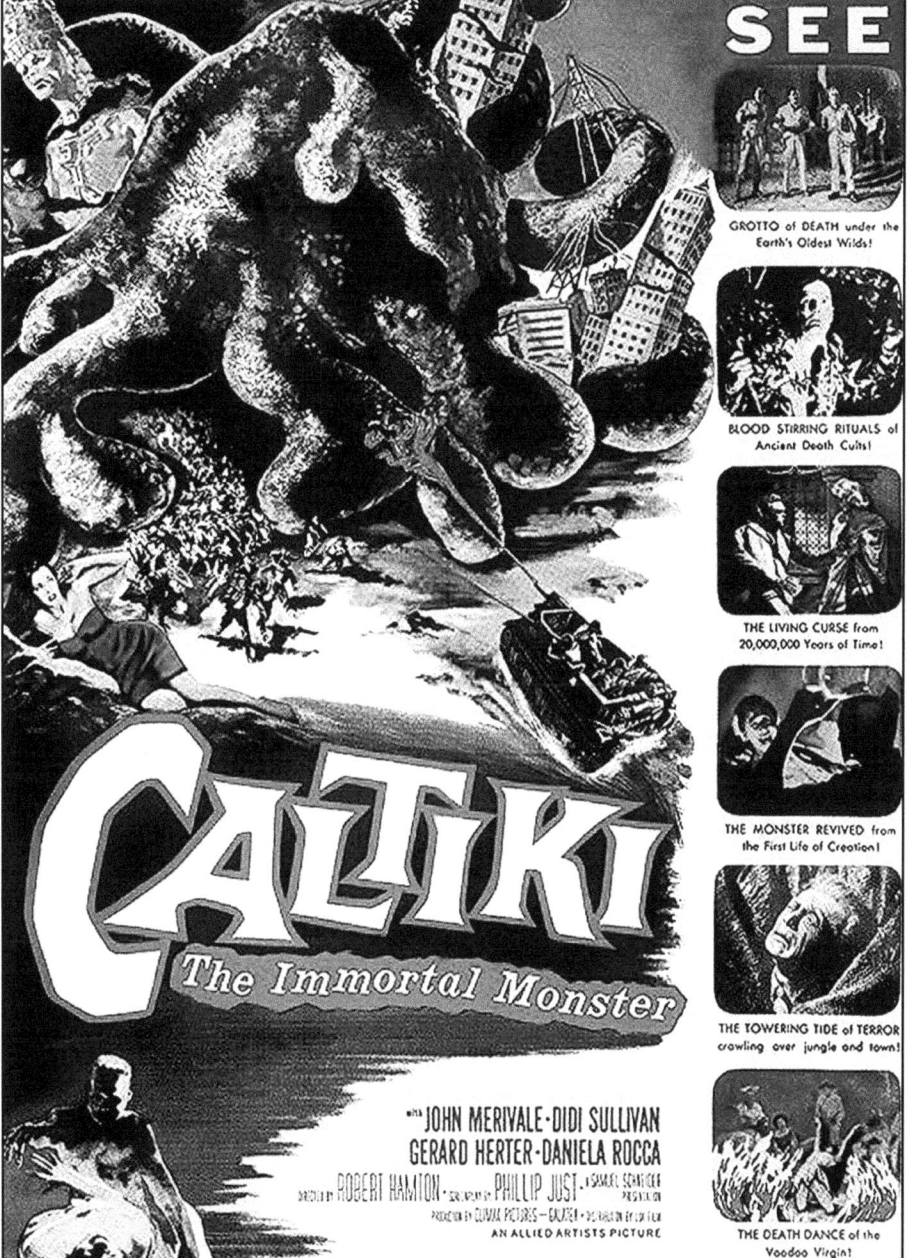

moved for critical focusing and also to change the optical axis of the lens, providing corrections of perspective distortion. The technique of essentially puppeting the mass of silicone over a photograph was used several times and, in short cuts, works just fine. I think Bart Sloane pulls off some minor miracles with the visual effects, including using cel animation to simulate electrical arcs dancing over the surface of the Blob as it tries to devour the diner.

After mentioning the miniature effects in *X the Unknown* and *The Blob*, I can't neglect the Italian film *Caltiki, The Immortal Monster* (1960), which is noteworthy for stretching its slim budget to execute over one hundred visual effects shots designed and photographed by Mario Bava, whose father, Eugenio Bava, had been a special effects cinemtographer during the silent era in Italy. Mario got early experience assisting his father in the special effects department of Mussolini's studio, the Istituto Luce. The bulk of *Caltiki*'s miniature shots, featuring the blob-like ancient god, were filmed at Bava's father's home.

The exteriors of Mayan ruins use photo cutouts mounted in front of the camera to embellish the location, a variation of the foreground matte painting technique used frequently by Emilio Ruiz del Rio and others.

By far the most impressive shot Bava designed and executed is in the beginning, when the lone survivor of Caltiki's first, off-screen attack, is seen in a distant part of a lush landscape littered with huge Mayan statuary—including a terra-cotta planter pressed into service as a "statue"—and dominated by a distant erupting volcano. In a continuous shot the man exits the background, steps in much closer to camera, and passes in front of the ruins until he arrives at the tents of his associates. It is bravura filmmaking by Bava, using all the tools he could.

What a pity Bava ordered the prints to be so damned dark! My educated guess is that the landscape, distant actor and volcano—which seems to have been filmed underwater—were combined, either in-camera or optically, resulting in a background plate that was rear projected on the same stage where the tent and actors were positioned. I suggest this as a solution because as the actor passes close to the camera, he casts a shadow on the background scene! The brilliance of this set-up compensates for the fact that Bava introduced the zoom lens to Italian cinema with *Caltiki*, which, on reflection, given its subsequent over-use, I am not sure was a good idea.

Above: Derek Meddings "pilots" the hero spaceship in the Gerry Anderson Marionation series **Fireball XL-5** *(1962).*

Below: Brian Johnson on the starship junkyard from the **Space: 1999** *Season 2 premiere episode, "The Metamorph." Some spaceships built earlier by Martin Bower dress the scene.*

A. Arnold Gillespie and crew film the naval battle for **Ben-Hur** (1959). The large hero models were radio controlled for rowing and other functions. Ships of different scales forced the perspective. Gillespie, Robert MacDonald and Milo Lory won the Oscar® for Visual Effects.

On the other hand, several shots of multiple Caltiki's marauding through Dr. Fielding's home—somewhat reminiscent of the ending of Les Bowie's work for **Quatermass II** (1957)—are atmospherically lit, but the inability to afford shooting at high speed reveals the small scale of the minimalist miniatures as the creatures tip over doll house furniture. The same problem robs the dramatic impact of the Army arriving to save the day, and the climax is further diluted by the use of motorized toy tanks. These are embarrassingly unconvincing, especially considering the posters promised tanks battling an immense, tentacled Caltiki... something audiences hadn't seen in either **X the Unknown** or **The Blob**. Incidentally, as adept as Bava was, the most convincing miniature shot in the film is from Republic's serial **The Crimson Ghost** (1946), done by the amazing Lydecker brothers.

When speaking of miniature military hardware, once can't help but think of the mind-boggling array of alien spacecraft, flying saucers, submarines, laser tanks, and futuristic jets created for the many Gerry Anderson productions in England. His earliest efforts were television series starring puppets filmed in Supermarionation, such as **Supercar** (1961), **Fireball XL-5** (1962), and **Stingray** (1964).

His most fondly-remembered puppet series, **Thunderbirds** (1965), about a family of daring rescue specialists, has gone through many incarnations including the feature films **Thunderbirds are Go** (1965) and **Thunderbird 6** (1968). Recently, there has been an all-CGI revival.

Little Things, Big Results • 19

Taken in the Lydeckers' Mascot Studio shop, possibly during *The Phantom Empire* (1935). Most—if not all—of these people became part of the crew at Republic. Ellis Thackery was a matte painter who later became a Director of Photography.

Anderson's team of outstanding craftspeople switched to live action productions requiring extensive, motion picture-quality miniatures and violent pyrotechnic explosions, such as the television series **UFO** (1970), supervised by Derek Meddings, who had started out working with Les Bowie on Hammer Films. In fact, dynamic explosions of miniatures became a hallmark of Meddings' work.

The Anderson studio kickstarted the careers of many technicians who would go on to earn nominations and Oscars® and BAFTA Awards, such as Roger Dicken, Ian Scoones and Brian Johnson (the Anderson series **Space: 1999** [1975] was supervised by Johnson).

Meddings supervised Anderson's first foray into live action feature films, **Journey to the Far Side of the Sun** (1969) and soon joined the James Bond family, delivering outstanding miniature work for **Live and Let Die** (1973), **The Man With The Golden Gun** (1974) and **The Spy Who Loved Me** (1977). For the latter he returned somewhat to silent-era methods, spending four months in the Bahamas shooting open-water footage of a sixty foot miniature of a super-tanker along with three scale nuclear subs. He also designed and fabricated quarter-scale models of James Bond's transforming Lotus Esprit car.

His spectacular miniature work for **Superman** (1978) won a Special Achievement Academy Award®. He soon re-joined the world of 007 with **Moonraker** (1979), which is packed with miniature effects including a space station and space shuttles, which earned Meddings an Oscar® nomination. He provided more pyro destruction of world-class models in **For Your Eyes Only** (1981) and **GoldenEye** (1995).

Returning to biblical times, the 1959 re-make of **Ben-Hur** used miniatures differently than the hanging miniature arena executed for the silent film version. For the exciting sea battle in this production, A. Arnold Gillespie and his MGM crew used different scale models of Roman warships and pirate vessels, as well as photo cut-out profiles for distant ships, which were filmed simultaneously to force the perspective. The water tank was filled with warring vessels and the battle looked appropriately massive. In the definitive book on Gillespie's prolific career, *The Wizard of MGM*, he recalled: "An amusing incident occurred during the Galley miniature shooting. All activity aboard, moving oars, miniature people, etc., were triggered by a radio signal. At 2:00 a.m. one black night the dozing watchman was awakened by strange noises coming from inside a huge covered 'hangar' which berthed the galleys at night. Stealthily entering, his eyes popped as he observed all oars operating and 12" people traversing the decks. Some wayward midnight frequency had tripped all the switches." **(7)**

One of the most notable accomplishments blending miniatures, mechanical and pyrotechnic effects for a catastrophe at sea was *The Poseidon Adventure* (1972), which won a Special Achievement Academy Award® for Visual Effects for L.B. Abbott's miniatures and A.D. Flowers' jaw-dropping pyrotechnics on sets with actors Gene Hackman, Ernest Borgnine, and others.

Aviation pioneers in the 1920s and 1930s encouraged interest in different kinds of flying machines, so miniatures were frequently used in storylines about the derring-do of barnstorming aviators and to show aerial combat. The Howard Hughes production *Hell's Angels* (1930) dramatically shows planes and zeppelins in aerial combat, and during WWII dozens of pictures such as *Destination Tokyo* (1944) and *Thirty Seconds Over Tokyo* (1944) used models.

In an interview, Theodore 'Ted' Lydecker recalled his and his brother Howard's Oscar®-nominated work on the Republic film *Flying Tigers* (1942): "I'll tell you something about *Flying Tigers*... there were no real airplanes of any type in that picture. We did 153 shots for it and they were all miniatures. The full-sized P-40s were just mock-ups with car motors, pulled by cables along the ground. Babe [Howard] and I sat in with the [Oscar®] nominating committee and they called us liars when we said there were no real planes in *Tigers*.

"As a result, while *Flying Tigers* received an Oscar® nomination for the Best Special Effects of 1942, it lost to Gordon Jennings, Farciot Edouart and William L. Pereira for *Reap the Wild Wind*." (8)

The Lydeckers put Republic on the map with fans of thrilling

Above: John P. Fulton combined a moving camera, natural sunlight, large-scale models and intense pyrotechnics into Oscar®-winning effects for **The Bridges at Toko-Ri** *(1954). The miniature US Navy F9F-2 Panthers have a ten foot wingspan, which hints at the large size of the landscape.*

Below: From "A Boom for Operating Miniature Airplanes" by Gordon Jennings, A.S.C., Head of Special Effects Department, Paramount. The publication is unknown, but looks to be the late 30s or early 40s.

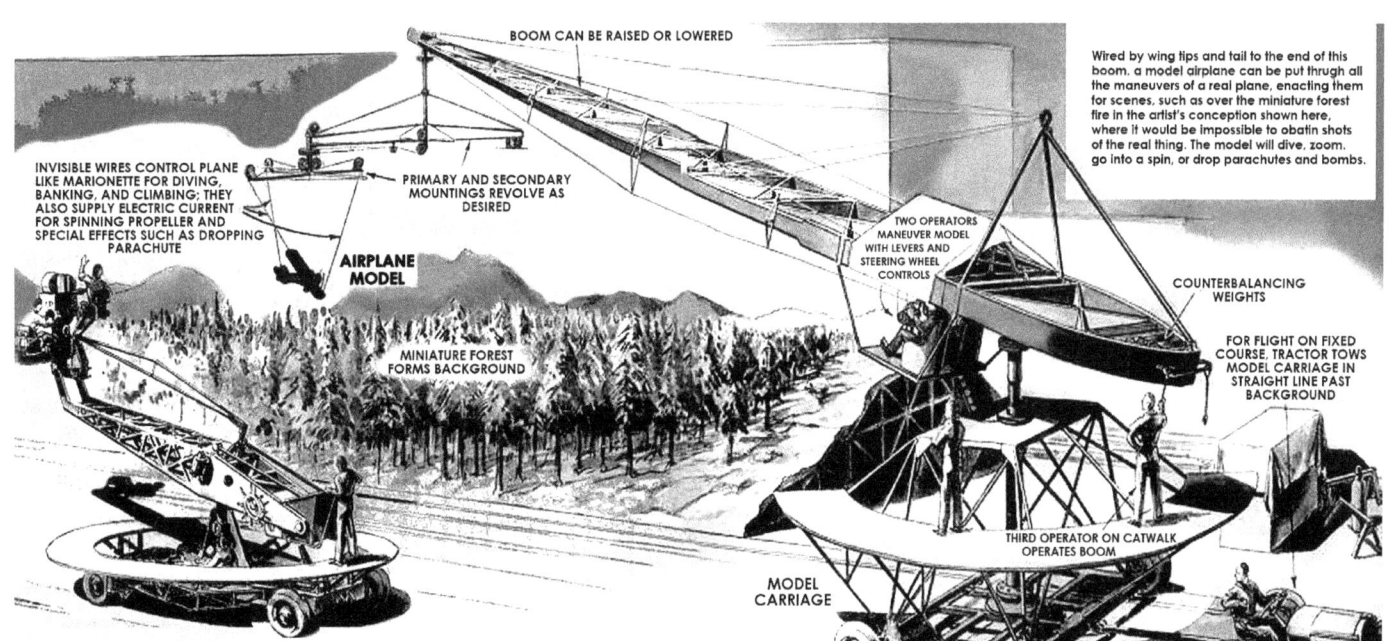

Little Things, Big Results • 21

serials and action films. *The Adventures of Captain Marvel* (1941), *Captain America* (1944), and *King of the Rocket Men* (1949) presented death-defying cliffhanger endings highlighted by wonderful miniature set-ups filmed by Howard and Theodore Lydecker.

Even more remarkable than the quality of their work, consider that in 1943 Republic did 50 films, compared to 19 for Warner Brothers and 27 for MGM—and the Lydecker brothers had to deliver the goods on significantly smaller budgets than the big studios. They were very savvy about using natural lighting—sunlight—to make the models look more realistic. All the best miniature specialists also knew that the larger the model could be built, especially if used in a water tank, the better the scenes would look. Filming miniatures suspended from overhead wires came to be called "Lydecker shots" in the industry.

The Lydeckers handled *all* the visual effects for a show, from flaming Apache arrows to hand grenade explosions to aerial dogfights. I cannot think of any other technicians with such a breadth and depth of abilities. I wouldn't have known about the extent of their skills if I hadn't had the great good fortune to meet Howard 'Babe' Lydecker in the early 1960s when I was a kid visiting Los Angeles and had the opportunity to hang out at Four Star Studios in Studio City. The studio had originally been Republic and Howard was there to shoot in their small water tank—which he had used on films like *Zombies of the Stratosphere* (1952).

A relative of mine worked at the studio and introduced me to Howard. I was tongue-tied but he was quick to put me at ease when he found out about my interest in special effects, and he graciously let me hang around and pester him with questions. Remember, in those days it was highly unusual for someone as young as me to express *any* interest in making movies, let alone special effects. After all these years—I can't say for certain—but besides shooting some commercials there, I am pretty sure I saw him shooting the S.S. *Minnow* in a storm-tossed sea for *Gilligan's Island* (1964).

The Lydecker model makers would produce a wooden car fender master, carefully wax and buff it, then build up layers of thin paper soaked with shellac. Once dry, it could be easily removed and finished, then attached to a model to realistically crumple, sparing them from having to replace the whole vehicle. They also used colored chalks to weather buildings.

Sadly, one day I saw large-scale miniature aircraft, 1940s-era automobile models, the clunky Republic robot suits and a mountain of photographs and press kits being tossed into the back of a large truck—to be hauled to the landfill. I did not get much of a chance to closely examine the aircraft, but they were made of metal. The cars were both wooden masters and a couple of finished models were made of metal.

Like ocean-going sequences, filming aircraft miniatures under controlled conditions made it possible to get action that would have otherwise been impossible to shoot. Oscar®-nominated films with elaborate aircraft sequences include **Flight Command** (1941), **A Yank in the R.A.F.** (1941), **One of Our Aircraft in Missing** (1942), **Air Force** (1943), **Bombardier** (1943) and the Oscar®-winning **Thirty Seconds Over Tokyo** (1944).

A seldom-mentioned use of miniatures came about during WWII: technicians built phony landscapes on top of the Lockheed aircraft manufacturing plant in Burbank, California, to hide the real configuration—and uses—of the actual wartime plants from overhead spies.

Opposite page:

Top: Theodore ("Ted"), left, and Howard ("Babe") Lydecker with unidentified associates.

Second photo: **Sink the Bismarck!** (1960). John Stears, later known for his special effects work on several of the James Bond films, was on the ship-building team.

Middle: Painting portholes on the twenty-four foot Japanese battleship which took twelve technicians six weeks to build for **Remember Pearl Harbor** (1942). A man sat inside to fire "cannons" made from old pistols.

Bottom: Howard, left, and Ted check out their advanced flying wing aircraft designed for the serial **Dick Tracy** (1937) which was also seen in a subsequent serial, **Fighting Devil Dogs** (1938).

This page:

Top left: Howard Lydecker checks a miniature car on rails hidden from camera.

Top right: Ted examines a set-up for **Great Train Robbery** (1941).

Middle: The Lydeckers' rocket ship in **Zombies of the Stratosphere** (1952).

Bottom: "The weather started getting rough, the tiny ship was tossed"—and their three hour tour turned into three seasons on **Gilligan's Island** (1964-1967).

Top: Ted Lydecker, director David Miller, and Howard Lydecker inspect the bridge miniature for **Flying Tigers** (1942).

Above: The bridge miniature blows up on cue in New Mexico.

Little Things, Big Results • 23

Just Imagine

Miniatures expanded the scope of stories, encouraging filmmakers to explore the realms of the utterly fantastic by showing audiences entire environments. One of the greatest examples of using models to realize an extensive imaginary reality was when UFA technicians in Germany used impressive miniatures and in-camera composites—often using mirrors—to overwhelm audiences with the awesome city of tomorrow for Fritz Lang's classic, **Metropolis** (1926).

In the U.S., the Fox film **Just Imagine** (1930) achieved the same goal through a brute force application; an Army hangar was filled with the massive Art Deco cityscape that took 205 technicians five months to build. Considering that Just Imagine is best remembered today for its futuristic City, the studio's $168,000 was well spent.

The structures were wired with fifteen thousand small-scale light bulbs while seventy-four arc lights were used to light the Metropolis-inspired structures from above. In terms of sheer dimensions, it may very well be the biggest miniature—ever. By comparison, at the other end of the scale, the silly Lum and Abner film, **Two Weeks to Live** (1943), has a few shots of a single Flash Gordon-style rocket ship miniature, with cel-animated thrust and smoke.

Willis O'Brien achieved the impossible for the iconic **King Kong** (1933) using the entire gamut of visual effects—while also creating new techniques. His world-class crew of extraordinary craftsmen used miniatures, matte paintings, animatronics, rear projection, traveling mattes and stop-motion model animation to populate Skull Island with ferocious dinosaurs and place a giant ape atop the Empire State Building. OBie and others who specialized in model animation will get the in-depth coverage they deserve in a separate volume dedicated to stop-motion.

Inspired by the surprise success of **Kong**'s 1952 re-release and Ray Harryhausen's 1953 smash box-office hit, **The Beast from 20,000 Fathoms**, the Japanese company Toho produced **Gojira** (1954), their first effort with a style of visual effects eventually dubbed "suitmation," which was devised and supervised by the brilliant Eiji Tsuburya, who had previously helmed first-rate miniature scenes for Japanese WWII movies. Their film was released in the U.S. as **Godzilla** (1956).

Suitmation refers to visualizing giant creatures for productions by using performers inside monster costumes, who interact with elaborate table-top landscapes, scale breakaway buildings and often times, other monstrosities.

Godzilla was an international hit that led to many descendants, such as **Rodan** (1956), which collectively ushered in a genre of films known as Kaiju (Japanese for "strange creature"). The continuing popularity of immense monstrosities created via suitmation has inspired a recent series of re-imaginings of the old characters, such as **Godzilla vs Kong** (2021).

Toho also produced **The Mysterians** (1957) and **Battle in Outer Space** (1959), colorful science-fiction films that relied heavily on visual effects including model spacecraft, matte paintings and traveling matte composites. **The Mysterians** also has suitmation in the form of a giant robot that looks like it is wearing Samurai armor. **The Last War** (1961) was a cautionary story that used visual effects to warn of the perils of atomic war and showed the destructive force of atomic bombs on major cities around the globe—all meticulously fabricated duplicates of the real places that were then blown up for the camera.

Inspired by George Pal's Oscar®-winning visual effects in **When Worlds Collide** (1951), Toho also threatened the Earth with a rogue celestial body in their seldom-seen **Gorath** (1962). All of these shows were made under the guidance of Eiji Tsuburaya.

*Above: Daei Film Company's **Daimajin** film series (1966) used both suitmation and special props to visualize the mighty statue-warrior.*

Left: **The Land Unknown** *(1956) featured Americanized suitmation for its T-Rex, better-crafted than the Godzilla suits from that same time. Bud Westmore's makeup lab at Universal employed gifted technicians who had considerable experience.*

Little Things, Big Results • 25

Above: George Pal (left) and A. Arnold Gillespie during the tank shooting for Pal's **Atlantis–The Lost Continent** (1961).

Right: **Destination Moon** (1950).

George Pal had emigrated to the U.S. where he first produced his stop-motion short films for Paramount starring his Puppetoons®. These rather surreal shorts won an honorary Oscar® in 1944, and by 1950 Pal was transitioning to making feature films. His **Destination Moon** (1950). the Technicolor® adaptation of H.G. Wells' **War of the Worlds** (1953), **Conquest of Space** (1955), **tom thumb** (1958) and **The Time Machine** (1960) all won Oscars® for visual effects. Pal's spectacular fantasy/adventure **The Wonderful World of the Brothers Grimm** (1962) was filmed in the original 3-strip Cinerama® process.

It's no understatement to call George Pal "The Godfather of Science Fiction." He was unique among producers for fully-appreciating what visual effects could bring to films.

Irwin Allen was an Oscar®-winning documentary producer who had employed Ray Harryhausen and Willis O'Brien to produce a superb dinosaur segment for **The Animal World** (1956). Allen's feature hit **Voyage to the Bottom of the Sea** (1960) was helmed by the L.B. Abbott team and made a star of the futuristic submarine, Seaview. Allen brought **Voyage to the Bottom of the Sea** to ABC-TV for four seasons (1964-1968), keeping costs down by using existing miniatures from the feature, supplemented by new models including a mechanical whale. Aurora released a model kit of the Seaview while the series was on the air and there have even been recent versions of larger-scale kits!

However, Irwin Allen wasn't content to rest on his laurels and produced **Lost In Space** (1965-1968), which chronicled the misadventures of the Robinson family on alien worlds and their encounters with bizarre beings. Two 1966 episodes starred Michael Rennie ("Klaatu" in **The Day the Earth Stood Still** in 1951) as "The Keeper," an alien who had amassed a large collection of inhuman specimens kept caged on board his spacecraft. With Allen's eye firmly on the budget, the menagerie was comprised of recycled creature suits and props from past episodes of **Voyage to the Bottom of the Sea** and **Lost In Space**. There were also guest appearances by Robby the Robot, such as the episode War of the Robots (1966), where Robby portrayed an evil Robotoid.

Howard Lydecker was part of the team shooting miniatures for the series, as was young Jack Polito. Jack was an animator and prop maker who was introduced to Abbott by Bart Sloane, of **The Blob** fame, and joined the Fox team on **Lost in Space** and **The Time Tunnel** (1966-1967). Polito remarked to me that L.B. Abbott was very kind to him.

Land of the Giants (1968-1970) used models, numerous large-scale props and split screens in what was arguably the most technically-demanding of Allen's TV series.

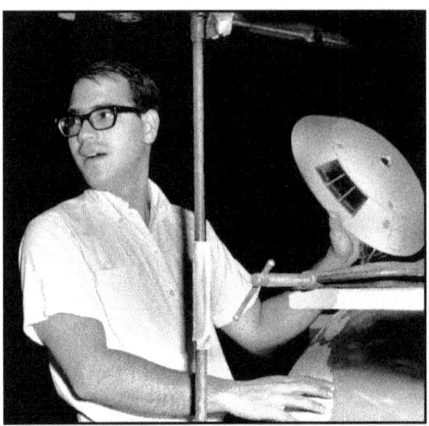

Top: Jack Polito with a small-scale Jupiter 2 miniature for **Lost in Space** (1965-1968).

Middle: The 18-foot Seaview (surface shots) and the 8-foot and 4-foot models (underwater shots) used on the **Voyage to the Bottom of the Sea** (1964-68) TV series. L.B. Abbott used the large tank (the "Sersen Lake"), newly-built at the Fox Ranch in Malibu for **Cleopatra** (1962). An open-top "camera boat" permitted filming at or beneath the water line, and the convex ports, necessary to counter water's refraction index, had been used previously on Disney's **20,000 Leagues Under the Sea** (1954).

Bottom: Abbott with his 1966 Emmy® for **Voyage to the Bottom of the Sea**.

26 · *Smoke and Mirrors – Special Visual Effects Before Computers*

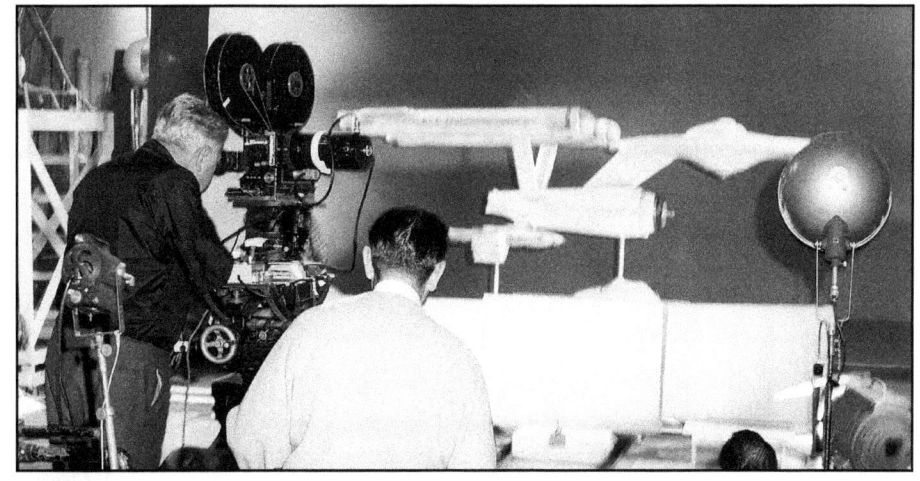

By the 1960s, the major studios streamlined their operations and trimmed what they perceived as fat—and visual effects departments were juicy targets. Enterprising professionals formed companies to pick up the slack. Linwood Dunn, Cecil Love and Don Weed founded Film Effects of Hollywood and provided miniatures, matte paintings and opticals for **West Side Story** (1961), **My Fair Lady** (1964), **Star Trek** (1966), **The Great Race** (1965), **Those Magnificent Men in their Flying Machines** (1965), **The Bible: In the Beginning** (1966), **Darling Lili** (1970) **Airport** (1970) and even **Alligator** (1980). (See Chapter 6 for more about Film Effects of Hollywood.)

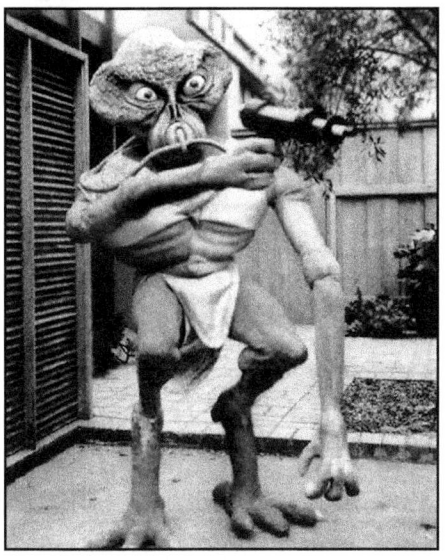

Project Unlimited was formed by Gene Warren, Sr., Wah Chang and Tim Barr in 1957 and was closed in 1966, leading to an auction of props, miniatures, costumes, and masks from **The Black Scorpion** (1957), **Master of the World** (1961), **The Outer Limits** (1963), **Star Trek** (1965), **Around the World Under the Sea** (1966) and many other films and TV series. In 1969, Gene Sr. founded Excelsior! Animated Moving Pictures, which is where I met him and Wah in 1973 during the **Land of the Lost** TV series.

Excelsior! closed in 1980 and was replaced by Gene Warren Jr.'s company, Fantasy II Film Effects, which supplied effects for scores of productions including the 3-D production of **Spacehunter: Adventures in the Forbidden Zone** (1983), **Gremlins** (1984), **The Terminator** (1984), **Fright Night 2** (1988), **The Abyss** (1989), **Tremors** (1990), Francis Ford Coppola's **Dracula** (1992), and many others. They won an Oscar® and BAFTA for visual effects in **Terminator 2: Judgment Day** (1991) and had earlier won an Emmy® for **The Winds of War** miniseries (1983).

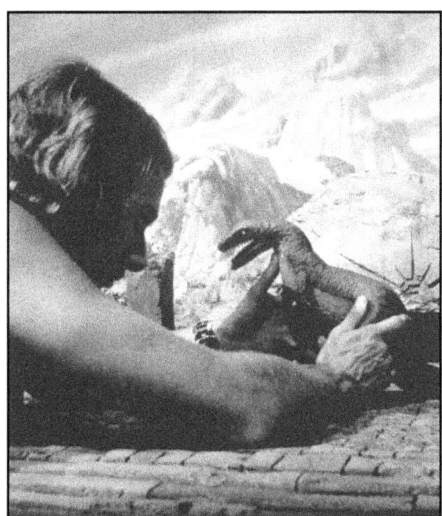

Top: Linwood Dunn lines up a blue screen shot for the episode "The Space Seed" (1966), the foundation for the feature **Star Trek** film **The Wrath of Khan** (1982).

2nd Row, left: Janos Prohaska tests the "Thetan" suit fabricated by Project Unlimited for **The Outer Limits** episode "The Architects of Fear" (1963), one of the earliest attempts to add leg extensions to a performer.

2nd Row, right: The "Keeper of the Purple Twilight" improves his mind on **The Outer Limits** set.

3rd Row, left: Joe Viskocil rigs a detonation (right) for **The Terminator** (1984).

Left: Harry Walton animates "Grumpy" at Excelsior! for **Land of the Lost** (1973).

Little Things, Big Results • 27

MGM PRESENTS A STANLEY KUBRICK PRODUCTION
2001: a space odyssey

Gordon Jennings first used a repeatable camera system for Cecil B. DeMille's *Samson and Delilah* (1949, Oscar®-nominated). A more sophisticated system was engineered for *2001: A Space Odyssey* but even then a week or more might be required to complete a single shot. *Star Wars* was the first film to benefit from a computer-controlled camera system that was capable of shooting multiple takes of a complex shot in a single day.

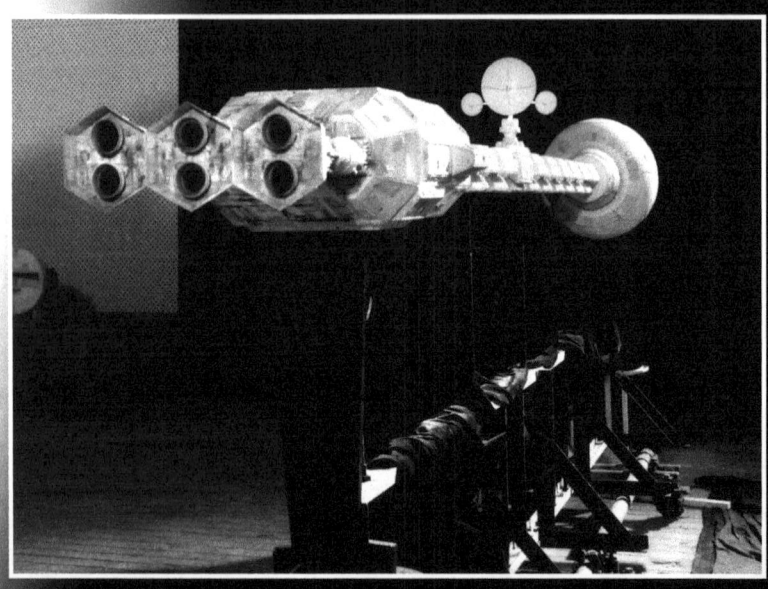

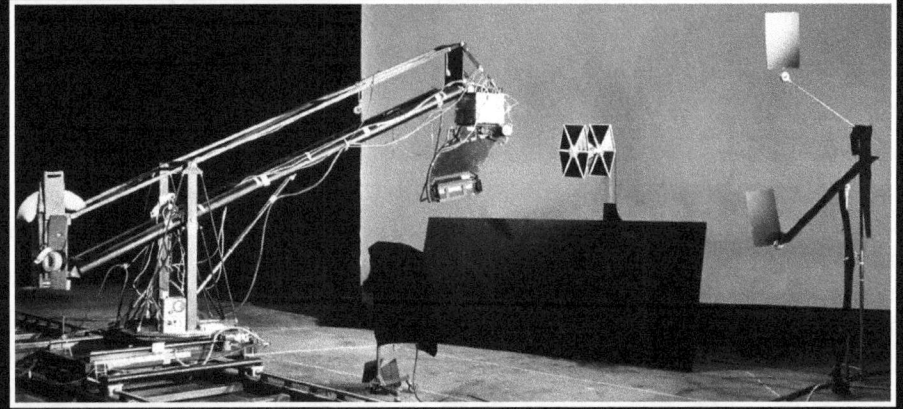

Star Wars (1977). *The model mover was programmable, and a combination of moving camera and model stand produced any desired action. John Stears, John Dykstra, Richard Edlund, Grant McCune and Robert Blalack each received an Oscar® for the innovative visual effects.*

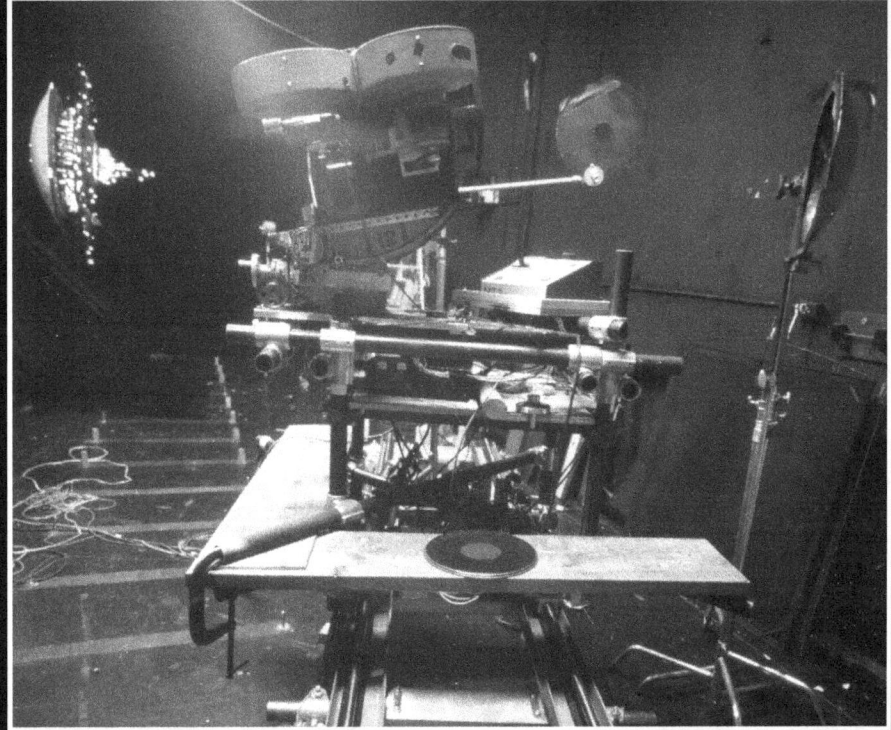

The massive motion control rig used to film the mothership for **Close Encounters of the Third Kind** *(1977). Roy Arbogast, Douglas Trumbull, Matthew Yuricich, Gregory Jein and Richard Yuricich received an Oscar® nomination for the Visual Effects.*

Melinda Dillon and Carey Guffey just barely avoid being hit by a speeding UFO in **Close Encounters.** *The UFO model was shot in multiple passes in a smoke-filled environment and then optically composited with a background made up of a miniature landscape with interactive lighting. That footage was, in turn, front-projected onto a Scotchlite screen with the actors, who reacted appropriately.*

A major breakthrough in miniature photography came about for *Star Wars: A New Hope* (1977), thanks to John Dykstra and his associates:

"We borrowed technology from everywhere," Dykstra said. Dykstra recruited Alvah J. Miller and Jerry Jeffress, who he'd worked with at Berkeley's Institute of Urban and Regional Development. Together they'd built a rig that slowly inched a 16mm camera around a tiny model of Marin County, California, to simulate traffic movement. They controlled the camera rig by programming a then state-of-the-art PDP-11 computer, 16-bit computers also used for factory automation, air traffic control and even controlling nuclear power stations.

That computer-controlled camera rig laid the foundations for ILM's first major breakthrough in motion and imagery. Where earlier sci-fi films flew a model around in front of the camera, motion control moved the *camera* and kept the *model* stationary. Dykstra, Miller and Jeffress took their experience from traffic research and applied it to *Star Wars*, replacing the 16mm camera with vastly higher-quality cameras and the tiny model cars with menacing Star Destroyers.

Miller and Jeffress custom-built ILM's motion control computers. "Computers at that time were the size of several refrigerators and had the power of a calculator," Dykstra said. "The iPhone I'm talking on now has hundreds of times the computational capabilities of those original systems."

They may not have been powerful by today's standards, but those lumbering 1970s computers were the key to motion control. Because the camera's movements were programmed into the computer, the motor-driven motions were absolutely precise, and could be repeated over and over. That was essential

Little Things, Big Results · 29

for compositing multiple models into each shot, paving the way for legendary action sequences like the Death Star dogfight.

In addition to building the computers, the team designed a user interface so camera operators could program the movement they wanted. "It wasn't even on a screen," Dysktra says of the method for operating the system. "It was knobs and buttons." The resulting motion control system earned the name Dykstraflex, though Dykstra stresses the label wasn't his idea.

The list of challenges was long. Dykstra's crew repurposed aging VistaVision cameras from the 1950s to make sure the effects shot had high-enough resolution for compositing. They figured out how to use fluorescent tubes to light their blue-screen backdrops without flickering. And they built a movie camera with swings and tilts, which allowed them to precisely control focus.

The hard work paid off, obviously. The effects pioneered in **Star Wars** entranced a generation and helped turn Lucas's space opera into a cultural touchstone. Dykstra and team took home the 1978 Academy Award® for visual effects. And the Academy also presented Dykstra, Miller and Jeffress with a special technical achievement award for the Dykstraflex system. **(9)**

At one point, 20th Century-Fox executives were so worried about what was happening at the small studio in Van Nuys (California) that they sent the Dean of Hollywood Special Effects, Linwood Dunn, to check out what these "crazy kids" were up to. Dunn told the studio to relax and leave them alone. Motion control went on to become a staple of miniature photography at studios around the world. Fox had no clue what **Star Wars** would become; two weeks before its premiere they were trying to sell it to any studio who'd take it off their hands. They had no takers.

And that, ladies and gentlemen, perfectly sums up typically clueless, unimaginative Hollywood executives. Thank heavens The Force was strong with Dykstra and his team, who understood the value of using miniatures to fulfill the vision of George Lucas. They were the latest in a long line of craftsmen using scale models to enhance a wide spectrum of stories, from **King Kong** (1933) to **Airplane!** (1980). Many people don't realize models are still used in films such as **Independence Day** (1996), **Titanic** (1997), **Moon** (2009), **Inception** (2010) and many others. I suspect miniatures will be used for a long time to produce big results that thrill audiences.

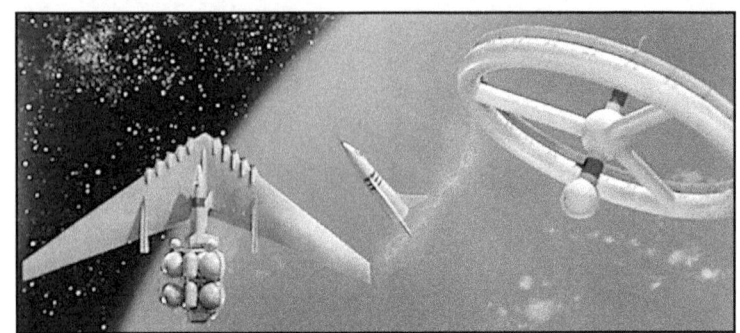

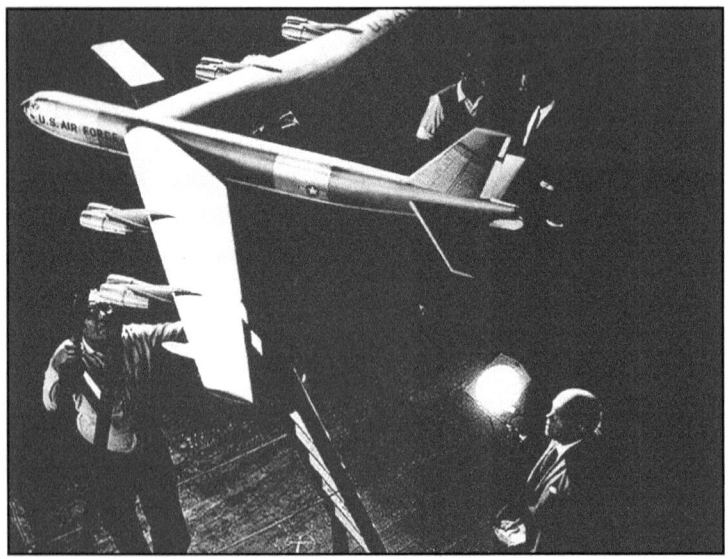

Top: In orbit with George Pal's **Conquest of Space** (1955).

2nd photo: **The First Spaceship On Venus** (1960) blasts-off.

3rd photo: Effects Supervisor Ernest Farino (left) and Cinematographer Tony Cutrono prepare for the landing of Apollo 11 for the HBO/Tom Hanks miniseries **From the Earth to the Moon** (1998).

Bottom: At Shepperton Studios Wally Veevers (lower right) prepares to film the B-52 model built for Stanley Kubrick's **Dr. Strangelove** (1964).

SCRAPBOOK

The night scenes for **In Harm's Way** (1966) were filmed on a lake in Mexico because they needed straits with mountains in the background. However, the day battles (above) were filmed in the gulf of Mexico, which gave the scenes a natural horizon. It is unknown who built the ship models.

Left: Director Otto Preminger seems like a giant aboard one of the ship miniatures for **In Harm's Way**.

A volcano miniature shot upside down in a water tank by Stephen C. Wathen for **The Age of Mammals** (1979). The "smoke" is colored latex house paint.

Only one of the nine cameras shooting the collapse of Hansen Dam for **Earthquake** (1974) worked. Frank Brendel, Glen Robinson and Albert Whitlock earned a Special Achievement Academy Award® for Visual Effects.

John P. Fulton in a water tank with an historical ship model ca. 1956 from an unknown film.

Steve Koch Studio created this shot combining a miniature landscape, water and Loch Ness serpent prop for the Disney Channel's **Legend of Firefly Marsh** (1987).

Little Things, Big Results • 31

THE "KELLISON STICKS"

A method of measuring proper visual distance from a foreground miniature to its live action component to ensure that the apparent scale of the miniature matches the scale of the background elements.

The markings on each stick are to scale with one another and when the heights and units of measurement on the sticks match each other visually (from the camera's P.O.V.), the scale and distance between the miniature and live action elements is correct for the shot.

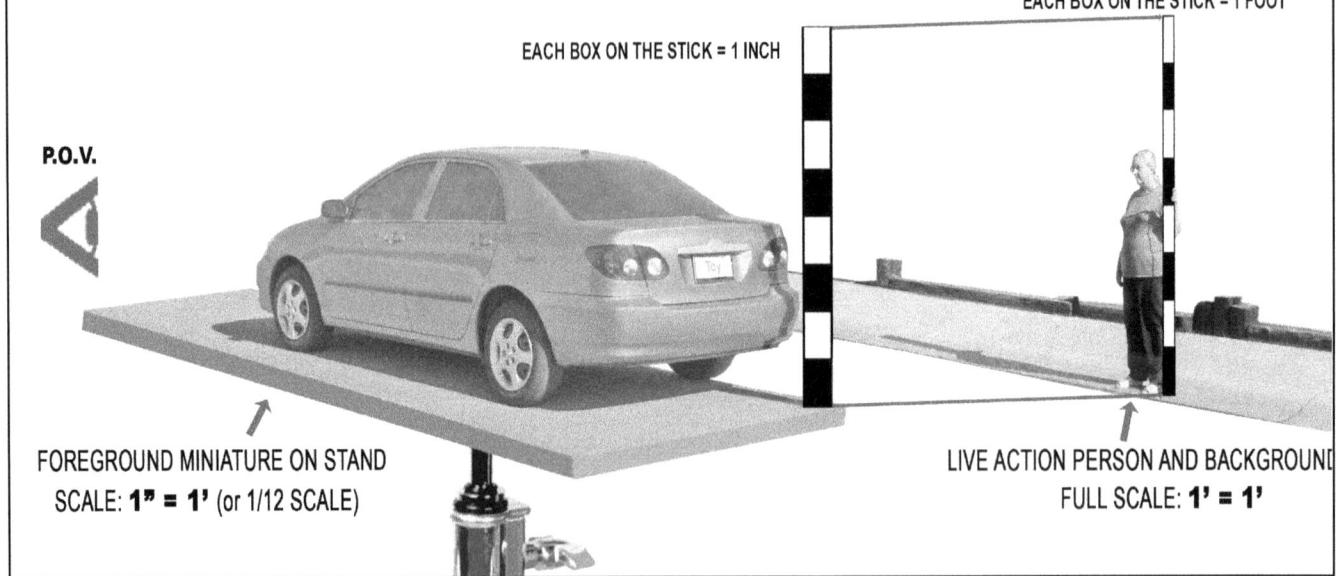

EACH BOX ON THE STICK = 1 INCH

EACH BOX ON THE STICK = 1 FOOT

P.O.V.

FOREGROUND MINIATURE ON STAND
SCALE: **1" = 1'** (or 1/12 SCALE)

LIVE ACTION PERSON AND BACKGROUND
FULL SCALE: **1' = 1'**

"The Kellison Sticks." Legendary animator/vfx supervisor Phil Kellison devised this simple method for ensuring that mixed-scale components could be most efficiently and effectively photographed.   *Copyright © 2019 by David Stipes and Kevin Hedgpeth*

When small stick with 1 inch marks matches full size stick with 1 foot marks then model is at correct distance from camera and in proper forced scale.

(View through camera lens)

32 · *Smoke and Mirrors – Special Visual Effects Before Computers*

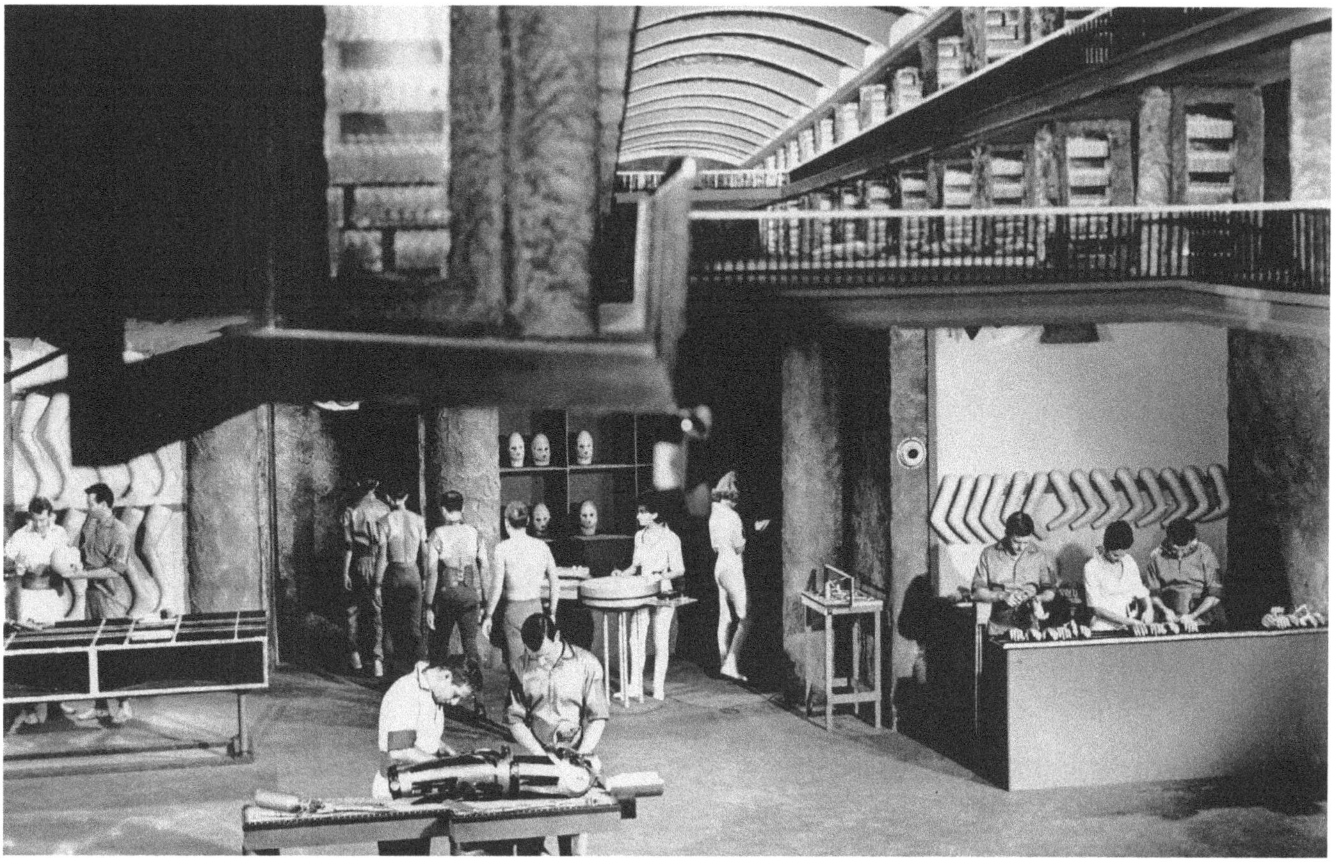

Above: The low-budget indie film **The Time Travelers** (1964) used clever, economically created effects. This futuristic android factory, complete with a moving conveyor belt, is a foreground miniature.

Left: Filmmaker David Hewitt attends to the factory model.

Below: Ray Harryhausen, Kit West and Les Bowie apply plaster dust to one of the miniature lunar mountains for **First Men "In" the Moon** (1964) at Bowie Films, Ltd. Bowie and his team had previously created miniatures and matte paintings for Harryhausen's **Jason and the Argonauts** (1963), and would go on to depict the "Creation of the World" for Ray's **One Million Years B.C.** (1966).

Gordon Jennings is dwarfed by the thirty-seven foot tall Temple of Dagon miniature seen in the epic finale of DeMille's **Samson and Delilah** (1950). Jennings used an early form of motion control that optically married the live action with the model, winning the 1952 Academy Scientific and Engineering Award "For the Design, Construction and Application of a Servo-Operated Recording and Repeating Device."

John P. Fulton, ca. 1931, was an avid flyer (his California flying license was No. 28) and he was friends with Ameila Earhart.

Fulton supervises filming **Airmail** (1932). The overhead rig mimicked real-life flight controls, allowing the operator to move the plane realistically.

34 · *Smoke and Mirrors – Special Visual Effects Before Computers*

Sue Turner with the miniature set she and James Belohovek built for **John Carpenter's The Thing** (1983). This set was built for a dramatic stop-motion climax animated by Randall William Cook. The animatronic effects by Rob Bottin and his crew were completed in time, so, unfortunately for animation fans, only two stop-motion cuts remain in the final film.

Kurt Zendler, Art Director for Wizard Works, touches up a miniature for Isaac Asimov's **Nightfall** (1988). A mirror added rear projected live action filmed at Vasquez Rocks outside of Los Angeles.

Douglas Trumbull works on the final surface detail of the "Moonbus" model for Stanley Kubrick's **2001: A Space Odyssey** (1968).

David Stipes and Dave Sharp with a motion-control miniature set-up for **V: The Final Battle** (1984).

Little Things, Big Results • 35

The space gun miniature from **Things to Come** (1936). Supervisor Ned Mann used every trick available, from rear projection to flying rigs.

At Fantasy II Film Effects in Burbank, Pete Kleinow (left) and Gene Warren, Jr., examine the stop motion model of the T-800 exoskeleton for James Cameron's **The Terminator** (1984). The model was combined with live action backgrounds using rear screen projection.

Mike Minor works on one of the tabletops he created for Sid and Marty Krofft's **The Far Out Space Nuts** (1975). His imaginative use of "found" items (such as plastic shapes, muffin tins, and styrofoam packing), kept costs down while creating a variety of fascinating alien worlds.

Terry Huud works on the Martian spacecraft for the cult classic **Spaced Invaders** (1990).

James Belohovek gives final touches to a miniature power loader used in a high-speed fight with a rod puppet of the Alien Queen in **Aliens** (1986).

Many of the Project Unlimited crew pose by sorcerer Pendragon's castle miniature, during **Jack the Giant Killer** (1962). Standing, from left to right, are Gene Warren, Sr., Tim Barr, Phil Kellison, Victor Delgado, Wah Chang, Paul LeBaron and Blanding Sloan. Seated are Marian Young, Marcel Delgado and Bill Brace. Dave Morrick and Don Sahlin are kneeling in front. Jim Danforth and Tom Holland are missing.

Little Things, Big Results • 37

PREVUES OF COMING ATTRACTIONS

Two of the most influential sci-fi films of the 1950s, **The War of the Worlds** and **Forbidden Planet,** deserve extensive coverage and will be featured in a special volume of this series.

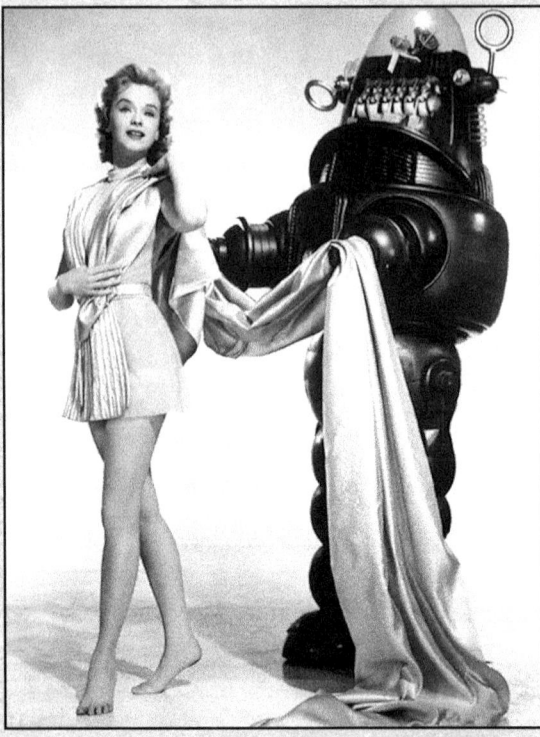

Chapter 2
Spectacle — On Glass

*Above: The lush, claustrophobic jungles of **King Kong** (1933) were designed under Willis O'Brien's supervision and painted on multiple glasses by world class artists Mario Larrinaga, Byron Crabbe, Albert Maxwell Simpson, Juan Larrinaga and others.*

*Below: This heart-wrenching vista of battlefield devastation for **Gone With the Wind** (1939) includes painted "bodies" of soldiers. A separately painted sky and rising smoke further enhanced the drama. The grueling visual effects workload was handled under the supervision of Jack Cosgrove.*

As audiences marched with the crew of the tramp steamer *Venture* thru the gnarled and twisted jungles of Skull Island in **King Kong** (1933) or watched the Old South transformed by the havoc of the Civil War in **Gone With the Wind** (1939), how many of them realized that much of the panoramas they were watching existed only as painted imagery that was combined with live actors? Such scenes were originally called glass shots and as methods evolved, came to be generally known as *matte paintings*.

While miniatures were useful for action scenes such as a steamboat race, an aerial dogfight or a building exploding, mattes were typically used in static shots. Directors came to appreciate their utility for expanding their visual horizons while producers welcomed the cost-savings from not having to build larger sets or travel to exotic locations.

For instance, a matte was a very efficient, reliable method of adding a grandiose ceiling and elaborate chandeliers to a scene in a period drama, while also serving the useful secondary purpose of hiding overhead catwalks, lights, studio workmen and rigging that would otherwise have been visible. In point of fact, building a real ceiling on a set might have been possible, but was seldom desirable from a production perspective; beyond the increased expense of physical set construction, the ceiling would have made it significantly more difficult to light the scene, which in turn would have required more personnel and lighting instruments. In other words, the combination of factors to make and photograph a real ceiling made it prohibitively expensive to do so.

*For Korda's **The Thief of Bagdad** (1940), the grandfather of the British special effects industry, Walter Percy Day, painted this atmospheric Temple interior, perfectly blending the surrounding painting of the gigantic idol to the small area of live action set on which Sabu performed.*

From the beginning, painters were regularly challenged to deliver naturalistic scenes of real world settings that the average viewer would be unaware had, in fact, relied on artistic trickery. Such unobtrusive effects were termed "invisible," because they were of essentially normal situations one might encounter in regular day-to-day life. However, precisely because people were readily familiar with "reality," these shots required consummate skill to execute flawlessly.

In other cases, such as **The Thief of Bagdad** (1940), mattes helped to exponentially elevate production values that would otherwise have been too dangerous, unaffordable or impossible to film.

In the early days, glass panes were set-up on location or at the studio and the painter rendered the desired components with artists' oil paints directly on the transparent glass; once completed, the camera filmed the glass and live action at the same time onto an original camera negative. As Earl Thiesen remarked in the November, 1936 edition of *Movie Makers*:

"Glass paintings are not simple, since the picture must be photographic in technique. The details, tone values and harmony of all parts of the painting must resemble a photograph and must match the perspective and photographic values of the setting. Very few artists have the ability necessary to do a glass painting." [1]

When such an image replacement scene is completed without requiring any post-production optical processing, it is called an "in-camera" or "O-neg" (original negative) effect and was always the preferred way to go for delivering the best negative possible. Glass shots by their very nature produce high quality footage because the artwork and live action are composited, that is, combined, at the same time onto a negative.

Matte paintings, on the other hand, are added to scenes in a specialized facility with dedicated equipment. The final composites blending live action and painted elements could be done with rear projection, bi-pack printing, or optical printing.

Norman O. Dawn's name is obscure today, but historically he was a true visionary, among the first to paint elements on glass to modify existing locations or sets. Like many technicians, he quicly started wearing many hats as a skilled cinematographer, special effects designer and gifted representational artist. Given his many talents, it should be no surprise that he quickly branched out as a producer and director.

He worked with many silent-era luminaries such as Mack Sennett, Carl Laemmle, Irving Thalberg, and Erich von Stroheim. In his career, Dawn executed an astonishing 861 effects shots in more than 80 movies, and his notebooks detail how he proceeded step-by-step.

Dawn's mastery of matte painting and special effects began while at the Thorpe Engraving Company in Los Angeles, where, among other things, he took photographs of real estate properties. His boss introduced him to the concept of shooting through a glass on which bits of oil paint were judiciously applied and soon, a photoengraver friend, Max Handschiegl, suggested Dawn could use the process on a current assignment.

On February 11, 1905, Dawn set up his Eastman 8x10 view camera with a glass in front of it for the express purpose of artistically improving a location, and his brush successfully replaced telephone poles with more aesthetically-pleasing trees. He had executed his first composite scene and coined the term "glass shot" to describe his method of image replacement.

A self-taught artist, he went to Paris in 1906 to refine his skills and met the brilliant film pioneer, Georges Mèliés, who exerted a profound affect on Dawn; the young American saw Mèliés as a kindred soul who also blended artistry with cinematography. Dawn also met the

Lumiere brothers and other pioneers who further encouraged his interest in filmmaking, and in early 1907, Dawn purchased a motion picture camera from the French innovator, Andre Debrie.

At that time, the monopolistic Motion Picture Patents Co. actively prevented the manufacture of cameras in the U.S. as well as the importation of equipment not licensed under its patents, forcing Dawn to smuggle his camera and raw stock into the country. The poisonous influence of the MPPC drove filmmakers on the East Coast to flee to California and Dawn joined them.

Because there were so few cameras—and cameramen—to feed the growing demand for filmed entertainment, Dawn was encouraged to create original productions, which led to his first entrepreneurial motion picture project in April, 1907, **Missions of California**. While he shot plenty of predictably scenic footage of various missions, the film is noteworthy because he applied himself to improving one location by executing a glass shot in which the structure's missing arches were restored: thanks to his painting skills, one could say he "miraculously" resurrected the building!

He quickly sold the one-reeler for the princely sum of $150.00 and was soon making more shorts. For **Hale's Tours** (1907), popular travelogues presented to audiences inside simulated railway cars, Dawn filmed railroad excursions in Mexico which also included glass shots at appropriate locations.

Dawn filmed shorts around the world for the next few years, occasionally using his glass shots, during which he realized that generating glass shots on location consumed a lot of time during which he was at the mercy of the weather. He began to consider a refinement to his process that would allow him to complete the compositing more comfortably in his studio; the first time he utilized his new approach was on January 14, 1911, for a film he photographed, produced and directed, **Story of the Andes**, a two-reel production shot on location in Bolivia. He considered it to be his earliest truly professional effort. His new technique proved beneficial for clients in Hollywood, by freeing directors from the constraints of being forced to shoot exteriors at a specific time when daylight on the set matched the glass art.

His solution to completing a composite in his workshop started by first filming the essential live action set or location through a glass on which he conformed black cardboard to create a hard-edged mask; this prevented the exposure on the negative of the area where the painted element would be added in a second step. The undeveloped film was then transported to his studio and threaded into a second camera mounted on a heavy lathe bed.

After processing a few feet of the original negative, Dawn traced the live action onto art board and painted that area flat black. His painting—done with pastels on art board—carefully matched the perspective, light direction and tone of the live action. The black area on the art board prevented that area from being re-exposed when the painting was filmed, and because the final composite was a latent image on the original camera negative, it was the best quality possible—comparable to a glass shot.

In his notebooks Dawn says he was still using his Debrie camera in 1910 and that his best early Hollywood work was for a Selig two-reel comedy, **The Black Pirate** (1911). By 1912, he had upgraded to a Bell & Howell Standard, the first all-metal 35mm motion picture

Norman Dawn's glass painting set-up in Port Arthur, Tasmania.

Dawn replaced a roof on the structure and extended the building itself.

Ferdinand Pinney Earle in his studio. He is believed to be surrounded by mattes painted by him for his "lost" film, **The Rubaiyat of Omar Khayam** *(1925).*

camera, with a major advance: a pin-registered intermittent movement, which guaranteed rock-steady frame registration during multiple passes through the camera. It was also engineered to enable cinematographers to employ handmade mattes that could be positioned inside the camera behind the lens.

Dawn prepared these mattes by laying a frame of test negative over a commercially-available "blank" made of red fiber board and cut away the area where the painting would be added. There were also readily available mattes to simulate looking through binoculars, for instance. Incidentally, Dawn did use glass shots from time to time in later films such as **Mr. Robinson Crusoe** (1932).

Dawn patented his invention on June 11, 1918, No. 1,269,061, for a process using photographs of the foreground as a cut-out mask, behind which a background was added. Three years later, he sued other matte artists for patent infringement. The co-defendants, including fellow-pioneers Ferdinand Pinney Earle and Walter Percy Day, counter-sued, claiming that the use of masks and counter-masks had been a long-standing process in the industry. Dawn lost his suit and left Hollywood, working in Australia for a number of years, where he directed the first talkie made "down under," a musical called **Showgirl's Luck** (1931), before eventually returning to America.

Some historians feel that Dawn founded the Universal matte department in the 1920's, and Albert Whitlock remarked that the easel he used to paint glasses on for years was originally put together by Dawn himself.

Assorted still photographers had used compositing techniques well in advance of the arrival of motion pictures, such as C. M. Coolidge, who in 1874 was granted patent No. 149,724 for a process of making composite prints by masking. Dawn's lawsuit clearly showed that a number of his motion picture contemporaries had cleverly devised their own similar image replacement methods and filed patents. One even pre-dated Dawn: in 1912, A. Engelsmann was granted patent No. 1,019,141 for combining actors and artwork on a glass placed in front of a painted backdrop.

J. Searle Dawley was arguably the first professional director in the U.S. He started working for Edison in 1907 and on August 17, 1914 filed a patent for "The Art of Making Motion-Pictures." Patent No. 1,278,117 was issued on September 10, 1918, and included a method of using an angled glass to reflect a photograph or artwork to enhance the scene being filmed.

In 1921, Walter G. Hall, a British Art Director, patented the so-called "Hall Process," which eliminated the glass, instead utilizing high-quality paintings on sturdy cardboard. These were carefully cut with the beveled edge slanted away from the lens and mounted in front of the camera, like hanging miniatures, via camouflaged supports. Like the glass shot, the composite was made on original camera negative, so the image was pristine and the production company could see the finished shot the next day. Decades later, the Spanish craftsman Emilio Ruiz del Río would use a variation on the technique to produce convincing in-camera composites on dozens of films.

No less than director D.W. (David Wark) Griffith was granted patent No. 1,476,885 in 1923 for using a painted screen with a hole cut in it, through which actors were visible and combined with the painted scene. Ralph Hammeras filed for a patent on a new glass shot technique and was granted patent No. 1,540,213 in 1925.

Eugene Schüfftan was granted patent No. 1,569,789 in 1926 for his novel method of combining miniatures or painted elements with live action using a front-silvered mirror. His mirror composites became known as "Schüfftan Shots" and helped Fritz Lang create the awe-inspiring settings in **Metropolis** (1927). In fact, the process was used extensively throughout Europe and the UK well into the 1930s. Schüfftan was also a renowned director of photography, later winning an Oscar® for black and white cinematography for **The Hustler** (1961).

Ferdinand Pinney Earle, one of the rival artists/technicians sued by Dawn, subsequently nursed a fierce grudge against Dawn while working in Hollywood. Earle studied at the Academie Julian in Paris under the great William Bouguereau and was a classically trained artist who created numerous paintings for productions like the Douglas Fairbanks **Robin Hood** (1922) and—like his nemesis, Dawn—had the ambitious vision of shepherding his own productions. He was the guiding light behind **The Rubaiyat of Omar Khayyam** (1925), which at this time remains a "lost" production from which many opulent matte shots survive.

Paul Detlefsen got his start the same way many other matte artists did, by painting scenic backings. His mattes helped bring to life ancient Egyptian settings for **Dancer of the Nile** (1923), done under the supervision of Ferdinand Pinney Earle—for which he was paid $24 a week (about $360 a week today).

Detlefsen said, "In the early days of silent movies I was my own camera technician. Following a stint with Cecil B. DeMille on **The Volga Boatman** (1926) and **King of Kings** (1927), the most rewarding experience I had as an independent special effects man was with Douglas Fairbanks on **The Iron Mask** (1929). That was when he was married to Mary Pickford and it was one of the 'Musketeer' pictures. He was so pleased with the way my partner and I did the ending—in which all four Musketeers are joined again in Heaven—that he just couldn't do enough for us. He gave us a print of the whole last reel in addition to paying us handsomely. Before long I became head at RKO and was able to design and equip my studio as I had long dreamed. That was just before the big stock market crash and the depression. RKO then changed hands and virtually closed down. I was temporarily out of work.

"After we lost our home and all of our savings it became apparent that I'd have to find work elsewhere. At long last I received a call from Warner Bros. They needed a scene with vast fields of cotton for **Cabin in the Cotton** (1932) with Bette Davis. There was a strong wind on location and I knew my painted trees would look strange without a single leaf stirring, so I devised a way of getting movement into them. The clouds I painted also transformed the scene into a thing of beauty, exceeding my own expectations. The director, Michael Curtiz, who made it very clear when we met that he had no faith in me, was so pleased that he insisted I be put under contract at once. That picture was the beginning of a long, fascinating and lucrative association with Warner Bros." (2)

He spent twenty years at Warner Bros., eventually heading the matte department, and painted mattes for **Dodge City** (1939), **They Died With Their Boots On** (1941), the Oscar®-nominated **The Adventures of Mark Twain** (1944), **To Have and Have Not** (1944), **San Antonio** (1945), **Mildred Pierce** (1945), **The Beast with Five Fingers** (1946) and many others. His last matte was for **Androcles and the Lion** (1952), after which Detlefsen become a celebrated calendar artist. His first collection of pastoral landscapes, *The Good Old Days*, was published in 1951 and by 1969, United Press International estimated that 80% of Americans had seen his art.

Ralph Hammeras, the first recipient of an Oscar® nomination for special effects (for his glass shots in Alexander Korda's **The Private Life of Helen of Troy** in 1927) was unique in that he was also an expert in photographing miniatures.

Working with Willis O'Brien on **The Lost World** (1925) was the beginning of a life-long friendship. Hammeras supervised the miniatures and also introduced OBie to the glass shot, which Hammeras was executing for the film. As an artist, himself, OBie immediately grasped the possibilities of the technique and would later execute and supervise mattes himself for various studios.

Left: The exterior live action and the final composite (right) featuring a painting by Paul Detlefsen, done in Warner Bros.' special effects department for **The Adventures of Robin Hood** *(1939).*

Ralph Hammeras

Supervisor of Miniature and Trick Department

FOX STUDIOS

After **The Lost World**, OBie and Hammeras prepared concepts for **Atlantis**, but that film was never made. Years later Hammeras painted moody art elements gratis to help OBie out on the micro-budgeted indie, **The Black Scorpion** (1957).

Ralph Hammeras was head of the effects department at Fox but for reasons that are now unclear, he was replaced by Fred Sersen but remained a part of the team, working on **Dante's Inferno** (1935), **In Old Chicago** (1937), the Jack Benny film **Charley's Aunt** (1941), **A Yank in the R.A.F.** (1941, Oscar®-nominated) and many others, as well as the first CinemaScope feature to be released, **The Robe** (1954).

Hammeras received Oscar® nominations for **Just Imagine** (1930) and **Deep Waters** (1948) and won an Oscar® for **20,000 Leagues Under the Sea** (1954) for which he was miniatures photographer. At the other end of the scale, he supervised miniature work for the notoriously so-bad-its-good **The Giant Claw** (1957) as well as **The Giant Gila Monster** (1959), which was directed by Ray Kellogg, a fellow matte artist from Fox, who had been Fred Sersen's right hand man.

*A glass painting setup for **King Kong** (1933), depicting the grotto in Kong's lair where he does battle with an Elasmasaurus. While this painting was likely rendered by Mario Larrinaga, the method of painting environments on glass was an approach that Ralph Hammeras introduced to Willis O'Brien eight years earlier for **The Lost World**.*

*Top: A Ralph Hammeras matte for the Fox epic **Cleopatra** (1963).*

*Middle two photos: The miniature street in **The Lost World** (1925).*

*Willis O'Brien's **The Black Scorpion** (1957) made extensive use of painted settings by Ralph Hammeras.*

44 · *Smoke and Mirrors – Special Visual Effects Before Computers*

The 20th Century-Fox matte department in the 1950s. L-R: Ray Kellogg, Lee Leblanc, Cliff Silsby, Emile Kosa Jr, and departament head Fred Sersen.

During WWII matte artist Ray Kellogg was a Navy Lieutenant and served as a cameraman with the O.S.S. Field Photographing Branch, where he became acquainted with director John Ford. Kellogg produced and directed **The Nazi Plan** (1945) using German-made documentary footage, which was presented as evidence at the Nuremberg War Crimes Trials. Much of the footage of the Trials was filmed by Kellogg and seen in subsequent documentaries.

In 1952 Kellogg became head of the effects department at 20th Century-Fox and one of his earliest assignments was the first CinemaScope production, **The Robe** (1953). Kellogg said he felt that CinemaScope was more important to the industry than the advent of sound and predicted matte paintings would become even more useful. He also contributed to **Deep Waters** (1948, Oscar®-nominated), **Les Miserables** (1952), **Titanic** (1953), **Demetrius and the Gladiators** (1954), **Hell and High Water** (1954, Oscar®-nominated), **The Rains of Ranchipur** (1955, Oscar®-nominated), **Soldier of Fortune** (1955), and **Desk Set** (1957). In 1957 he passed the torch to L.B. Abbott to concentrate on being a second unit director at Fox and worked on **Cleopatra** (1963, Oscar®-winner), **Batman: The Movie** (1966), **Castle Keep** (1969) and **Tora! Tora Tora!** (1970, Oscar®-winner).

Ray Kellogg later directed the independent films **The Giant Gila Monster** (1959) and **The Killer Shrews** (1959).

*Above: Ray Kellogg, second from left, and associates during the documentary filming of the Nuremberg war crimes trials in 1945. Although Kellogg ventured into feature films as a director with **The Giant Gila Monster** and **The Killer Shrews**, he should not be confused with the **actor** Ray Kellogg, who racked up some 199 credits ranging from **The Man From U.N.C.L.E.** to **Green Acres**.*

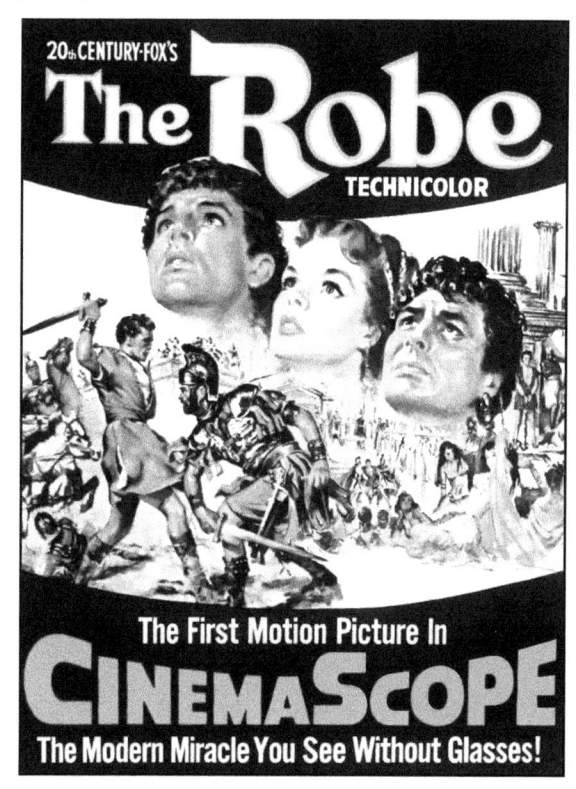

Spectacle On Glass

Above: This panoramic view of Alexandria for **Cleopatra** (1963) used two panes of glass, with the join hidden by the statue. This staple technique of Fox visual effects was executed by Joseph Natanson (who was trained by Percy Day) and British muralist Mary Adshead Bone. Infamous for many years as the most expensive film ever made, the cost overruns and exhorbitant excesses of **Cleopatra** forced 20th Century-Fox to sell off the valuable real estate that made up its back lot, and that business and shopping district is now known as Century City. Ironically, the "Nakatomi Plaza" building that is the central location of the first **Die Hard** movie in 1988 is a prominent feature of Century City.

Above: Joseph Natanson and Mary Adshead Bone with one-half of their panoramic glass shot.

46 · *Smoke and Mirrors – Special Visual Effects Before Computers*

GLASS SCREEN — OPENING FOR FILMING ACTION

Only the steps and pillars of this set are built. The rest of the sultan's palace is painted on a piece of glass through which the camera photographs.

ACTION FILMED THRU THIS UNPAINTED OPENING

HOW GLASS LOOKS TO EYE

Left: A vintage diagram of the basic glass shot setup as published in the magazine **Modern Mechanics and Inventions** in the 1920s.

Below, left: The glass painting setup by Paul Grimm for **Noah's Ark** (1927).

Below, right: The finished composite of live action and unusual architecture.

Spectacle On Glass • 47

"Each day do loyal men rally to our cause. 'Twill not be long ere we storm the very castle itself."
— Robin Hood
(Douglas Fairbanks)

Robin Hood *(1922). The above scene features a matte painting by F. P. Earle and such sequences utilized as many as 1,200 extras. The live action portion of the castle set is reputed to be the largest Hollywood set built for any silent movie. Under the guidance of supervising art director Wilfred Buckland, set designer Lloyd Wright (Frank Lloyd Wright's son) designed one set which he later remodeled as a temporary band shell for the Hollywood Bowl. Requiring a million feet of lumber and thirty tons of nails, the design, labor and materials for the massive sets for this film came to a cost of $248,000 (about $3.8 million today). The top-grossing U.S. film of 1922,* **Robin Hood** *has the distinction of being the first to have a gala premiere, conceived by theater owner Sid Grauman and held at Grauman's then-brand new Egyptian Theater in Hollywood.*

In July, 1929, when he was Chief of the Art Department at William Fox Studios, Fred Sersen wrote *Making Matte Shots: Some of the Intricacies of Making Things Seem What They Are Not—Explained for the Amateur by an Expert with Years of Experience* for **American Cinematographer** magazine.

Writing this article is rather an unusual way of expressing my thoughts, as I have seen used to doing so by means of paint and brushes for the last twenty years, and juggling the pen is somewhat clumsy. The editor of this magazine asked me to write something about 'matte shots' as we call them in this studio, and I will try to describe the process of making them and how they can be used to best advantage.

"Some will say 'we have glass shots and miniatures, why use matte shots at all?' There are cases when some process will do better than others. I will enumerate some instances when the matte shots can be used to better advantage than anything else.

"Sometimes the sets are not exactly as they should be, due to many reasons—incidents that come up daily—such as changing the script at the last minute, or the director may have some idea of his which came to him on the spur of the moment. Or the cameraman may see better composition if he shoots the set from a different angle, due to change of light or some other unforeseen reason, or to create a beautiful scene where one did not exist.

"The use of a matte enables a cameraman to make the picture he visualizes. He is no longer limited by the size of the set, poor light, etc. It makes it possible for him to create and carry out the ideas he has for the enrichment of the production. I have seen cameramen by the use of ingenuity and mattes double the value of a production.

"For instance: a company went to Nevada to photograph some battle scenes in a snow storm. To build the sets there would have been very costly, while without them the desired Russian atmosphere could hardly be obtained. (It happened to be a Russian picture). While they were walking around looking for the most suitable locations, they happened to run across an old concrete dam. The cameraman, being of a highly creative mind, began to visualize an old fortress connected with that wall of concrete, and before long he had a matte cut out of a piece of card-board and placed in the matte box so as to block out that piece of scenery where the fortress was supposed to be. The scene was photographed and was finished in the studio very successfully showing a fortress of great production value.

"In cases of this kind it is necessary for the cameraman to be able to visualize the complete scene so as to be able to make a matte in the right place and provide enough space for the object to be painted in. He has to use good judgment as to how sharp a matte to make. If there are definite lines in the picture it is easier for an artist to match to the sharp lines and it is best for the matte to be placed about thirty inches from the camera, even further if the glass or the material to be used for the matte is easy to obtain. Again when matting to the foot-

48 · *Smoke and Mirrors – Special Visual Effects Before Computers*

age (especially when there is any wind blowing) or when dust is created by action in the scene, in a rain or snow storm, very soft blend is desirable and the matte should be placed four to six inches from the lens."

"It is a difficult thing to make a good combination shot of rain, snow or dust storm with a glass or miniature, because of the distance between the real set being so much greater than that between the glass or miniature and the camera. In this case the matte shot is much the best. By double exposing or double printing the rain or whatever it may be, all over the film, makes it a perfect shot.

"Where the mechanism of the miniature is too complicated, or if there are any other reasons that might delay the company while shooting, mattes are the most plausible remedy. The process is very practical—when putting two or three exposures together, by matting out the undesirable portion of the picture one can double expose or double print anything right on the original negative, which eliminates the process of duping which means much to the quality of the film.

"The cameraman conceives the effects or settings he desires and directs his camera as if the scene existed. By using opaque paint on glass or snipping out a piece of black cardboard and placing it in a rigid position between the subject and the lens those portions of the scene are blocked out so that the film is unexposed in those parts to permit the subsequent exposure of the painting. The camera is 'planted' [that is, securely bolted down and made absolutely immobile] to prevent further movement, and a test scene is made as nearly under the same lighting conditions as is possible. Then the actual scenes are made, a record being kept of the footage, fade-outs, etc.

"The test film, of which we usually have about one hundred feet, and the scene itself is turned over to the artist undeveloped. We take a few feet of the test and develop it, and this is used for lining up. There are several methods that can be used for lining up a 'matte shot.'

"One can project the film through a camera on to a highly colored surface on which the artist is going to paint, and draw the outlines of the objects of the first exposure, which gave the base to draw to. After the drawing is completed, it is laid in with oil paint in black and white, and on the artist's ability and experiences depends the matching of the tones of the first exposure, which is ascertained by making the hand test and comparing the tones. He does this repeatedly by correcting the painting until the match is perfect. Another system is to line up the shot by using auxiliary aperture and looking through it to guide the drawing of the picture.

"The third method is to double expose over the original exposure a black screen divided by white lines into one inch squares which are duplicated on the surface of the would-be painting, and the image of the original exposure is transferred by aid of these squares. It is the same system that is used by artists in enlarging a drawing. In all cases enlargements of 9x12 inches should be made in order to better see the details of the picture.

"The system we are using in this studio and which is most practical in about seventy-five per cent of 'matte shots' is to make an enlargement of the picture on the paper which is mounted on a specially prepared board. This gives the artist a perfect picture of the scene and he can work out his drawing, tones and composition and see the picture as a whole before he paints his reverse matte on. It eliminates a long and tedious job of lining up, which is connected with the methods previously mentioned. One can appreciate the advantages of this system better when there are numerous objects to match to a very accurate printing. To demonstrate this, I would describe a shot I made of changing Michigan Avenue in Chicago from a day to a night shot.

"We took a day shot of Michigan Avenue with automobiles and pedestrians in busy commotion as only American thoroughfares can be, and had an enlargement made of it. I painted the enlargement of the day shot into a night effect and the match was so perfect that in a four-foot lap dissolve one could not detect any variation in form whatever. It was a rather complicated shot and here is the process we used. Day shot was duped with a four-foot grid laid out. Into that we lap the painting of the city at night, and the automobile traffic was double printed in by using positive of a film we photographed on the local street which was exactly the same width and same elevation as in the day shot. The shot had to be photographed at dusk when the head-lights of the automobiles were on. The pedestrians on the side walk were printed in from the day shot as well as the lower part of the first stories of the buildings, with automobiles parked against the curb. Only those acquainted with this type of work can fully understand what it takes to balance the lighting and painting of these separate parts of a picture and what perfect mattes had to be used in printing hard edges of the automobile contours.

"The enlargement comes handy when we have three or more exposures to be put into one picture. By making separate enlargements on the same piece of enlarging paper will give us perfect outlines to the mattes which are used for double printing as well as the connecting painting which is double exposed in. For instance, we had part of a boat built for the action of people moving about on deck which was backed up by painted backing. This was to be made into a picture of the boat cutting through ice in the Arctic sea, with the clouds passing by. We built the hull of the boat in miniature which matched the set boat built for the scene, and photographed it with speed camera, the miniature ice floating by. This was double printed into the original take, and painted to connect the two, and the rigging was double exposed afterwards. The real clouds were photographed moving in the proper direction, aided by panning the camera, and then double printed in, which required some fine matting.

"Too much attention cannot be paid to the steadiness of the exposure, as the least movement in the film will cause a distinct movement between two exposures. The films should be measured so the perforations would be perfectly cut into the film when intended for matte shots, and the camera buckled down securely. All the work should be done through a camera fastened to a title block fastened to a concrete pedestal." (3)

Fred Sersen

(Sersen's actual painted signature)

Another matte artist at Fox was Lee LeBlanc who had started at Disney for a salary of $10 per week. When he had a chance to see a bump in income he moved to Leon Schlesinger's unit at Warner Brothers. In 1941, friends helped him get into the Fox effects department, where he started out building miniatures before becoming an accomplished matte painter.

LeBlanc departed Fox in 1955 to replace Warren Newcombe as the head of the matte department at MGM. LeBlanc worked on **Cat on a Hot Tin Roof** (1958), **Ben-Hur** (1959, Oscar®-winner), **Tarzan the Ape Man** (1959), **Cimarron** (1960), **Mutiny on the Bounty** (1962), George Pal's **Atlantis the Lost Continent** (1962), **The Four Horsemen of the Apocalypse** (1962) and others.

In 1962 LeBlanc began a new phase of his life, creating fine art featuring wildlife for calendars, children's books, national magazines and Gibson Greeting Cards, in the same way Paul Detlefsen had left Hollywood to become an acclaimed landscape painter.

Throughout the 1970s LeBlanc received acclaim for his wildlife illustrations, including winning the Federal Duck Stamp Design contest in 1973-1974. In 1975 he received the Golden Mallard Award from the Arkansas Wildlife Federation and in 1976 he was honored as Artist of the Year by Tennessee Ducks Unlimited. In 1979, he received the Michigan Ducks Unlimited Waterfowl Artist Award.

*Fred Sersen was Oscar®-nominated for **The Blue Bird** (1940), **A Yank In The R.A.F.** (1941), and **The Black Swan** (1942), and won for **The Rains Came** (1939) and **Crash Dive** (1943). He was also responsible for the UFO in the 1951 classic **The Day the Earth Stood Still** (above).*

The Matte Department at 20th Century-Fox, November, 1953.

50 · *Smoke and Mirrors – Special Visual Effects Before Computers*

*Matte artists Paul Detlefsen and Mario Larrinaga add to the dramatic climax of **Casablanca** (1942). The work was done at Warner Bros.' own in-house special effects unit, Stage 5, headed by Lawrence Butler.*

Warren Newcombe, the respected head of MGM's matte department, studied fine art in Boston at the Normal Art School. After graduating in 1914, he moved to New York City and worked as a teacher and commercial illustrator. He first worked on a film in Boston in 1918 as a set designer for an Atlas production. In 1920 Newcombe worked as an artist and designer for producer Louis Selznick in Ft. Lee, New Jersey while continuing to pursue his passion for fine art by painting landscapes in his spare time. In 1921 he left the studio to work with screenwriter Clarence Doty Hobart on **The Woman God Changed**, a courtroom melodrama, during which time Newcombe was conceptualizing the principles of matte painting.

In 1922 he created a new title sequence for the re-release of Enrico Guzzzoni's **Quo Vadis** (1912), the first feature-length epic. Some sources claim he worked on **The Headless Horseman** (1922), the first movie based on Washington Irving's story, which starred Will Rogers.

Following his artistic muse, Newcombe created the short "art films" **The Enchanted City** (1922) and **The Sea of Dreams** (1923), today respected as significant early experimental films. The inventive visuals caught the eye of director D.W. Griffith who had built a studio on Long Island, and in 1923 Griffith hired Newcombe to design sets for Griffith's historical epic, **America** (1924, aka **Love and Sacrifice**). Mattes made the 18th-century Revolutionary War settings believable and Newcombe received one of the earliest credits for matte paintings.

Newcombe moved to Los Angeles in 1925, bringing with him matte painter Neil McGuire. Reportedly it was McGuire who painted most of the mattes through the 20s and 30s. Soon after, Newcombe began his long association with MGM where he treated his department as his personal fiefdom. He was a supervisor with a large stable of accomplished artists, often from commercial illustration backgrounds. Staff painters Irving Block and Matthew Yuricich stated that Warren never picked up a paintbrush. During his forty years in the film business Newcombe collaborated with directors such as King Vidor, George Cukor, William Wyler and Vincente Minnelli.

His 175 productions include **Dr. Jekyll and Mr. Hyde** (1941), **A Guy Named Joe** (1943), **30 Seconds Over Tokyo** (1944, Oscar®-winner), **Gaslight** (1944), **They Were Expendable** (1945, Oscar®-nominated), **Green Dolphin Street** (1947, Oscar®-winner), **An American in Paris** (1951), **Singin' in the Rain (1952), Forbidden Planet** (1956, Oscar®-nominated), and was Assistant Special Effects Supervisor for the classic,**The Wizard of Oz** (1939, Oscar®-nominated).

His original lithographs are part of many public collections, including the Frederick R. Weisman Art Museum, Minneapolis, and the Nelson-Atkins Museum of Art, Kansas City. Only his 1937 lithograph, *Anna Karenina in Hollywood*, shared a knowing glimpse into his life in motion pictures; it is an outstanding piece of art that also offers an amusing insight into the realities of production, with a bored crew member waiting while a scene starring Greta Garbo is being filmed.

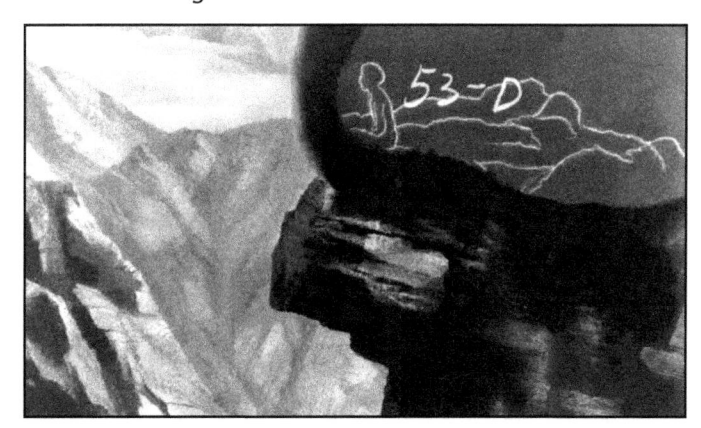

*Above: An incomplete matte by Warren Newcombe's department for Willis O'Brien's **War Eagles** (1938), which Merian C. Cooper was producing at MGM prior to the outbreak of WWII. Many feel this would have been one of the greatest fantasy-adventures ever made.*

Spectacle On Glass • 51

*Chesley Bonestell poses with his concept painting of the new world Zyra for George Pal's **When World Collide** (1951). This art was used as an editorial "place-holder" but ended up being left in the final cut of the movie (below) to save the costs of producing and filming the properly executed final art.*

Over at Paramount Jan Domela was a part of Gordon Jennings team and later worked for John Fulton, adding atmosphere and set extensions to countless films such as Cecil B. deMille's **Union Pacific** (1939, Oscar®-nominated), **Reap the Wild Wind** (1942, Oscar®-winner), **Samson and Delilah** (1949, Oscar®-nominated) and **The 10 Commandments** (1956, Oscar®-winner). Perhaps some of his most memorable mattes were done for George Pal's **When Worlds Collide** (1951, Oscar®-winner), **War of the Worlds** (1953, Oscar®-winner) and **Conquest of Space** (1955).

Chesley Bonestell was a fine artist who had studied architecture at Columbia University in New York (but did not graduate). Between 1910 and 1938, he worked as an architect/architectural illustrator and was involved in building the Chrysler Building in New York and the Golden Gate Bridge in San Francisco.

His film work included backings and/or mattes for **The Adventures of Robin Hood** (1938), **The Hunchback of Notre Dame** (1939), **Citizen Kane** (1941), **The Magnificent Ambersons** (1942), and **The Adventures of Mark Twain** (1944, Oscar®-nominated)).

The mood at the beginning of George Pal's **War of the Worlds** (1953) when the audience is treated to a Technicolor tour of the solar system is highlighted by scientifically accurate vistas of the canyons of Jupiter, the rings of Saturn, and more. To realize these impossible scenes, Pal turned to Bonestell, who had previously helped create the other-worldly visual effects for **Destination Moon** (1950) and **When Worlds Collide** (1951)—which, with **War of the Worlds**, completed a trifecta of visual effects Oscar®-winners.

Most of the astronomical art was painted on stretched canvas, but Jupiter was executed on a 7'x4' glass with black areas where lifelike streams of molten lava would later be added optically. Miniature foregrounds enhanced the effectiveness of the paintings, such as wind buffeting surface dirt and ice crystals on Mars. But wait—could that be a Martian city in the distance? *(opposite page, bottom)*. Incidentally, this approach inspired Academy Award®-winner Dennis Muren to use the same methods for his 1972 educational film, **The Solar System: Islands in Space**.

52 · *Smoke and Mirrors – Special Visual Effects Before Computers*

George Pal *(left)* described his working relationship with Chesley Bonestell: "As technical adviser he was also our troubleshooter. He's the one who questioned accuracy when screenwriter Barré Lyndon gave the night temperature on Mars... we have never seen the night side of Mars through telescopes so we can only guess at the temperature. Better cut it out. Then the script presented Saturn as peaceful and quiet. Bonestell advised that the bands around Saturn—not the famous rings—appear stormy. As contact man between us and scientists at California Institute of Technology—which we call Pacific Tech—Bonestell kept us on the right track." [4]

Bonestell's visionary astronomical illustrations appeared in a series of articles called *Man Will Conquer Space Soon* (1952-1954) in **Collier's** magazine, inspiring those who would ultimately take us to the Moon. He also contributed to books, including Willy Ley s **Conquest of the Moon** (1953 and Wernher von Braun's **The Exploration of Mars** (1960).

Byron Haskin—the director of *War of the Worlds*—described the problems color presented to the artists who laboriously matched tones in black and white renderings to live action elements shot on black and white stock: "It is obvious that the coloring of the actual set or landscape of the live-action portion of the shot must be precisely matched by the coloring of their respective continuations in the painting. This is by no means easy.

"It is entirely possible that the pigments used to paint a set may not photograph with the same Technicolor values as will visually identical pigments used in producing the matte painting. Therefore, the matte painter must not only know what colors were used in the set, but what paints were used to produce those colors. Where it is possible, he should have samples of the colors and paints used. The same, of course, is also true of fabrics and the like where they enter the matte painter's problem.

"Equally important is the color of the lighting used in photographing the matte painting. Most Technicolor interiors are lit with special arc equipment which gives a light very closely matched to natural daylight." [5]

Spectacle On Glass · 53

Walter Percy "Pop" Day

In England, a remarkable man created black and white mattes and transitioned to color, and in so doing, created some of the most sumptuously elegant paintings ever done. He was one of the influential early matte artists sued by Norman Dawn for patent infringement, and over the course of his career Day exerted a profound influence on England's visual effects industry.

Walter Percy Day began his career in 1919 at Ideal Films Studios in Borehamwood and it was there that he mastered the skills for matte painting. Unfortunately, the British film industry was stagnating while the French film industry was robust, which encouraged Day to emigrate in 1922, where he introduced the glass shot in Henry Roussel's *Les Opprimés* (1923). Another of his early assignments, André Hugon's *L'arriviste* (1924), inadvertently caused a furor when an angry member of parliament saw the film and was incensed that a foreigner had been permitted to film inside the Chambre des Députés! Day had skillfully painted the interior so effectively that the politician was fooled—which undoubtedly angered him even more.

This compliment to his skills brought him to the attention of leading directors like Jean Renoir, Julien Duvivier and Abel Gance. Day was one of three visual effects creators working on the epic *Napoléon* (1927) and painted glass shots of the Club des Cordeliers, while also playing a bit part, Admiral Hood, the British general defeated by Napoléon at Toulon. The next time a matte artist would step in front of a camera was when Mel Brooks cast Albert Whitlock for a role in *High Anxiety* (1977).

In 1927, while still based in France, the Elstree studios hired Day to shoot visual effects for Alfred Hitchcock's *The Ring* (1927). For the first time in a British film, Day employed a mirror composite for the boxing ring scene at the Albert Hall. Eugen Schüfftan, who invented the mirror process which is named after him, personally taught Day how to do the set-ups. Namely, a mirror angled at 45° to the camera would reflect a miniature, painting, or photograph, except for where the silvering had been carefully removed to allow the camera to see through the glass and film the live action (i.e., simultaneously with the reflected element).

Arthur George Day, his son, joined his studio as draughtsman while his other son, Thomas Sydney Day, served as both cinematographer and still photographer, all working together for the first time on Léon Poirier's production of *Verdun: Visions of History* (1928). From that point on he was called "Poppa Day" or "Pop Day" and would be joined in the 1930s by his stepson Peter Ellenshaw (himself a mainstay of Walt Disney productions for his matte paintings years later).

A scene for Julien Duvivier's film *Au Bonheur des Dames* (1929) presented a challenge: the narrow street wouldn't permit placing the camera back far enough to get the right angle. Further, because Day preferred

DEBORAH KERR
"Black Narcissus"

Black Narcissus (1947) was set in the Himalayas but never left Pinewood Studios for that distant location (or even sent a second unit to shoot background plates) as Day's paintings supplied the dramatic mountain peaks. Many critics regard **Black Narcissus** as the best British film ever made, and for many it is highlighted by some of the most exquisitely-realized mattes ever done.

The pictures on these two pages show how **Black Narcissus** took audiences to a far-off land without leaving the studio.

Left: The top picture shows what little was required for the live action, the middle shows the scene without the matte, and the bottom picture shows how Day's stunningly executed painting completely sells the illusion of being high in the Himalayas.

---

working with larger glasses than his contemporaries, there were safety concerns about working with a twelve-foot-wide sheet of glass on a busy street. But Day had been formulating a different approach since his time at Elstree: like Norman Dawn, he used a black holdout matte during photography of the live action to prevent the area of his painted component from being exposed. The painting was later composited in Day's studio onto the original (unprocessed) negative. This latent image matte technique became known as the "Day Process" in France.

Returning to England in 1932, Pop Day worked with Alexander Korda on **The Private Life of Henry VIII** (1933). Faced with the prospect of more work, he established a studio in Iver, Buckinghamshire. In 1936, he was put in charge of the matte department at Denham Studios and created trick shots for productions by Korda, William Cameron Menzies, Michael Powell, David Lean and other notable British filmmakers. In 1946 Day joined the Korda group as Director of Special Effects at Shepperton Studios, where he remained until his retirement in 1954. He trained promising young matte painters, including Judy Jordan, Les Bowie, George Samuels, Albert Julion and Joseph Natanson. His cinematographer, Wally Veevers, took over the matte department when Poppa Day retired.

Like his American counterparts during WWII, Day was kept busy working on visual effects for morale-boosting films such as **49th Parallel** (1941), **In Which We Serve** (1942) and **The First of the Few** (1942) as well as general productions like Korda's **The Thief of Bagdad** (1940, Oscar®-winner), **Henry V** (1944), **A Matter of Life and Death** (1946), **Anna Karenina** (1948), and **The Third Man** (1949).

In 1948, Day was awarded the Officer of the Most Excellent Order of the British Empire (O.B.E.) for his services to British cinema. In his autobiography, Michael Powell proclaimed Percy Day as "the greatest trick-man and film wizard that I have ever known..." [6] Furthermore, in 2008, the British daily The Independent included Day in the same league as the much-better-known French visual effects pioneer, Georges Méliès. [7]

Spectacle On Glass • 55

*Above: In 1964 Walt Disney discusses the movie magic found in **Mary Poppins** with Peter Ellenshaw whose aerial view of London is behind him.*

Poppa Day's stepson, Peter S. Ellenshaw, worked with him on a number of those classic productions, beginning as an assistant on Korda's adaptation of H.G. Wells' ***Things to Come*** (1936) and ***The Thief of Bagdad*** (1940). After serving in WWII as a pilot for the Royal Air Force, Ellenshaw resumed his film career working with Poppa Day on ***An Ideal Husband*** (1947) and ***Black Narcissus*** (1947). At the British MGM Studio he worked with opticals expert Tom Howard and painted mattes for ***Quo Vadis*** (1951), re-creating ancient Rome in all its splendor.

His most enduring association was with Walt Disney and began with ***Treasure Island*** (1950). For ***The Sword and the Rose*** (1953) Ellenshaw produced 62 matte shots in only 27 weeks. In fact, he was unbelievably fast, often generating color sketches in only a few minutes and full four-foot-wide mattes in three days.

He worked at Disney over 30 years on ***20,000 Leagues Under the Sea*** (1954), for which he executed over a dozen matte shots, as well as ***Darby O'Gill and the Little People*** (1959), ***The Absent-Minded Professor*** (1961) and the original ***Mary Poppins*** (1964), which earned him an Oscar® for visual effects. Ellenshaw retired after ***The Black Hole*** (1979), for which he was nominated for an Academy Award® but later helped out with mattes for ***Dick Tracy*** (1990).

While visiting the Disney lot during ***The Black Hole***, I saw the stored glasses from many of Ellenshaw's films. All of them were stunning but I was especially struck by an aerial view of London he had painted for ***Mary Poppins***—it was not the representational art I had expected, but an impressionistic piece which revealed a mastery of light and color that "sold the scene."

When Walt was developing Disneyland, Ellenshaw contributed to popular original attractions such as ***Rocket to the Moon*** and ***Space Station X-1*** (later called ***X-1 Satellite View of America***). For the grand opening Ellenshaw painted an aerial view of the attractions which was used on the first Disneyland postcard and souvenir guidebook. The painting can be seen behind Walt during many of the introductions to his TV shows.

Walt's Disneyland TV series fueled a national obsession with ***Davy Crockett*** (1954) and ***Zorro*** (1957), and Ellenshaw's atmospheric mattes helped to immerse audiences in the heroes' adventures.

Once freed from the rigors of studio deadlines, he dedicated himself to artistic pursuits, becoming a premiere illustrator of landscapes and seascapes. Having fallen in love with the California coastline in the 1950s,

*Above: The set built for **Quo Vadis** (1951) and how Peter Ellenshaw's artistry showed magnificent ancient Rome at the height of its power.*

*Below: Harrison Ellenshaw puts the final touches on a glass painting for **The Empire Strikes Back** (1980).*

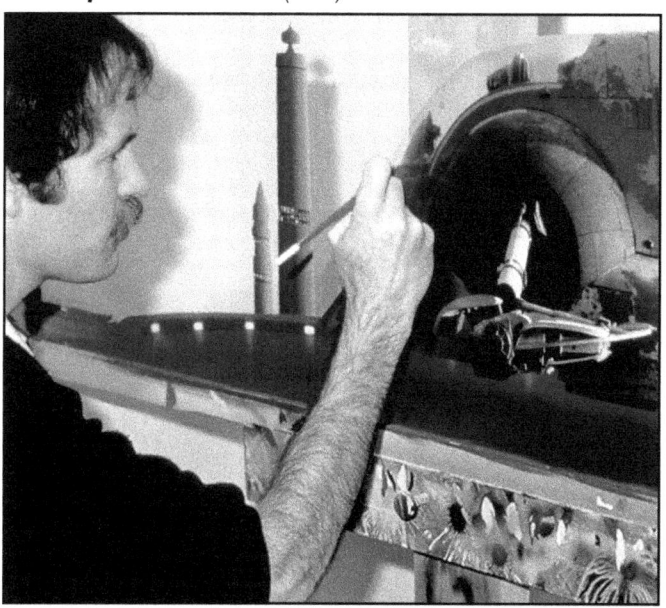

he escaped from the studio on weekends and painted the dramatic vistas along the ocean, many of which were sold to collectors through the renowned Hammer Galleries in New York. I saw several of his pieces at a fine art gallery in San Francisco and marveled at the photographic quality of such purely artistic visions. Ellenshaw also captured the entrancing landscapes of the Emerald Isle and his dramatic paintings were in a special exhibition at the American Embassy in Dublin.

In 1993 Disney CEO Michael Eisner and Roy E. Disney officially designated Ellenshaw a "Disney Legend" and commissioned him to paint scenes from Disney productions, several giclées of which have delighted collectors.

Harrison Ellenshaw, Peter's son, followed him as a matte artist. With a degree in psychology from Whittier College, he was steering for a career in business administration when his father suggested taking a temporary job in the matte department at Disney.

Working under English emigré Alan Maley—a Best Visual Effects Oscar®-winner for **Bedknobs and Broomsticks** (1971) who had worked with the elder Ellenshaw in the UK on Disney's **In Search of the Castaways** (1962)—Harrison contributed to Nicolas Roeg's **The Man Who Fell to Earth** (1976). He soon found himself involved with George Lucas on a little film called **Star Wars Episode IV: A New Hope** (1977) but soon returned to Disney to join his father on **The Black Hole**, for which they both received Oscar® nominations. After that, he joined Industrial Light and Magic (ILM) where he was responsible for the mattes on **Star Wars Episode V: The Empire Strikes Back** (1980).

He returned to Burbank to supervise fixes for **The Watcher in the Woods** (1980), and was soon involved in the production of **Tron** (1982), one of the earliest features to embrace CG—and for which Harrison was the first person to receive a credit as Visual Effects Supervisor. He was also involved with **Captain Eo** (1986), a 3D theme park film starring pop star Michael Jackson and produced in 65mm by Francis Ford Coppola and George Lucas. He was also a visual effects supervisor for **Superman IV** (1987) and contributed to the hugely successful romantic fantasy, **Ghost** (1990).

After **Dick Tracy** (1990), Disney asked him to head up a new effects facility on the Burbank lot and over the course of its six year existence, Buena Vista Visual Effects earned respect for its outstanding work servicing the industry on productions including **Honey I Blew Up the Kid** (1992), **The Santa Clause** (1994), **James and the Giant Peach** (1996), **Mortal Kombat** (1995), **Escape from LA** (1996) and nearly 60 more.

Like his father, he also nurtured a fine art career, producing one man shows for galleries in New York, San Francisco and Tokyo. In 2002 he teamed up with his father to create Disney-themed giclées.

Spectacle On Glass

It is impossible not to discuss matte paintings without acknowledging two artists who worked with Willis O'Brien ("OBie") on the motion picture many consider the most influential effects film of all time, **King Kong** (1933). Mario Larrinaga and Byron Crabbe brought the menacing jungles of Skull Island to life by meticulously painting the Gustave Doré-inspired trees and foliage on layers of glass while OBie supervised the many effects shots and, of course, personally animated Kong. OBie's multiple glasses and tabletops built depth few films have achieved since; the stegosaurus encounter is one of the most thrilling moments ever put on film, as the enraged dinosaur charges the astonished Carl Denham and his sailors—and us!

OBie generated highly-detailed master renderings for the required mattes and designed a special projector that could give the artists a precise guide for the paintings. However, Mario Larrinaga relied solely on his very practiced "eye." Starting in 1911 as an apprenticeship at Universal's scenic department mixing paints, it wasn't long before his natural talent led to painting scenic backdrops on canvas. It was relatively easy for him—as with many others similarly trained—to transition to painting mattes.

Both Larrinaga and Crabbe made contributions beyond the large glass paintings by creating concept art. Larrinaga defined the look of the native village, for instance, and both contributed designs for settings in **Son of Kong** (1933). Larrinaga retired in 1951 and moved to Taos, New Mexico with his wife and joined the art colony there.

Byron Crabbe and OBie produced an initial presentation painting depicting a semi-nude "jungle girl" brandishing a knife while a ferocious, wounded gorilla glares at an intrepid hunter.

The art used in Cooper's final pitch for **King Kong** consisted of dynamic black and white renderings of scenes guaranteed to thrill the viewer, including Kong's defiant stand atop the recently-completed Empire State Building. The impressive artwork did its job, persuading the studio to proceed with a one reel demonstration. Cooper had recently canceled a film called **Creation** on which OBie and his team had labored for a year, and no doubt Cooper pointed out that the expenses for his demo would be held down by using existing miniatures and animation puppets.

Crabbe worked on Cooper's **The Most Dangerous Game** (1932) and would again work with OBie on the mattes for Cooper's **The Last Days of Pompeii** (1935). Crabbe had a long relationship with David Selznick and worked for Jack Cosgrove on films such as **The Prisoner of Zenda** (1937). Sadly, Crabbe passed away during the early stages of **Gone With The Wind** (1939), on which he was Cosgrove's primary matte artist.

The huge workload of art for **Kong** necessitated several other artists had to be brought on board too, such as the Polish emigre Stanislaw Suzukalski, and also Albert Maxwell Simpson, whose career began with D. W. Griffith's **The Birth of a Nation** (1915). His work spanned the decades from **The Ten Commandments** (1923) to **Gone With The Wind** (1939), **Rebecca** (1940), **Swiss Family Robinson** (1940) and **Hawaii** (1966), where he worked for Linwood Dunn's Film Effects of Hollywood.

From the top:
Kong atop the Empire State Building, the first concept drawing made for the film.

Mario Larrinaga smiles from behind a painted glass for Kong's rampage through the native village.

Willis O'Brien shares a lighthearted moment with his good friend, artist Byron Crabbe.

*Byron Crabbe at work on a painting for **The Last Days of Pompeii** (1935) ultimately not used.*

*Above: Al Whitlock poses by one of the many scenes he created for **Earthquake** (1974), for which he won an Oscar®. The entire frame consisted of this painting, to which he carefully added smoke and fire.*

A much more well-known matte artist also worked as an independent contractor for Linwood Dunn's facility: Albert "Al" Whitlock provided impressive production values for the original incarnation of Gene Roddenberry's **Star Trek** (1966) by visualizing imaginative outer space locales. He also worked for Lawrence Butler and Donald Glouner at their optical house known as Butler-Glouner, supplying some sumptuously gothic artwork for several of Roger Corman's Edgar Allan Poe pictures such as **The Fall of the House of Usher** (1960) and **The Pit and the Pendulum** (1961).

British-born Whitlock started at Gaumont Studios in London in 1929 at the tender age of 14, where he made use of his carpentry skills building scenery, as well as painting sets and signs. He began a long working relationship with Alfred Hitchcock, first assisting in the elaborate miniature effects for **The Man Who Knew Too Much** (1934), and later he painted all the signs for **The 39 Steps** (1935) when he was 19.

Whitlock painted his first mattes in the late 1940s and would be lead matte artist at Pinewood for several years. He worked on **The Sword and the Rose** (1953) in the UK with Peter Ellenshaw, possibly painting titles and credits on glass, which was his specialty.

Whitlock came to the U.S. in early 1954, and applied for work at the studios, but no one was hiring. Just before he was about to return to England, Disney studios asked him to design the titles for their prestigious **20,000 Leagues Under the Sea**, which led to him staying gainfully employed at the studio for several years, working under his fellow-Englishman Peter Ellenshaw on **The Great Locomotive Chase** (1956), **Darby O'Gill and the Little People** (1959) and **Pollyanna** (1960). He also contributed to the design of the Disneyland park before moving to Universal in 1961 to head their matte department. There, he became an invaluable collaborator with Alfred Hitchcock on **The Birds** (1963), **Torn Curtain** (1966) and **Frenzy** (1972).

Whitlock received his first Oscar® nomination for the war film **Tobruk** (1967) and won his first Academy Award® for depicting the catastrophic destruc-

*Left: George Roy Hill, who had specific ideas of what he wanted when he directed **The Sting**, says "Al convinced me to put in one of the best shots in the movie, which was an elevated train approaching a window. He can create sets that are impossible to get. You can't get an elevated railway running on a back lot. However, that scene was shot on the back lot, using the existing El on a New York street set. The lower part of the picture included pedestrians, traffic, buses. The upper part was painted to look like a 1930 Chicago skyline at dawn." (8)*

"It was an economical way of telling a story visually within a few feet of film and served many purposes," said Whitlock. "It provided the necessary sound to wake Robert Redford in the morning, to open the sequence, to establish time of day and that it was 1930 Chicago." (9)

Spectacle On Glass • 59

tion of Los Angeles for *Earthquake* (1974), for which his department produced over 70 matte paintings. He worked with Robert Wise on *The Andromeda Strain* (1971) and later on Wise's *The Hindenburg* (1975), brilliantly returning the infamous zeppelin to flight, and in so doing, earned a second Oscar®.

A few of the other productions his department serviced included John Wayne's *Big Jake* (1971) and his *The Train Robbers* (1973). In 1979 Whitlock brought Universal back to its glory days by producing mattes for the Frank Langella version of *Dracula*. He later produced the shots of the crashed ufo in *John Carpenter's The Thing* (1982), the dream sequences for *Cat People* (1982), spectacular African vistas for *Greystoke: The Legend of Tarzan, Lord of the Apes* (1984), and returned to sci-fi for the alien worlds in David Lynch's *Dune* (1984). He also worked on TV productions such as the mini-series *A.D.* (1985), for which he won an Emmy.

In these days of advancing Artificial Intelligence, it is worthwhile to watch Whitlock's *Colossus—The Forbin Project* (1970) which seems downright prescient in its cautionary warning about AI gone too far. It has one of my favorite Whitlock scenes as the scientist, Dr. Forbin, activates his brain-child, a gargantuan computer complex built into a mountain. Innumerable banks of hardware switch on, lighting up and heading towards us down an infinitely-long corridor as the machine comes to life, instilling a sense of awe and foreboding, exactly as intended. I consider it to be one of the very finest matte shots ever done, superbly designed and executed by Whitlock, who said it was the most difficult shot he'd ever done.

Helen Kaufman wrote about Whitlock in 1978:

"Al Whitlock's office at Universal—he is the only visual effects consultant under exclusive contract to a studio—is up a flight of stairs. The simply lettered sign on the door ('Matte Department' on one line, 'Albert Whitlock' on the next) belies the complex workings within.

"Paintings all over the walls—with blacked-out portions—are pictorial reminders of just what Whitlock has done on many movies.

"On the wall beside his desk, a painting of the Capitol used in *Airport 1977* reveals how much easier it was to do a painting than shoot an actual scene. A $10 Revell miniature plane moved over the painting during the opening credits—the only way direc-

*The unforgettable activation of the vast artificial intelligence in **Colossus— The Forbin Project** (1970) is a unique use of a matte painting in that it dramatically conveys tremendous depth as bank after bank of lights turn on, racing towards the audience. This was achieved using an intricate series of painted overlays to animate the blinking lights in patterns as well as provide subtle interactive light effects across the cavernous room.*

Right: The vast system-of-systems was entirely painted by Whitlock, except for a small black area for the live action. The original negative composite was produced by Universal visual effects cameraman, Roswell Hoffman.

60 · *Smoke and Mirrors – Special Visual Effects Before Computers*

*Above: Al Whitlock stepped out from behind the camera briefly to appear in Mel Brooks' productions of **High Anxiety** (1977) and **History of the World, Part I** (1981). Whitlock was following in the footsteps of Walter Percy Day, the grandfather of British mattes, who had done mattes for—and appeared in—Abel Gance's **Napoleon** (1927).*

tor Jerry Jameson could get this shot since planes are prohibited from flying that low over the Capitol.

"Seated behind his desk, Whitlock says modestly of the things he does, 'You could do them in your own garage. They're not as esoteric as they appear. All you need is a painting with some light on it and a steady camera.'

"The directors he has worked for would disagree.

"Robert Wise said that, when asked if he would take on *The Hindenburg*, he first went to Whitlock before giving Universal an answer. 'Al,' he asked, 'can we show this airship outside Frankfurt, get it in the air, sail it across the ocean, sail it past New York City and bring it into Lakehurst in bad weather?' When Whitlock told Wise that it could be done believably and realistically, Wise agreed to direct the film.

"Whitlock enjoys working with directors like Hitchcock who, he says, know what they want and why. 'You know, Hitch will say 'I don't want scenics, Al. I want this to be a story scene—so let's have a car coming up the road, but I want to make the point of a lowering mood, so let's have some of your clouds there.'

"'Directors who say, 'Well, I don't know whether we need a shot here or maybe you can make a suggestion,' are, Whitlock says the ones likely to wind up with a superfluous picture-postcard shot.

"Nothing Whitlock does is superfluous. He has found that a more realistic scene was produced when the paintings are animated and other 'tricks' are employed.

• When the water for a lake scene is agitated by various gadgets, then filmed through a glass with Vaseline on it, the lake shimmers with reflections.

• A bit of styrofoam properly lit can pass for snow in front of a painted scene.

Whitlock used enlarged photos of a 25-foot-long 'miniature' of the Hindenburg (photographed by expert miniatures cinematographer Clifford Stine) as the basis for a series of paintings that depicted the airship in flight against varied skies and changing patterns of light and shadow.

Spectacle On Glass • 61

- Using mattes with a painting of a cloud photographed in three horizontal sections gives the effect of moving clouds. Each section moves on a track at a separate speed, the top section moving fastest. When finished, the full cloud appears to change shape. Creating the holocaust in *Earthquake* came about with a combination of both the mattes and real fires: Special effects men gradually moved seven rows of fires upward, interspersing them with mattes that placed the flames in front or back of the buildings, as desired.

"Whitlock's studio, near his office, is filled with the tools of these tricks: cables, cameras, large windows in frames for the glass paintings, splicing tables, cans of film, easels and paint brushes, a light table draped with strips of film, a large workbench. Nearby are several darkrooms.

"He doesn't do it all singlehandedly, however. Whitlock has a small staff, starting with cameraman Bill Taylor, camera assistant Mike Moramarco, and Mark Whitlock, Al's son, who is learning his father's craft starting as camera loader. Syd Dutton is assistant painter and Larry Shuler is key grip; he and his assistant, Henry Schoessler, rig everything and solve construction problems. Susan Rodgers is the rotoscoper, painting cels frame by frame to superimpose a moving figure over a background, and Dennis Glouner is the optical matte/cameraman."

"For Whitlock, work is like catching fish—and he likes fishing. His enthusiasm never seems to flag. 'You know,' he reflects, 'you say to yourself I wonder how it's come back from the lab. That sense of wonder is a big part of it for me. That's like catching fish.'

"After he finishes *The Wiz,* Whitlock goes to Vienna to scout locations for *The Prisoner of Zenda*. For him, Emerald City is right in his own backyard." (10)

Hitchcock summed up Al Whitlock: "He is the finest technician that we have in our business today." (11)

"Even a man who is pure in heart—"

Above: Russell Lawson provided this magnificent setting for Lon Chaney's return to his ancestral estate in **The Wolf Man** *(1940). It is a perfect "invisible effect" matte painting that takes the pains to include tree leaves gently swaying in the breeze over the art element. The leaves were filmed separately and added in a bi-pack matting pass.*

Russell Lawson, who spent the majority of his career working at Universal, retired after receiving a substantial inheritance. He had painted mattes for the original disaster epic **Deluge** (1933), a previously "lost" film best-remembered for providing stock shots of cataclysmic devastation for Republic serials like **Commando Cody Sky Marshal of the Universe** (1953). He worked initially under John Fulton, who was apparently a very difficult person to deal with. Lawson teamed with artist Jack Cosgrove on such films as **The Invisible Man** (1933) and **The Bride of Frankenstein** (1935). His many other productions include **Showboat** (1936), **Never Give A Sucker an Even Break** (1941), Hitchcock's **Saboteur** (1942), **Arabian Nights** (1942), **Abbott and Costello Go To Mars** (1953), **The Land Unknown** (1957), Stanley Kubrick's **Spartacus** (1960) and countless others. His only on-screen credit was for **Taras Bulba** (1962), his final film. Interestingly, his successor at Universal, Al Whitlock, also worked on that production.

—can still travel to distant galaxies.

It was more practical for Lawson to travel from **This Island Earth** *(1955) to the interior of Metaluna via matte painting than to send a crew on location! Here, a small area of live action is combined with an extensive painting. Violent pyrotechnics were added optically.*

62 · *Smoke and Mirrors – Special Visual Effects Before Computers*

*Above: Matthew Yuricich's painting of the "Mount Rushmore House" for Alfred Hitchcock's **North by Northwest** (1959). A former art director himself, Hitchcock was the rare filmmaker who understood the value of miniatures and mattes.*

Below: Chief matte artist Lee LeBlanc painted the vertiginous United Nations Building down view while Yuricich painted the lobby interior.

Another matte artist with a long career encompassing more than 100 films from the 1950s until the 1980s was Matthew Yuricich, who got his start working in the Fred Sersen matte department at Fox and later moved to MGM. Yuricich painted mattes for **Logan's Run** (1976), for which he received an Academy Award®. Accepting the Oscar®, Yuricich gave one of the best acceptance speeches ever:

"I'd like to thank Bill Adler for twenty-seven years of help and guidance. And to my fellow members of the Special Effects Committee, for this honor. And especially to my wife Clotilde, without whose fierce loyalty I couldn't have gotten through these difficult years. Without her I couldn't have gotten very far, and this is very, very far. And I want to thank myself, because I think I earned it." (12)

Yuricich went on to another nomination for **Close Encounters of the Third Kind** (1977) and also a year later for his second Spielberg film, the comedy **1941** (1979). He provided mattes for **The China Syndrome** (1979) and for Ridley Scott's Oscar®-nominated **Bladerunner** (1982), where his art reinforced the oppressive environment the director envisioned for a dreary Los Angeles.

Other noteworthy productions that benefitted from his brush were the grand expanses of imperial Rome for **Ben-Hur** (1959, Oscar®-winner), James Mason's eye-catching cantilever house perched above Mount Rushmore for Hitchcock's **North by Northwest** (1959), the Universal horror film-inspired castle in Mel Brooks' **Young Frankenstein** (1974) and several mattes for the **Planet of the Apes** franchise, such as the ruined stock exchange in **Beneath the Planet of the Apes** (1970). He also contributed to the original **Ghostbusters** (1984), **Fright Night** (1985), **Poltergeist 2: The Other Side** (1986), **Die Hard** (1988), **Field of Dreams** (1989) and **Dances with Wolves** (1990).

His alma mater, Miami University in Oxford, Ohio, awarded him a Distinguished Achievement Award for his stellar career in 2006. His brother is Academy Award®-nominated special effects cinematographer Richard Yuricich.

Spectacle On Glass• 63

By the 1980s, several small companies had replaced the studio matte departments. Bill Taylor and Syd Dutton founded Illusion Arts in 1984, the descendant of the Universal matte department where both had worked with Al Whitlock. They purchased Universal's equipment and worked on more than two hundred productions, from TV series like *Beauty and the Beast* (1987) and *Star Trek: Next Generation* (1987) to films such as *Spaceballs* (1987), *Coming to America* (1988), *Tremors* (1990), *Chaplin* (1992), *Batman Forever* (1995), *From Dusk Till Dawn* (1996), and *The Age of Innocence* (1993).

*Syd Dutton and Bill Taylor created this **Just Imagine**-like setting of towering buildings for an episode of the **Buck Rogers** (1979) TV series.*

Visual Effects Supervisor Bill Taylor and Matte Painter Syd Dutton discussed the famous, highly-complex shot of Robert De Niro leaving prison for Martin Scorsese's re-make of *Cape Fear* (1991) following a screening of the film at the New York Film Academy/Los Angeles (www.nyfa). This image left such an indelible sense memory for movie goers that it was parodied in a *Simpsons* episode where Side Show Bob leaves prison.

Bill said that "the shot was originally designed for De Niro to walk below the frame but Scorsese wanted him to walk directly into the camera. A special ramp was built that allowed the actor to do just that (the last few frames of the original footage showed De Niro, still in character, licking the lens). Because of the compositional change, the shot became much more complex, involving hand drawn silhouettes of the actor allowing him to appear in front of the painting. The shot took eight hours to execute, with a fan blowing on the camera motor that had to run at an extremely slow speed to prevent it from burning out."

Syd added, "The older studio system allowed for tremendous care and planning to create the seamless shots that appear in the film. One thing he shared with the current generation of matte painters is to always remember that the Earth only has one sun and one horizon line. Adhering to these facts is essential to create a believable and realistic painting." (13)

Bill concluded by emphasizing the value of control, and advocated that shooting the real thing as much as possible reduces variables and allows the image to remain based in reality.

Matte Effects was founded in 1982 by Bruce Block, cinematographer, and Ken Marschall, matte artist. Working out of Gene Warren, Jr.'s facility, Fantasy II Film Effects, their films included **The Terminator** (1984), **Cherry 2000** (1987), **Fright Night 2** (1988) and the Chiodo Brothers' cult classic **Killer Klowns from Outer Space** (1988). They also contributed "invisible" mattes to **Stand By Me** (1986) which would have made the old-timers from the 1930s and 1940s very proud.

Ken recalled working on the Emmy-winning effects for Dan Curtis' miniseries **The Winds of War** (1983): "Atmosphere and a sense of distance is key. Bruce often added a diffusion filter over the matte camera lens to help in that regard. A scene where a distant structure is too crisp, with too much contrast, and too warm in hue, will scream 'matte painting.'

"One of the paintings I did for **The Winds of War** had distant Moscow observed through binoculars from nearby hills. Director Dan Curtis wanted the Kremlin, which was miles away, to look more red. "It's Red Square... the Red Army. It has to look red." He was in charge, so I had to adjust it despite protests until he was satisfied, but of course Bruce and I knew that it reduced the believability of the scene." (14)

Baby Boom (1987): Ken Marschall painted almost this entire location. In the second photo, his hand reveals the small size of the painting and points to the live action area. A classic "invisible" matte shot!

Above: Bruce Block shoots a VistaVision plate in 1982. Bruce has been a hero to me—he hired me for one of my first professional jobs in Hollywood, building and animating the stop-motion demon for the TV movie **Dr. Strange** (1978).

Above and right: Ken shows the relatively small size of his painting of the hanger housing a UFO for the TV movie **Roswell** (1994).

Spectacle On Glass · 65

Above: **How Rare A Possession: The Book of Mormon** (1987) clearly illustrates the breadth of David Stipes' projects.

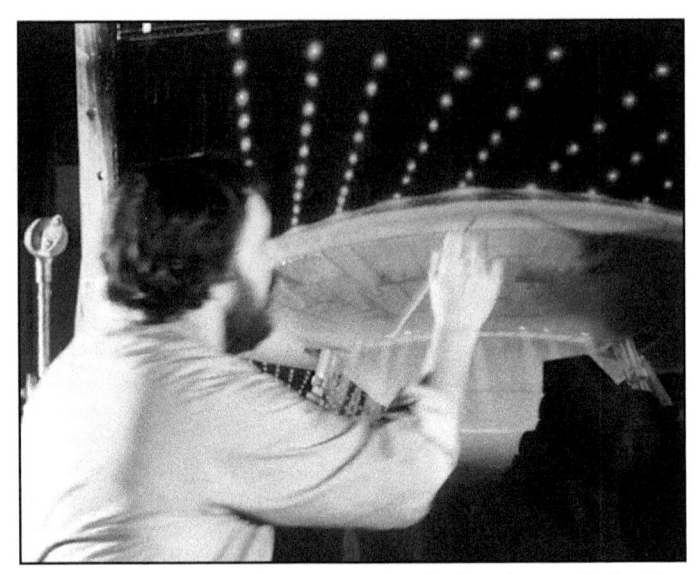

Above: Dan Curry paints the saucer on glass for **Battlestar Galactica** (1978), Below:

The original negative composite of the finished shot.

David Stipes could paint mattes, build miniatures, light a set-up, shoot motion control and even push puppets for stop-motion, having started out working with David Allen on **Equinox** (1970) where he made miniatures and a prop corpse affectionately dubbed "Charlie." He is well-known for his work on **Star Trek: The Next Generation** (1987) and **Star Trek: Deep Space Nine** (1993), for which he won a Special Visual Effects Emmy. Previously he provided matte work at Universal Hartland on **Battlestar Galactica (**1978), **Galactica 1980** (1980) and **Buck Rogers** (1979). He executed some shots using stop-motion camera moves while the motion control cameras were tied-up. He also animated a scene for an episode of **Buck Rogers** where the *Hawk* ship's claws—which he made—emerge from inside the vessel.

David described how he coped with a nearly-impossible time-frame to create a gas planet:

"It was one of the things where [supervisor] Peter Anderson said: 'We really need this planet shot and we only got about three hours to do it and it's supposed to be a gas planet!' We had no time to experiment and we just did it. We set this thing up with the motion control camera and tracks and created a camera 'fly-over' move. I quickly painted the planet white, which gave us a matte then I painted some black over it. Then I painted red, yellow, blue and purple over the black and spun the planet at different speeds. So it was just a series of double exposures on different rotational speeds. Basically it became a multi-exposure shot. When they fly over the gas planet you see bands swirling around like Jupiter at different speeds." (15)

David's extensive credits, many compiled by his own company, include **The Lawnmower Man** (1992), **Get Smart, Again!** (1989), **Night of the Creeps** (1986), **V: The Final Battle** (1984), **The Ice Pirates** (1984), **Darkroom** (1981) and many others.

Stipes transitioned from traditional visual effects into mastering CGI and eventually became an instructor at The Art Institute of Phoenix, sharing his expertise with students who were very fortunate in benefitting from his wealth of knowledge.

Above: A matte painting by David Stipes for **V: The Final Battle** (1984).

66 · *Smoke and Mirrors – Special Visual Effects Before Computers*

*Above: Jim Danforth's second version of the crashed Swan Ship from **Flesh Gordon** (1974). His many excellent mattes helped elevate the film above the usual adult fare.*

*Above: Mark Sullivan's palace glass painting for the TV series **Bring 'Em Back Alive** (1982).*

On **Star Trek: The Next Generation** (1987) David worked with Dan Curry, who has been a major influence on the many versions of the Roddenberry-inspired series.

"While I was in grad school," recalled Dan, "an influential person in the film industry happened to see an exhibition of paintings, found me, and suggested I look into matte painting. On that person's recommendation Universal Studios hired me to do matte paintings for **Buck Rogers**, **Battlestar Galactica**, **Cheech and Chong's Next Movie** and others. When I left Universal I went to work as art director for Modern Film Effects, then I went on to Cinema Research Corporation as Vice President and Director of Creative Services. During that time I was involved with 117 feature films and over 40 television productions. I left CRC to join **Star Trek** 12 years ago and have been concentrating on **Star Trek** ever since." (16)

I worked with Dan at CRC and found him to be meticulous, a very effective communicator, and mighty clever. He approached jobs with good humor, keeping the work day lighthearted but getting the job done right. Dan's book, **Star Trek: The Artistry of Dan Curry** is packed with rare photos of his design work, visual effects, and adventures in the **Star Trek** Universe—including a one-of-a-kind guitar!

Jim Danforth's company, Effects Associates, provided Civil War settings for the miniseries **The Blue and the Gray** (1982) and then shifted gears for the sci-fi political allegory **They Live** (1988). I could fill an entire book about his work! Fortunately, Jim has written **Dinosaurs, Dragons, and Drama: The Odyssey of a Trickfilmmaker** consisting of three volumes that document his career, filled with his encyclopedic recollections of productions and illustrated with scores of behind-the-scenes photos. As far as I'm concerned, they should be required reading at all film schools.

Mark Sullivan began his career at Jim Danforth's studio on TV shows like **Bring 'Em Back Alive** (1983). Mark's films include **Pee-wee's Big Adventure** (1985), Paul Verhoven's **RoboCop** (1987), **Throw Momma from the Train** (1987), **Rain Man** (1988), **Killer Klowns from Outer Space** (1988), **Indiana Jones and the Last Crusade** (1989), **The Abyss** (1989), **Bugsy** (1991), **Rocketeer** (1991), and **Death Becomes Her** (1992).

I built a model helicopter for **Ishtar** (1987) and was part of the motion control crew at Cinema Research. The chopper was matted over one of Mark's paintings. Unfortunately, as is often the case in Hollywood, the shot was cut from the film.

Mark was nominated for a BAFTA (British Academy of Film and Television Arts) award for Best Special Effects for **Indiana Jones and the Last Crusade** and received an Oscar® nomination for **Hook** (1991).

Spectacle On Glass • 67

Harry Walton created mattes for the TV series *Salvage 1* (1979) as well as the TV movies *Once Upon a Spy* (1980), the delightfully fanciful *The Night They Saved Christmas* (1984) and the documentary *Creation of the Universe* (1985). He also worked on features such as *Hopscotch* (1980) and the cult-classic *The Stuff* (1985).

Rocco Gioffre is a well-respected matte artist whose first job was on *Close Encounters of the Third Kind* (1977) as assistant to Matthew Yuricich, and Gioffre soon contributed mattes to *Star Trek–The Motion Picture* (1979) and *Blade Runner* (1982) where he worked once again with his mentor.

Gioffre went on to become one of the founding members of Dream Quest Images and contributed to *Blue Thunder* (1983), *Gremlins* (1984), *The Adventures of Buckaroo Banzai Across the 8th Dimension* (1984) and *Short Circuit* (1986). He received a British Academy of Film and Television Arts nomination for Best Special Effects for his work on *RoboCop* (1987) which also earned him a Saturn award for Best Special Effects. Along with mattes for that production, he did a stop-motion stunt of "Dick Jones" (Ronny Cox), the chief villain of the story, falling from a skyscraper.

Some of Gioffre's other projects include *Caddyshack* (1980), *Dreamscape* (1984), *Throw Momma from the Train* (1987), *RoboCop 2* (1990), *Dances with Wolves* (1990), *Predator 2* (1990), *City Slickers* (1991), *Hook* (1991), *RoboCop 3* (1993) and *Cliffhanger* (1993), to name a few.

Turning again to Europe, an undisputed master of painted mattes as well as being skilled in the use of foreground miniatures, Spanish craftsman Emilio Ruiz del Río started in 1942 as an assistant to scenic painter Enrique Salva and soon transitioned to matte work.

After laboring on a glass painting which accidentally broke, costing him time and effort, del Rio was anxious to avoid another such catastrophe. So, he began painting on cut-out masonite and mounting the rigid art in front of the camera, eliminating the problems of working with glass. He later modified this to using thin sheets of cut-out aluminum, a technique that was effectively used in Ray Harryhausen's *The Golden Voyage of Sinbad* (1974). He had earlier worked for Harryhausen on *The 7th Voyage of Sinbad* (1958) and *The 3 Worlds of Gulliver* (1960).

In over six decades Ruiz del Rio contributed to 450 films, servicing studios in Europe and the U.S. He worked with some of the finest directors including Orson Welles (*Mr. Arkadin*, 1955), Stanley Kubrick (*Spartacus*, 1960), Anthony Mann (*El Cid*, 1960), Nicholas Ray (*55 Days in Peking*, 1963), David Lean (*Doctor Zhivago*, 1965), and John Milius (*The Wind and the Lion*, 1975). He also contributed to low-budget "sword and sandal" films like *The Last Days of Pompeii* (1959), *Legions of the Nile* (1960) and *The Colossus of Rhodes* (1961).

*Harry Walton stretched his creative muscles for **The Night They Saved Christmas** (1984), expanding a whimsically fantastic setting at the North Pole.*

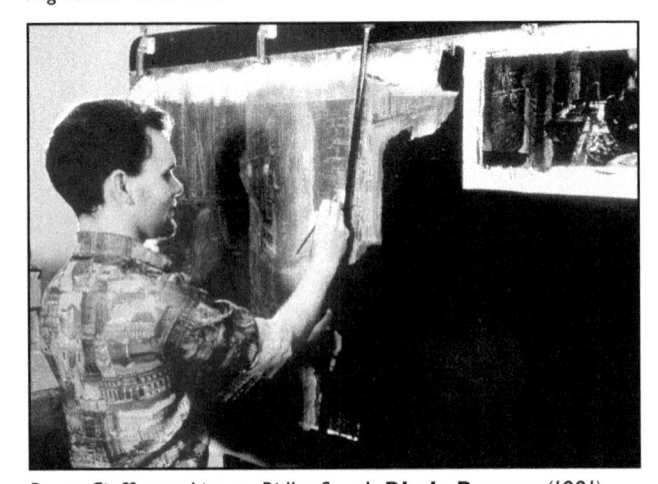

*Rocco Gioffre working on Ridley Scott's **Blade Runner** (1981).*

*Emilio Ruiz del Rio on location painting a glass shot for **Conan the Barbarian** (1982), later replaced by a more upbeat matte executed by Jim Danforth.*

In spite of saying that I would not cover companies who had previously had whole books dedicated to them, I would be remiss in not acknowledging Industrial Light And Magic ("ILM"), if for no other reason than the sheer volume of outstanding mattes produced at Kerner Optical.

The checklist of ILM's nearly 300 productions is the stuff of legend: **Dragonslayer** (1981), **Star Trek II: The Wrath of Khan** (1982), **E.T.–The Extra-Terrestrial** (1982), **Poltergeist** (1982), **Back to the Future** (1984), **Howard the Duck** (1986), **Star Trek IV: The Voyage Home** (1986), **Harry and the Hendersons** (1987), and **Who Framed Roger Rabbit?** (1988). Matte department supervisor Christopher Evans remarked about **Willow** (1988): "There are real advantages to using miniatures with matte paintings. Miniatures have incredible perspective, but matte painting can create a sense of atmosphere and distance better than a model. Combining the two techniques is like making an alloy in metallurgy—the combination of the two ingredients is stronger than either by itself. The miniature is shot latent image and then we add the paint to it—so it is actually a blending and intermixing of the two." [17] Yet, in a few short years, ILM would bring CGI to fruition with **Jurassic Park** (1993) and cause an upheaval in the world of visual effects as producers abandoned mattes, miniatures and other traditional techniques to jump on the CGI bandwagon.

Whatever they were required to paint, from the real world to the fantastic, matte artists have been able to blend film and art. While hand-painted mattes have gone the way of the dinosaurs, digital matte paintings thrive as a vital part of motion pictures today.

I bet we will see mattes for many years to come and I look forward to seeing what technological advances will bring.

Can holographic matte paintings be that far off...?

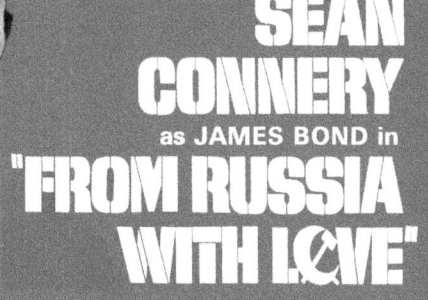

While Kronsteen (of Czechoslovakia) works his magic on the chessboard to defeat MacAdams (of Canada), Cliff Culley (of Great Britain) works his own magic with a paintbrush to top off (literally) the grand hall hosting the championship chess match. One of the few but effective matte paintings seen in the early Bond films.

SCRAPBOOK

A diagram by Norman Dawn of a multiple element matte shot for **The Spoilers** (1914). He coined the term "glass shot."

Preparations for a glass shot by Paul Detelfesen for **Dancer of the Nile** (1923), which Ferdinand Pinney Earle supervised.

Left: Behind-the-scenes of the French production of **Napoleon** (1927) showing how large Walter Percy Day preferred his glasses to be, and the finished composite (above).

One of many matte shots done by Walter Percy Day for Alexander Korda's adaptation of H.G. Wells' **Things to Come** (1936).

Noah's Ark (1929) showcasing a glass painting by Paul Grimm of the ark, made even more convincing by adding real animals.

70 · *Smoke and Mirrors – Special Visual Effects Before Computers*

Above: A few years after working on the epic **Quo Vadis** (1951), Peter Ellenshaw revisited the grandeur of Rome by painting spectacular vistas of the city for the Kirk Douglas/Stanley Kubrick production of **Spartacus** (1960).

Middle and above: Matthew Yuricich carries on the long tradition of using mattes to provide spectacular ancient Roman settings for movies, in this case for the multiple Oscar®-winning **Ben-Hur** (1959).

Spectacle On Glass · 71

THE BIRDS

One of Alfred Hitchcock's "impossible angles," this time a "God's Eye view" of Bodega Bay, the setting for his 1963 film—

The final composite consists of live action and pyro (fires) filmed on the Universal lot, live seagulls added to the scene optically (filmed by former actor Jon Hall), and a breathtaking Al Whitlock painting of the town.

72 · *Smoke and Mirrors – Special Visual Effects Before Computers*

*Above: Main title background painting by Luis McManus for TV's **The Addams Family** (1964-66). McManus is perhaps best known to special effects fans for his concept drawings of the creatures for Edward Small's production of **Jack the Giant Killer** (1962).*

Above: Neil E. McGuire as part of a trade ad placed before he and business partner Warren A. Newcombe relocated from New York to Los Angeles in the 1920s.

*Butler-Glouner hired Al Whitlock to produce atmospheric mattes for (L-R) Roger Corman's **The Fall of the House of Usher** (1960) and **The Raven** (1963). I'm sure that even penny-conscious Roger thought the money was well-spent. Now **that** is a sorcerer's castle!*

*Russell Lawson's matte painting for **House of Dracula** (1945) blends studio live action with dramatic location footage of waves crashing on a rocky shoreline.*

*Mark Sullivan in a gag shot, using a ridiculously-huge brush on his painting for **What Waits Below** (1985).*

Spectacle On Glass • 73

Rocco Gioffre's picture-postcard matte for Joe Dante's **Gremlins** (1984). This charming shot really hit the right emotional chords for the audience.

Emilio Ruiz del Rio painting a glass shot for **Le Legioni di Cleopatra** (1959; U.S. title **Legions of the Nile**). 20th Century-Fox bought up the film for $1 million and shelved it so it wouldn't compete with Fox's own upcoming epic, **Cleopatra** (1963).

Below: In **Mighty Joe Young** (1949), Willis O'Brien's design uses tremendous depth to establish a memorable African residence.

Jim Danforth and Roger Dicken's work on **When Dinosaurs Ruled the Earth** earned the only Oscar® nomination for a Hammer film. For the Mother Dinosaur's entrance, Danforth blocked in the matte painting which was then painted by Ray Caple.

Below: Below: An unidentified artist paints the matte of the lush African vista for **Mighty Joe Young**.

74 · *Smoke and Mirrors – Special Visual Effects Before Computers*

How Projector and Camera were used to composite matte paintings over live action (not to scale)

Projector with previously filmed live action

RP image on screen

Matte Painting on Glass

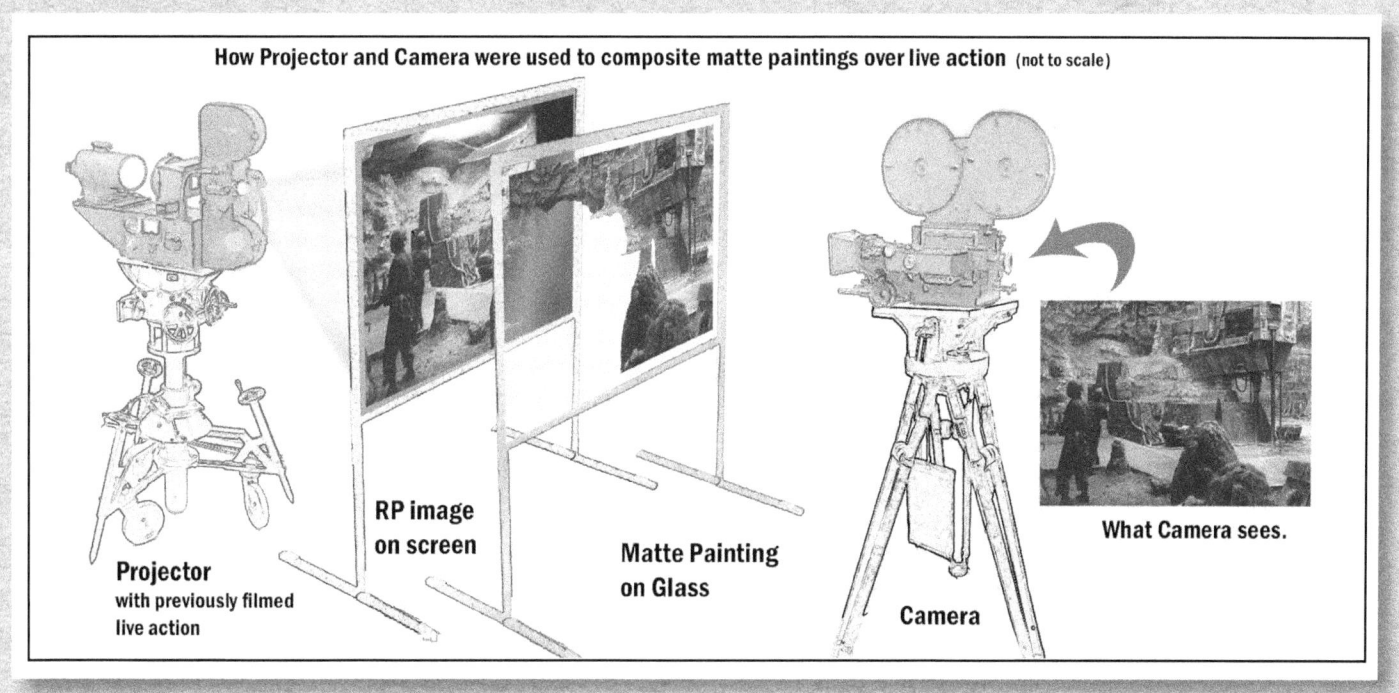

Camera

What Camera sees.

For **What Waits Below** (1985), this schematic clearly shows how David Stipes used rear projection to add the live action element of the shot.

Below: The final composite blending the live action with Mark Sullivan's matte.

Spectacle On Glass • 75

Above: Castle Dracula, a matte by Les Bowie for Hammer's wildly successful color re-imagining of the world of gothic supernatural terror, **Dracula** (1958), known in the US as **Horror of Dracula**.

Left: Jack Cosgrove stands beside a background projector used for compositing live action with his paintings via rear projection.

Below: Perhaps the most intentionally surreal matte painting ever done, from Alfred Hitchcock's **Spellbound** (1945), executed by Jack Cosgrove with the design influence of Salvador Dali.

76 · *Smoke and Mirrors – Special Visual Effects Before Computers*

Universal's **Dracula** (1931) made a movie star out of Bela Lugosi. Some sources suggest the mattes may have been done by Conrad Tritschler.

Below: For **Mighty Joe Young** (1949) extensive use of mattes were as essential as they had been in **King Kong** (1933).

*Perhaps one of the most famous climaxes in any science fiction film: the reveal at the end of **Planet of the Apes** (1968), when Charlton Heston discovers the truth about the world he has crashed on—thanks to a matte by Emil Kosa, Jr.*

*Mark Sullivan contributed several paintings to the Chiodo Brothers' cult classic, **Killer Klowns from Outer Space** (1988), including this power room.*

*A tremendous vista provided by the Newcombe matte department for **Tarzan's Secret Treasure** (1941).*

Jan Domela prepares to shoot a live action exposure with the matte area masked off on a foreground glass.

78 · *Smoke and Mirrors - Special Visual Effects Before Computers*

For **Hopscotch** (1980), Harry Walton describes how he matched his matte to an anamorphic background plate: "I got photos of the capitol building, rephotographed them, and made 12x16-inch prints. I then drew perfect squares over all parts of the building, especially the dome. On another sheet of paper I drew rectangles that were 2 units high by 1 unit wide (2:1 squeeze). I then drew the corresponding parts of the capitol from the squares to the 'squeezed' rectangles, which allowed me to draw the art with a 2:1 squeeze. When this was done, I photographed this sheet and projected the drawing onto my matte glass."

Below: Skull island, as realized by Willis O'Brien's crew for **Son of Kong** (1933), blending a menacing real location with a carefully executed painting.

Spectacle On Glass • 79

The matte painting and final composite from the Warren Newcombe unit at MGM for **The Picture of Dorian Gray** (1945). Newcombe preferred using pastels for the artwork; Norman Dawn had also done some of his matte work in that medium instead of oils.

Left: Samuel Fuller's **China Gate** (1957), featured special visual effects supervised by Linwood Dunn.

Below: Mark Sullivan works on a painting for the Cohen Brothers' **Hudsucker Proxy** (1993). Could it have been at least partly inspired by the end of **Raiders of the Lost Ark** (1981)?

80 · *Smoke and Mirrors – Special Visual Effects Before Computers*

*Above: A matte done by Warren Newcombe's artists for **Salute to the Marines** (1943).*

*Mammy (Hattie McDaniel), Pork (Oscar Polk), and Prissy (Butterfly McQueen) arrive at Rhett Butler's newly-built mansion in Atlanta, one of numerous matte paintings by Jack Cosgrove in **Gone With the Wind** (1939). An "invisible matte shot" if there ever was one.*

*An impossible angle looking down on Dorothy and her friends on the witch's battlements—thanks to Warren Newcombe—in **The Wizard of Oz** (1939). These two images illustrate the breadth of stories in the best year ever for motion pictures.*

Above: Who can ever forget joining Dorothy and her friends on the yellow brick road? One of the most endearing films of all time, MGM's **The Wizard of Oz** (1939) owes much of its special magic to a host of Warren Newcombe's Technicolor mattes, such as this one showing the fantastical Emerald City.

Below, left: Ray Harryhausen's **Mysterious Island** (1961) featured seven lush landscape matte paintings executed by the Shepperton Studios matte department under Wally Veevers' supervision (Veevers was later one of the four principal visual effects supervisors on Stanley Kubrick's **2001: A Space Odyssey** in 1968). The mattes were painted by Bob Cuff and George Samuels.

Below, right: From the cowboys-vs.-dinosaurs adventure **Valley of Gwangi** (1969), Gerald Larn's matte painting of the entrance to "Forbidden Valley."

82 · *Smoke and Mirrors – Special Visual Effects Before Computers*

Chapter 3
Men In Suits
(and the Men Who Put Them There)

This chapter will focus on methods of altering the physical appearance of actors. In the early days of filmmaking artists were limited to techniques which had originated with stage performances and made use of standard theatrical items like greasepaint, spirit gum and mortician's wax, which were applied to faces. That was fine for undemanding stories, but as time progressed, more sophisticated enhancements became necessary. Eventually, new materials and technologies made it possible for full suits to be created.

From the beginning, films required actors to wear basic makeup so they photographed properly, and costumes were everyday components of productions. However, one of the first thespians to expand beyond the norm was John Barrymore, who relied on the power of his performance—and minimal makeup—to electrify audiences with his metamorphosis from the handsome, noble Dr. Jekyll into the ugly, depraved Mr. Hyde in his 1920 version of Robert Louis Stevenson's story. By the time Paramount mounted their version in 1931, more sophisticated audiences demanded greater thrills from the filmmakers, and makeup artist Wally Westmore delivered superb design and execution that enhanced a stellar performance by Frederic March. Together, they set the standard for future collaborations between artists of radically different disciplines—acting and makeup—and earned March his first Oscar®.

Men In Suits • 83

Over the years, the demands of storytelling would drive the necessity of developing increasingly advanced techniques to empower performances, until in the 1950s, full monster suits appeared, most notably with the groundbreaking *Creature from the Black Lagoon* (1953), which completely disguised the actor beneath a new character. By the 1980s, "special makeup effects" had progressed significantly to include fiberglass sub-skulls, push-pull cables and computer-actuated servo-motors that essentially eliminated previous limitations for filmmakers who wanted to bring fantastic characters to life.

Incidentally, some sources acknowledge Tom Burman, brilliant five time Emmy-winning and Oscar®-nominated makeup artist, as the first to use the term "special makeup effects" to define this brave new world of makeup: however, if we go back to the British film *X...the Unknown* (1956), we see Philip Leakey receiving the first such credit. Leakey brought makeup into the modern era so vividly that the studio, Hammer, had to coin a new way to acknowledge his achievements.

As techniques and materials have evolved, in some cases the actor was entirely replaced by a mechanical version, sometimes called an animatronic. Fully-mechanized fabrications—also called mechanicals or props in the past—will be examined in the next chapter. Modern animatronics offered the advantage of going beyond what could be glued onto an actor, allowing the staging of intense physical alterations such as in *The Howling* (1981), where audiences were electrified by the "in your face," real time transformations that were light years beyond the simple dissolves seen in Universal's classic films of the 1940s.

*Frederic March menaces Miriam Hopkins in Paramount's **Dr. Jekyll and Mr. Hyde** (1931), for which he won an Academy Award®. Wally Westmore created a series of progressive makeups that captured Hyde's descent into evil dehumanization.*

*Rob Bottin stages a close angle of a werewolf attack for **The Howling** (1981). He wears a claw and also puppeteers an animatronic head which had internal mechanics for secondary actions that were activated by push-pull cables operated by crew members.*

LON CHANEY

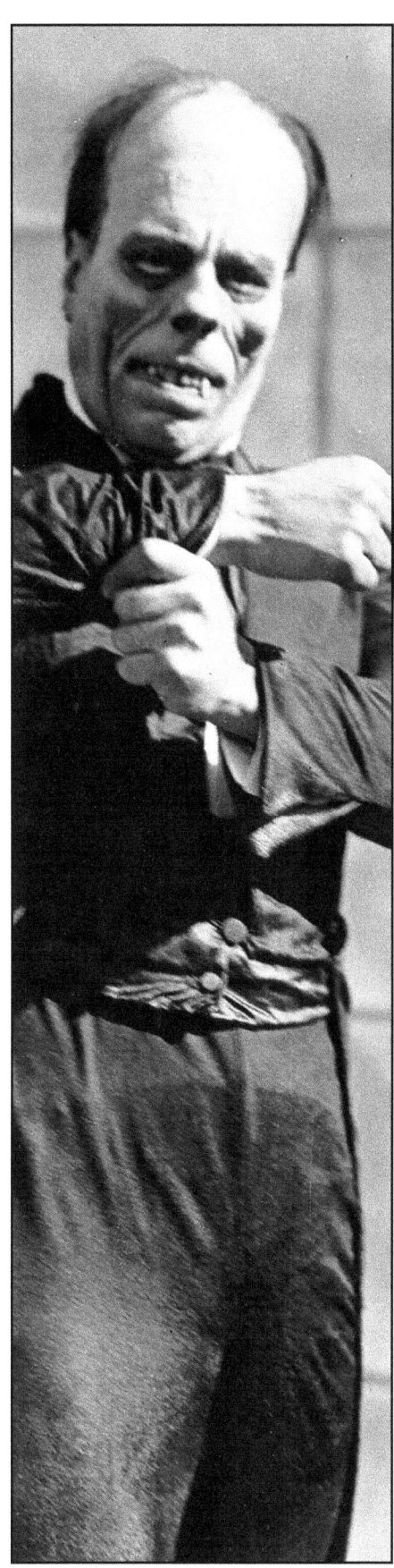

*Universal released **The Phantom of the Opera** (1925) as a super-production that featured an early color sequence and was re-released with a special soundtrack in 1929. Even today, scholars and makeup artists discuss the exact approaches Chaney used to achieve these unforgettable results for the character of Erik.*

In the days of the silents such extremes were beyond the scope of the materials and abilities of the technicians. However, one remarkable performer rose to the challenge, skillfully pushing the limits of makeups in unusual roles: Lon Chaney, Sr. By 1923, his combination of talents in portraying a bewildering assortment of unusual personalities led to his being known as "The Man of a Thousand Faces." In 1957, this phrase that showed deep respect for his versatility, was appropriated as the perfect title for a Universal biography about Chaney. In that production, James Cagney wore versions of the late actor's most famous roles, which replaced his old-fashioned techniques with state-of-the-art foam latex appliances from Bud Westmore's lab.

Men In Suits • 85

Chaney was a unique artist, rising to the heights of stardom in the 1920s by cleverly specializing in roles that only he could perform. He carved a niche in the emerging industry by successfully marketing himself as the rare actor-technician who could design, apply customized makeups and, crucially, deliver a performance. Whether he was a clown, an elderly Mandarin, an ape-man, a legless criminal or a pirate, in over 150 films he was a true hyphenate and hiring him enabled producers to stretch their dollars.

From his makeup box, Chaney unleashed iconic characters like **The Hunchback of Notre Dame** (1923) and **The Phantom of the Opera** (1925), which he imbued with an inner humanity and pathos that elevated them above being one-dimensional "monsters."

In a time before molds and foam latex appliances were the standard for makeup effects, Chaney needed three hours to physically model Quasimodo's deformities on his face, building up the changes using mortician's wax, spirit gum—a sticky rosin-based adhesive that was safe to use on skin—and nose putty, as well as a combination of cotton and collodion. Collodion is a solution of cellulose nitrate suspended in alcohol and ether which is highly inflammable and dries to a plastic, similar to nail polish. Incidentally, collodion can be used by itself to produce effective scars once dried and is still sold for makeup uses today.

Because Chaney was not using molds that allowed for mass duplication of the facial configuration for every day of shooting, subtle differences can be discerned in Quasimodo from scene to scene. Regrettably, in the grueling process of applying and removing the materials, Chaney suffered irreparable damage to his eyes, forcing him to wear glasses from that point on.

While some reviewers felt the bell ringer was repulsive, Chaney said he made a dedicated effort to be faithful to Hugo's description of Quasimodo during a rare interview for *Movie Weekly* magazine:

"The idea of doing the picture was an old one of mine and I had studied Quasimodo until I knew him like a brother, knew every ghoulish impulse of his heart and all the inarticulate miseries of his soul. Quasimodo and I lived together—until we became one. At least so it has since seemed to me. When I played him, I forgot my own identity completely and for the time being lived and suffered with the Hunchback of Notre Dame." [1]

Over the years, it has been reported that Chaney wore a seventy-pound rubber hump but in fact, he fabricated a plaster one that weighed around twenty pounds, which left him relatively unencumbered, so his natural athleticism wouldn't be hindered as the Hunchback clambered about Notre Dame.

Regarding Erik, the Phantom of the Opera, makeup effects experts still debate how Chaney achieved his masterpiece, especially regarding the alteration of his nose. A recurring hypothesis is that fish skin was used to pull his nose up. Fish skin is an incredibly thin, delicate sheet of translucent material that gets its name from its resemblance to actual fish skin (or dried, colorless seaweed). It is still used in special effects makeup, as well as fashion and stage shows.

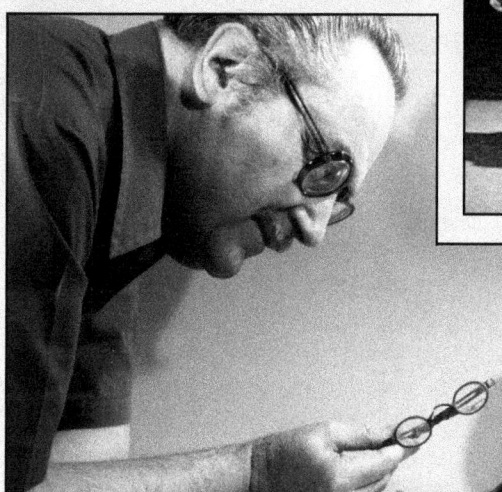

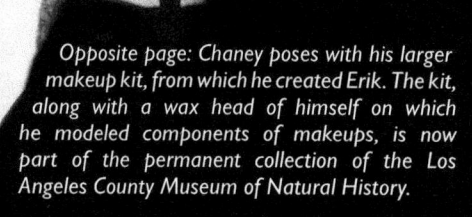

Opposite page: Chaney poses with his larger makeup kit, from which he created Erik. The kit, along with a wax head of himself on which he modeled components of makeups, is now part of the permanent collection of the Los Angeles County Museum of Natural History.

Top middle: Lon Chaney as Quasimodio and Nigel De Brulier as Don Claudio inside Notre Dame.

Top left: **Laugh, Clown, Laugh** *(1928), co-starring 14-year-old Loretta Young. This was supposedly Chaney's favorite film role.*

Left: **Famous Monsters of Filmland** *magazine editor Forrest J Ackerman in the 1960s with one of Lon Chaney's smaller makeup kits.*

Above: Chaney in **The Unholy Three** *(1930).*

However, original publicity stills reveal a thin string or wire running from the tip of Chaney's nose, up under his skull cap. At the time, observers reported Chaney's nose often bled during filming, suggesting the wire/string was somehow attached inside his nostrils and caused the bleeding. There have also been suggestions that he employed fish-hooks, which seems extreme to say the least, but no one can say for certain exactly what he did.

Chaney used a head piece that featured an enlarged forehead designed to reinforce the impression of a cadaverous skull while his eyelids were pulled down by spirit gum and, as with Quasimodo, his cheekbones were built up with a combination of cotton and collodion. Custom-made dental inserts simulating rotted, misshapen teeth—likely carved from wood—were fitted with some type of controls like his nose, drawing his mouth into a hideous grin. The death's head was further refined by taping or gluing his ears flat against his head.

The final illusion was achieved by an exceedingly skillful application of greasepaint, with highlights and shadows perfectly complimenting the physical elements. His eye orbits were blackened, with a thin highlight added just below the lower eyelid to make the eyes seem buried deep in their sockets. Thin, painted wrinkles gave the skin a withered appearance.

In addition to his makeup wizardry, Chaney's grasp of the technical aspects of cinematography was unprecedented; he understood lenses, the latitude of raw stock, and the limitations of the lighting units. For him, such education ensured that his characters were recorded on film the way he wanted them to look.

In **Outside the Law** (1920) Chaney's talents enabled him to portray more than one role and he experienced being shot by another character he was also playing. Chaney brought to life such a vast assortment of characters that were so different from each other, that an oft-repeated joke at the time was "Watch out! Don't step on it! It might be Lon Chaney!"

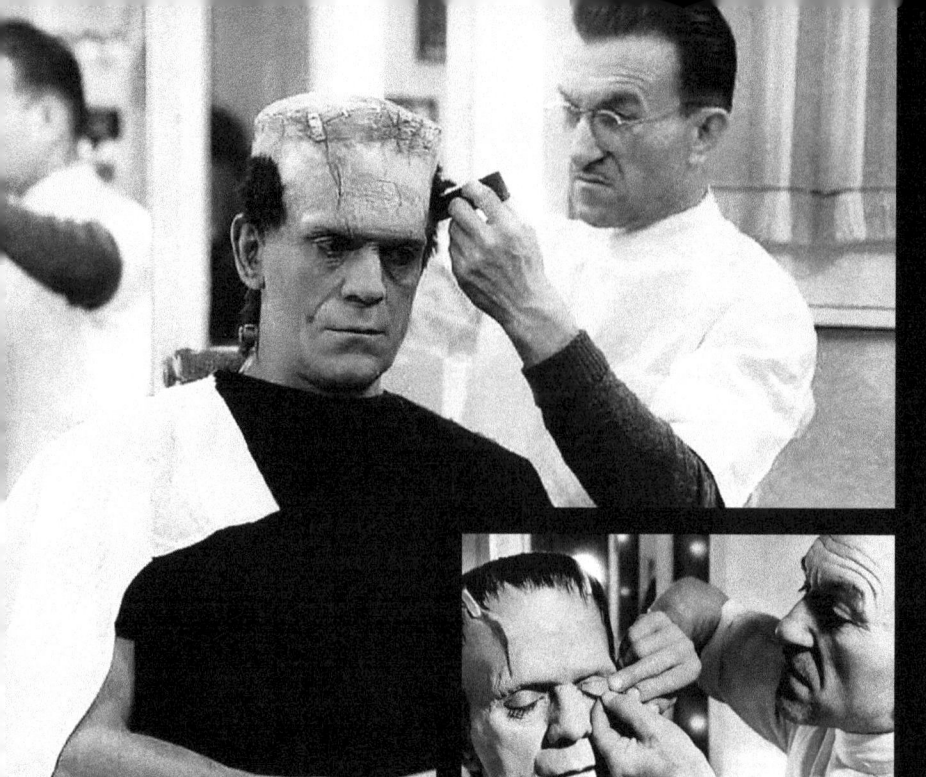

Chaney left Universal after *The Phantom*, signing with MGM, where he made several films, including his only talkie, a re-make of one of his silent hits, *The Unholy Three* (1930). Even though Universal lost its resident monster creator, in just a few short years, the studio would unleash the first of many classic horror films starring a host of monstrous personalities created by the new head of the makeup department, the legendary Jack P. Pierce.

Where Lon Chaney was a one-of-a-kind who did his own makeups for roles he himself played, Pierce's specialty was to turn performers such as Boris Karloff and Bela Lugosi into a legion of unforgettable characters, including supernatural monstrosities whose popularity floated the studio through the 1930s. Ironically, many of the films in the 1940s starred Chaney's son, who built upon his father's legacy by wearing various makeups—however, in his case they were the triumphs of Pierce, especially the iconic *The Wolf Man* (1941). The "things" Pierce was called upon to fabricate were unlike anything seen before in Hollywood.

After being rejected from his dream of being a pro baseball player, Pierce had a number of jobs, including being a theatre-chain manager, before being exposed to film production as a stuntman, clapper/loader, assistant director and bit-part actor. He analyzed the career of Lon Chaney and quickly surmised he could generate work for himself the same way, by mastering makeup so he could play any role.

When Raoul Walsh's 1926 Fox Pictures production *The Monkey Talks* was having problems creating the makeup for a man who impersonates a simian, Pierce rose to the task, designing and executing a meticulously crafted makeup that got him a job at Universal. Carl Laemmle, head of the studio, quickly assigned Pierce to work with Chaney on *The Man Who Laughs* (1928), hoping another Victor Hugo novel would be a box-office hit for Universal, as *The Hunchback of Notre Dame* (1923) had been.

The prospects of working with Chaney must have been both gratifying and daunting to Pierce, but when Chaney left the studio, the role went to German actor Conrad

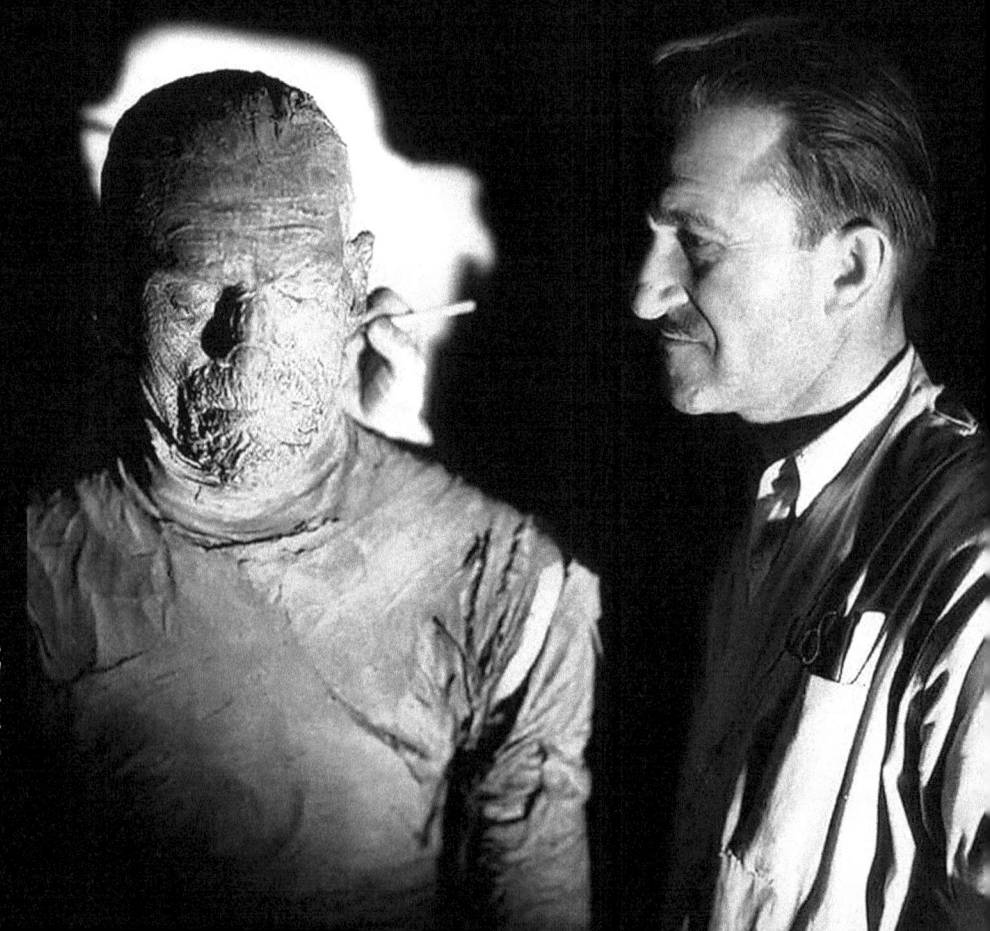

Right: Pierce turns Karloff into the 3700 year old title character of **The Mummy** *(1932). Im-Ho-tep. the disgraced High Priest, was a striking accomplishment as an elaborate full-body makeup that did not completely hide the actor.*

Smoke and Mirrors

Veidt, with whom Pierce would collaborate closely. Pierce embraced visualizing the victim of a hideous punishment, whose mouth was forever frozen in a hideous grin. In looking at the monstrous disfigurement, it is easy to understand why some scholars insist the leering visage inspired Batman creator Bob Kane's bizarre character The Joker. It has been said that Pierce's approach emulated Chaney's *Phantom*, employing a set of custom-made misshapen teeth with hidden controls that pulled Veidt's cheeks back into a perpetual grin. Light green greasepaint was applied for an appropriately unhealthful pallor on black and white film.

Bela Lugosi's ***Dracula*** (1931) was the answer to the studio's prayers for a financial windfall after a disastrous 1930; as the biggest hit of the year for the studio, Carl Laemmle, Jr., the head of production, was prompted to order more horror films. From that momentous decision came the film that put Pierce and Boris Karloff on the map and filled the studio's coffers: ***Frankenstein*** (1931). While the film is the sum of many parts, including direction by the gifted James Whale, inspired art direction by Charles D. Hall and superbly evocative cinematography by Arthur Edeson, the film's runaway success was truly fueled by the shocking originality of Karloff and Pierce's collaboration on Frankenstein's Monster. It was so effective, it went on to inspire a franchise of releases with different actors wearing the scars and neck bolts...

Pierce did extensive research for six months, then sculpted a clay maquette of his conception of Frankenstein's Monster to present for approval. In my own experiences in Hollywood, I quickly learned that a three dimensional representation of a creature design was invaluable for communicating concepts to those concerned with a production.

In an interview in *Monster Mania*, Pierce said: 'It was a lot of hard work, trying to find ways and means; what can you do? Frankenstein wasn't a doctor; he was a scientist, so he had to take the head and open it, and he took wires to rivet the head. I had to add the electrical outlets to connect electricity in here on the neck. I made it out of clay and put hair on it and took it in to Junior Laemmle's office. He said, 'You mean you can do this on a human being?' I said, 'positively.' He said, 'All right, we will go to the limit.'" **(2)**

Pierce set about working with Karloff and developing his take on Mary Shelley's modern prometheus, starting by building a wig with cotton padding that simulated the flat cranium. Then, thick eyebrows were built using the familiar combination of cotton and collodion, while a putty customized by Pierce produced the drooping eyelids. Next, a sky grey greasepaint was applied that Pierce had formulated in conjunction with the Max Factor Foundation, followed by black lipstick and discolored fingernails to complete the look. In an instance of an actor giving his all, Karloff bore scars on his neck for the rest of his life, the direct result of gluing and removing the electrodes again and again... and again.

Pierce was concerned with every aspect of how the monster would be presented, not just the makeup; he had the costumer shorten Karloff's coat sleeves so that his arms protruded to reinforce the illusion the monster was huge, and he also had the asphalt spreader's shoes padded, to increase the monster's menacing height. Showing the extent of their working relationship and how they trusted each other, Pierce convinced Karloff to remove a dental appliance to help with that gaunt, fresh-from-the-grave appearance.

James Whale knew that Karloff's performance combined with the appearance of the monster would electrify moviegoers. He heightens the audience's anticipation of coming face-to-face with Frankenstein's manufactured being by first showing its "birth"—unholy science goes insane thanks to Kenneth Strickfadden's bizarre electrical props spit sparks and fling electrical arcs in a laboratory that would have been at home in a German expressionist production. In fact, the 1920 Paul Wegener film *Der Golem* is widely credited for having been a major influence on the art direction and cinematography for *Frankenstein*. And, of course, both used a man-in-a-suit to portray their fantastic title characters.

Whale forces the tension to percolate as the audience listens to Dr. Waldman describe his former student's creation as "a fiend" and "a monster." Then, Waldman informs Frankenstein that the brain stolen from him was abnormal, reminding the audience about Fritz's "uh-oh" moment stealing that brain. As the two men discuss what to do, footsteps shuffle closer from outside their room—the only sound, because Whale refrains from music, ratcheting up the audience's dread to fever pitch as the horrible, as-yet-unseen creature approaches...

The director mercilessly stretches our nerves to the breaking point as the first glimpse of Karloff is of him backing slowly into the room. WHAT DOES HE LOOK LIKE?! As the monster turns, his face partially enters a pool of light, and Whale cuts to successively closer angles until there is a tight closeup of the pasty, sunken-cheeked countenance, on which Whale unhesitatingly lingers because the makeup holds up to our intense scrutiny. This remains one of the greatest entrances ever filmed, as Whale masterfully primed the viewers for the revelation, holding them riveted and unable to look away as Pierce and Karloff delivered "the goods!"

Right, top: Karloff in full makeup and costume, presenting a terrifying figure that was considered so extreme, Universal added a prologue featuring actor Edward van Sloan giving audiences "...a little friendly word of warning" about what they were going to see. The sets, lighting and the hulking monster echo Paul Wegener's expressionistic **Der Golem** *(1920).*

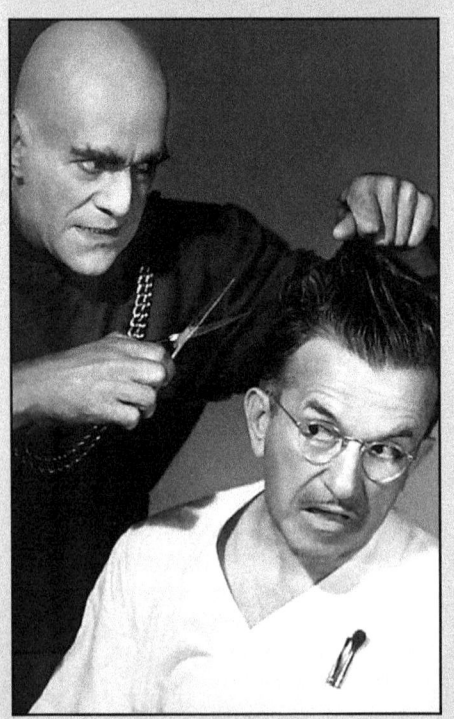

Above: Karloff turns the tables on Jack Pierce while filming of **Tower of London** *(1939).*

Perhaps the ultimate testimony to Pierce and Karloff is that their version of the monster is the one most people think of when they hear the name Frankenstein. And from the studio perspective, it represents a continuing source of revenue, and Universal is ever-watchful of anything infringing on that world-famous creation.

After the significant returns on **Frankenstein**, Universal embarked on a succession of roles for Karloff with makeups by Pierce, starting with one of their most elaborate collaborations, **The Mummy** (1932).

"The complete makeup, from the top of the head to the bottom of his feet took eight hours," said Pierce. Starting with the bandages, which had to be secured with tape, Pierce then added a further set of bandages treated with acid and burned in an oven, and finished the costume with clay. The whole procedure was designed to give the effect of the bandages breaking and dust falling off as the mummified creature steps out of the sarcophagus. Despite the arduous process, this incarnation of the creature Im-Ho-Tep only appeared on screen in the opening moments of The Mummy." (3)

Once the bandages were in place, a layer of neutral-colored liquid grease paint was applied like a primer for the detailing to come. Next, fuller's earth, a natural clay, was dusted onto the bandages and Karloff's hair to simulate a desiccated look. After the actor took position in the prop sarcophagus on stage, Pierce wrapped Karloff's legs and sealed the actor's eyes closed with rice paper with a tiny slit. A final application of powders reinforced the shadows and highlights of the long-entombed mummy.

On January 14, 1933, the *Hollywood Filmograph Journal*, a rival to *Variety*, honored Pierce for his masterful work with a special award presented to him at a ceremony at the Hollywood Roosevelt Hotel, by his victim/collaborator, Boris Karloff, who generously said:

"I want to publicly acknowledge to you, Jack Pierce, the deep debt of gratitude I owe, for were it not for your wonderful makeups, the success I had in *The Old Dark House*, *Frankenstein* and *The Mummy* would have been impossible." (4)

After Pierce's death in 1968 the trophy was believed lost; however, when a sink was removed from the makeup lab at the studio, it was recovered and later auctioned off.

Pierce would soon top himself with the remarkable makeups for *The Bride of Frankenstein* (1935), on which he was assisted by Harry Thomas (who would go on to a lengthy career creating monstrosities for productions like *Neanderthal Man* (1953), *Killers from Space* (1954), *Frankenstein's Daughter* (1958) and many more).

Pierce's design for the "bride" was based partly on the Egyptian queen Nefertiti and actress Elsa Lanchester was given a permanent wave over a wire frame to achieve the distinctive hair style. There have been some reports that Lanchester disliked working with Pierce because she thought he had a God complex; to be fair, it is hard to find many creators who don't have it to some degree.

For me, Pierce's masterpiece was his lycanthrope, who was introduced to the Universal monster roster in *The Wolf Man* (1941). Some sources say it had been designed a decade earlier for an unproduced Karloff vehicle, while others feel it was left over from *Werewolf of London* (1935) after Henry Hull insisted on a design that didn't completely obscure his features. Considering Pierce's admiration for Chaney Sr., it is likely he thought about "the old man" as he worked on Lon Chaney, Jr.

Chaney made the wolf man character his own, being the only actor to portray cursed Larry Talbot in five films, but he also tackled roles that had been done first by others, such as playing Dracula in *Son of Dracula* (1943), the Frankenstein monster in *Ghost of Frankenstein* (1944) and the Mummy in several films.

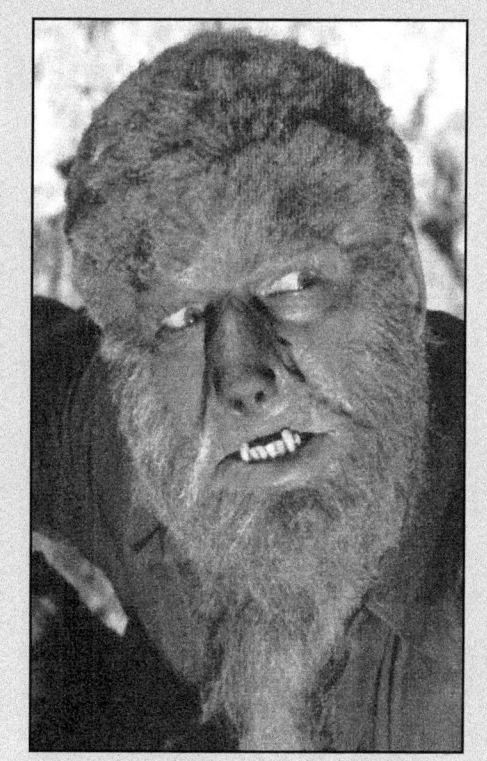

The werewolf makeup represented an advance for Pierce, in that the nose appliance was rubber cast from a mold, meant to streamline getting Chaney out of the lab and onto the set faster. The hirsute horror sported yak hair singed by a curling iron and affixed with spirit gum, taking two-and-a-half hours to apply and an hour to remove. Custom-made fangs completed his animal-like appearance.

Of special interest were many shots in this and subsequent films of Chaney transforming intro the wolf man via a series of dissolves; these scenes were filmed in reverse order as the makeup was removed. For *Frankenstein Meets the Wolf Man* (1943), Chaney claimed he was given numbing injections so the flesh of his neck could be pinned to a prop pillow to ensure his head

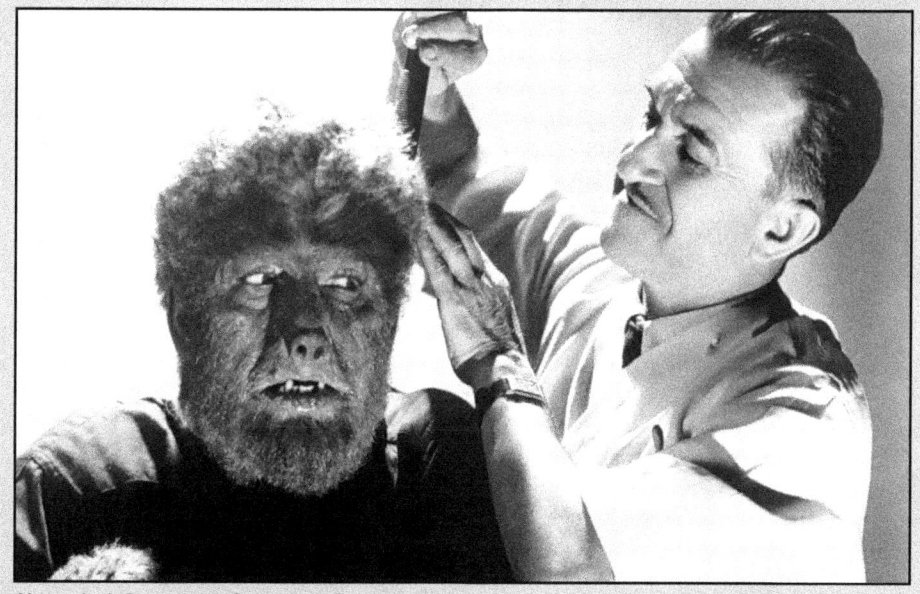

*Above: Lon Chaney, Jr., in **The Wolf Man** (1941), suspiciously eyes his predecessor, Henry Hull in **Werewolf of London** (1935).*

Above: Jack Pierce transforms Lon Chaney into the tormented Wolf Man. Pierce used a rubber nose piece to reduce the time it took to get Chaney ready for filming.

Dracula   Frankenstein

was in proper register for the takes that would comprise the transformation. He also spoke of having tiny nails driven through the flesh of his fingers to hold his hands in place, though these extremes have never been verified.

In *Monster Mania* #1, Russ Jones interviewed Pierce and asked about the many reported difficulties working with Chaney, Jr.; his terse response was "Yes and no. That's all I can say." (5)

Pierce was notorious for being short-tempered with performers who complained about his painstaking processes. In ***Lon Chaney Jr.: Horror Film Star 1906-1973*** by Don G. Smith, Chaney said: "What gets me is after work when I'm all hot and itchy and tired *[I've still]* got to sit in that chair for forty-five minutes while Pierce just about kills me, ripping off all the stuff he put on me in the morning." Chaney gave his tormentor an autographed picture that read, "To Jack Pierce, the goddamndest sadist in the world." (6)

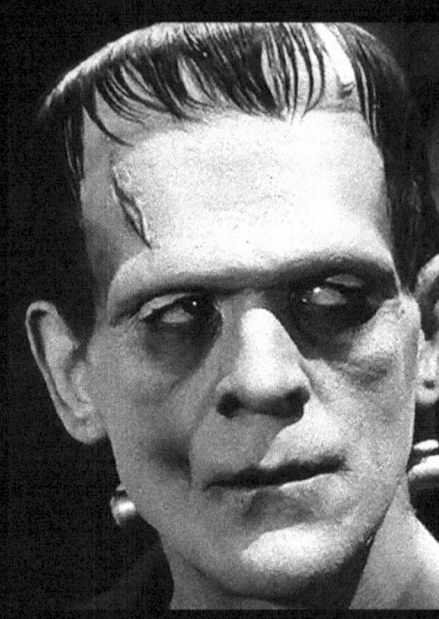

The Bride   The Mummy   The Wolf Man

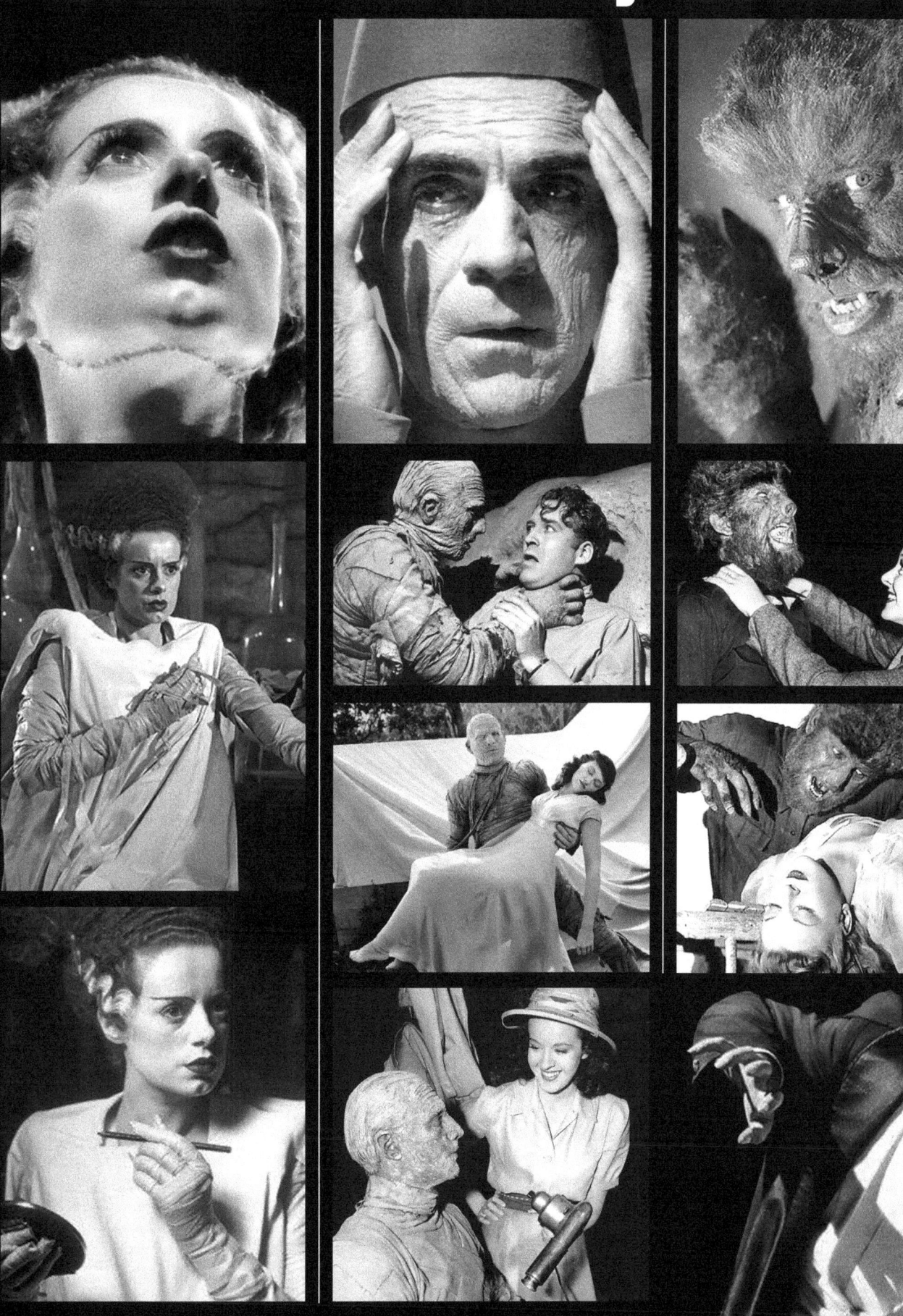

Creature from the Black Lagoon

Time marches on. By the end of the 1940s Universal was adamant about trimming expenses in the makeup department by exploiting technological breakthroughs, such as using molds and foam rubber for appliances instead of Pierce's time-consuming hand-applications—but Pierce was unwilling to adopt the new methods.

After having helped push the studio into profitability, he was replaced by Bud Westmore, whose team of designers, modelers, fabricators and mold-makers would bring to life the next generation of monsters for the studio. Perhaps their most memorable achievement was *Creature from the Black Lagoon* (1954) and output from producers like William Alland and directors like Jack Arnold ushered in Universal's stories of hybridized science fiction and horror that abandoned the gothic elements from the '30s & '40s.

The Gill Man presented a major hurdle because it was a truly "naked" monster, with its whole reptilian appearance fully-unveiled "in front of God and everyone," which offered no potential for cheats such as when Chaney's clothing was used to eliminate hair work for *The Wolf Man* a decade earlier.

The Creature was designed by Milicent Patrick, a former Disney animator and one of the few women working in the male-dominated special effects field. The fabrication of the suit was supervised by Jack Kevan, who had helped Jack Dawn produce the appliances for *The Wizard of Oz* (1939). The head of the costume was sculpted by Chris Mueller, Jr., who was also responsible for work on the huge animatronic squid for Disney's *20,000 Leagues Under the Sea* (1954). Ben Chapman played the Creature on land while a fellow champion swimmer, Ricou Browning, appeared in the underwater scenes; they could both hold their breath for over four minutes underwater.

Both Chapman and Browning had to undergo the rigors of having full body molds made of themselves so the lab staff could duplicate their physiques in plaster, on which the details for the suit were sculpted in clay. The clay master was, in turn, molded and sections of the suit were cast in foam rubber, then adhered to a one piece body stocking made of latex; approximately a half dozen suits were made for Chapman for use over the course of production.

The suits were painted with tinted rubber cement, which bonded to the foam like a second skin and would not rub off during strenuous land action or disintegrate during the water sequences; gold/copper paint was used to apply highlights that echoed fish scales—and certainly helped the figure photograph better underwater. The eyes were yellowish and the basic body color was a mid-tone green. They did not have the red lips seen in some color publicity pictures.

The suit was a masterpiece of originality in its conception and jaw-dropping in its fabrication, one of many creations that would be generated by the Universal lab for shows like *Abbott and Costello meet Dr. Jekyll and Mr. Hyde* (1953), *This Island Earth* (1955), *Tarantula* (1955), *Revenge of the Creature* (1955), *The Creature Walks Among Us* (1956), *The Mole People* (1956), *The Land Unknown* (1957), *Monster on the Campus* (1960) and many others. The assorted monsters and aliens have turned into perpetual money-makers for Universal, selling countless VHS tapes, laserdiscs, DVDs, Blu-rays, masks, model kits, action figures, coloring books and more!

DESIGNING THE CREATURE

MILICENT PATRICK

The Westmore family of makeup artists was considered "royalty" within the studio system in the 1940s and 50s, and, as Mallory O'Meara described in her book ***The Lady From the Black Lagoon*** (Hanover Square Press, 2019), each of the major Hollywood studios clamored to have a Westmore on staff. That culture, combined with the enormous ego of Bud Westmore (photo above), obscured for decades the proper credit for the real designer of the Creature From the Black Lagoon, Milicent Patrick. An accomplished artist who often sketched portraits of film stars, Milicent began as a Disney animator and also appeared in small bit parts in several movies.

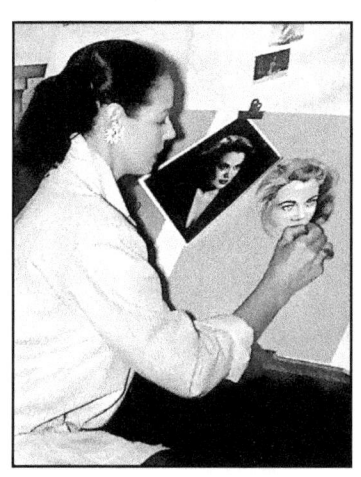

Men In Suits • 95

BACK TO THE DRAWING BOARD

Jack Arnold's original concept of the Creature was inspired by the Oscar® statuette and Julie Adams called it "eel like." A maquette was sculpted (below, left) and the initial suit—which truly looked like a man in a suit—was filmed, but wisely abandoned.

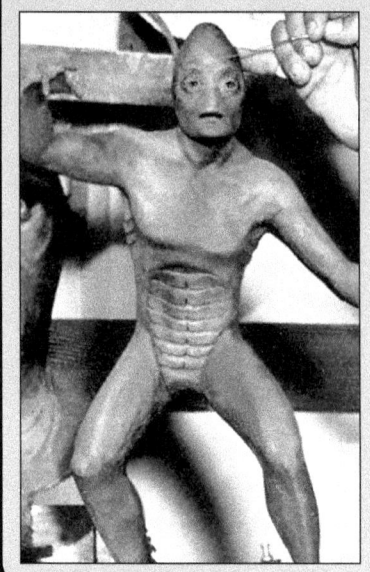

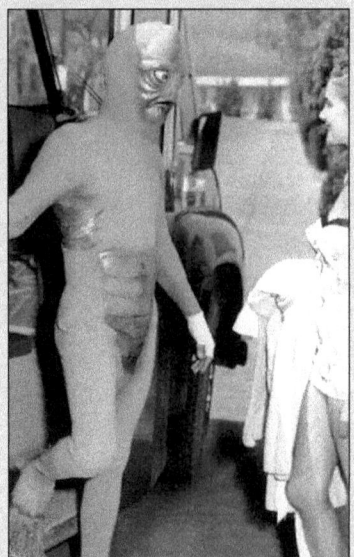

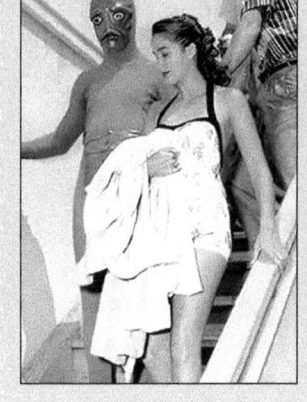

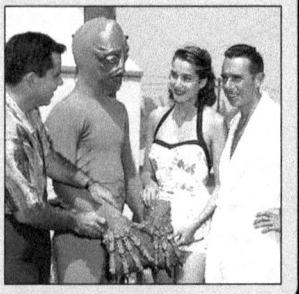

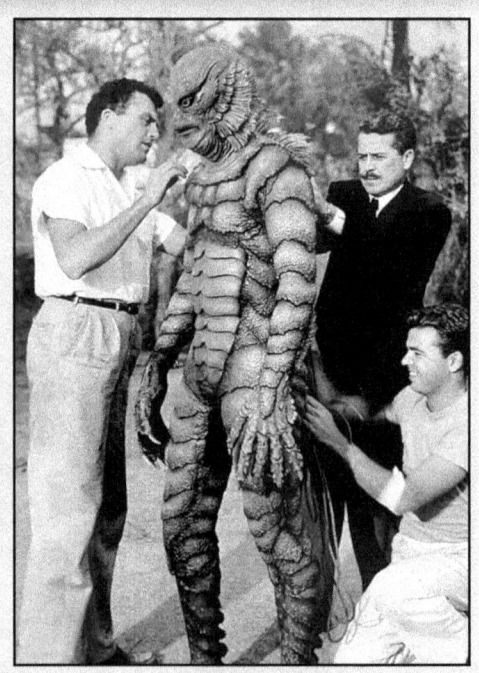

96 · *Smoke and Mirrors - Special Visual Effects Before Computers*

Men In Suits • 97

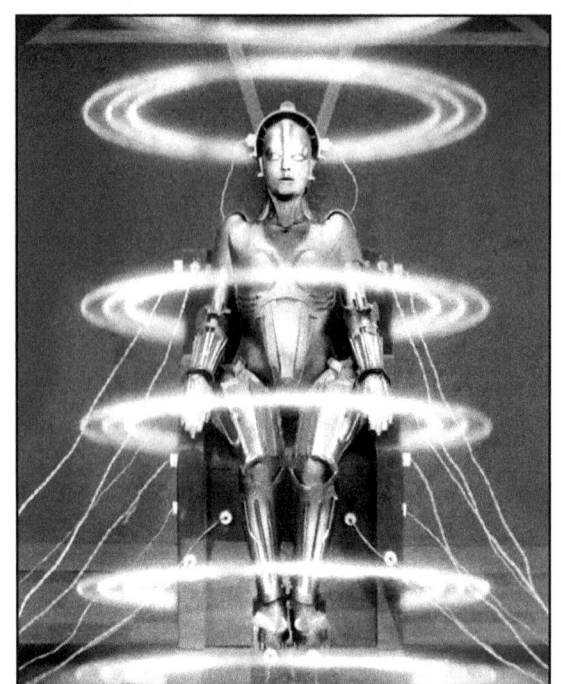

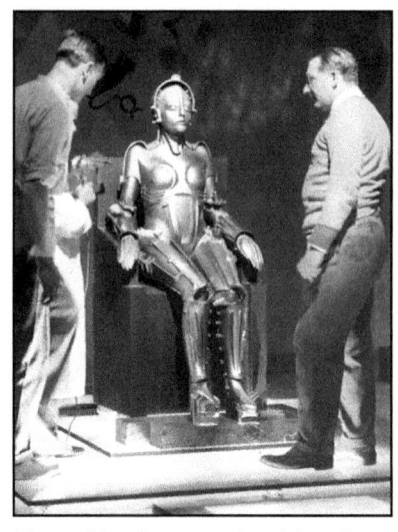

*Above: Fritz Lang, at the right, directs Brigitte Helm as the robot in **Metropolis** (1927). The brilliant design was a key inspiration for George Lucas and Ralph McQuarrie fifty years later when conceptualizing C3PO.*

Today robots are real. But in the movies robots usually relied on human performers inside custom-made suits. Some have become archetypal, forever etched in the minds of audiences. Unquestionably, the most recognizable robot from the silent era was in Fritz Lang's **Metropolis** (1927).

At that time, no one had ever made such a complex suit, so creating this vital character was an extraordinarily challenging task. In the book **Fritz Lang**, sculptor Walter Schultze-Mittendorf said:

"An accident helped us. A workshop making architectural models gave us decisive assistance unintentionally. I went there because of another job. My attention was drawn to a little cardboard box labeled 'Plastic Wood—trade sample.' A postal parcel. This 'trade sample' was not interesting for the workshop and was given to me. One trial brought the proof straightaway that the material for our 'machine creature' had been found. 'Plastic wood' turned out to be a kneadable substance made of wood, hardening quickly when exposed to air, allowing itself to be modeled like wood.

"Now it needed a procedure that was not very pleasant for Brigitte Helm: namely the making of a plaster cast of her whole body. Parts resembling a knight's armor, cut out of Hessian, were covered with two millimeters of the substance flattened by means of a kitchen pastry roller. This was then stuck onto the plaster Brigitte Helm, like a shoemaker puts leather over his block. When the material hardened, the parts were polished, the contours cut out. This was the rough mechanism of the 'machine creature' that made it possible for the actress to stand, to sit and to walk. The next procedure was furnishing it with detail to create a technological aesthetic. Finally we used 'Cellon' varnish mixed with silver bronze and applied with a spray gun, which gave the whole it's genuinely metallic appearance, so it even seemed convincing when looked at from close range. The work took many weeks however. In those days, films were carefully prepared and thus the realization of a piece of work unusual for a film like this one was ensured. In striking contrast to the present-day German film industry!" (7)

But in the 1939s producers reverted to the "tin woodsman" approach as seen in Bela Lugosi's comically-scowling mechanical monster in **The Phantom Creeps** (1939) and Republic's walking water-heater in **The Mysterious Dr. Satan** (1940).

*Left: First seen in Republic's serial **Undersea Kingdom** (1936), these "walking water heaters" made guest-appearances in other serials, such as **The Mysterious Dr. Satan** (1940).*

*Right: Bela Lugosi and friend in **The Phantom Creeps** (1939).*

However, in 1951, Robert Wise's *The Day the Earth Stood Still* (1951) took a radical leap away from that trend by introducing Gort, the imposing interstellar peace officer able to spit death rays.

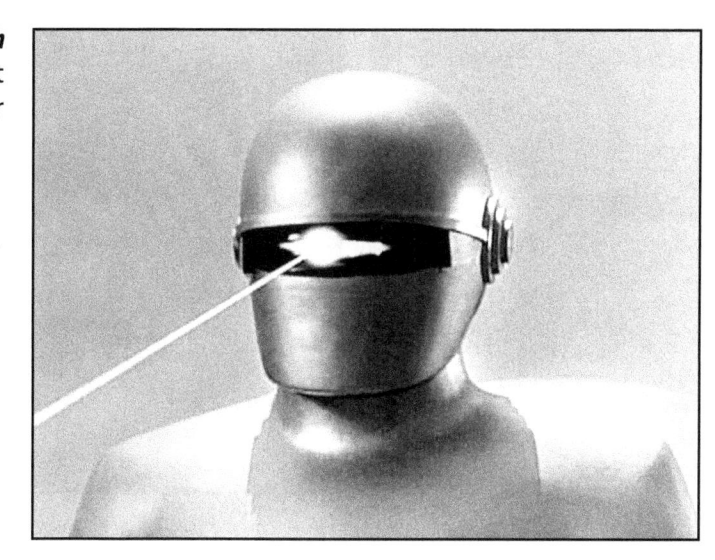

Gort retained the same basic humanoid shape of the earlier robots—after all, a human was going to be inside—but he was elegantly futuristic and imposing looking, topped by a brilliantly-conceived head. His powerful presence made him a natural for use in marketing the movie; in looking though the pressbook, exhibitors could order "Lifesize Robot Masks" of Gort, novelty accessories that were ideal for Children's Matinees!

Designed by Addison Hehr and Lyle R. Wheeler, once sculpted and molded in the 20th Century-Fox prop shop, castings were made from what sources alternately claim was foam latex or neoprene rubber (with foam backing inside).

The suit was worn by 7'-7" tall Lock Martin, who was discovered working as a doorman at Grauman's Chinese Theatre in Hollywood; he was, however, relatively weak and had serious difficulty carrying Patricia Neal, requiring the use of supporting wires when the actress was visible but they used a lightweight dummy when he was carrying her away from camera. Martin could only work in the suit for about a half an hour at a time and note in the final scene, with resurrected Klaatu addressing the scientists, his right arm seems to be twitching from painful cramps.

Unlike *The Creature from the Black Lagoon* where one suit could be filmed from all sides, Gort was manufactured as two costumes. When the robot moved towards camera, the suit's seams opened at the back, while a second Gort opened at the front for angles when "he" was seen from behind; both were laced up and a hollow head—with air-holes below the chin—was then placed on top of the actor. The somewhat rigid suits had a tendency to crease noticeably at the hips, knees, and elbows which helped convey an unnatural, alien-like quality of fluid metal - long before James Cameron used the idea in *Terminator 2: Judgment Day* (1991).

There was also a rigid fiberglass duplicate made for lighting purposes and also to stand-in for Gort when he is entirely static, such as when the military authorities immobilize him in a huge block of plastic.

An additional head with a functioning visor was manufactured for close-ups to which Fox's head of visual effects, Fred Sersen, and his team of Ray Kellogg, Emil Kosa, Jr., and L.B. Abbott added Gort's ray-beams and disintegration effects in post-production.

Republic took note of the popularity of Gort and abandoned their trusty "water heaters"... er, robots, for a more modern concept in *Tobor the Great* (1954). They had the good sense to put the design chores in the hands of art director Robert Kinoshita, who would later develop the iconic Robby the Robot for *Forbidden Planet* (1956) and B9 seen in Irwin Allen's *Lost in Space* (1965). (More about Robby in the next chapter.)

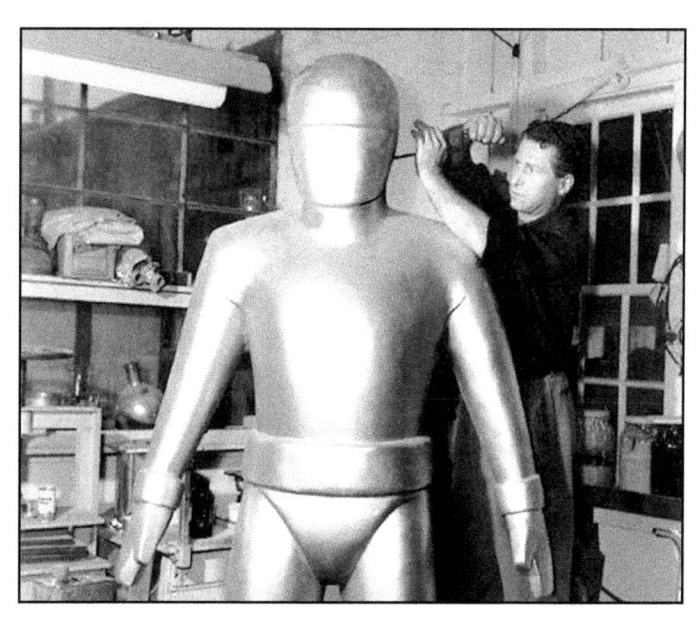

Klaatu, Gort's alien associate in **The Day the Earth Stood Still**, was virtually identical to us humans and didn't require anything unusual for his makeup. But at Paramount, producer George Pal needed some "thing" noticeably other-worldly for his latest sci-fi project.

Pal had brought science fiction to mainstream audiences with a huge hit, **Destination Moon** (1950) and while he was in post on **When Worlds Collide** (1951), he was gearing up to make War of the Worlds (1953), based on the classic science fiction novel by H. G. Wells. But Pal had a major concern about visualizing the alien invaders.

In the film, a radio interview with Dr. Forrester (Gene Barry) teases how bizarre the aliens may be. In the novel, the Martians are described as:

"A big greyish rounded bulk, the size, perhaps, of a bear... rising slowly and painfully out of the cylinder. As it bulged up and caught the light, it glistened like wet leather... There was a mouth under the eyes, the lipless brim of which quivered and panted, and dropped saliva. The whole creature heaved and pulsated convulsively. The peculiar V-shaped mouth with its pointed upper lip, the absence of brow ridges, the absence of a chin beneath the wedge-like lower lip, the incessant quivering of this mouth, the Gorgon groups of tentacles... There was something fungoid in the oily brown skin, something in the clumsy deliberation of the tedious movements unspeakably nasty... " (8)

Production designer Albert Nozaki—also responsible for the unique Martian manta-shaped war machines—came up with a design and Pal turned to Paramount's makeup and special props wizard, Charles Gemora, who had been Lon Chaney Sr.'s apprentice. Gemora sculpted the facade of the Cathedral for **The Hunchback of Notre Dame** (1923) and designed and supervised the construction of the opera house stage for **The Phantom of the Opera** (1925).

Gemora presented his completed Martian suit in Pal's office in late October, 1951, and both Pal and Nozaki were delighted that he had hit the target, being both economically-built and quite realistic; Pal hired the diminutive Gemora to also perform inside the suit, which just happened to be made for a person matching his dimensions. Perhaps he had learned from Chaney Sr. about making himself indispensable for the character performances, not just the manufacturing.

Ably assisted by his 12-year-old daughter, Diana, the Martian was made of chicken wire, latex sheets, papier mache, plaster bandages, 2"x2" lumber and—in what might have been a first—wet foam latex modeled directly onto the suit. The long arms meant the alien's fingers were too far away to fit his own hands, so Gemora cleverly devised ring pulls that fed cable to the individual Martian digits; when his fingers tugged on the rings, the Martian fingers responded.

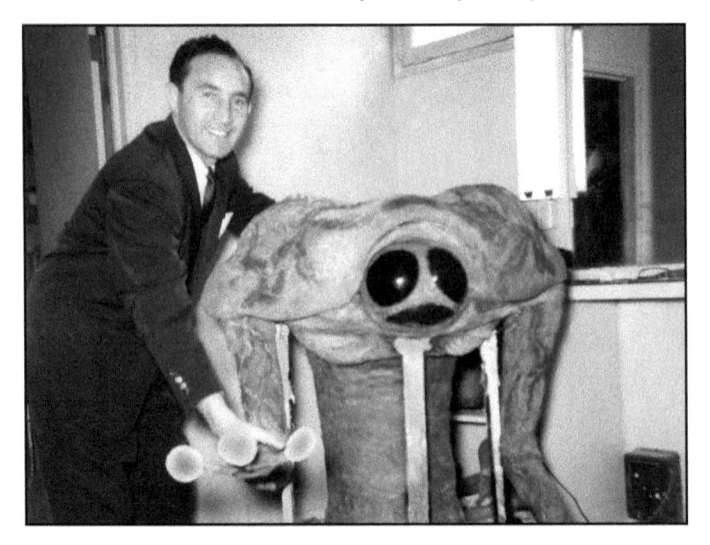

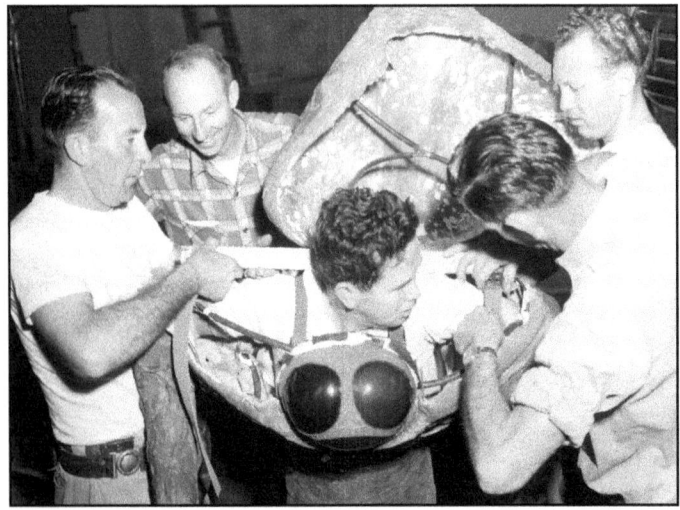

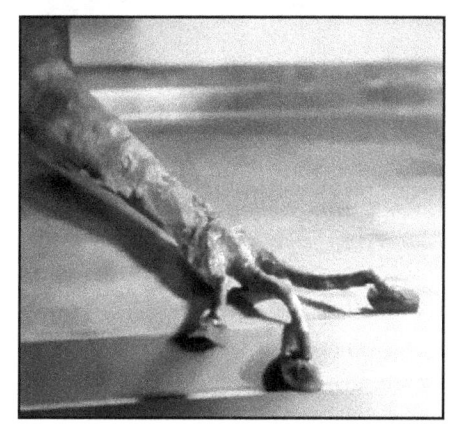

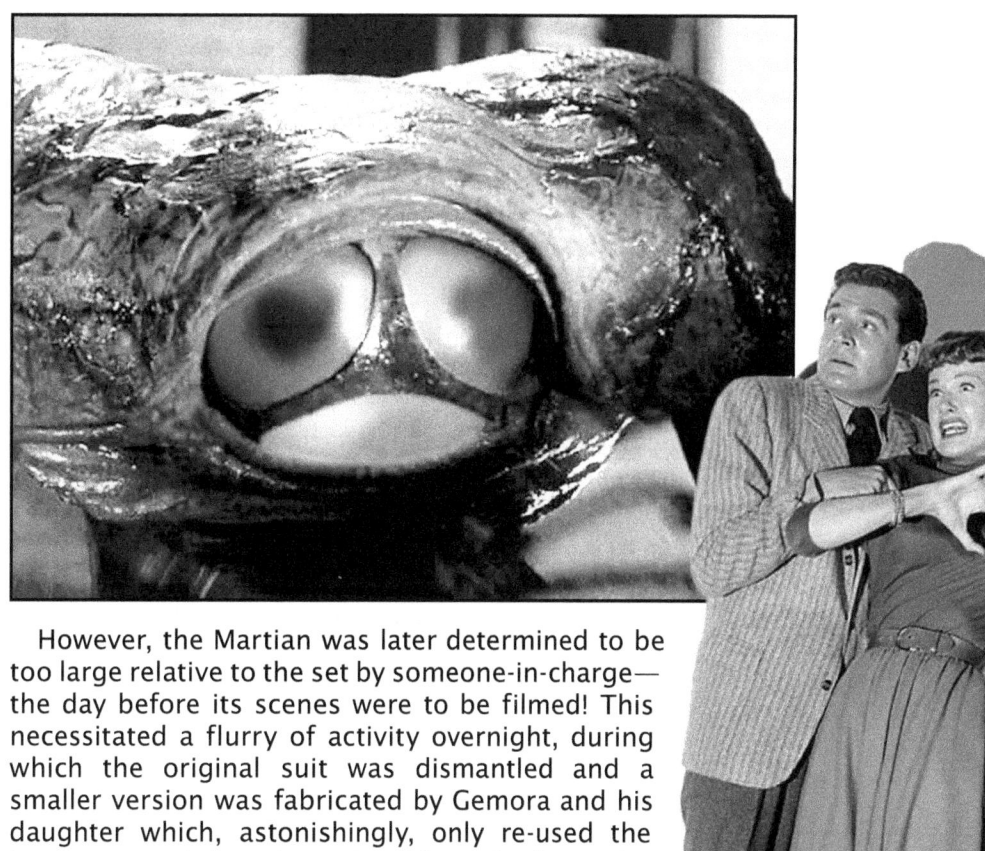

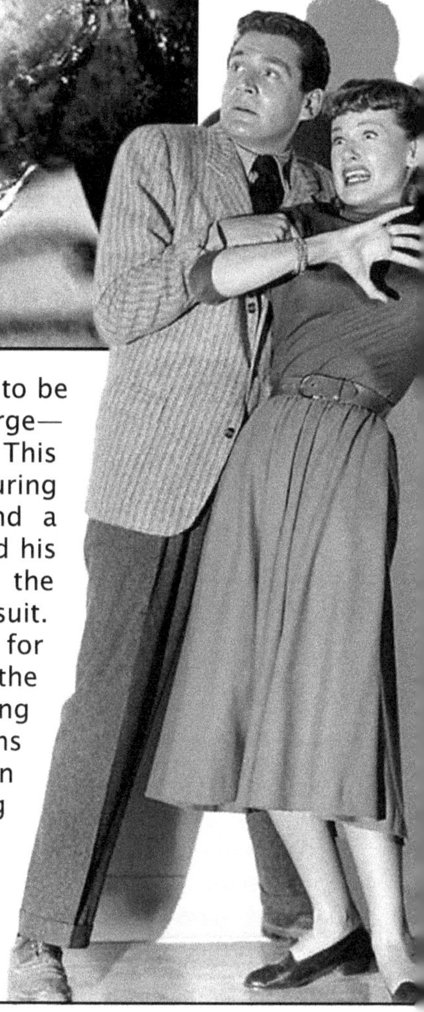

However, the Martian was later determined to be too large relative to the set by someone-in-charge—the day before its scenes were to be filmed! This necessitated a flurry of activity overnight, during which the original suit was dismantled and a smaller version was fabricated by Gemora and his daughter which, astonishingly, only re-used the long arms and three-lensed eye from the first suit.

Their professionalism delivered the Martian for its debut and Gemora wore the suit, handling the broad actions, while Diana operated breathing tubes from under the set that made its veins pulse, a detail that truly brought the Martian to life. The hastily-made suit lasted just long enough to finish its day's work! Gemora delivered a believable alien that, while not on screen for more than a few scenes, more than holds its own in a film packed with impressive moments.

At about the same time Gemora was building his alien, in late summer of 1953, a British Broadcasting Corporation serial showed a different type of Martian in a half-dozen forty-minute episodes of *The Quatermass Experiment*, which captivated audiences across the U.K. The insect-like aliens in it were accomplished as special props because they were never required to "act." The series' popularity encouraged Hammer Studios to produce a theatrical version, *The Quatermass Xperiment* (1955), which was a significant success and features some startling makeup effects that were so shocking, the UK censor insisted on trims and awarded the film an "X" certificate, which meant only those over age 16 could attend.

Hammer turned the tables on the censor with a clever strategy that used the 'X' (Xperiment) in advertising to make the film even more appealing to adults. The marketing stunt worked; audiences got the promised shocks and the company was saved by a substantial influx of cash. United Artist released it in the U.S. as *The Creeping Unknown* (1956) with four minutes of footage clipped.

Hammer was temporarily denied the rights to produce a sequel to their hit by the *Quatermass* author, Nigel Kneale, so the studio shifted gears to make *X the Unknown* (1956), an atmospheric shocker. In the titles, there are two credits for Philip Leakey, for Make-up and—for the first time—Special Make up Effects (no hyphen appears in the second credit). Leakey was a very inventive artist who devised imaginative effects for *X* and would later create a new look for Christopher Lee's monster in *Curse of Frankenstein* (1957).

Men In Suits • 101

X the Unknown

Our first glimpse of what happens when humans come into close contact with X, a never-seen-anything-like-it marauding mud "thing," is when a soldier reveals horrific burns on his back; it is no accident that the damaged tissue is based on the survivors of the A-bomb attacks on Japan, as the film is a cautionary tale about radioactivity unleashed. The burns appear to be a mix of latex stippling and cast components glued onto the actor.

Other makeup effects in the film are likely the most intense that audiences had seen up to that time, building on the transforming astronaut seen in **The Quatermass Xperiment**. Jack Curtis, chief electrician at Hammer, was given a special effects credit for helping Phil Leakey create some of these ghastly effects.

Leakey turned to Curtis to engineer a special prop, an articulating mechanical hand over which Leakey slid a hollow foam rubber casting which he had molded off of the electrician's hand. Leakey ran rubber tubes inside the prop in which he had made pinholes, so that injected liquid would spurt out where he wanted it. As Curtis gave some life to the hand by gently pulling on cables, Leakey injected red-dyed acetone, which instantly reacted with the foam; the on-screen illusion of the joints swelling and spewing blood was an horrifically-impressive first for makeup effects.

This was followed by an even more grotesque scene where a human head literally *melts*. Leakey made a life mask of the actor, from which the actor's face could be reproduced in wax. (Some sources claim a paraffin wax was used, but that can be highly inflammable, so I suspect a carnuba wax.) Jack Curtis added heating elements to a plaster skull, over which the wax head—including a wig—was mounted. The camera rolled as the melting wax sloughed away from the skull, allowing the jaw to drop—a horrifying illusion that set the bar for gore in later movies.

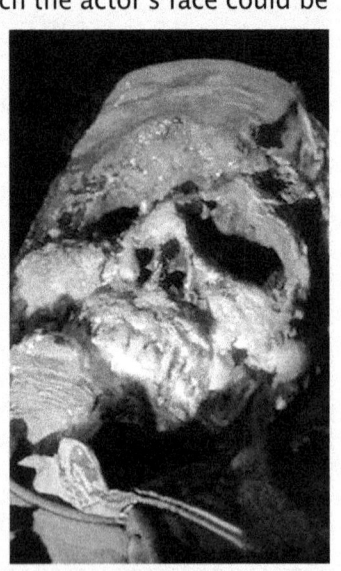

PHIL LEAKEY

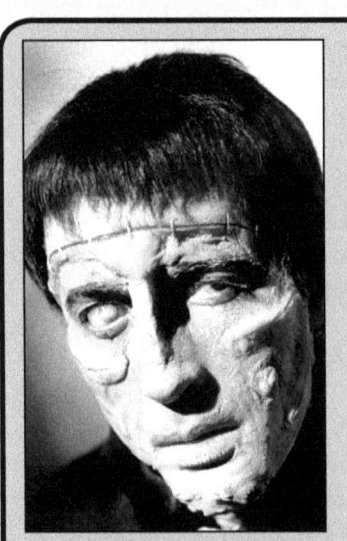

The Curse of Frankenstein (1957)
Christopher Lee.

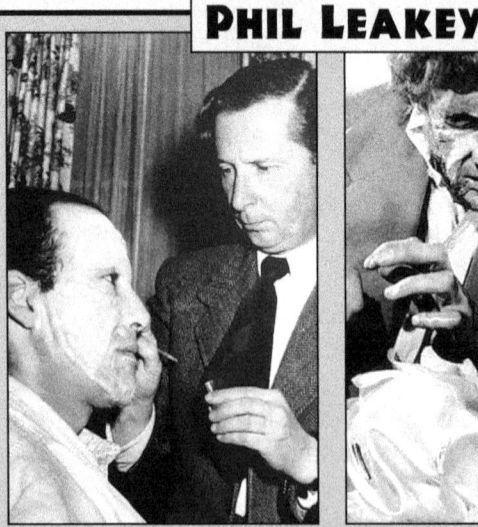

The Curse of Frankenstein (1957)
Christopher Lee, Phil Leakey.

The Revenge of Frankenstein (1958)
Michael Gwynn, Eunice Gayson.

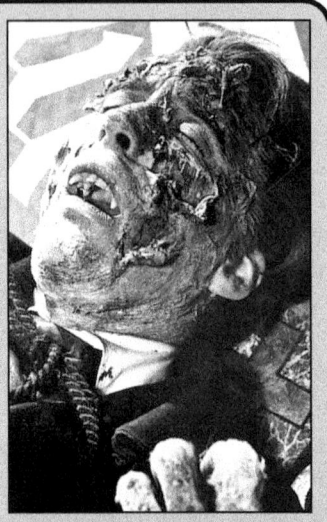

Horror of Dracula (UK: **Dracula**) (1958)
Christopher Lee.

102 · *Smoke and Mirrors – Special Visual Effects Before Computers*

PAUL BLAISDELL

As the fifties progressed, the big studio films inspired imitators and for the first time since Chaney, Sr.'s films, a talented artist began designing and manufacturing fantastic characters which he would generally perform himself, primarily for American International Pictures, a studio known for "slim budgets."

His name was Paul Blaisdell and he had the ability to work economically and deliver the goods on short time frames, often for filmmakers like Roger Corman and Bert I. Gordon. Lacking the studio budgets that enabled the complex procedures used at Bud Westmore's lab at Universal, Blaisdell devised a simplified method of building monster suits by cutting out shapes from thick sheets of foam rubber and gluing them onto a pair of long johns, followed by applying latex details and finishing with paint to add personality.

He followed in Lon Chaney Sr.'s footsteps, performing in his suits for shows like **The Day the World Ended** (1955) and **The She-Creature** (1956). For **Invasion of the Saucer-Men** (1957), however, the script called for several small invaders, which meant he was too large to play a proverbial "little green man." The solution was to make several over-the-head masks slush-cast in latex from a mold, conveniently and affordably supplying multiple heads for the little people playing the invaders. Blaisdell also made slip-on alien hands with eyeballs on them.

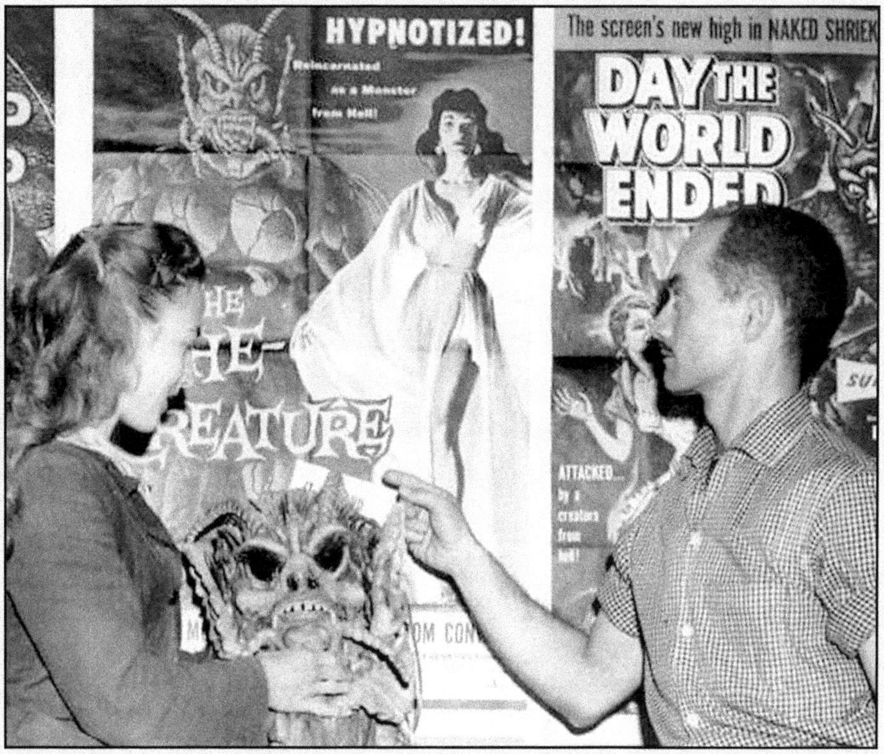

Above: Jackie and Paul Blaisdell. Paul started as an illustrator, painting covers for science fiction novels (below) and publications like **Spaceways**, **Other Worlds**, and **Universe**, This work led to him meeting **Famous Monsters of Filmland** magazine editor Forrest J Ackerman, who became his agent. Forry is seen below with **The Voodoo Woman** (1957) and the real woman (Marla English).

Below: Trophy heads on the wall illustrate **How to Make a Monster** (1958).

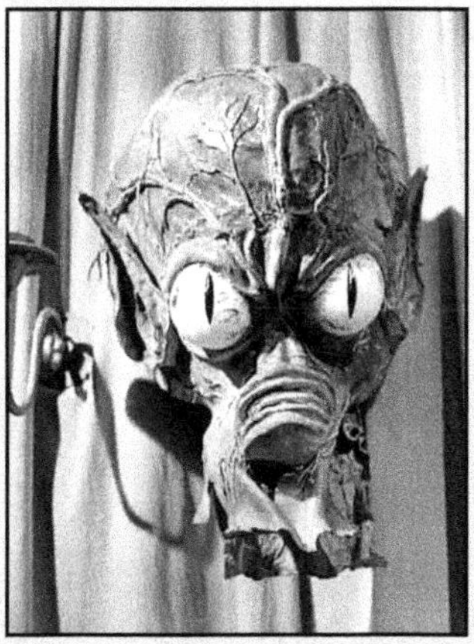

Men In Suits • 103

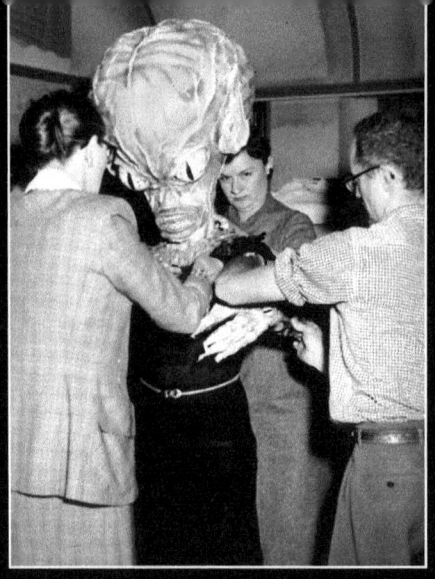

Above left: **The Beast With a Million Eyes** gets an eyeful of co-star Dona Cole.
Middle: Paul (right) and assistants suit up one of the Saucer Men in preparation for their invasion.
Right: AIP recycled the **She Creature** suit (slightly modified) for **Voodoo Woman** (1957) and **The Ghost of Dragstrip Hollow** (1959), and just her head in **How to Make a Monster** (1958).

However, Paul Blaisdell's masterpiece was his "Martian vampire" for—

THE TERROR from BEYOND SPACE

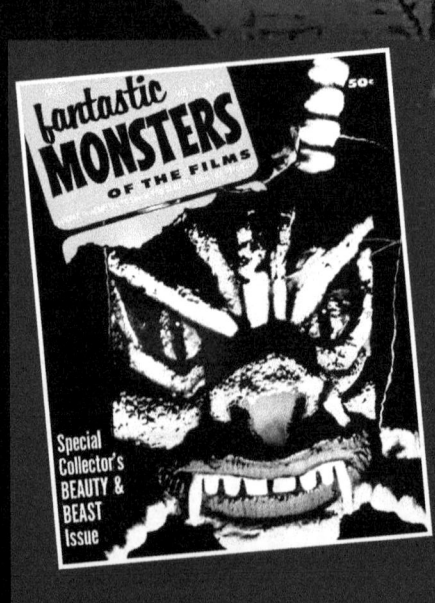

It! The Terror from Beyond Space (1958) was one of the key inspirations for Ron Shusett and Dan O'Bannon when they formulated their story for *Alien* (1979). Here's a description of the process used to manufacture the suit written by Blaisdell himself, which appeared in *Fantastic Monsters of the Films* #5 (left), a magazine the artist produced with his good friend Bob Burns:

"After the original sketches of *It! The Terror from Beyond Space* were approved by producer Bob Kent, director Eddie Cahn, and script writer Jerry Bixby, it was time for the 'prop builders' to go to work, and this is how they did it—and on time.

"First a clay head was constructed over a plaster replica of a normal human being's head and shoulders. This would insure a reasonably good fit when it came time to wear the completed rubber head. The script called for a scaly desert creature that lived on Mars, and the sketches were carefully followed.   *(continued...)*

Men In Suits • 105

...Reaches Through Space!
...Scoops Up Men And Women!
...Gorges On Blood!

"When the clay head for It was completed, a row of aluminum plates, the size of playing cards, were pushed into the clay. They ran up the side of the neck, over the top of the head and down the other side, dividing the head into two parts, front and back. Casting plaster was mixed with water to the consistency of heavy whipping cream and brushed into the first half of the head. Since the plaster mold was to be a large, strong one, a layer of wet burlap strips was applied over this first layer of plaster before it dried. Extra layers of plaster and burlap were built up, until the mold was over an inch thick. When the casting plaster burlap mixture was thoroughly dry, a similar mold was made over the back half of the head, This, when dry, completed the mold for the entire head. The two halves were pried apart with a screwdriver, and all clay 'scraps' were carefully removed from the mold.

"At this point, a recount of the materials used involved the following: Modelling clay from the five and ten cent store. A sheet of 'do it yourself' aluminum, from the local hardware store, and some casting plaster from the local lumber company. The phone book, as usual, gave us the nearest company that sold liquid latex rubber, and a few quarts were purchased for the next phase of the operation.

"The liquid latex was applied inside the head mold until sufficient layers were built-up to the desired thickness. Each layer of latex was allowed to dry at room temperature, according to the instructions on the jar. A few drops of brown poster paint were mixed with each application of rubber to give the final product a desert beige 'lizard' color. When dry, the two halves of the head were peeled from their respective molds and seamed together with additional applications of latex. Ears for the head and teeth for the mouth were cast in rubber, following the same clay-to-plaster-mold technique as the head. Artificial eyes were also made at this point, but discarded later in favor of letting the actor (Ray Corrigan) use his real eyes, for greater realism and better vision. "Additional shading and coloring with make-up and grease paint would 'polish off' the head, but there still remained the hands, feet, and body to be constructed. There were two ways this could be accomplished. The first way would be to construct a giant mold of the body in two parts, similar to the one for the head. This idea was discarded on the grounds it would be a clumsy, time-consuming operation that, while effective, could only be indulged in by the largest of studios.

"A study of some old-fashioned suits of armor seemed to indicate a faster and more time-proven way. Half a dozen one piece molds of "lizard-like scales" were made up, in varying sizes, over original clay modelings. A multitude of rubber castings was made from these plaster molds. These, in turn, were glued over a proper-size suit of heavy winter underwear, with a good brand of 'contact bond' cement. The whole effect was remarkably like Medieval armor, in that the overlapping allowed for bending and flexing on the part of the actor, while still retaining enough rigidity so that the suit tended to support its own weight. 'Claws' were constructed in the same way, over heavy work gloves, and the three toed "feet" were built entirely over a pair of 'sneakers.' Entry into the suit was effected by a 'zipper' that ran the entire length of the spine, and it was concealed by the 'lizard man's' backbone.

"The completed suit was given final minor adjustments to insure adequate fit and ventilation; then, in Jerry Bixby's action filled script, Ray Corrigan in full monster dress went on to survive heavy caliber gunfire, grenades, bazooka shells and a radioactive furnace!

"From the time of the agreed-upon sketches to the completion of the operable suit, six weeks elapsed. The deadline? The 'prop builders' beat it by 24 hours. *It! The Terror from Beyond Space* became It, the terror that got there on time!" (9)

[Note: Paul modestly neglected to mention that the "prop builders" are he and his wife Jackie.]

All in all, Blaisdell's versatility provided his clients with services they could afford—miniatures, hand puppets, monster suits, custom props—and his contributions helped make possible some of the most fondly-remembered genre films of the 1950s.

Dick Smith

Dick Smith was a makeup innovator utilizing molds and foam latex appliances to push the boundaries light years beyond mortician's wax and spirit gum. Known affectionately as "The Godfather of Makeup," Dick Smith was a mentor to artists who followed in his footsteps, including multiple Oscar®-winner Rick Baker.

In 1967 Smith provided foam appliances for two episodes of the Dan Curtis gothic soap opera *Dark Shadows*, transforming actor Jonathan Frid into a 175 year old vampire. Smith said that *Dark Shadows* turned out to be valuable preparation for his astonishing old-age transformation of Dustin Hoffman for Arthur Penn's *Little Big Man* (1970). Smith had earlier helped devise Hoffman's Ratso Rizzo for *Midnight Cowboy* (1969). In 1968 he transformed Jack Palance for *The Strange Case of Dr. Jekyll and Mr. Hyde*, and was Emmy-nominated.

Smith further advanced the art with *The Godfather* (1972), which, in the wake of Sam Peckinpah's *The Wild Bunch* in 1969, included realistically violent and bloody bullet hits using rubber bladders positioned under foam appliances. An electrically-fired "squib" blew a hole in the bladder and blood gushed out. (The method later used condoms to hold the blood.)

He really hit his stride with his electrifying work on *The Exorcist* (1973), with challenges that required Smith to combine makeup, appliances, special props and stage effects to produce moments that terrorized audiences. For instance, when the possessed girl's head does a 360 degree spin without breaking her neck (photo below), Smith staged the horrifying moment with a dummy that perfectly duplicated actress Linda Blair. And who can forget the projectile vomiting scene?

In *Altered States* (1980) William Hurt seemed to endure a painful metamorphosis via Smith's carefully inflated bladders and specially-designed appliances.

Smith won an Academy Award® for Best Makeup for his work on *Amadeus* (1984)—another utterly convincing old-age makeup—and in November, 2011, became the first make-up artist to receive an honorary Oscar® for Lifetime Achievement.

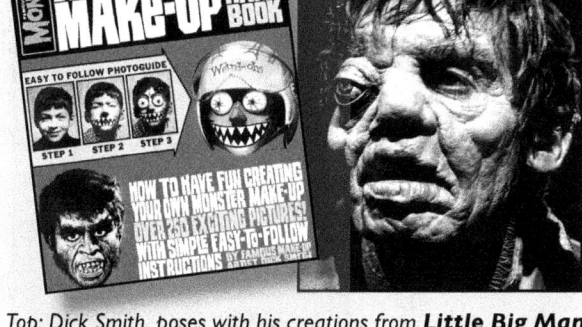

Top: Dick Smith, poses with his creations from *Little Big Man* (1970), *Ghost Story* (1981), *Altered States* (1980) and *The Exorcist* (1973).

Above, left: In 1965 Warren Publishing released Smith's *Do-It-Yourself Monster Make-up Handbook*, a very welcome one shot that gave solid advice to budding makeup artists on how to do the work themselves. I know I almost wore those pages out!

Above, right: For the Roald Dahl series 'Way Out (1961), Smith created his version of Quasimodo, the Hunchback of Notre Dame.

Below: For 'Way Out, Smith removed half of Barry Morse's face.

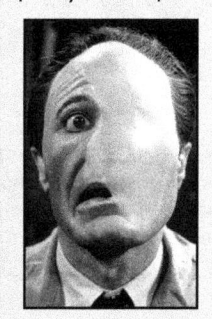

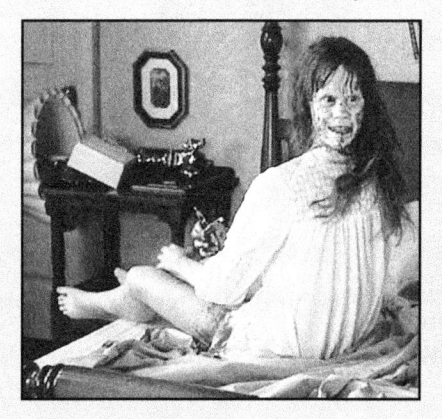

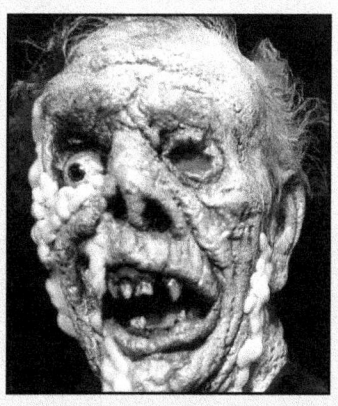

Men In Suits • 107

John Chambers

John Chambers began by supplying medical prosthetics for disfigured veterans before moving to Hollywood production in 1945. He was active with TV during the 1960s on **The Outer Limits** (1963), **The Munsters** (1964), and **Rod Serling's Night Gallery** (1969).

One of his best-remembered TV projects from that period were Leonard Nimoy's Spock ears, produced for the original **Star Trek** series (1966). Lee Greenway, who had done the makeup for James Arness in RKO's **The Thing** (1951), was Desilu's resident makeup expert and for the pilot, he built-up papier-mache and liquid latex directly onto Nimoy's ears. A number of tests over four or five days left the actor aghast at the results and, as Marc Cushman and Susan Osborn pointed out in their book **These are the Voyages: TOS, Season One** (Jacobs Brown Press, 2013), "Fred Philips was subsequently asked to make the ears, but he passed this task onto John Chambers so [Philips] could concentrate on achieving the right shade of red for Spock's skin." (10)

Chambers' first step was to generate new ear molds to replace the originals that had been damaged and the fresh molds pumped out scores of foam latex castings. The volume of appliances was required because they were irreparably damaged during the removal process, necessitating a new pair of ears for each day of shooting.

Some of his most outlandish creations were never seen by the public; he generated faithful versions of the bizarre Dick Tracy comic strip villains for a pilot that wasn't picked up. Chambers received another Emmy nomination for **Beyond Westworld** (1980).

However, Chambers' enduring masterpiece has to be **Planet of the Apes** (1968) which required transforming a horde of actors into different species of primates. Before 20th Century-Fox would commit, they ordered a ten minute test reel featuring Charlton Heston in a scene with Edward G. Robinson as the orangutan, Dr. Zaius. In the past, gorilla suits hid performers who were never "name" stars; the test footage would be a proof of concept that such talent could truly act from under the makeups. Robinson wore an initial ape makeup by Ben Nye, Fox's department head from 1944 to 1967, who was preparing to retire after contributing to 500 films. While not perfect, the test clearly demonstrated that the unique concept was viable and the studio moved ahead—with no inkling of the franchise that would be born, thanks in large part to the immense talents of John Chambers.

From *Variety's* July 10, 2017 retrospective article by Tim Gray: "They wanted to maintain "the surprise element," as producer Arthur P. Jacobs said, for audiences. They also wanted to keep rivals in the dark. There was fear that the $5 million film could be ripped off in a lower-budget version.

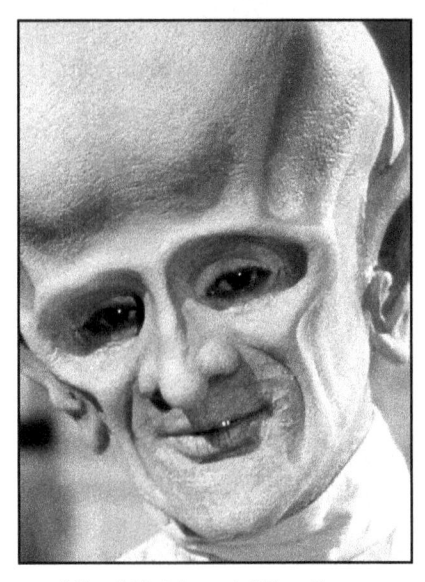

It's All About The Ears

Above: David McCallum in **The Sixth Finger** episode of **The Outer Limits**.

Below: Fred Phillips (right) applies Spock's signature ears to Leonard Nimoy.

Above: John Houston's **The List of Adrian Messenger** exploited Chamber's work with the tagline, "5 Great Stars Challenge You to Guess the Disguised Roles They Play!" His appliances on Burt Lancaster, Tony Curtis, Kirk Douglas, Robert Mitchum and Frank Sinatra earned him plaudits.

Left: John Chambers' Emmy-nominated suit for the **Night Gallery** (1969) episode of H.P. Lovecraft's **Pickman's Model**.

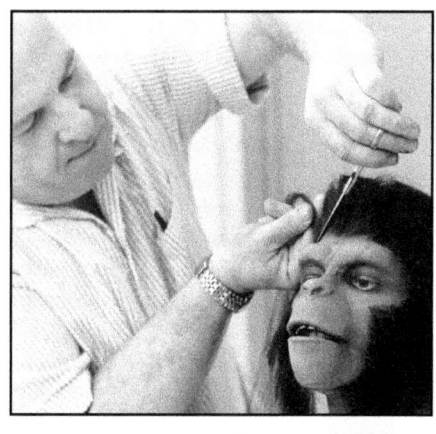

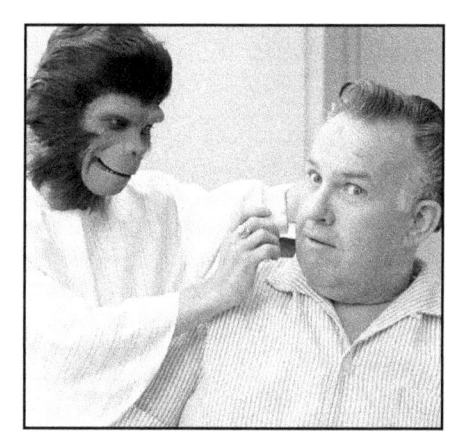

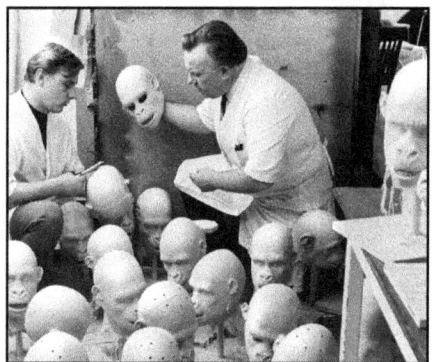

Above: Tom Burman (left) and John Chambers in the lab. His revolutionary approach made it possible for Rod Serling's script to be produced.

Below: Serling visits the set.

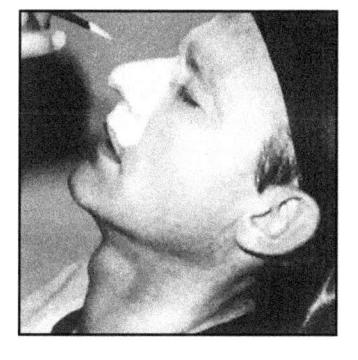

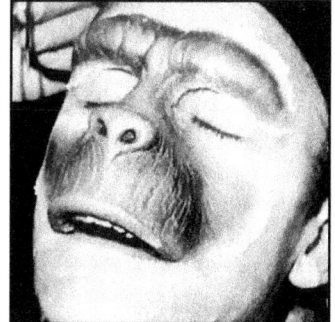

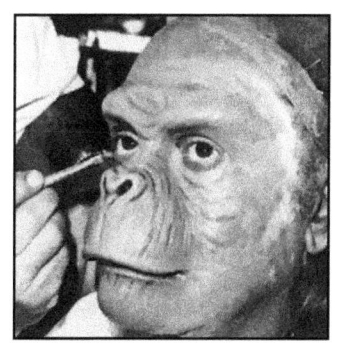

"Jacobs said that the makeup tests had started back in 1965 when he acquired the book: 'The makeup was our biggest expense on the film—costing about $1.5 million, or nearly one-third of the budget—and applying and removing it used up almost 60% of our total shooting time.

"There weren't enough makeup men in Hollywood so we had to train them. We had 10 trailers that were turned into classrooms for makeup," Jacobs said. "It took three to four hours to put it on every day and about an hour and a half to get it off." (11)

John Chambers had recommended Tom Burman as an apprentice at Fox and they began work on the film in January, 1967. They were joined by Daniel Striepeke, but to meet the overwhelming demand, young artists were hired: Larry Abbott (Charlton Heston's former hairstylist), Ken Chase, John Inzerella, Leo Lotito Jr., Werner Keppler, Maurice Stein and Dana Nye.

Chambers innovated a foam rubber formula that allowed the actors' skin to breathe and he was the first to accelerate prep time by pre-painting appliances.

Without doubt, the most unusual aspect of Chambers' career involved his participation in the CIA's "Canadian Caper," for which he was honored with their Intelligence Medal of Merit. The operation was built around a science fiction film supposedly being made in Iran, which served as cover to rescue six Americans held during the 1979 hostage crisis. The events were portrayed in the film ***Argo***, the 2012 Best Picture winner. (One wonders what the late makeup maestro would have thought of the casting of John Goodman to play him...)

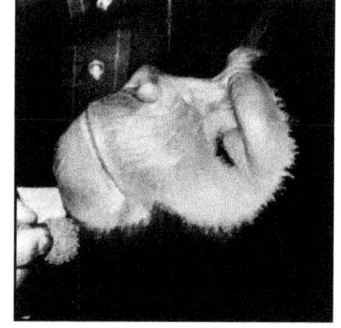

Men In Suits • 109

WILLIAM TUTTLE

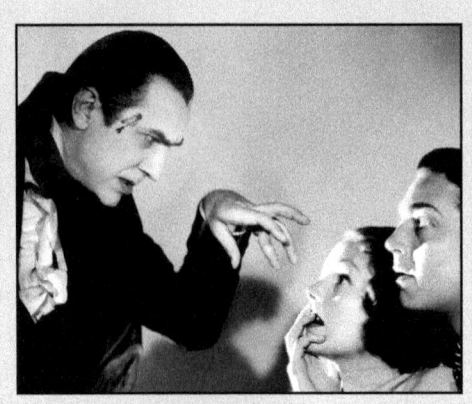

Once married to actress Donna Reed (above, left), star of **From Here to Eternity** and **It's a Wonderful Life**, MGM's makeup chief William Tuttle began in 1935 by assisting on **Mark of the Vampire** (above middle) for which he produced an effective bullet hole in the head of Bela Lugosi. He then assisted department head Jack Dawn, most notably on **The Wizard of Oz** in 1939 (above right). In 1965 Tuttle received the Academy's first Special Honorary Award for Makeup for his work on George Pal's—

7 FACES OF DR. LAO

Star Tony Randall wore a number of foam appliances and wigs to play widely diverse characters such as the God Pan, Merlin the magician and even Medusa, with her tresses made of snakes. The abominable snowman also appears, as a costume worn by the producer's son, Peter Pal, a bodybuilder who was also in **Atlantis: The Lost Continent** (1961), which spared Randall from having to wear the heavy suit.

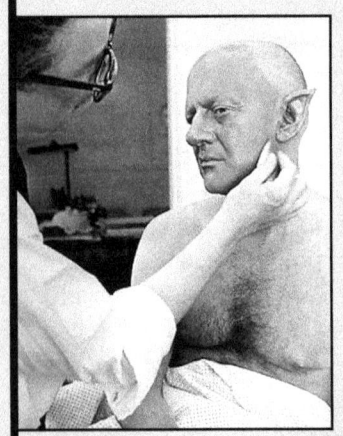

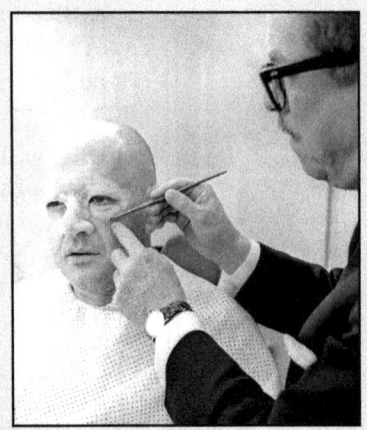

110 · *Smoke and Mirrors – Special Visual Effects Before Computers*

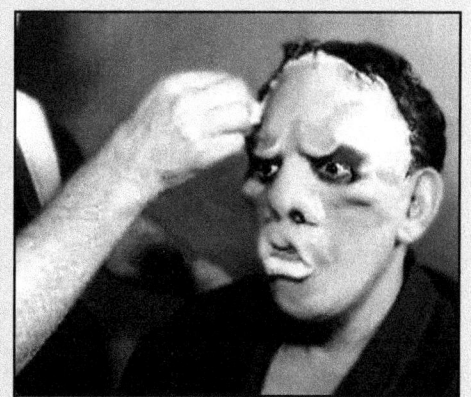

William Tuttle created the cannibalistic Morlocks in George Pal's *The Time Machine* (1960). Some people suggest that these same appliances were re-used in the *The Twilight Zone* episode *Eye of the Beholder* (1960), but, in fact, those makeups, while similar, were newly created from designs by episode director Douglas Heyes.

A noteworthy Tuttle makeup for *The Twilight Zone* was the gremlin for *Nightmare at 20,000 Feet* (Nick Cravat) in which an ugly creature torments William Shatner from the wing of an airliner in flight.

Project Unlimited and The Outer Limits

Project Unlimited was formed by Wah Chang, Gene Warren, Sr. and Tim Baar and covered the gamut of special effects, from props to costumes to stop-motion animation.

For *The Outer Limits* (1963), Project created the suit for the Thetan in *The Architects of Fear* (worn by Janos Prohaska), the Megazoid for *The Duplicate Man*, and over-the-head masks and gloves for *The Keeper of the Purple Twilight*, *Children of Spider County* and *Fun and Games*. They also built the close-up mechanical prop of the plant monster for *Counterweight*, which also included a stop-motion model animated by Jim Danforth. Project also created the alien insect prisoners for one of the series' most popular episodes, *The Zanti Misfits*, which featured stop-motion by Al Hamm and Pete Kleinow. Wah Chang made the puppets, giving them individual facial features, and mass-produced the disposable props used in scenes with the live actors.

Later, Chang designed the tricorder prop for *Star Trek* (1966-1969) and the Romulan spacecraft. He also designed and supervised the fabrication of the Gorn costume for the episode *Arena* with fangs for the reptilian alien hand-modeled from wood putty.

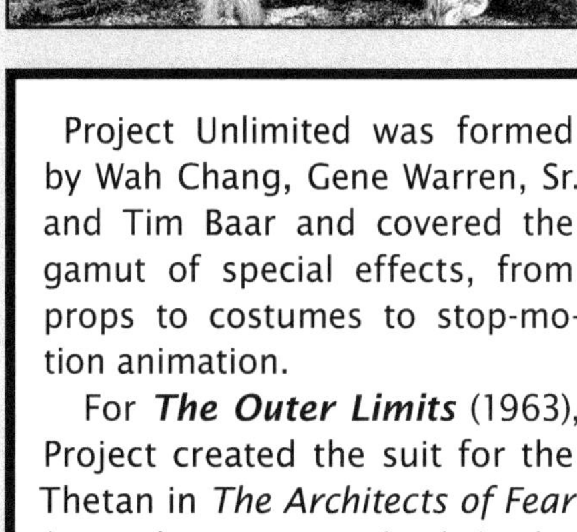

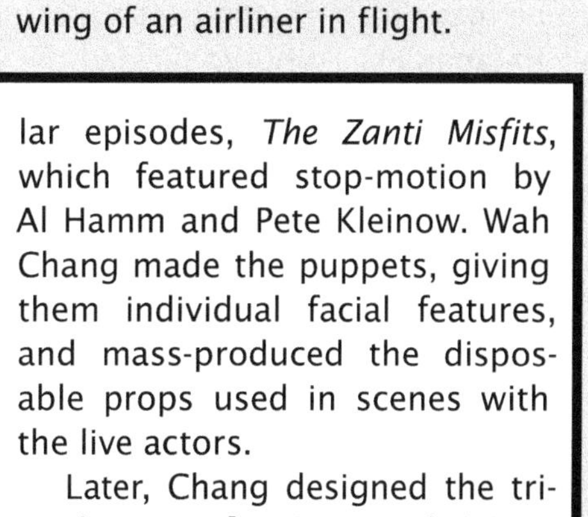

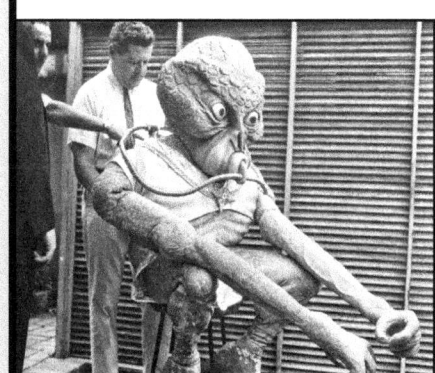

Men In Suits • 111

The 1960s and 1970s saw the emergence of Italian genre filmmaking, and the film that got the ball rolling was ***Caltiki, il mostro immortale*** (1959; U.S. 1960, as ***Caltiki the Immortal Monster***). It presaged "Giallo" (Italian murder mysteries) with horror and eroticism. It also introduced staple elements like found footage—possibly the first use in horror films—plus steamy lust, unbridled avarice and increasingly graphic gore, directly impacting the films of Lucio Fulci (***Zombie***, 1980) and others.

Caltiki's most atmospheric moments are at the beginning when researchers investigate a shadow-drenched cavern dominated by a statue of Caltiki, the goddess to whom victims were sacrificed in a nearby black-water pool. The grotto sequence surpasses the gore effects seen in both ***The Quatermass Experiment*** (1955) and ***X the Unknown*** (1956) when a skin diver is hauled back up from the depths of the pool and is seen to have his face nearly melted off! The horrific impact is amplified as he struggles to draw his last breaths! The prop appears to be made from gelatin over a plaster skull.

In Japan Eiji Tsuburya tackled the effects for Toho's ***Gojira*** (1954; U.S.: ***Godzilla***, 1956) utilizing a custom-built suit stomping puny human buildings flat—a process that came to be dubbed "suitmation." Contrary to popular opinion, Tsuburya also used stop-motion for a few brief shots in both ***Godzilla*** and ***King Kong vs. Godzilla*** (1962).

Tsuburya understood how to design scenes using the best techniques he could afford to give the director what he wanted. Among the films featuring his suitmation and miniatures are ***Godzilla Raids Again*** (1955), ***Rodan the Flying Monster*** (1956), ***Varan the Unbelievable*** (1958), ***Gorath*** (1962), ***Godzilla vs. the Thing*** (1964), ***Ghidrah, the Three-Headed Monster*** (1964), ***Frankenstein Conquers the World*** (1965), and ***Destroy All Monsters*** (1968). ***The Mysterians*** (1960) is noteworthy for a broad spectrum of visual effects methods including a wildly imaginative giant robot in samurai armor that fires death rays from its eyes! The robot is a prime example of Tsuburya's "suitmation" techniques, the performer in the suit filmed on tabletop landscapes. The raybeams were cel animation added optically in post-production.

Doctors slowly peel away the sticky, gooey remnants of Caltiki from a man's arm. The camera dwells on the action and the shocking revelation of only bones being left set a standard for on-screen outrageousness for years to come.

British filmmakers did their Japanese counterparts one better with a life-sized giant monster that was driven around London for *Gorgo* (1961)! Actually, just the full-sized head and claw sticking out from under a tarpaulin on a flat-bed trailer. They built a mechanical head with illuminated eyes and an elaborate costume for suit-mation. Arthur Hayward, who later sculpted animation models for Ray Harryhausen, worked on the creature.

*Inside the Gorgo suit (alternating with another man and a woman): stunt man Mick Dillon. Mick started out as a jockey before embarking on a career in films: he was Ringo Starr's stuntman in **HELP!**, doubled for Buster Keaton in **A Funny Thing Happened on the Way to the Forum**, slid down a rope into a volcano in **You Only Live Twice**, fractured his skull when he fell out of a vintage racing car in **Chitty Chitty Bang Bang**, appeared as a plant mutation in **Day of the Triffids**, and was the Dalek that disappeared down an elevator shaft in **Dr. Who and the Daleks**.*

Men In Suits • 113

A Hammer Film Production

Roy Ashton

By the end of the 1950s Hammer Films in England had turned to making color updates of the earlier Gothic horror films, which took the world by surprise. Phil Leakey devised a radical new version of Frankenstein's Monster for actor Christopher Lee, seen in **The Curse of Frankenstein** (1957), which was sufficiently removed from Pierce and Karloff's monster that Hammer could avoid a lawsuit from Universal. He was assisted by Roy Ashton, who took over when Leakey departed after the studio cut Leakey's retainer.

Ashton's first big success was **The Man Who Could Cheat Death** (1959) in which actor Anton Diffring withered away at the climax. The results prompted Dick Smith to consult Ashton when Smith was preparing to age Dustin Hoffman for **Little Big Man** (1970).

Hammer relied on Ashton for new versions of the creatures that had populated Universal's original series, including **The Mummy** and **Frankenstein's monster**, as well as original creations such as **The Gorgon** (1964). **Curse of the Werewolf** (1960) features one of the most beautifully executed lycanthropes ever put on film, made all the more compelling by a powerful performance by Oliver Reed.

114 · *Smoke and Mirrors*

Gorillas in Our Midst

Charles Gemora

Charles Gemora was an innovator who developed "blood" that wouldn't stain wardrobe. He also refined foam latex by injecting air into the mixture to increase volume, which also made it softer and more flesh-like. Gemora was renowned as a "Gorilla Man" and wore his hand-made suit in the Our Gang short **Bear Shooters** (1930), **Murders in the Rue Morgue** (1932), Laurel and Hardy's **The Chimp** (1932) and **Swiss Miss** (1938), **At the Circus** (1939), **Road to Zanzibar** (1941), **Africa Screams** (1949) and **White Witch Doctor** (1953). He also appeared on screen with Lon Chaney, Sr., his mentor, in the remake of **The Unholy Three** (1930).

Ray "Crash" Corrigan

Ray "Crash" Corrigan, a former stunt man and cowboy star, built a western town set in Simi Valley north of Los Angeles, which he rented to dozens of productions. He wore his own gorilla costume in many productions such as **Tarzan and his Mate** (1934), **Flash Gordon** (1936), **The Ape** (1940), **Dr. Renault's Secret** (1942), **Captive Wild Woman** (1943) and **Unknown Island** (1948). Over the years some refinements to the inner mechanisms of his suit were engineered and a new face was created. His final film was wearing Paul Blaisdell's Martian suit for **It! The Terror from Beyond Space** (1958).

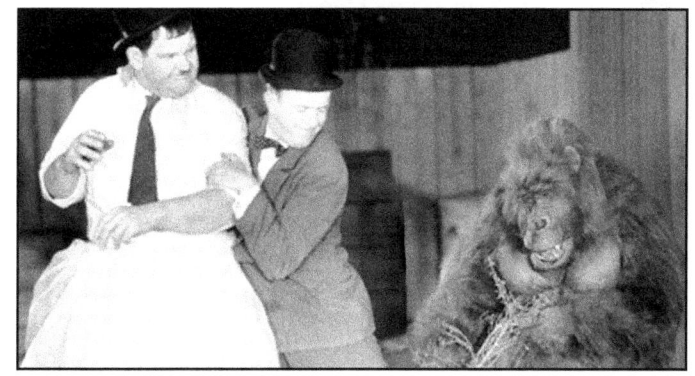

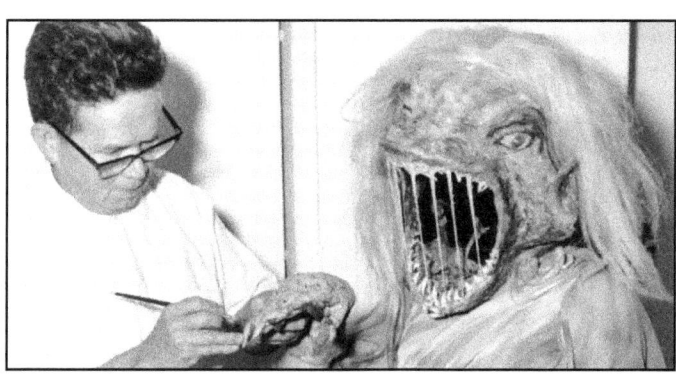

*Top to Bottom: Charles Gemora prepares to don his ape suit; menaces Laurel and Hardy in **The Chimp** (1932); and puts final touches on one of the ghostly demons for **Jack the Giant Killer** (1962);*

*Above: Ray "Crash" Corrigan menaces Jim Hawthorne and Joe Besser in **Fraidy Cat** (1951), directed by Three Stooges veteran Jules White. This short is a scene-by-scene remake of the Stooges short **Dizzy Detectives** (1943) as Besser and Hawthorne play detectives who go after a gorilla trained to rob an antique store after hours. It was remade yet again as **Hook a Crook** (1955).*

STEVE CALVERT

Steve Calvert (who named himself after Calvert whiskey), purchased Corrigan's suit in 1948 and was seen in *Bride of the Gorilla* (1951), *Road to Bali* (1952), *Bela Lugosi Meets a Brooklyn Gorilla* (1952), *The Bowery Boys Meets the Monsters* (1954) and Ed Wood's *Bride and the Beast* (1958). He was also inside the absurd robot suit for *Target Earth* (1954).

*Above: Charlotte Austin is menaced by Steve Calvert's gorilla in Ed Wood's film **The Bride and the Beast** (1958).*

Below: Steve Calvert puts final touches to his gorilla suit.

GEORGE BARROWS

George Barrows built his first gorilla suit after doubling for Johnny Weismuller in *Tarzan and his Mate* (1934) and played a gorilla in that film (as did "Crash" Corrigan). He played the vicious one-horned "orangopoid" in Universal's 1936 *Flash Gordon* serial and donned the suit for the 3D films *Gorilla at Large* (1954) and the inept *Robot Monster* (1953), as well as *Frankenstein's Daughter* (1958), *Ghost in the Invisible Bikini* (1966) and *Hillbillys in a Haunted House* (1967), and TV series such as *The Beverly Hillbillies* (1962), *The Man from U.N.C.L.E.* (1964) and *The Addams Family* (1964).

Konga (1961) was shot in the U.K. and because they could not afford to fly Barrows over, Paul Stockman played *Konga*—uncredited—because he fit the suit and had brown eyes (no need for expensive contact lenses). Barrows was paid $750/week for five months. When the suit was returned Barrows was dismayed to discover the costume had been mistreated—ventilation holes had been cut into it and the lip mechanisms that created a menacing snarl were wrecked. Nevertheless, he later used his suit for *The Black Zoo* (1963), produced in the U.S. by *Konga* producer Herman Cohen.

*Above: Before she was Mrs. Robinson, even before she was Mrs. Mel Brooks, Anne Bancroft (left) joined Charlotte Austin in the clutches of George Barrows' gorilla suit in **Gorilla At Large** (1954). Today, the suit resides in the Los Angeles County Museum of Natural History.*

*Below: **Konga** (1961) threatens a miniature greenhouse and has eyes for actress Claire Gordon.*

116 · *Smoke and Mirrors – Special Visual Effects Before Computers*

2001: A SPACE ODYSSEY

STUART FREEBORN

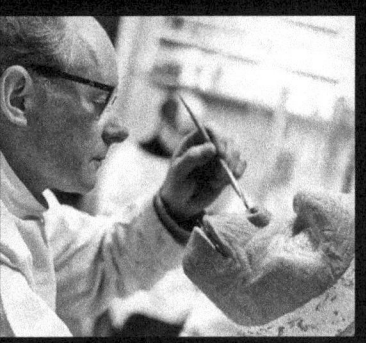

Above: Early Neanderthal tests, a concept deemed unsuitable.

For the extensive makeups in *2001: A Space Odyssey* (1968), perfectionist Stanley Kubrick turned to Stuart Freeborn, with whom he had worked on *Dr. Strangelove* (1964). Freeborn would later helm the first three *Star Wars* films: (*A New Hope*, *The Empire Strikes Back*, and *Return of the Jedi*). for which he created Yoda, performed by Muppet-master Frank Oz.

Freeborn, who had transformed Alec Guinness into Fagin for *Oliver Twist* (1948), created a stunning old-age makeup to Keir Dullea for the end of *2001*. However, his biggest challenge was ape-men for the opening "Dawn of Man" sequence, which Kubrick initially planned to shoot in close angles from the waist up because they were going to be nude. Tests with a caveman-like makeup convinced Kubrick that he couldn't get what he wanted and he pushed the timeline further back so the characters would be more ape-like. The wardrobe department couldn't get the ape suits right so Kubrick dumped the task on Freeborn.

Freeborn made full-body molds of each performer (selected because they were thin) so every suit could have form-fitting padding covered with plenty of hair to hide the "naughty bits." For the leader, "Moonwatcher" (performed by mime Daniel Richter, who also choreographed the apes), Freeborn devised the most sophisticated over-the-head "hero" masks seen on film up to that point, and far more advanced than the appliances for *Planet of the Apes*. They had toggle switches in the mouths which the actors could control with their tongues to drive lip action, and the combination of quality makeup execution with top-notch acting made the ape-men completely believable.

Colin Arthur

Working alongside Freeborn creating the hominid makeups was Colin Arthur, a gifted sculptor who had attended the Guildford School of Art, after which he worked at Madame Tussaud's, in London, the world-famous wax museum. His considerable skills were refined working as an apprentice to her descendant, Bernard Tussaud, before he migrated into film work.

Arthur brought his craftsmanship to films made by visual effects legend Ray Harryhausen. For *The Golden Voyage of Sinbad* (1974), he produced the disfigured face of the Grand Vizier (Douglas Wilmer), looking somewhat like the burned face of Vincent Price in *House of Wax* (1953). Working from Harryhausen's conceptual art, Arthur also fabricated the Golden Mask worn by the Vizier to hide his disfigurement.

For *Sinbad and the Eye of the Tiger* (1977), again guided by Harryhausen's detailed pre-production art, he created two suits that were hoped would cut down on the time-consuming stop-motion workload. The metal statue brought to life by dark sorcery, the Minoton, appears in several scenes worn by Peter Mayhew, in his first film role. When George Lucas called to ask if the actor might be useful for a little film he was about to make called *Star Wars: Episode IV—A New Hope* (1977), he was given high marks for his professionalism. Another suit, of the character Trog was made and used on location for long shots, but it seems all but one shot of it was left on the cutting room floor.

For Harryhausen's last film, *Clash of the Titans* (1981), Arthur made several noteworthy contributions including the makeup for Calibos (Neil McCarthy), which had to intercut with the stop-motion version of the character. He also made the prop head of Medusa which Perseus (Harry Hamlin) uses to stop the formidable Kraken. Arthur also created a fifteen foot long Kraken suit to be worn by a scuba diver for some underwater scenes.

Over a fifty year career Colin Arthur worked on scores of films including the original *Conan the Barbarian* (1982) and is now based in Spain. I was fortunate to meet him while he was at Cannon Films in Hollywood, having recently completed *Allan Quartermain and the Lost City of Gold* (1986) for them. He was discussing special effects for the spoof *It Ate Cleveland*, which sadly was never made. I would have enjoyed working with him!

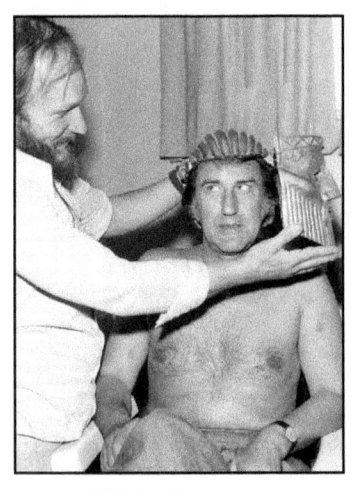

Above: The Vizier's mask in ***The Golden Voyage of Sinbad.***

Above: ***Sinbad and the Eye of the Tiger.*** *Below:* ***Clash of the Titans.***

STAR WARS— AND BEYOND...

Towards the end of the 1970s, decades after the robot Maria was made for **Metropolis** (1927), the basic process was duplicated for C3PO in **Star Wars IV: A New Hope** (1977), starting with a full life cast being made of the performer who would be inside, Anthony Daniels. Liz Moore and Brian Muir sculpted the final design and, after preparing masters and molds, a number of modern materials including fiberglass, vacuum formed plastic and aluminum shapes yielded components that were metallized to create the golden outer skin of the protocol droid.

In spite of the many years separating them, both robots shared the trait of being very warm for the performers inside and I salute Daniels as a better man than me—I cannot imagine working in the Tunisian desert while wearing that form-fitting sauna!

The bar for robots was raised high by James Cameron's **The Terminator** (1984), featuring Stan Winston's duplicate of Arnold Schwarzenegger and the unforgettable life-sized T-800 robotic menace, a magnificently engineered prop which was a primary factor in the birth of a franchise that is still chugging along.

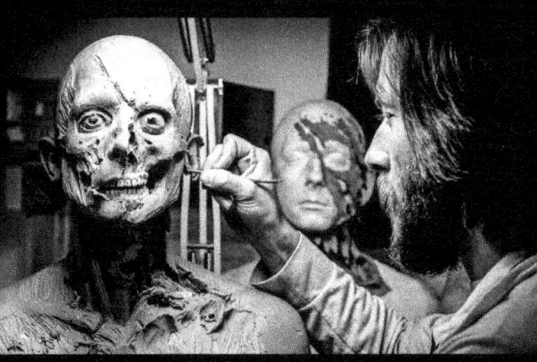

In the 1980s, special makeup effects and animatronics/props took a giant leap forward with the in-front-of-God-and-everyone werewolf transformations in Rick Baker's Oscar®-winning collaboration with John Landis, **An American Werewolf in London** (1981) and Joe Dante's **The Howling** (1981), with effects by Rob Bottin.

Bottin later capitalized on the experiences gained on the werewolf show to provide **John Carpenter's The Thing** (1983) with utterly nightmarish transformation effects beyond anything seen previously, ranging from appliances worn by actors to fully-mechanical creatures. Baker has won seven Oscars® of eleven nominations, as well as other awards. Bottin has won an Oscar® out of two nominations. Winston had four Oscar® wins out of ten nominations.

From top: **Star Wars, Terminator 2-Judgment Day; An American Werewolf in London; The Howling.**
Right: **John Carpenter's The Thing** (1983).

Men In Suits • 119

Several companies appeared in the 1980s such as MMI, Magical Media Industries, which was founded by John Carl Buechler. MMI provided special makeup effects and props for a host of films, especially for Charles Band. Buechler also directed **Troll** (1986), **Cellar Dweller** (1988), **Friday the 13th Part VII: The New Blood** (1988) and **Ghoulies III: Ghoulies Go to College** (1991). He wrote the story for **Demonwarp** (1988) but the script was written by marketing expert Jim Bertges. My company, Wizard Works, provided the visual effects, the second time I worked with John, the first time when he provided a prop head, robot costumes and a monster suit for my production, **Slave Girls from Beyond Infinity** (1987). Buechler was nominated for Saturn Awards for **Forbidden World** (1983), **Re-Animator** (1986) and **From Beyond** (1987).

Makeup effects legend Tom Savini—"The Sultan of Splatter"—took gore to new heights, highlighted by an enduring relationship with George A. Romero. Savini carried on Romero's zombie apocalypse with **Dawn of the Dead** (1978) and provided a broad range of effects for **Creepshow** (1982), including the full suit of "Fluffy." He created effects for **Friday the 13th** Part 1 (1980) and Part IV (1984) and worked with Tobe Hooper on **The Texas Chainsaw Massacre 2** (1986). In 1985, Savini received a Saturn Award for Romero's **Day of the Dead**. He also directed the 1990 re-make of Romero's 1968 film, **Night of the Living Dead**. These days he concentrates on Tom Savini's Special Make-Up Effects Program at the Douglas Education Center in Pennsylvania, sharing his wealth of knowledge to keep makeup skills alive.

The Chiodo Brothers—Stephen, Charles and Edward—have provided prosthetics, animatronics and stop-motion and are perhaps best known for their cult film **Killer Klowns from Outer Space** (1988), a showcase of outstanding visual effects. They also contributed to **Sword and the Sorceror** (1982), **Pee-Wee's Big Adventure** (1985), **Critters** (1986) and many other productions.

Founded in 1988 by Robert Kurtzman, Greg Nicotero, and Howard Berger, KNB EFX Group has become one of the preeminent specialty vendors for makeup effects, animatronics and prosthetics. Initially providing gore effects, they expanded into realistic animatronics with Kevin Costner's **Dances with Wolves** (1990). Some of their credits include **Misery** (1990), **City Slickers** (1991), **Army of Darkness** (1992), and **Reservoir Dogs** (1992).

Amalgamated Dynamics, Inc., helmed by Alec Gillis and Tom Woodruff, Jr., was also founded in 1988 to provide world-class makeup efx, prosthetics and animatronics. Some of their films include **Tremors** (1990), **Alien 3** (1992), which earned an Oscar® nomination, **Death Becomes Her** (1992), which received an Oscar®, and **Demolition Man** (1993).

Makeup effects artists have continually pushed the technological limitations of their times, helping directors and producers bring to the screen imaginative and compelling characters. Collaborating with actors, they represent a perpetually evolving force within the industry, and this close relationship will continue well into the future.

John Carl Buechler.

*Nicolas Rashby (left) assists Kirk Graves and Mark Wolf with the android suit fabricated by John Buechler's crew for **Slave Girls from Beyond Infinity** (1987). It was made in part using foam core, reflecting the minimal budget on the film!*

*Tom Savini sculpting "Fluffy," from the 1982 film **Creepshow**.*

Klowns among us! L-R: Edward, Stephen and Charles Chiodo.

SCRAPBOOK

In the October, 2020 issue of **RetroFan** magazine (#11), Dan Johnson interviewed Julie Ann Ream, an investigative agent on the TV series **Unsolved Mysteries** and producer of the Western Legends and Silver Spur Awards and the Roy Rogers Festival. More to the point here, Ms. Ream's grandfather was Taylor 'Cactus Mack' McPeters,' first cousin to Glenn Strange. Ream recalled hearing that "Glenn was having lunch inside the Universal commissary, Also lunching was Jack Pierce. Due to the amount of time Boris Karloff had to spend in the make-up chair, Pierce was hoping to find another candidate to play the Monster. He looked over at Glenn and said to himself, 'If I only had him, I'd be halfway done with my makeup before I got started.' He offered Glenn $25 to stay late and let him 'make him up' and 45 minutes later he had his new Monster. Glenn's response in seeing himself for the first time? 'Wow! You've turned me into Boris Karloff!'"

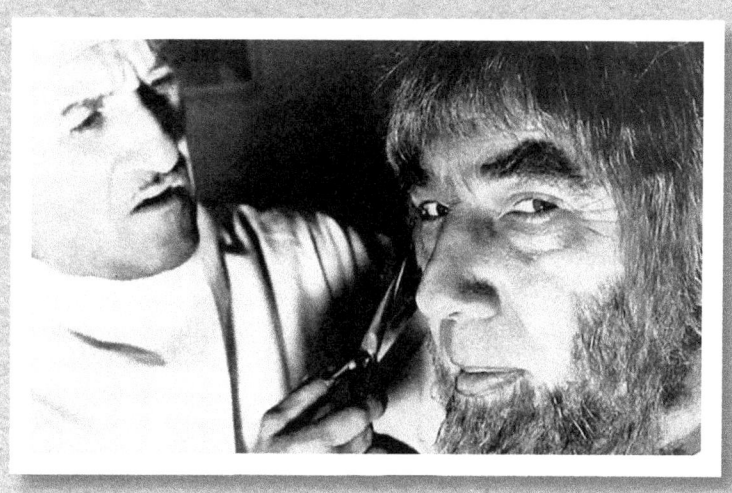

Above: Jack Pierce works on Bela Lugosi's superb makeup for "Ygor" in **Son of Frankenstein** (1939). Lugosi's outstanding performance revitalized his career.

Below: Basil Rathbone, the son of Frankenstein, examines Karloff. Lugosi's grizzled "Ygor" would return in **The Ghost of Frankenstein** (1942) opposite Lon Chaney, Jr.'s monster.

Lon Chaney and his assistant, Charles Gemora, appeared together on-screen in Chaney's final film, the sound re-make of his silent movie, **The Unholy Three** (1930).

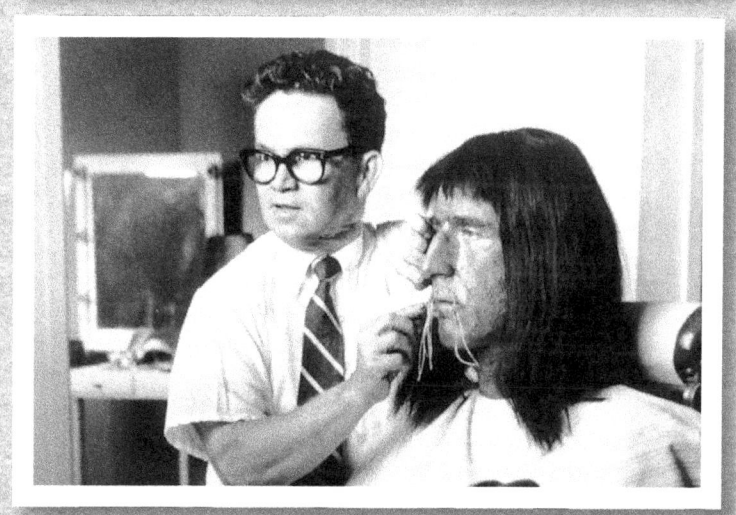

Charles Gemora applies voodoo makeup for **The Four Skulls of Jonathan Drake** (1959). Elgen B. "Buzz" Gibson, who worked on **King Kong** (1933) and **Son of Kong** (1933), is credited as the Chief Technician.

Men In Suits • 121

Lon Chaney, Jr., as Kharis, the mummy. Tom Tyler played Kharis in the first seuqel, **The Mummy's Hand** (1940), and Chaney got all wrapped up in it for the three sequels that followed: **The Mummy's Tomb** (1942), **The Mummy's Ghost**, (1944) and **The Mummy's Curse** (1944).

Above: Virginia Christine removes a speck of Egyptian dust from Lon Chaney, Jr.'s eye during the filming of **The Mummy's Curse** (1944). Ms. Christine's "resurrection" scene in the film is one of the highlights of this film, the last of Kharis mummy sequels.

Below: Lon Chaney, Jr., wonders how mummies kept cool in Egypt. Southern California is tough enough.

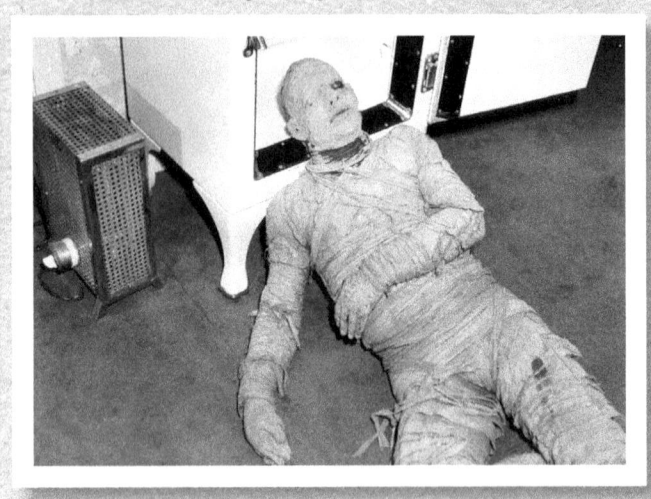

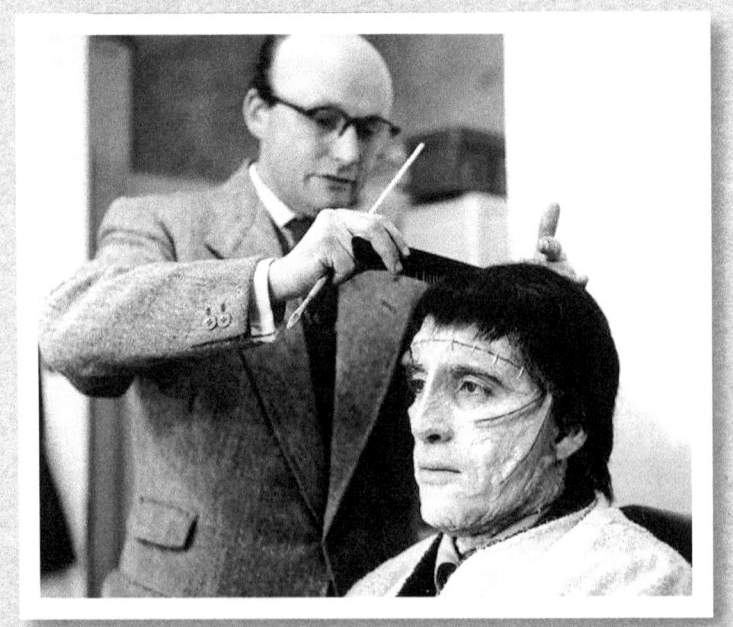

Makeup assistant George Turner puts final touches on a radically-different monster for Hammer's **The Curse of Frankenstein** (1957), The new concept avoided copyright infringement of Universal's version of the monster.

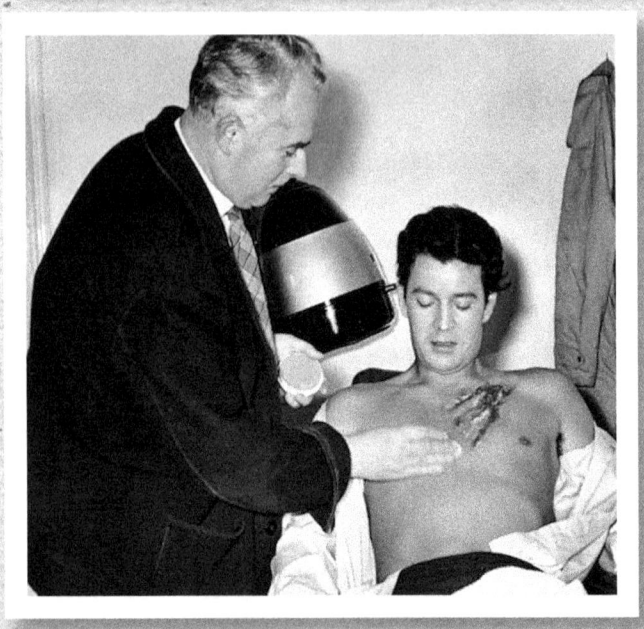

Roy Ashton, who became Hammer's resident makeup genius after the departure of Phil Leakey, applies scars to the chest of Edward de Souza for **Kiss of the Vampire** (1963).

122 · *Smoke and Mirrors – Special Visual Effects Before Computers*

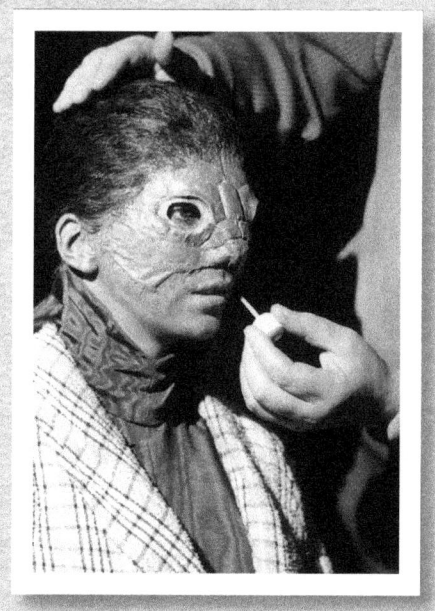

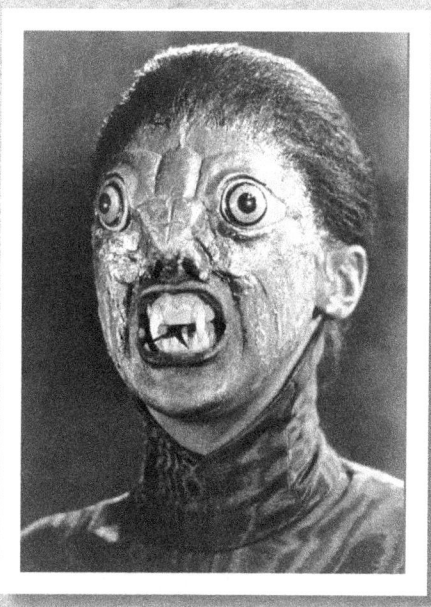

Beyond remaking and updating characters from Universal's heyday, Roy Ashton created all-new creatures. Actress Jacqueline Pearce goes from Beauty to Beast in Hammer's **The Reptile** *(1966). Ashton even gave her a forked tongue!*

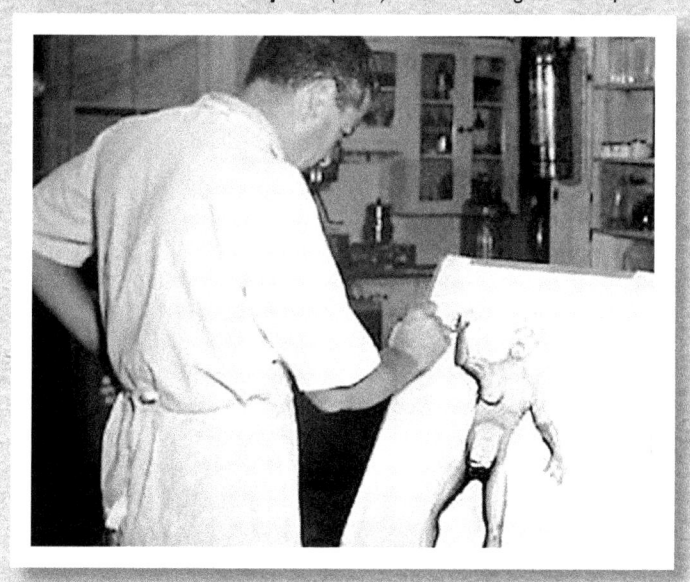

Illustrating a "sleek" Gill Man, based on director Jack Arnold's initial concept using the Oscar® statuette as inspiration.

The Creature from the Black Lagoon *(1953), swims directly towards the camera, capitalizing on the 3D process. The Creature was a huge success in large part because of the effective suit designed by Millicent Patrick and fabricated by Bud Westmore's lab.*

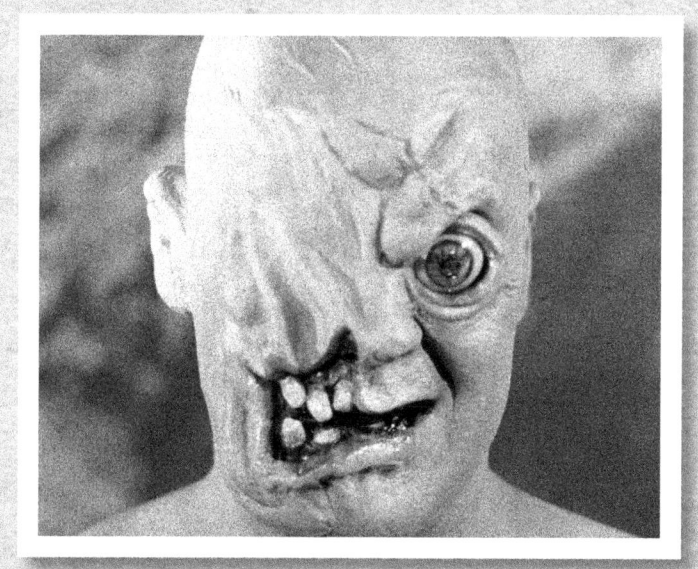

Bert I. Gordon's **The Cyclops** *(1957) growls at the camera. Several latex collectors' masks have been based on this character design.*

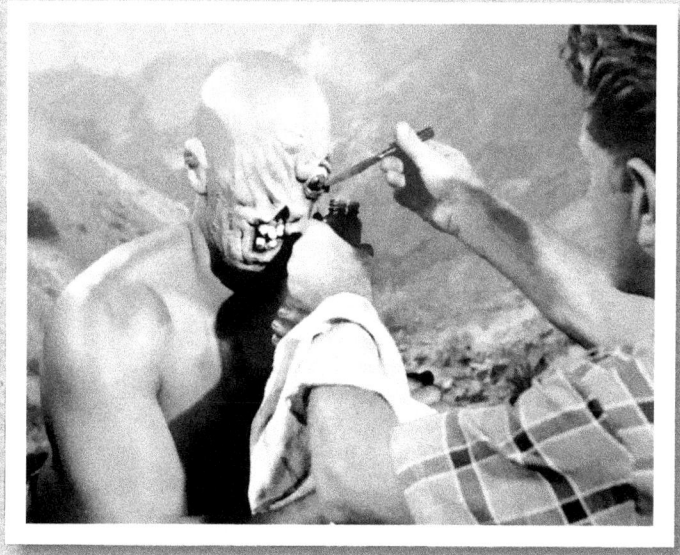

The grotesque special makeup effects were created by Jack H. Young, later nominated for an Emmy for the TV version of **Salem's Lot** *(1979).*

Men In Suits • 123

Charles Gemora made invaders with only one thing on their minds in **I Married a Monster from Outer Space** (1958).

Actress Valerie Allen cuddles with her alien co-star before she reports to the set—to be disintegrated! A woman's work is never done...

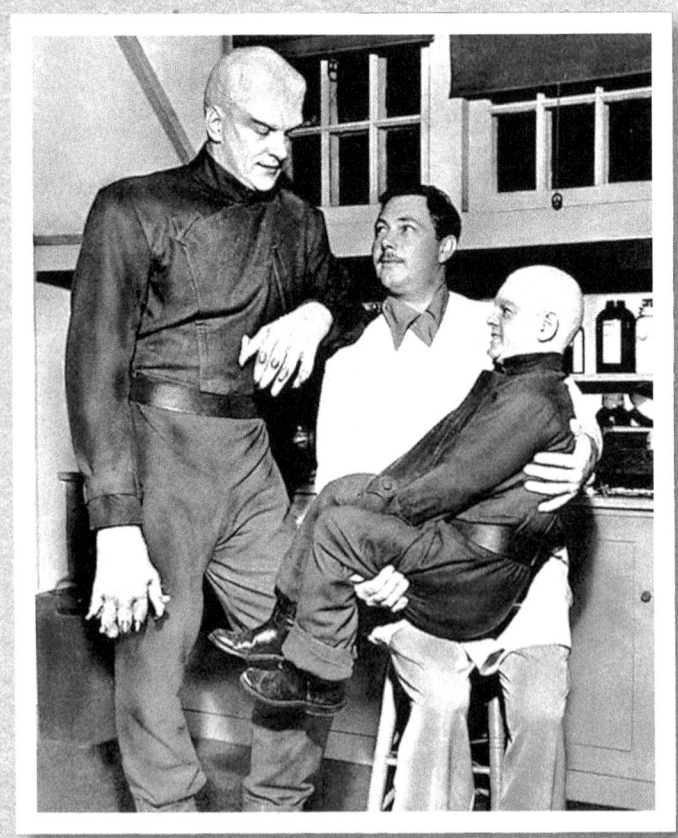

Actors James Arness (6' 7") and Billy Curtis (4' 2") with RKO's head of makeup, Lee Greenway. Curtis appeared at the climax to help simulate the melting of **The Thing from Another World** (1951).

Donald Steward and Thol Simonson rigged James Arness outside the sound stages to test the smoky demise of the alien.

124 · *Smoke and Mirrors – Special Visual Effects Before Computers*

Gordon Bau, head of the Warner Bros. makeup department, supervised the grotesque disfigurement of Vincent Price for **House of Wax** (1953). His brother, George, ran the prosthetics lab, using a foam rubber formulation they had devised and sold to other technicians.

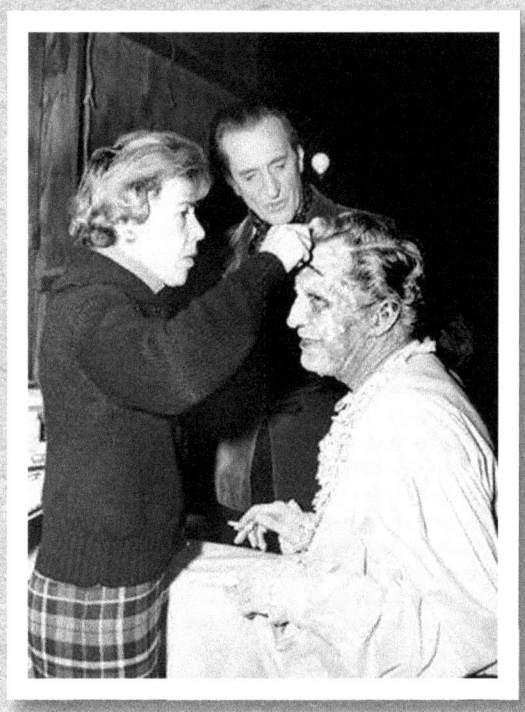

Basil Rathbone is amused by the "goop" applied to Vincent Price for "The Strange Case of M. Valdemar" segment of Roger Corman's anthology **Tales of Terror** (1962).

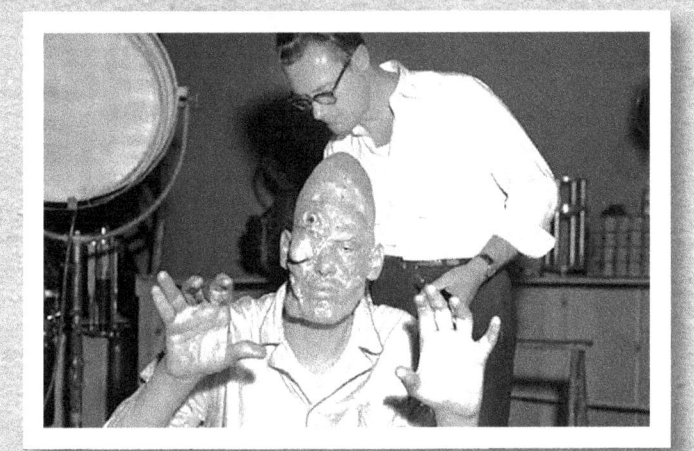

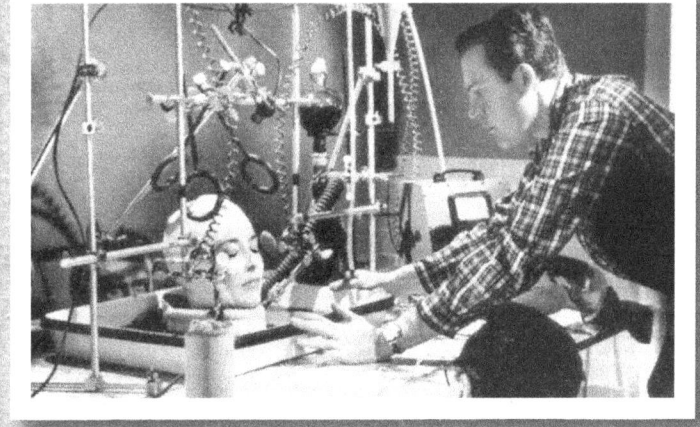

The Brain that Wouldn't Die (1962) focused on Virginia Leith's "decapitated" head (right, known as "Jan in the Pan") but mad doctor Jason Evers also had a large monster in his closet. Eddie Carmel is made up by George Fiala, who later worked on **Santa Claus Conquers the Martians** (1964).

Margaret Field, mother of future Oscar®-winner Sally Field, confronts **The Man from Planet X** (1951). Director Edgar G. Ulmer had worked in Germany and brought an expressionistic style to the production, atmospherically filmed by John Russell (**Psycho**, 1960).

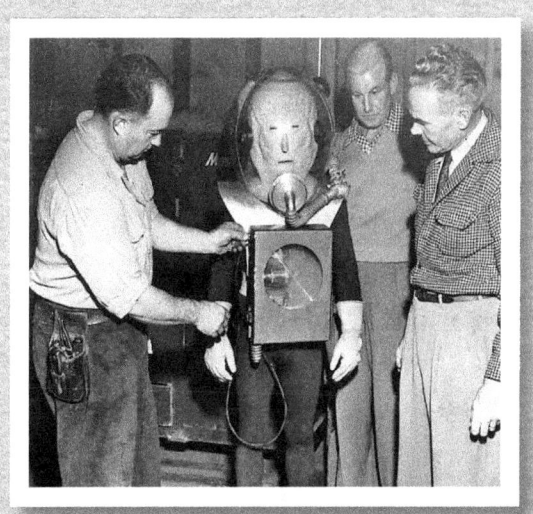

The alien, rumored to be played by Pat Goldin, reports to the set. Ulmer stretched a $41,000 budget to buy six days of shooting using left over sets from **Joan of Arc** (1948).

Robert Clarke starred as **The Hideous Sun Demon** (1958, UK: **Blood on His Lips**) menacing Nan Peterson. He told me he did his own stunts and that the suit by Art Director Robert Cassarino was miserably uncomfortable.

Lou Costello does one of his signature double-takes when he realizes Lon Chaney, Jr. has transformed into the Wolf Man in **Abbott and Costello Meet Frankenstein** (1948).

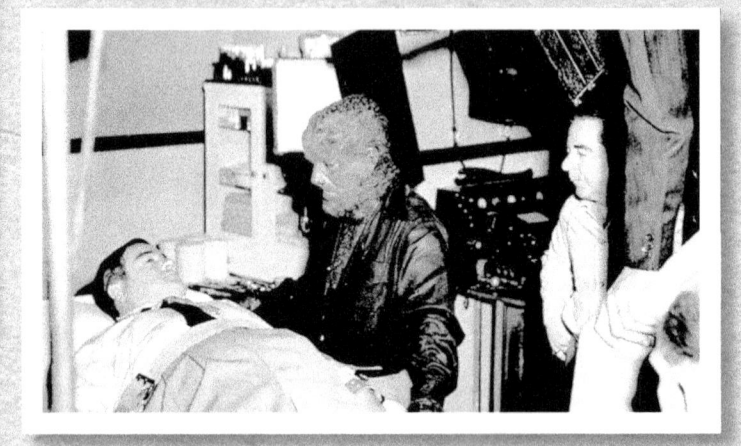

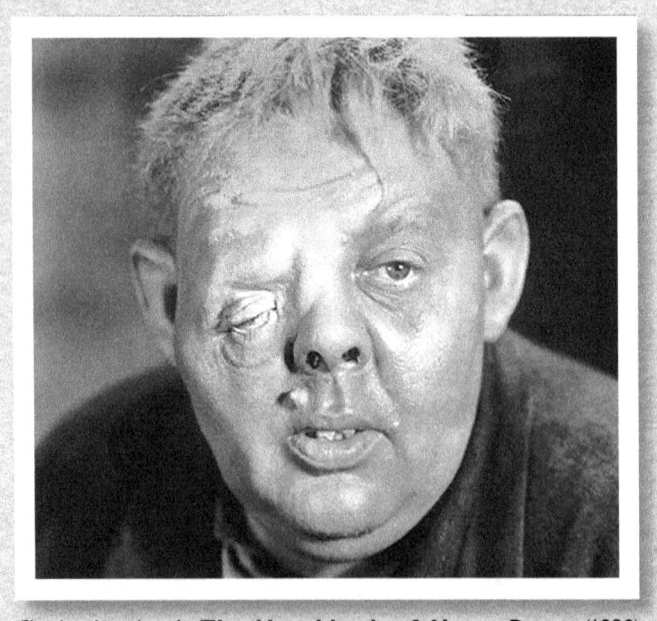

The Monster of Piedras Blancas (1959) interrupts Jeanne Carmen's sunbathing ritual. Jack Kevan's design is invariably compared to his earlier **Creature From the Black Lagoon** (1954).

Charles Laughton's **The Hunchback of Notre Dame** (1939) foam latex face and hump were created by Perc Westmore on loan from Warner Bros. Lon Chaney, Jr. was offered the part and did tests, but the studio chose Laughton once his tax issues were resolved.

Brigitte Helm takes a refreshing sip of a beverage while a hair drier (with the heating filament removed) blows air into the marvelous robot suit for Fritz Lang's masterpiece, **Metropolis** (1927). This film was **Famous Monsters** magazine editor Forry Ackerman's all-time favorite movie.

Bull Montana as the "Missing Link" in **The Lost World** (1925), by Clay Campbell, later head of the makeup department at Columbia.

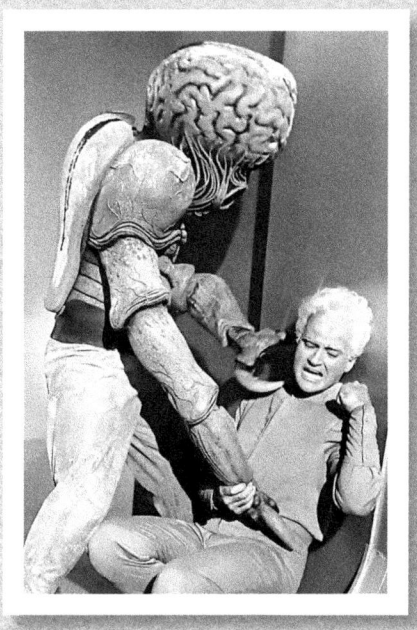

Jeff Morrow and mutant on **This Island Earth** (1955), suit by Chris Mueller, Robert Hickman, Milicent Patrick and Jack Kevan.

One of the most unusual cheescake photos—ever—for American International's **Invasion of the Saucer Men** (1957). That's Paul Blaisdell's monster head.

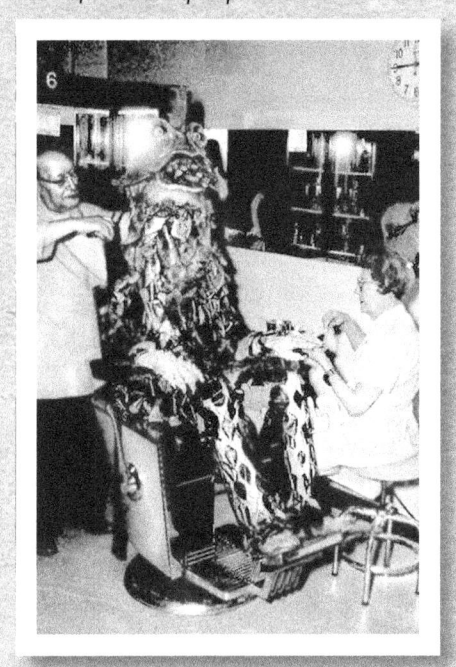

Work underway at Gutzon Borglum's Stamford, Connecticut, sculpting studio on one of two suits designed by art director Bob Verberkmoes for **The Horror of Party Beach** (1964).

Production assistant Ruth Glassenberg Freedman's 16-year-old son, Charles Freedman, fit perfectly into the suits and he was recruited to portray a monster in the film.

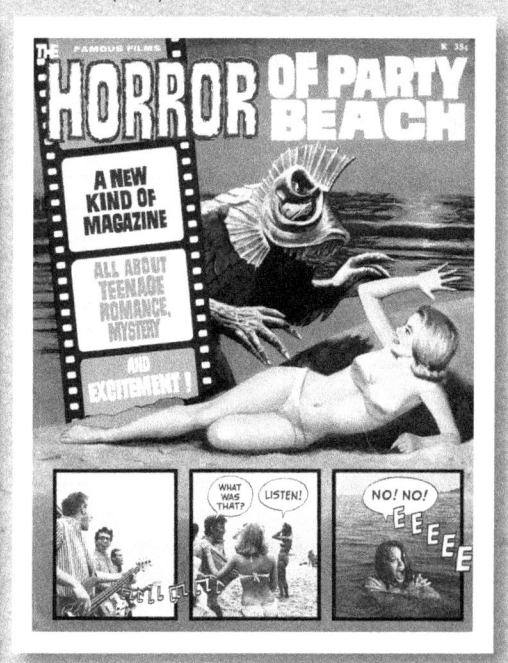

A "fumetti" photo magazine published by James Warren in 1964. During a commentary on the 2018 Blu-ray, director Del Tenney professed no awareness of the magazine, an odd memory lapse even if 54 years later.

Bela Lugosi's werewolf servant in **Return of the Vampire** (1943), played by Matt Willis in a distinctly wild makeup by Clay Campbell.

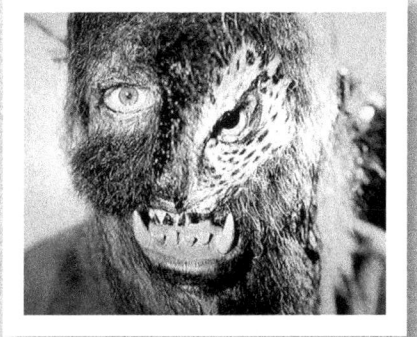

Only stills survive of makeup tests for Dr. Moreau's more perverse experiments in **The Island of Lost Souls** (1932).

Fay Wray reveals Lionel Atwill's horribly scarred face in **Mystery of the Wax Museum** (1933). Makeup by Perc Westmore and Ray Romero.

Men In Suits • 127

Anatole Robbins created the Martian makeups for **Invaders from Mars** (1953), and, like Gort, it was Lock Martin in the suit.

The "Sleestaks" in the orginal version of **Land of the Lost** (1974) series were fabricated by Michael Westmore.

Former basketball players Bill Laimbeer (Detroit Pistons) and John Lambert (Cleveland Cavaliers) transform into Sleestaks.

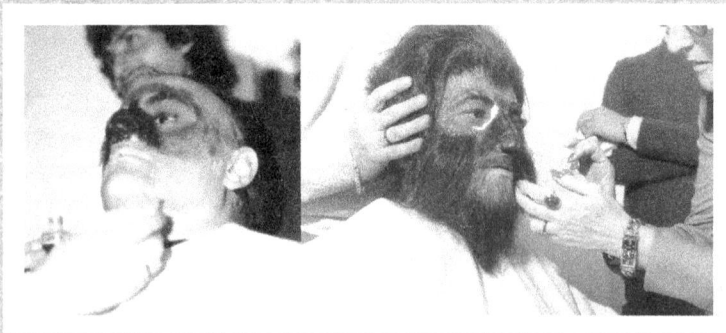

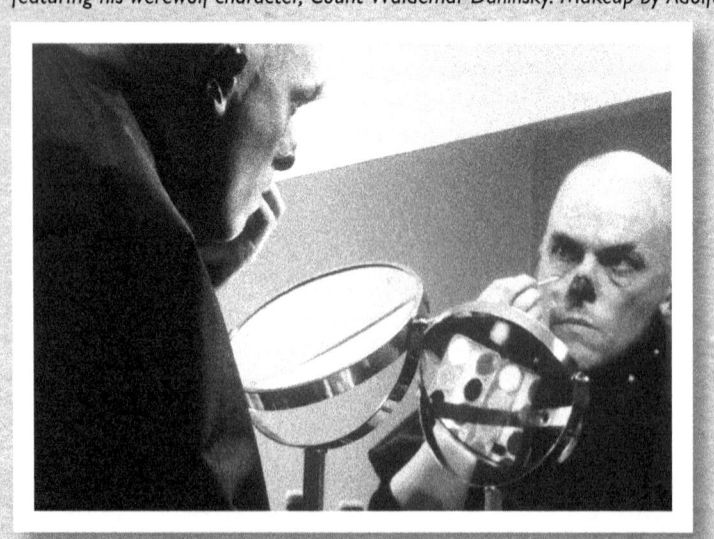

Paul Naschy undergoes the arduous makeup process for **La Maldicion de la Bestia** (1975; U.S.: **Night of the Howling Beast**), the eighth film featuring his werewolf character, Count Waldemar Daninsky. Makeup by Adolfo Ponte and Manolita G. Fraile.

Randall William Cook follows in the footsteps of Lon Chaney, Sr. as he applies his own makeup, which he designed, for his role as "Brand" in **I, Madman** (1989).

Randy Cook achieved what no one had accomplished since Willis O'Brien with **The Ghost of Slumber Mountain** (1919): acting, creating makeup for his role, and staging the stop motion sequences.

128 · **Smoke and Mirrors – Special Visual Effects Before Computers**

The 20th Century-Fox makeup department devised this suit for the pilot episode of Irwin Allen's series **Lost in Space** (1965), which incorporated palm tree trimmings.

Producer/director George Pal poses with his son, Peter, who is wearing the William Tuttle makeup to portray the Abominable Snowman in **7 Faces of Dr. Lao** (1964).

Above: Mark Wolf directs second unit with the monster from the Phantom Zone, supplied by John Buechler's Mechanical and Makeup Imageries (MMI) for Wolf's production of **Slave Girls from Beyond Infinity** (1987).

Left: Mark Wolf with a hand puppet he built for **Monster, the Legend That Became a Terror** (1980; aka **Monstroid**). It had to match a larger mechanical version (at left) built by Stephen Czerkas. Stephen also made a large section of the creature's back for water scenes with actors.

Jack Dawn chose to use foam latex for the special makeups in **The Wizard of Oz** (1939). The winged monkeys had special harnesses to "fly."

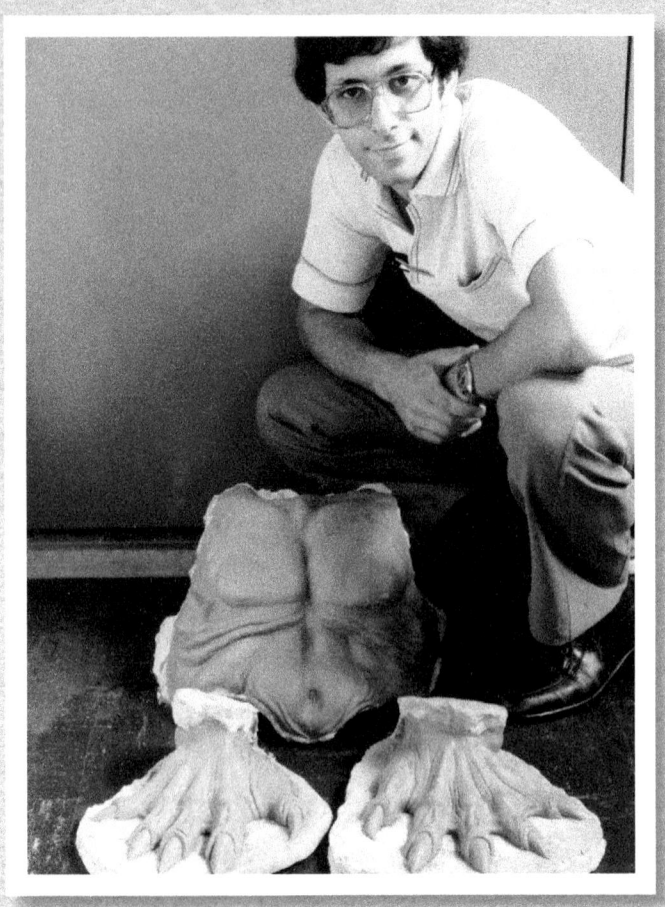

Sculptor/animator Richard Catizone poses with his contributions to the creation of "Fluffy" for George Romero's **Creepshow** (1982).

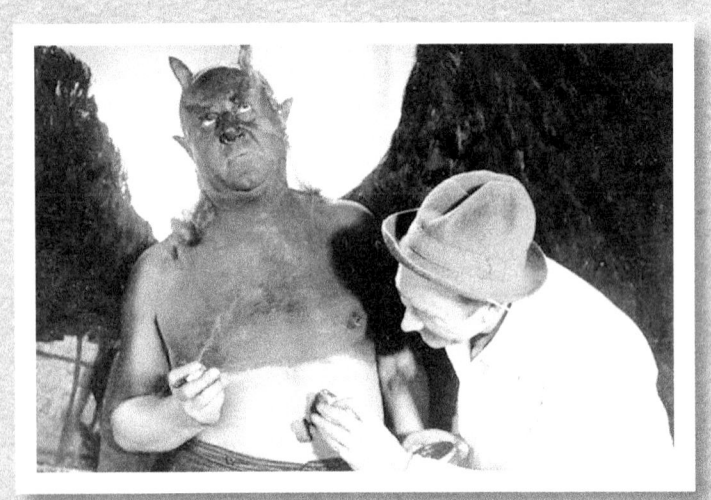

Haxan (1922; U.S.: **Witchcraft through the Ages**, 1929). Several sources claim this is Swedish director Benjamin Christensen playing Satan.

A modern Golem in **IT!** (1967) carries the mummified remains of Roddy McDowall's mother.

Enemy Mine (1985), directed by Wolfgang Petersen, featured an alien performed by Louis Gossett, Jr. in makeup effects created by Chris Walas.

Several of the malevolent Minions seen in **The Gate** (1987). The suits were built by Emmy-winner Craig Reardon.

Ben Nye's original concept for **The Fly** (1958) used scores of beads to simulate the compound eyes. This version was rejected.

Al Hedison's shocking reveal at the end of **The Fly** (1958) in a startling appliance by Ben Nye, who also prepared a claw and foot.

The larger head designed for **The Return of the Fly** (1959). Note the straps to help hold it on stunt man Ed Wolff.

Octaman (1971) on a rampage! An early project with suit and makeup effects by Rick Baker and Doug Beswick with Harry Walton (above, right) lending a hand.

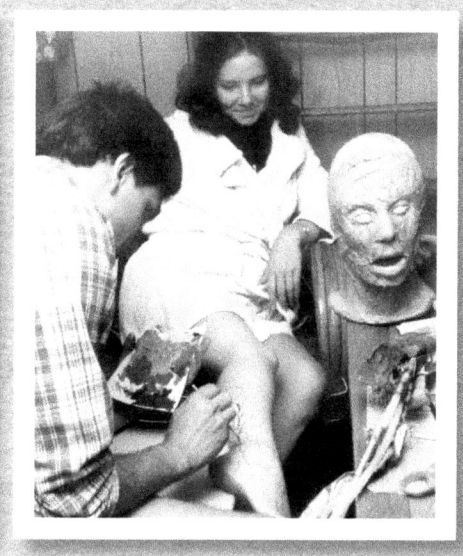

Tom Sullivan paints veins on actress Betsy Baker's leg for Sam Raimi's **The Evil Dead** (1981).

Actress Beverly Garland (left) told Tom Weaver in his book, **Interviews with B Science Fiction and Horror Movie Makers** (McFarland 1988), "**The Alligator People** was a fast picture, but [director Roy Del Ruth, above] really tried to do something good with it. And I think that shows in the film. It is such a ridiculous story. But there really was no way to end it. What could they do? Were we going to live happily ever after and raise baby alligators?"

Above: In **Unknown Island** (1948), a ceratosaurus built by Ellis Burman combats Ray "Crash" Corrigan in his gorilla suit. The heat of the Mojave desert caused a dino-stuntman to pass out—which was used in the picture.

Right: Paul Wegener as **Der Golem** (Germany, 1920), which he co-wrote and co-directed, a blueprint for **Frankenstein** (1931) with expressionistic cinematography by Karl Freund, who would direct **The Mummy** (1932).

While the primary Selenite characters in **First Men "In" the Moon** (1964) were created using stop motion animation, including The Grand Lunar, Ray Harryhausen spared himself the unwieldy task of animating an army of puppets by using children wearing costumes for scenes with many Selenites.

Lorena Velazquez, Miss Mexico in the 1958 Miss Universe contest, is menaced by the Martian prince Tagual. **La Nave de Los Monstruos** (Mexico, 1960; U.S.: **Ship of the Monsters**), features lackluster suits and a robot recycled from **The Robot vs. the Aztec Mummy** (1958).

American International struck gold with **I Was A Teenage Werewolf**, their first "teenage" monster movie. Shot in seven days, Philip Scheer created the makeup.

Right: Michael Landon attacks 22-year-old Dawn Richard, **Playboy** centerfold in the May, 1957 issue, which hit the newsstands just ahead of the movie's release.

Middle: Dawn Richard sits with producer Herman Cohen.

Far right: Covergirl Dawn on the British one-shot **Screen Chills** (1958), one of the rarest and most desirable monster magazines in the collector market.

132 · *Smoke and Mirrors – Special Visual Effects Before Computers*

Chapter 4
Prop It Up

Throughout the long history of human beings entertaining their fellows with performances, there has been a need for supplemental items to enhance their roles and sets, which were generally referred to as "properties." In the earliest days of stage plays, whatever object an actor needed to hold in their hands was unsurprisingly known as a "hand prop." Today, the term most commonly used is the simplified catch-all, "props," which has come to cover not just anything handled by the talent, but anything custom-fabricated for a particular film's needs.

As the entertainment industry evolved with the arrival of motion pictures and later, television, a vast spectrum of stories became possible and the demand grew for props of all kinds, from the historically accurate to the most imaginatively fantastical. Many years ago, I worked at The Hand Prop Room in Los Angeles, which specialized in providing productions with a ready-supply of rental items covering everything conceivably useful to whatever kind of story was being produced. They had an endless array of items from every historical period and country: watches, eyeglasses, police badges, belt buckles, wallets, purses, men's and women's hats, license plates, all types of mobile phones, dishes and cutlery, artificial food, chandeliers, spacesuits, bullion bars (gold-plated resin), scientific devices, a drivable location TV satellite vehicle, plus a cold-storage room with actual animal skin rugs—and much, much more.

All of the Hollywood rental houses combined couldn't supply everything that the screenwriters came up with, so the studios' Property Departments were kept busy servicing productions with one-of-a-kind items from every genre.

Let's consider some famous films and a few of their custom-made props...

In this specially posed publicity photo, Humphrey Bogart, as surly detective Sam Spade, examines the Maltese Falcon, made for the 1941 Warner Bros. film of the same name. It is not very often that the title of a production translates into a special prop!

When you mention ***King Kong*** (1933), everyone thinks of the monarch of Skull Island, but what about the map Carl Denham showed to Captain Englehorn and First Mate Jack Driscoll? Do you think it was made by the skipper of a Norwegian barque? There were also the natives' spears, drums, and the witch doctor's stick, which I saw in storage at the old Selznick studio, and were recently sold at auction. And don't forget Denham's gas bombs—carved from wood—one of which resided at Forry Ackerman's Ackermansion for years.

For the beloved ***The Wizard of Oz*** (1939), the Wicked Witch's hourglass was produced under Cedric Gibbons' supervision in a highly-detailed "hero" version for scenes with Margaret Hamilton. Lightweight duplicates were made for the scene where it was smashed, constructed from hand-blown glass, wood and papier-maché. When something must be destroyed on camera, extras are made to give the production crew options in case several takes are necessary. Small holes were drilled so the hourglass could slide down guide wires and always hit exactly where required.

Incidentally, a pair of Dorothy's ruby slippers—costuming that could be called props—sold at auction for $2 million.

Orson Welles' masterpiece ***Citizen Kane*** (1941) ended by revealing that the elusive "Rosebud" was Charles Foster Kane's beloved sled. Three balsa wood sleds, thirty-four inches long, were handmade in the RKO shop. Two ended up being burned shooting the ending of the film, while the surviving sled was sold at auction in June, 1982, to Steven Spielberg for $60,500.

The Maltese Falcon (1941) required a special prop of the invaluable statuette and director John Huston commissioned a master sculpt from his friend, acclaimed Los Angeles-based artist, Fred Sexton, for $75.00. A rubber mold was prepared in the Warner Bros. properties department and castings were made. Exactly how many six-pound plaster Falcons were made is the subject of debate. Persistent rumors of a fifty or sixty pound lead falcon have been debunked by people who worked on the film.

In 1975 the original rubber mold was used to make another pull, but the mold had so deteriorated that the cast was flawed; that level of damage suggests to me a sizable number of pulls had been taken from that mold. A new mold, of that final casting was generated to make duplicates for the Warner Bros. production, ***The Black Bird*** (1975). An original, screen-used plaster prop was sold in November, 2013, at a Bonhams, New York, auction for $4,085,000—including a buyer's premium of $585,000. Another plaster falcon had sold in 1994 for $385,000.

The stone tablets in Cecil B. DeMille's ***The Ten Commandments*** (1956) were carved from a slab of granite imported from the Sinai to ensure biblical accuracy. A lightweight pair made of painted plaster was used for rehearsals.

Indiana Jones was introduced to audiences in ***Raiders of the Lost Ark*** (1981) by retrieving a relic inspired by an Aztec jade carving of a fertility goddess. It was sculpted then molded and reproduced several times in resin castings that were painted gold.

Sam Raimi's ***The Evil Dead*** (1981) and ***Evil Dead 2: Dead By Dawn*** (1987) benefitted substantially from Tom Sullivan's prop of the unholy book *The Necronomicon*. For the "cost-conscious" first film, Sullivan cleverly stretched the budget by using an existing mold to produce a face which was

Above: Producer Merian C. Cooper shows Fay Wray the wooden "gas bombs" constructed in the RKO prop shop for the 1933 **King Kong.**

Above: Charlton Heston proclaiming **The Ten Commandments** *on granite tablets imported from the Sinai to ensure biblical accuracy.*

Below: Say it slowly, and with feeling: "Rosebud..."

mounted onto corrugated cardboard. For the second film, Raimi wanted a more elaborate cover, which Sullivan created by sculpting and molding a clay master. The interior pages were based upon his original book, with added weathering and appropriate blood splatters courtesy of red paint.

Blade Runner (1982) presented many requirements for special props in its unique universe, such as Deckard's pistol, the Voight Kampf Machine, and Chew's glasses and origami unicorns, which, despite their delicate appearance, were made from metal foil to ensure they would last through production.

Bob Clark's **A Christmas Story** (1983) needed several versions of "the leg lamp," made by modifying mannequin legs: one could break on demand, one was electrified, and one could be handled by the cast.

Westerns also demanded special props: sheriff's badges, cartridges, jail cells, gatling guns and scores of phony bottles to be broken during a saloon brawl. During war movies, hand grenades, rocket launchers and armored vehicles had to show up on set.

Laurel and Hardy were always being clobbered by bricks and stones, in actuality lightweight props. The Three Stooges regularly walloped each other with assorted saws, crowbars, hammers, and pick-axes—made from rubber. Some of their shorts, such as **Cactus Makes Perfect** (1942), had elaborate one-of-a-kind props that had to be fabricated.

When I asked acclaimed artist Wah Chang what he was the most proud of creating in his long and distinguished career, he didn't miss a beat before saying he was proudest of the original decorative props he designed and fabricated for the musical **The King and I** (1956).

*Over the years the studios accumulated mountains of properties, many of which they rented to other companies. At 20th Century-Fox I repaired some of the magnificent costume jewelry from **Cleopatra** (1963), above right, as well as created new art deco sculptures from plasticized ceramic that were destined for set-dressing. Universal stored many noteworthy props, such as the flying vampire bat used in films such as **House of Dracula** (1945) and the silver wolf-headed cane for **The Wolf Man** (1941), shown above left with Lon Chaney, Jr. and Evelyn Ankers.*

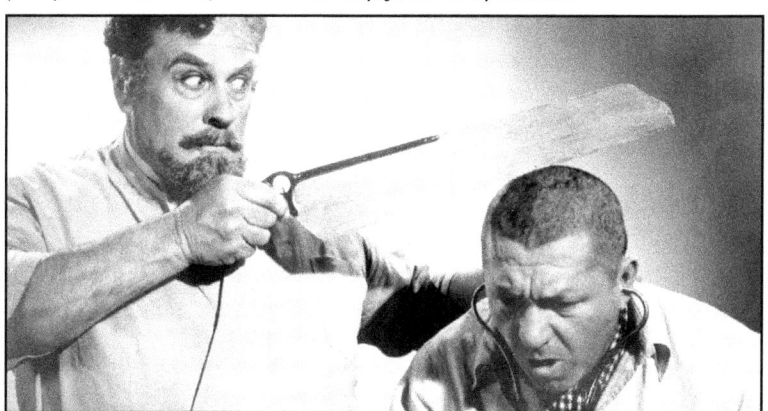

*Above: In **A Bird in the Head** (1945) perennial Three Stooges foil Vernon Dent plays a mad doctor looking to use Curly's brain. The prop saw appears to be made from a wooden handle and sheet rubber.*

*Below: In **Cactus Makes Perfect** (1942) Larry and Moe are incredulous about Curly's invention to retrieve lost gold collar-buttons. The elaborate working prop was complete with flashing lights.*

*Tom Sullivan with his props for **The Evil Dead** (1981), including the Necronomicon and the demon-slaying Kandarian Dagger.*

Prop It Up • 135

PLANES, TRAINS, AND AUTOMOBILES
(AND SUBMARINES)

While science fiction and fantasy productions present the most obvious needs for unusual props, we must not forget that every genre can require some form of props and right from the beginning, different modes of transportation were integral to the plots spun by silent filmmakers.

PLANES

Flight was new and exciting at the same time cinema was experiencing its birthing pains, so it is not unexpected that the amazing technological wonder of flying machines were showcased in movies right from their mutual beginnings.

After World War I, a group of daredevil fliers helped make it possible to stage enthralling scenes with real planes for *Wings* (1927), which won the first Oscar® for Best Picture (the only silent film to do so) at the first Academy Awards May 16, 1929. The spectacular film also won for Best Engineering Effects, for which the Oscar® was awarded to Roy Pomeroy, who had parted the Red Sea for Cecil B. DeMille's original *The Ten Commandments* (1923). As head of Paramount's effects department, he was responsible for pyrotechnic/physical effects as well as miniatures.

Among the skilled pilots who brought authenticity and thrills to *Wings* was Dick Grace, who had survived WWI and later served as a co-pilot on B-17 bombing missions during WWII. He specialized in flying a plane directly into the ground, church steeples, cliffs and the sides of buildings, exactly where the camera was set up to record the "catastrophe." Amazingly, he walked away from dozens of such stunts in *The Flying Fool* (1925), *Young Eagles* (1930), *The Lost Squadron* (1932) and *Devil's Squadron* (1936).

He took great pride in his methodical approach to analyzing the physics of a crash event and modifying the aircraft per his experience into props capable of flying long enough for a single use in a "safe" stunt. Dick Grace was a pioneer who uniquely combined the best of scientific savvy, special effects engineering and—plenty of guts.

The WWI-era was the time period for *Hells Angels* (1930) and *The Dawn Patrol* (1938), and later productions like *The Blue Max* (1966), Roger Corman's *Von Richthofen and Brown* (1971) and Robert Redford's *The Great Waldo Pepper* (1975). Many of these followed in the tradition of using real planes, prop sections for close-up work, and occasionally miniatures. At Four Star Studios, I got to examine a custom-made prop section of a Spad used in shooting close angles for an ABC TV pilot about WWI flying aces; a wooden propeller was used when the plane was static on the ground but for scenes simulating flight, it was replaced with one consisting of several exceptionally thin and flexible wires that were as long as the wooden propeller. When spun by a belt attached to an electric motor, the wires reproduced the blur of a spinning propeller with the added advantage of preventing a tragedy if someone inadvertently walked into it while it was operating. In this case, the prop cockpit was used in conjunction with rear projection of aerial stock shots.

*Opposite page: Dick Grace with an airplane he just crashed for **Wings**.*

*Top Director William Wellman (left) and Dick Grace, center, during production of **Wings**.*

*Left: William Wellman filming **Wings**.*

Above: James Stewart with the replica of The Spirit of St. Louis.

Prop It Up • 137

THE FLIGHT OF THE PHOENIX

"It should be remembered that Paul Mantz, a fine man and a brilliant flyer, gave his life in the making of this film."
—On-screen credit at the end of the film.

Paul Mantz

The Last Flight of the Phoenix

The Flight of the Phoenix (20th Century-Fox, 1965) starring **James Stewart**, **Richard Attenborogh**, **Peter Finch**, **Hardy Krüger**, **Ernest Borgnine**, **Dan Duryea**, **Ian Bannen**, **Ronald Fraser**, **Christian Marquand**, **George Kennedy**, and **Barrie Chase**. Produced and directed by **Robert Aldrich**, based on the 1964 novel by **Elleston Trevor**.

Preston Lerner wrote in the October 31, 2012 issue of *Air & Space Magazine*: "***The Flight of the Phoenix*** dramatized the aftermath of the crash of a Fairchild C-82A Packet—called a Salmon-Rees Skytruck in the movie. The survivors piece together a new airplane out of the wreckage and fly it out of the desert.

"20th Century Fox commissioned a scratch-built—and airworthy—airplane from Tallmantz Aviation, a company formed by Hollywood stunt pilots Frank Tallman and Paul Mantz. To design the mongrel, Mantz and Tallman hired Otto Timm, an aeronautical engineer who in 1922 had given Charles Lindbergh his first airplane flight. Timm created the inner wings, wheels, tail section, and fuselage of tubular steel with wooden bracing and a plywood skin. To this he attached a Pratt & Whitney R-1340, a cowling and cockpit from a North American T-6G Texan, the outer wings from a Beech C-45 Expeditor, and the tailwheel from a North American L-17 Navion.

"Predictably, the Frankenstein-like airplane was hard to handle. While Mantz was flying the climactic takeoff, the skids dug in on a sand hummock, the fuselage split in two, the plane flipped over and the 62-year-old Paul Mantz was killed instantly. To complete the shoot, the filmmakers substituted a North American O-47A modified to look like the *Phoenix*."

The "Phoenix" under construction at Orange County (California) Airport in the spring of 1965.

A frame from the actual film footage of the fatal flight, clearly showing the fuselage splitting in two.

138 · *Smoke and Mirrors – Special Visual Effects Before Computers*

TRAINS

When enjoying Buster Keaton's brilliant 1926 film *The General* (above left), it is hard not to be stunned when a real trestle, locomotive and cars are destroyed! Filmed on location in Cottage Grove, Oregon, a 300-foot wooden bridge was constructed for the train's destruction, widely acknowledged as the single most expensive shot in the silent era. The entire town gathered to watch the spectacle, which wasn't capable of being repeated. When it went off flawlessly, Keaton and his team heaved a sigh of relief.

Decades later, David Lean's award-winning masterpiece *The Bridge on the River Kwai* duplicated the feat (above middle and right) by demolishing a real bridge and train cars on March 10, 1957, with government dignitaries of Sri Lanka (then known as Ceylon) in attendance.

Because of the impossibility of re-filming it, multiple cameras were positioned at the best locations to record the event, a standard procedure for any company facing a similar situation. Due to the Suez crisis, the exposed footage could not be shipped to London by boat, so the priceless film cans were sent by air freight and—never arrived. A week later the errant cans were traced to a Cairo airport, baking in the relentless sun. Miraculously, the footage was unaffected and the shots were cut into the film.

David Lean blew up a real train once again in *Lawrence of Arabia* (1962) his followup film to *The Bridge on the River Kwai*. Even better than composite shots using miniatures, live action (with dialog) could be filmed on location against the backdrop of the demolished train (above right).

Several years later director John Frankenheimer's WWII drama *The Train* (1964) also used real-world components when the film needed a railroad yard to be devastated by Allied bombs. The production had good timing, being able to achieve tremendous production values affordably by working with the French railway authorities to destroy obsolete structures that they wanted to get rid of but couldn't afford to demolish. *The Train* goes even further than *The General* or *The Bridge on the River Kwai* by showing several real train wrecks (left).

Prop It Up • 139

AUTOMOBILES

An entire book could be dedicated to specially-made or modified vehicles used in films such as *The Great Race* (1965), *The Love Bug* (1968) and *Bullitt* (1968). In *The Joy Rider* (1921) comedian Snub Pollard has a hard time controlling his runaway car—which even drives up the side of a building courtesy of stop-motion (which had also been done very cleverly in Robert W. Paul and Walter R. Booth's 1906 British production *The '?' Motorist*).

Kings of comedy, Mack Sennett and Hal Roach, frequently used prop automobiles—often in coordination with special effects—to help actors get laughs. In countless one and two reel films, the Keystone Cops, starting in 1912, careened wildly around the streets of Culver City in their modified paddy wagon. Laurel and Hardy were often seen in a Model T that suffered various catastrophes such as in *Hog Wild* (1930) when their flivver was crushed between two street cars. That prop has survived and is preserved in the Petersen Automotive Museum in Los Angeles. In *Busy Bodies* (1933), The Boys watched in disbelief as a specially-prepared version of their tin lizzy was sawed in half, another instance of special effects and props working together.

Production designer Ken Adam took a break from James Bond's Aston Martin to devise another unusual car for the musical *Chitty Chitty Bang Bang* (1968), based on Ian Fleming's novel *Chitty-Chitty-Bang-Bang: The Magical Car* (1964). Six versions of the car were built, two of which were road-worthy (though one was somewhat smaller), and specific scenes and functions dictated the need for versions that could transform, hover, fly and be towed for conveniently shooting angles of Dick Van Dyke and his passengers. Peter Jackson bought

Busy Bodies (1933). The split car was engineered by machinist Fred Harryhausen (Ray's father).

Pat Priest poses with George Barris' Munsters Koach (1964)

Batman (1966)

Bullitt (1968)

Blade Runner (1982)

the larger road car on auction in 2011 for $805,000.

The ABC-TV series *Batman* (1966) starring Adam West is fondly remembered today for—among other things—the sleek Batmobile made by custom-car king George Barris. Starting with a 1955 Lincoln Futura concept car, Barris modified the fins, grille, and headlights, and then added rocket boosters, machine guns, and, of course, the essential Bat-Radar and Bat-Phone. Total cost: $15,000 ($125,500 today). The immediately-recognizable vehicle still sells diecast toys and model kits. In January, 2013, the first of six Batmobiles used for the show was the top-selling car in the Barrett-Jackson Salon Collection, Arizona, selling for $4.62 million.

Full-sized vehicles built for *Blade Runner* (1982) included "spinners"—flying cars—one of which could be lifted by cables to simulate taking off. One interior was made and re-dressed as necessary, but motion-controlled miniatures were used for the long shots to more easily show graceful flight.

If a company needed a duplicate, lightweight car body to be used for stunt purposes or to saw in half to make an insert vehicle for use on rear projection stages, the place to go in Hollywood was 20th Century-Fox, which had the largest vacuum forming device in the industry. Smaller machines were used in many shops but the process was the same: a warmed sheet of plastic was lowered onto a wooden, plaster or metal master (a "buck") and then a vacuum pump would quickly draw the plastic around the shape that was to be reproduced. The plastic would be trimmed, painted and finished with the addition of a rear window, steering wheel, etc. The technique relied on the operator's experience to get the plastic pliable but not too gooey.

"An ejector seat? You're joking!"

"I never joke about my work, 007."

The Most Famous Car in the World

"You'll be using this Aston Martin DB5 with modifications…"

And what modifications! Bulletproof windows, revolving license plates, a "Homer" tracking device, smoke screen, oil slick, rear bulletproof screen, tire-slashers, right and left front-wing machine guns, and the passenger ejector seat.

The silver birch Aston Martin DB5 attained classic status when introduced in *Goldfinger* (1964). Seeing Daniel Craig driving the DB5 in *Skyfall* (2012) was like seeing an old friend.

One of the DB5s went on tour to promote *Thunderball* (1965). In August, 2019, it sold at auction for $6.4 million, beating the price for the DB5 driven in *Goldfinger* which sold for $4.1 million in June, 2010.

Prop It Up • 141

SHIPS AND SUBMARINES

In Burbank, Disney's craftsmen built a partial full-scale Nautlius submarine for shooting exteriors for *20,000 Leagues Under the Sea* (1954, Oscar®-winner) and also fabricated custom-made properties for the interiors. These sets and props were so well-done, they continued earning their keep after the picture wrapped by becoming a *20,000 Leagues* exhibit in the early days of Disneyland.

Around 1960, on my first visit to the park, I still remember drinking in the sets as part of my early education learning how hand-made sets and props could look on film; the most awesome moment, however, was coming face-to-tentacle with the gigantic full-sized mechanical squid! Also on exhibit was a miniature of the *Nautilus* that was exquisite in its details.

142 · *Smoke and Mirrors – Special Visual Effects Before Computers*

Other productions making use of full-sized submarine elements—and miniatures—include **Destination Tokyo** (1943), **Hell and High Water** (1954, Oscar®-nominated), **The Enemy Below** (1957) and **Fantastic Voyage** (1966, Oscar®-winner), to name a few. And who could forget the full-sized submarine-tank—and miniature—made for **The Three Stooges in Orbit** (1962)?

For Ray Harryhausen's **Mysterious Island** in 1961 *(above)*, Captain Nemo's submarine was again built as a full-scale exterior section and interiors, as well as an eleven-foot miniature. The interior included props such as the pump that sent air to fill the balloon inside the sunken pirate ship. The work was the product of expert Spanish craftsmen under the supervision of Francisco Prosper. Several years later, he and his crew made another full-sized *Nautilus* that was shot on location in real caves for **The Mysterious Island of Captain Nemo** (1973).

An earlier version of **Mysterious Island** (1927) featured a *Nautilus* with an interior filled with "advanced technology," possibly featuring some work by Kenneth Strickfaden. Lionel Barrymore and Montagu Love are nearly upstaged by the glowing props. The exteriors also make extensive use of a miniature submarine.

*Below: The full-sized flying tank prop built for **The Three Stooges in Orbit** (1962) takes to the air—with three hardy stunt men standing-in for the Stooges. For the flying scenes, it was suspended by cable from a crane, but it was also capable of driving under its own power. Some people have suggested it was made using a surplus WWII Army amphibious vehicle.*

Prop It Up • 143

Submarines are not the only instance of a "real" ship being simulated with a combination of life-sized props and miniatures. Warner Bros.' **Captain Blood** (1935) used a full-sized ship on which star Errol Flynn would begin to carve out his career. In the following years, dozens of pirate films would follow the tradition of using stage-bound prop vessels as well as miniatures shot in water tanks, lakes and harbors.

For **The Golden Voyage of Sinbad** (1974) Ray Harryhausen needed to show Sinbad's vessel docked at port. He turned again to Francisco Prosper to help him accomplish the task. Spanish visual effects historian Domingo Lizcano shared this story:

"They built the ship in the middle of a field near Verona Studios outside Madrid. Benjamín Fernández, the assistant art director, told me, 'You could see the ship from the road, and one day, an engineer passing on the road came to the set and told us that we were crazy!' He said that because we were filming with the huge sail deployed, that was very dangerous. He was right, because the ship mast began to creak under the force of the wind. Luckily nothing happened, but for a moment we feared that it would split and there would be a catastrophe."

To complete the illusion of the ship in the harbor, Prosper´s crew created building facades, wooden tents, and other prop elements to hide the surrounding landscape and horizon line. The expanse of the city was created by Emilio Ruiz, who painted two separate aluminum cut outs which were supported horizontally from each side of the frame, and everything was filmed as an in-camera composite. [1]

Over his extensive career, Francisco Prosper built several ship decks for many maritime-themed movies, such as **Krakatoa—East of Java** (1969), for which he and his team built a life-sized replica of the *Batavia Queen* deck at Seville Film Studios. Mechanical effects expert Dick Parker built a hydraulic system that moved the set to simulate the normal rocking motion of the sea, as well as turbulence when the volcano erupts. Pyrotechnics supervisor Alex Weldon controlled fires on the ship deck. From the overhead lighting catwalks, Weldon's Spanish crew dropped fireballs to simulate debris from the volcano.

Ships of all periods, real or imagined, have needed custom props to take audiences on adventures above and below the oceans.

Right, top and middle: A land-locked ship and painted cutout of the city create the illusion of Sinbad's ship docked at the fictional ancient city of Marabia in **The Golden Voyage of Sinbad**.

Right: For **The 7th Voyage of Sinbad** *in 1958, a mockup of Sinbad's ship was moored to the dock in Madrid. Fire hoses and buckets showered the cast with water from the bay during the storm sequence.*

CARL FOREMAN'S PRODUCTION
THE GUNS OF NAVARONE

Gregory Peck "rescues" Anthony Quinn in what turns out to be knee-deep water in the giant "Stage H" at Shepperton Studios in England during the filming of Carl Foreman's production of J. Lee Thompson's film **The Guns of Navarone** (1961). Stage H measured 250 feet by 120 feet, offering 30,000 square feet of space. The balloon sequence in Ray Harryhausen's **Mysterious Island** (1961) was filmed on Stage H, as well as the massive set of the monolith excavation site (TMA-1, Tycho Magnetic Anomaly-1) in Stanley Kubrick's **2001: A Space Odyssey** (1968).

CREATURES WALK AMONG US

After the tremendous challenges of making **King Kong** (1933) and **Son of Kong** (1933), producers were reluctant to follow in their huge footprints with stories that required similar costly visual effects. After all, Universal showed that men in costumes could give audiences plenty of thrills for less bucks, optimizing the chances for financial success.

Therefore, it is a significant surprise that **The Flying Serpent** (1946) would be produced by a poverty row "almost-studio," Producers Releasing Corporation (PRC). It was a re-make of the studio's successful Bela Lugosi-starrer **The Devil Bat** (1940), which featured a large prop bat that didn't do much, and a separate prop hung from wires to attack Lugosi's victims. Considering how little was done for that film, one wouldn't expect that the **Serpent** team would stretch their minuscule budget to a whole new level.

The Serpent is by far the most complex monster since King Kong and worthy of a major studio. It outdoes the flying shots in **The Devil Bat** by light years, in some cases diving directly at camera. The filmmakers cleverly shift from a larger prop suspended from a wire rig to long shots of a miniature with flapping wings.

But the truly extraordinary thing is when it is in its cage being admired by its crazed master, George Zucco: the prop breathes, lashes its tail, exhales smoke and flicks its tongue! It is amazingly sophisticated for such a no-budget enterprise and it is a true pity that we don't know who made the props, though Bud Westmore has credit for makeup.

PRC's **The Flying Serpent** (1946) is mind-boggling, in that such a low-budget company could produce such an ambitious monster. Sadly, there are no better film prints available to study more closely. This publicity still shows a version of the creature flown from an overhead rig.

Prop It Up • 145

In the previous chapter, we looked at some of Paul Blaisdell's monster suits, but he had gotten his start creating the alien henchman of **The Beast With A Million Eyes** (1955), a small-scale prop he manipulated in a miniature spaceship setting.

Blaisdell was more than up to the challenge of stretching his creative muscles and technical craftsmanship to deliver a non-humanoid creature for Roger Corman's **It Conquered the World** (1956). Delivered on a paltry budget, the Venusian invader has been a joke to some and an inspiration to others (and was even marketed as a vinyl model from the Billiken company in Japan). In any case, the production expanded Blaisdell's horizons for what could be built.

In fact, Blaisdell outdid Lon Chaney, Sr. for sheer versatility, doing much more than just acting in the costumes he made. He also constructing special props, such as a huge syringe for **The Amazing Colossal Man** (1957). And who could forget Blaisdell's "umbrella monster," seen in Corman's **Not of this Earth** (1957)?

For Gordon's **Earth vs. the Spider** (1958) Blaisdell provided a repulsive desiccated corpse sucked dry by the spider, as well as a full-size spider leg.

Mechanicals had been used during the silent film era to simulate portions of giant creatures, such as the full-sized head, neck and tail sections of a brontosaurus in **The Lost World** (1925). Three decades later Russian fantasy-filmmaker Aleksandr Ptushko used a full-sized prop—as well as a miniature for flying scenes—for a three-headed, flame-spitting dragon in **Ilya Muromets** (1956; U.S.: **The Sword And The Dragon**, 1960).

Bert Gordon had a mechanical, fire-belching 2-headed dragon in what many regard as his best film, **The Magic Sword** (1962). This dragon was built on a smaller scale and matted into the live action. As of this writing, no one has been able to identify who built the creature, although I suspect it was done by Augie Lohman.

Right: Blaisdell's so-called "cucumber creature" for **It Conqured the World** *was fabricated from a wooden lattice covered with latex foam sheet which was detailed and painted, the arms built separately. He also built and operated the flying bat-things, suspending them from a fishing pole-like device.*

Below: For **Attack of the Puppet People** *(1958) Paul Blaisdell provided doll-sized replicas of the human cast and would later re-use a female figure in a one reel short,* **The Cliff Monster** *(1960), directed by Bob Burns and starring Paul's wife, Jackie. 8mm reels of the production were sold through their magazine,* **Fantastic Monsters of the Films**.

Above: Aleksandr Ptushko reached deep into his considerable bag of tricks to tell the epic Russian folk-tale of **Ilya Muromets** *(1956), which was highlighted by a life-sized, gigantic three-headed dragon that could exhale streams of fire and smoke.*

Right: Bert I. Gordon's roaring two-headed dragon in **The Magic Sword** *was the most memorable part of the film. Unfortunately, BIG's choice of matting solutions meant that the interaction was minimal, except for the use of a large prop tail.*

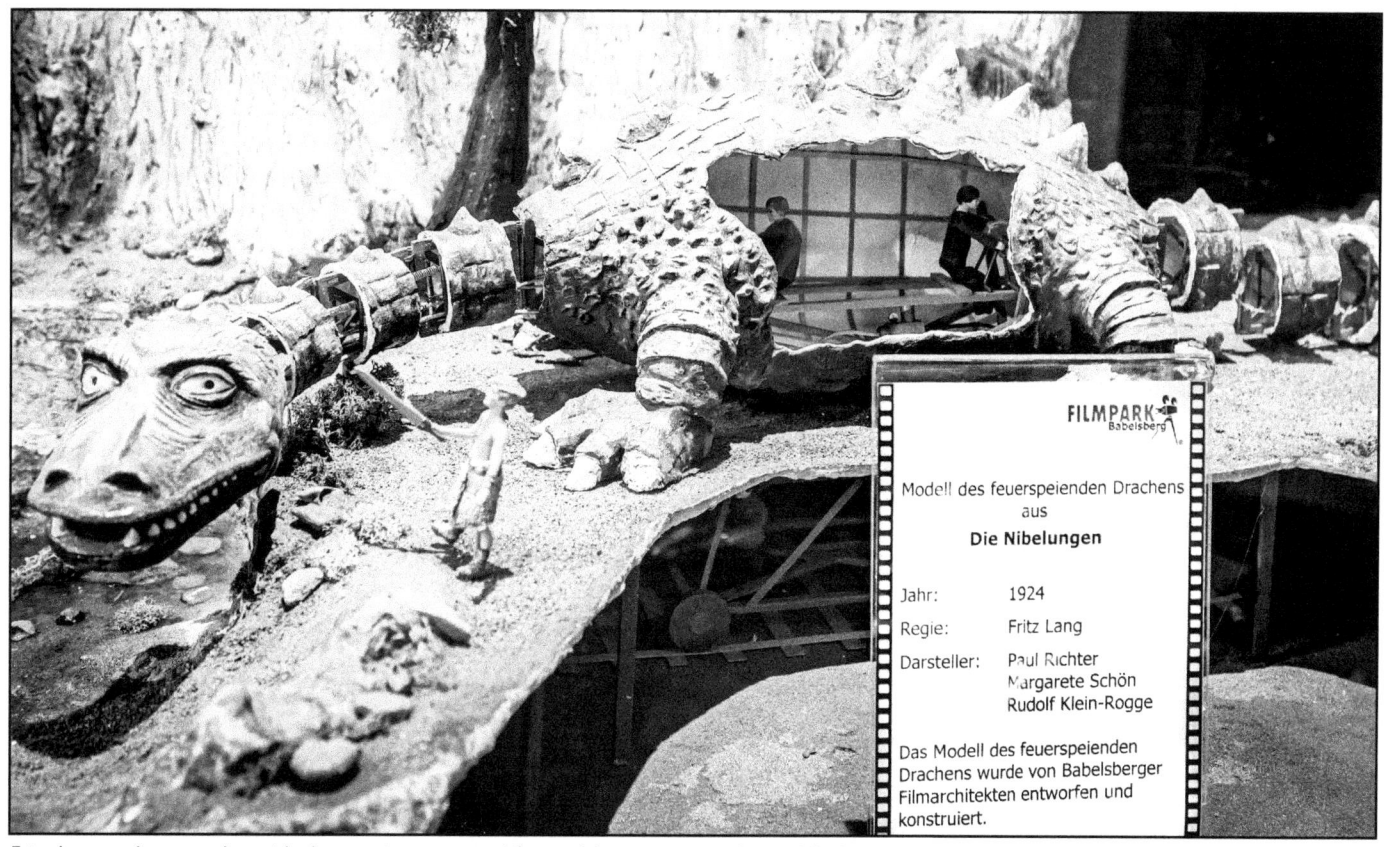

*Fritz Lang took tremendous risks by creating an entire life-sized dragon as a mechanical for his **Siegfried** (1924), complete with breathing flames. I am indebted to historian/author Rolf Giesen for the above photo of a diorama he commissioned that shows how the creature was brought to life.*

By far the best mechanical dragon props yet seen were made for the fantasy-adventure **Dragonslayer** (1981), fabricated under the supervision of Danny Lee at Walt Disney Studios, which was a producing partner with Paramount. Sections of the dragon, *Vermithrax Pejorative*, were built full-sized, such as a sixteen-foot head and neck for scenes requiring intimate interaction with performers. A Boeing 747 airlifted the props to Pinewood Studios near London. Chris Walas created a highly-detailed hand puppet close-up head fitted with cable controls that made it easier to stage certain shots rather than struggling with the large mechanicals.

Prop It Up • 147

Attempting to pitch the classic giant bug film, **Them!**, director Ted Sherdeman ran some 16mm documentary footage of desert specimens for Jack Warner and his right hand executive, Steve Trilling. Unfortunately, both executives were utterly disinterested and promptly walked out of the screening. Knowing he needed a better way to sell the concept, Sherdeman had Larry Meiggs in the Warner Bros. art dept make a three-foot wooden ant with a working head, antennae and mandibles that was painted black and placed inside a case with flocking on the inside. Sherdeman set the case on Trilling's desk and with some showmanship, he unveiled the contents. Trilling was so excited that he insisted on shooting a test with the ant model right away. Trilling then showed the test footage to Jack Warner and **Them!** went on to be Warner's biggest success of 1954. It also inspired the 'Big Bug' craze of the 1950s and earned a place in the history books as one of the period's best sci-fi films.

With advances in technology, engineering entire creatures as mechanicals had become somewhat easier. Under the supervision of Dick Smith, Warner Bros. studio craftsmen worked with Gordon Douglas, the final director, to build the ant props for a color production, including a unique approach to the creatures' eyes: a soapy mixture of reds and blues was injected into the eyes to add an extra dimension of life. But two days before production commenced Warners slashed the budget. Black and white photography couldn't capture the full impact of the eyes.

There was one complete "hero" ant as well as a "half"-ant for scenes of actors struggling in the mandibles. The mechanicals were maneuvered from a dolly by a crew of twenty operators. Additional ants with minimal functions were made for scenes inside the nest, such as the winged ant juveniles, as well as extras that could be burned.

Incidentally, rumors persist the film was shot in 3D, but that is incorrect.

In 1957 Pat Fielder, a young UCLA Theater Arts graduate, was working as a production assistant when she persuaded her employers to give her a shot at writing. Ultimately, she wrote a quartet of sci-fi/horror films for them, and **The Vampire** (1957) and **The Monster That Challenged the World** (1957) were released on a double-bill. The last two were **The Return of Dracula** (1958, UK: **The Fantastic Disappearing Man**) and **The Flame Barrier** (1958). Of this series, **The Monster that Challenged the World** was the most expensive at $254,000 (about $2.3 million today), primarily because of the title character.

After a maquette had been approved, effects maestro Augie Lohman fabricated the eleven foot tall creature. A crew of five men operated levers attached to three miles of intricate wiring to get a performance out of the mechanical mollusk. The pressbook includes a story that a monster was sucked down a drain during location shooting around the All-American Canal near El Centro, California, and locals were alerted to be on the lookout for an escaped sea monster. But honestly, that seems to be more likely something from a publicity agent's fevered imagination.

Prop It Up • 149

ALIEN

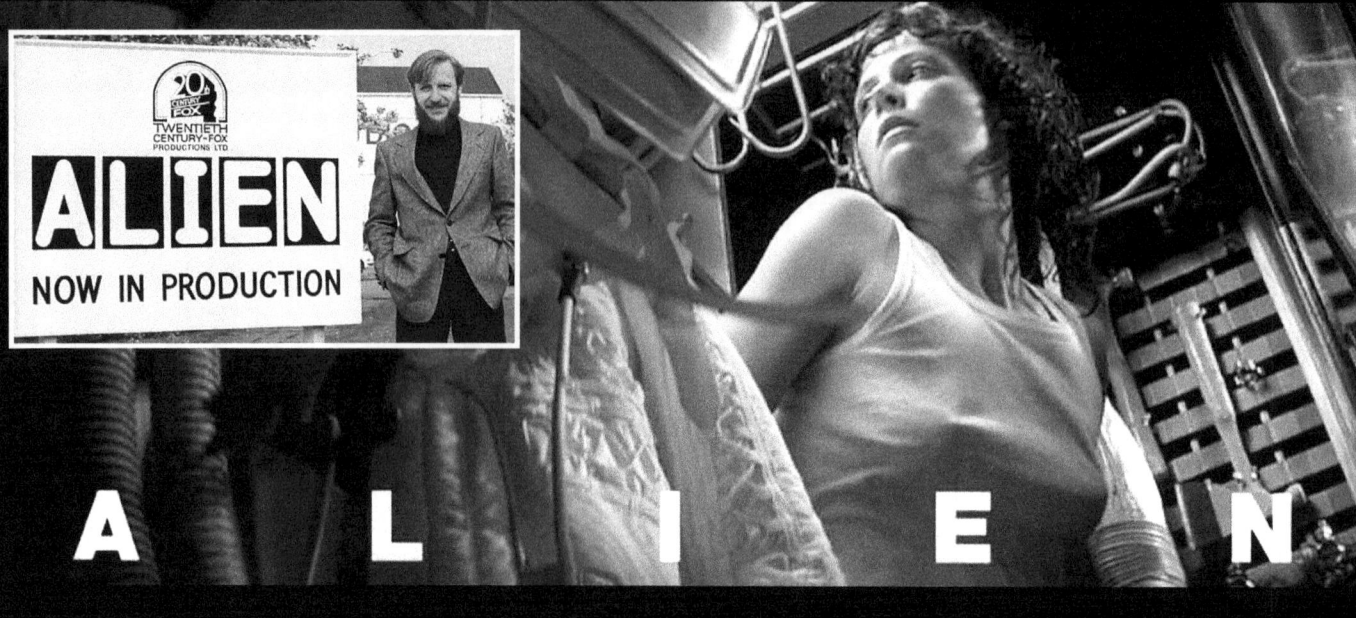

Alien (1979) had revolutionary production design by Swiss surrealist H. R. Giger, who had been hired to design the titular creature and the environment of a seriously inhospitable alien planet. The Space Jockey, an alien corpse of a wildly original concept merging organic and machine—a "biomechanical" life form—discovered inside the derelict spacecraft, was one of many props which he had hands-on participation in generating for the film. Typically, the studio had wanted to eliminate the unique prop as too expensive.

It was sculpted, molded and fabricated from fiberglass and then painted, after which it was coated with latex rubber textured to look like dessicated skin. When completed, it was 26 feet tall and Ridley Scott positioned his young sons wearing scaled-down spacesuits near it to make it look larger. A smaller version of the prop was also built, which was displayed with other artifacts from the production during the opening of the film at the Egyptian Theater in Hollywood. Sadly, that version of the Jockey was destroyed by inconsiderate jerks who set it on fire.

The film had other "alien life cycle" prop requirements that included a cargo of 130 custom-made plaster eggs with a few hero versions placed near camera; only one had a rubber top capable of opening using manual action. Some sources claim that the interior used membrane from a sheep's stomach and there are reports that the movement within was provided by director Ridley Scott while wearing long rubber gloves. The Facehugger flying out of the egg used sheep's intestine and some sources report that when pressurized air didn't yield the desired results, Ridley Scott tossed it himself.

Incidentally, some preliminary tests were shot using textured chicken eggs and that footage ended up being used in early theatrical teasers. One of these eggs ended up in the advertising and marketing campaign, on posters, despite not being remotely like the actual props.

Model maker Roger Dicken shows the Face Hugger to Sigourney Weaver.

Smoke and Mirrors – Special Visual Effects Before Computers

Star Wars: Episode V: The Empire Strikes Back (1980) features Luke Skywalker riding across the snowy landscape of Hoth on a bipedal mount. The "tauntaun" was depicted by both a mechanical prop *(above)* and a stop-motion puppet for long shots where it has to gallop *(above, inset, with animator Phil Tippett)*. The prop was manufactured under the supervision of Stuart Freeborn, who had built the ape suits for Kubrick's ***2001 A Space Odyssey*** (1968), Chewbacca in ***Star Wars Episode IV: A New Hope*** (1977) and Yoda as a hand-puppet for ***Star Wars V***, (performed by puppeteer Frank Oz).

A stranded alien has adventures with kids in Steven Spielberg's box-office hit, ***E.T. The Extraterrestrial*** (1982). In spite of his unhappy experience with the mechanical shark for ***Jaws*** (1975), Spielberg had Ed Verreaux build a $700,000 mechanical alien. But Spielberg rejected it and turned to Carlo Rambaldi, who had been Oscar®-nominated for designing the 'Puck' alien for ***Close Encounters of the Third Kind*** (1977).

Spielberg asked Rambaldi to be inspired by the faces of Carl Sandburg, Albert Einstein and Ernest Hemingway. Producer Kathleen Kennedy hired the Jules Stein Eye Institute to create E.T.'s eyes, vital for eliciting empathy from the audience. One animatronic E.T. head was used for the main filming and three others for extreme facial expressions.

A costume was also fabricated to be worn by a little person, primarily Pat Bilon, but in some scenes by Tamara De Treaux. Twelve-year-old Matthew De Meritt, who was born without legs, also wore the costume, depending on the scene. Caprice Roth, a professional mime, wore prosthetics to play E.T.'s hands. The finished hero prop was created in three months at a cost of $1.5 million. It is a testimony to all their hard work that the entirely artificial E.T. captured the hearts of millions of people.

Prop It Up • 151

Director Wolfgang Petersen.

Colin Arthur supervises the application of fur to Falkor, the luck dragon.

The German production of **The Neverending Story** (1984) features a furry, white 'luck dragon,' named Falkor, which like the tauntaun was realized as both a life-sized mechanical prop and a stop-motion puppet. There were also other creatures which combined mechanics and performers, such as the Rock-Biter, made under the supervision of Colin Arthur. The director, Wolfgang Petersen recalled in an interview with *HuffPost* that the dragon was "...the result of weeks and weeks of training. Each of the puppets required a team of puppeteers, who mastered intricate coordination prior to production." Petersen recalled a team of about 25 behind Falcor, with multiple people assigned to facial expressions alone. "One person was responsible for operating Falcor's nose, one for eyebrows, one for the upper lip and one for the lower lip," Petersen said. "You cannot imagine. It was just unbelievably ridiculous to watch it from the outside."

He saw the process in action, and the magic that came into being when the mechanicals behind the puppets were out of sight. They would record the creatures' voices in advance and much of the work was spent synching up movements with words. Although, there was always something off: an eyebrow out of place or the dialogue not quite lining up. Even with practice, it was impossible to shake human error. The challenge, however, Peterson always felt gave it the sense of being true art. "Perfection can close everything off. It pressures you and rolls right over you," Petersen said. "It feels like art because you feel the human beings behind it and not the technology behind it... This sort of humanity behind this very simple technique. It's interesting that it still works 30 years later.

"Actors now often complain they have nothing on stage to work with," he said. "They have to imagine everything. This was not like that. The creatures were there and they were talking to them. They felt alive. That made it easier and also adds to the warmness and the humanity. I didn't have to say, 'Look, Atreyu, you are here and there is a rock biter coming towards you.' If there was a rock biter coming his way, the rock biter was coming his way." (2)

Back in the U.S. terrifying supernatural creatures were about to undergo a renaissance thanks to the new technologies and innovative thinking by brilliant artist/creators. At long last werewolves were given the vivid treatment they deserved, advancing lightyears beyond Universal's simple dissolves that showed Lon Chaney Jr.'s transformations.

In one of those odd Hollywood coincidences (such as **Armageddon** and **Deep Impact** coming out in 1998), two werewolf films with jaw-dropping makeup and prop effects were released in 1981. Rick Baker had started on Joe Dante's **The Howling**, but left to work on **An American Werewolf in London**, directed by his friend and associate from **Schlock!** (1973), John Landis.

Rob Bottin, Baker's assistant, took on the challenge of completing Dante's film—and would later surpass himself with the wildly imaginative, over-the-top creature effects for **John Carpenter's The Thing** (1982).

An American Werewolf in London and **The Howling** were incredible leaps in setting new standards for physically altering a prop

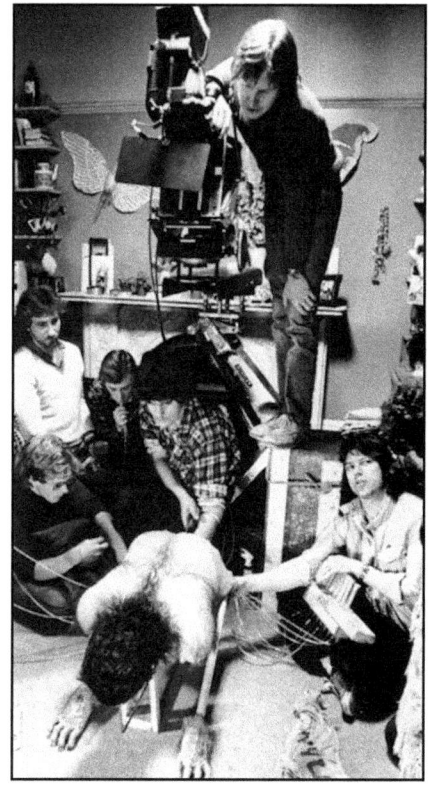

Above: Rick Baker, David Naughton, and director John Landis.

Left: Filming the transformation sequence for **An American Werewolf in London**.

Below, left: Wes Shank adds final fur to the full-size werewolf for **The Howling**.

Below, right: Actress Dee Wallace Stone with a stop motion werewolf for **The Howling**.

Bottom: **The Company of Wolves** *used cable-operated animatronic figures created by Chris Tucker requiring numerous crew members.*

in real-time, on-screen "in front of God and everybody." Their elaborate transformations required the use of foam-rubber appliances with internal cables and push-pull mechanisms that extended the muzzle, for instance, blending art and craft to empower previously impossible real-time metamorphoses.

With **American Werewolf**, the final creature was a four-legged mechanical version operated from a dolly and required a crew activating cable controls to turn the head, open the jaws, and move the legs.

For **The Howling**, a different approach was taken to show the full lycanthropes in action, with David Allen carrying on the "tradition" of using stop-motion to execute scenes that were impossible to stage just with props. In this case, the animated versions also eliminated potential risks to performers wearing suits around fire gags. Sadly, the director felt the stop-motion, while very interesting, didn't cut with the live action and eliminated those scenes, only opting to use a shot of three full werewolves on a road.

It is worth mentioning that around this time, people in the industry introduced the term "animatronic" into the lexicon to help distinguish modern production solutions from the earlier, broader definition of "mechanical effects." I think one could argue that the **King Kong** (1933) full-sized head was one of the earliest animatronics. As both a producer and special visual effects supervisor, I often heard the terms animatronics, special props and special makeup effects used interchangeably.

In England, Chris Tucker brought a different approach to the werewolves in **The Company of Wolves** (1984), for which he received a BAFTA nomination. The production was inspired by ancient folklore, where the wolf literally exited from the body via the mouth of their human selves.

Prop It Up • 153

Legendary makeup artist Dick Smith's transformations for *Altered States* (1980) were accomplished with inflatable bladders that simulated the internal distortions *(right)*, a technique also used in *American Werewolf*, *The Howling* and in Tom Burman's metamorphosis effects for *The Beast Within* (1982).

After describing the complexity of making some props, let's not forget our old friend *The Blob* (1958), a formless, oozing prop that uniquely had no fabrication. It was just a mass of silicone. Collector Wes Shank, author of *From Silicone to the Silver Screen: Memoirs of The Blob*, purchased the actual prop from director Irvin 'Shorty' Yeaworth in 1965 and displayed it at numerous fan conventions thereafter.

The Quatermass Xperiment (1956) and *The Blob* inspired *Caltiki, il mostro immortale* released in Italy in August, 1959, and the following September in the U.S. as *Caltiki—The Immortal Monster* (1960). This story did require a full-sized prop to stage shots of it interacting with humans *(right, bottom)* and in those scenes, Caltiki appears to be comprised of fabric/canvas stretched over a frame and operated by assistants on the inside. Think of it as an extremely primitive forerunner of Jabba the Hut from *Return of the Jedi* (1983).

Caltiki director Mario Bava claimed that cow entrails—animal intestines & other organs—were used to make the monster, and that the biggest problem was keeping flies away. Others have mentioned that 100kg of beef tripe—the first, second or third stomachs of cattle—were used every day to fabricate Caltiki. After analyzing the Blu-ray, I am unconvinced that viscera were directly applied to the full-sized prop. On the other hand, the miniature versions of Caltiki suggest that sheep tripe may have been used for them. At least these anecdotes make good Caltiki stories...

The musical *Dr. Dolittle* (1967) starred Rex Harrison cavorting with props that were prominent in marketing the movie. Foremost were the two-headed pushmi-pullyu and the Giant Pink Sea Snail *(below)*, the latter being a large, full-sized construction that was quite unconvincing. Just to keep the record straight, the movie won an Oscar® for Best Original Song and, unaccountably, for Special Visual effects. The storm at sea is quite good but hardly Academy-worthy. Because it was a box-office bomb, for years afterwards it was forbidden to mention the film at Fox.

Below: John Merivale valiantly tries to save Gérard Herter from the ravages of the flesh-eating dishcloth known as **Caltiki– The Immortal Monster**.

Sculptor Mike Trcic on the set with a friend.

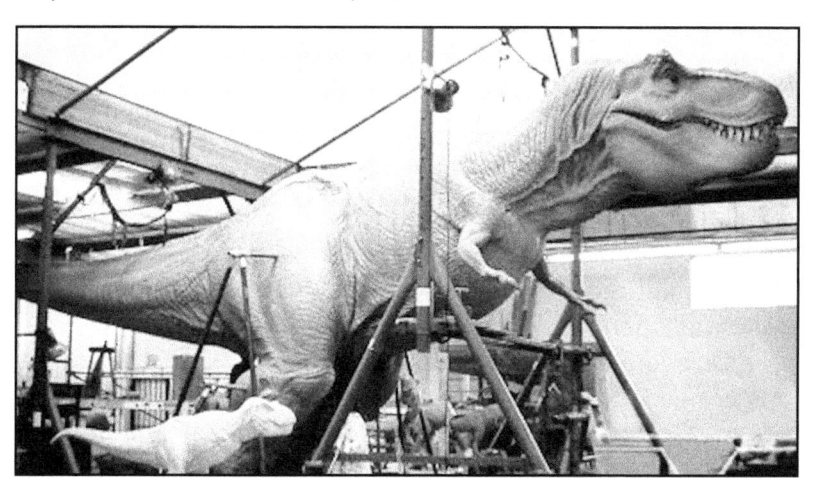

From the ridiculous to the sublime, we come to the largest and most sophisticated mechanical creature built (to that time): the T-rex for Steven Spielberg's *Jurassic Park* (1993). Supervisor Stan Winston was no stranger to large creatures, having made the Queen for James Cameron's *Aliens* (1986), but no one had done anything this ambitious for film work. Because of the mass of the creature, Disney imagineer Bob Gurr designed it to use hydraulics, though Winston had optimistically hoped initially to use manual activation or electric motors.

McFadden Systems built the primary T-rex on a custom-platform based on their flight simulators which provided gross movements. Controlled by four operators, a telemetry device used a miniature duplicate of the platform, and the immense legs were operated separately on tracks.

Mechanical effects coordinator Richard Landon designed and supervised the making of the support armature of steel, wood, chicken wire and fiberglass. Joey Orosco, Mark Jurinko, Bill Basco, Robert Henderstein, and Greg Fiegel sculpted the beast's body, while Len Burge and Christopher Swift sculpted the legs. Michael Trcic worked on the head and neck and constructed the subskull. The master sculpt consumed three tons of Roma plastalina oil-based clay and needed sixteen weeks to finish. Once completed and sealed, Steve Patino made fiberglass molds that were then used to generate the huge foam latex skins.

The finished T-rex was encased in a two-inch thick foam rubber "hide" and weighed four-and-a-half tons. At forty feet long and capable of rising twenty-four feet into the air, it damned near seemed like a real animal.

As in the days of *Them!*, a partial T-rex with extra attention to the skin texture and painting was built for closeups. Motion control was used to activate this prop's repeatable moves.

The project was a herculean undertaking, blazing a new path for mechanical props, for which Stan Winston more than deserved his Oscar® for visual effects. I wonder what Carlo Rambaldi thought about it, given his disastrous robotic *King Kong* back in 1976...

DENIZENS OF THE DEEP

Co-star Peter Lorre joked that one of the most menacing marine monsters ever built played the part usually reserved for him! Lorre was referring to the remarkably effective giant squid built for Walt Disney's magnificent production of—

20,000 Leagues Under the Sea

The squid was sculpted in clay under the supervision of Chris Mueller, who had helped create **The Creature from the Black Lagoon** (1953), and rigged by mechanical effects expert Robert Mattey, who had worked on **King Kong**'s mechanicals and, more importantly, the squid for **Wake of the Red Witch** (1948). That film brought him to the attention of production designer Harper Goff. The tentacles were molded and rubber castings were pulled for skins.

Mattey spent several weeks engineering a system to operate the tentacles using a pneumatic tube and thin spring interior. When pressurized, the tentacle would uncurl and straighten out while releasing pressure would reverse the action. Each tentacle was supported from overhead by six lengths of music wire. The squid's ten-foot long body was mounted onto a hydraulic ram that could raise it several feet out of the water. Because the ram was attached to a dolly, the body could be moved as desired. The menacing beak was operated pneumatically. On average, the one-ton monster needed sixteen technicians to manage its' performance, but for some shots as many as fifty people were needed to marionette the tentacles from the overhead catwalks.

After a week of staging the action on a calm sea at sunset in the tank specially built at Disney Studios Stage 3, director Richard Fleischer became concerned that the bright lighting showed all the defects of the squid, such as the many wires helping move the huge tentacles. Disney wisely understood Fleischer's misgivings and, to his eternal credit, approved re-designing the action to take place during a violent storm. He hired veteran second unit director James C. Havens to re-stage the scenes, which added six weeks to the schedule and upped the budget by $200,000. While the end result did become the dramatic highlight of the movie, Disney was savvy enough to hedge his bets by bringing in Willis O'Brien for several days to consult about a possible stop-motion approach if the second attempt failed.

*John Wayne and Ray Milland engage in hand-to-tentacle combat with a giant squid in Cecil B. De Mille's **Reap the Wild Wind** (1942). In some shots wires helped pull the tentacles through their paces.*

*Roger Dicken prepares his octopus model for an appearence in **Warlords of Atlantis** (aka **Warlords of the Deep**) (1978).*

*Gregory Peck is strapped to the great White Whale in **Moby Dick.***

*The full size mechanical head is prepared in the studio for **Moby Dick.***

Cephalopods have been enduring villains in movies. In the Robert Youngson film, **Days of Thrills and Laughter** (1961), there is a segment from an unidentified 1920s silent serial, where a large octopus in a cave pulls a struggling victim into the water with its tentacles. In **S-H-H-H The Octopus** (1937), based on a stage play, tentacles reach out to grab the cast from behind doorways in a lonely lighthouse, and Bob Hope had a humorous altercation with an ornery, ink-spitting octopus in **Road to Zanzibar** (1941).

Cecil B. DeMille's epic **Reap the Wild Wind** (1942) climaxes with a hair-raising encounter aboard a sunken ship between stars Ray Milland and John Wayne and an aggressive giant squid, a prop later stolen from the studio by Ed Wood for **Bride of the Monster** (1955). Republic's **Wake of the Red Witch** (1948) also has an underwater fight between John Wayne and a tentacled terror, this one engineered by Robert Mattey and shot by Howard Lydecker.

Frogmen in Irwin Allen's **Voyage to the Bottom of the Sea** (1960) have a brief encounter with a prop giant squid and Ray Harryhausen's **Mysterious Island** (1961) includes scenes with a gigantic cephalopod which is primarily done as a stop-motion puppet, but in some shots a full-sized tentacle is also used underwater with the live actors.

Moby Dick (1956), directed by John Huston from a screenplay by Ray Bradbury and Huston, had the courage to not only tackle a ponderous masterpiece of literature but to shoot with life-sized props in the sea off of Youghal in County Cork, Ireland. Dunlop, Ltd., a large multinational firm specializing in rubber products, manufactured a seventy-five foot long, twelve ton whale. Star Gregory Peck almost "went down with the prop" when its tow line snapped and it got lost in the fog. After losing the prop, the production resorted to using individual sections comprising fins, hump back and tail.

Close angles of the sailors' life and death struggles with the gigantic whale were shot in the relative safety of Elstree Studios using a life-sized animatronic head with movable jaw and eyes.

Augie Lohman was involved with the special effects and the vast bulk of the shots of the white whale interacting with the whaling ship *Pequod* and lifeboats with harpooners are miniatures supervised by him and filmed in a water tank at Shepperton Studios.

BANG! ZAP! POW!
Swords and Guns and Light Sabers

When **From Russia With Love** completed filming in 1963, noted British documentary photographer David Hurn was hired to do a photo spread with Sean Connery and the actresses in the film. But the prop master had forgotten to bring Bond's famous Walther PPK. Improvising, Hurn, an amateur marksman, got his Walther LP-53 air pistol, assuring the producers that no one would notice *as long as the graphic designers removed the long barrel.* They neglected to do that, of course, and the resulting iconic photo has since depicted the most famous secret agent in the world holding... an air pistol.

Director Terence Young briefly stands in for Pedro Armendariz as Sean Connery picks up some last minute weapons instructions about assassinating Krilencu in **From Russia With Love**.

Nothing spells drama more than a good war or swordfight, so for years the studios stocked armories of swords, pikes, shields, knight's armor, flintlocks, pistols, rifles and virtually any other weapon imaginable. In time, such equipment became the province of dedicated prop houses like Stembridge Gun Rentals, located on the Paramount lot, where you could rent anything from bazookas to gatling guns. Stembridge could also supply rubber versions of weapons for use in crowd scenes and battles. All fully automatic weapons, whether firing live ammo or blanks, were federally regulated.

For DeMille's **Unconquered** (1947) 1,000 antique flintlocks were needed for a large battle sequence. Stembridge modified old military rifles with new stocks and locks cast with flints. From a distance they looked genuine (foreground performers were given real flintlocks).

Vintage cannons have metal sleeves to protect the muzzle from damage when two or six ounce black powder charges are fired. At least once during cannon-firings in **Captain Blood** (1935) the actual detonation happens at the side of the cannon, protecting the prop from possible damage.

Before effects techniques had progressed significantly—and insurance companies could dictate to production companies—marksmen shot at trees, buildings, and vehicles near performers. This practice was wisely abandoned and replaced by the judicious use of pellet guns, electrically-fired squibs, and compressed air to simulate bullet hits.

The studio prop shops also fabricated imaginative weapons for sci-fi films like **Forbidden Planet** (1956), which included hand blasters, Colt-Vickers raygun rifles and large disintegrator cannons.

In a more mundane reality, for **Dead Men Don't Wear Plaid** (1982), Hand Prop Room in Los Angeles supplied custom-made .38 calibre handguns cast in rubber so Steve Martin wouldn't accidentally clobber another actor with a real metal gun. HPR also made polyfoam knives which when finished and painted or metallized would photograph like the real things but would not cause injury.

STAR WARS

Star Wars Episode IV: A New Hope (1977) was filled with assorted rayguns made by Roger Christian—who won an Oscar® for *Episode IV*'s set decoration—using actual firearms as a starting point to provide a robust foundation so they could hold up to handling by cast and crew. Extensive modifications made them look "cool." He also made the lightsabers because the effects department under John Stears, who had won an Oscar® for *Thunderball* (1965), kept delivering what looked like flashlights, which George Lucas rejected.

Roger Christian recalled, "I knew it was such an amazing invention by George and I knew this, if anything, would be the iconic image of the film, just as Excalibur is as important to King Arthur. It confounded me to find something, because by then I had to find objects to base things on, and I realized the advantage of that is there are things that you wouldn't necessarily design. I was under huge pressure because everything had to go in advance to Tunisia, because that's where we started shooting. They were pressuring me to get this and it was pure accident. It looked so beautiful. It had the red firing button, it had another button, and it was weighty and exactly the right size. So I got in my car and ran back to the studios. I thought, I've got to have a handle. So I stuck the t-strip that I'd used for the handle of the stormtroopers' weapon. I stuck that around the handle. I had broken-down calculators, and I loved the little bubble strip which illuminated the numbers underneath, and magnified them so you could read it on the screen. That fit perfectly into the clip. And I called George over and he just held it and smiled. That's the biggest approval from George that you can get. He doesn't have to say, "That's great," or "Do this." The only thing we agreed was [Luke] wouldn't use it in Tunisia, but he would have to hang it on his belt. So I stuck a d-ring on the end of it, and that was it. Then I made five or six of them. The two that I made went out to Tunisia, and then that's the one that Obi-Wan brings out of his box and gives to Luke. When he says, "This is your father's weapon," you know this is a turning point in the film, and it's a beautiful object." (3)

In 2012 the two original lightsabers were sold to the Seattle Museum of Pop Culture for $250,000.

Props: From a .44 Magnum to The Guns of Navarone

"I know what you're thinkin'—'Did he fire six shots or only five?' Well, to tell you the truth, in all this excitement I kind of lost track myself. But bein' that this is a .44 Magnum, the most powerful handgun in the world and would blow your head *clean off*, you've got to ask yourself one question: 'Do I feel lucky...?'

Well, do ya, punk...?"

Sergio Leone demonstrates his particular way to handle firearms to Lee Van Cleef in **For a Few Dollars More** (1967) and Claudia Cardinale in **Once Upon a Time in the West** (1969).

Disintegrator cannons and "blasters" provide firepower for the crew of the C57-D in **Forbidden Planet** (1956).

Left: Sherry Jackson and Mercedes McCambridge in *The Space Croppers* episode of **Lost in Space** (S1/Ep5, March 30, 1966), and *(right)* director J. Lee Thompson confers with star Gregory Peck while construction of **The Guns of Navarone** (1961) continues behind them.

160 · *Smoke and Mirrors – Special Visual Effects Before Computers*

Mad Scientists' Mad Labs

Forrest J Ackerman first pointed out that every good— er, evil—"mad scientist" needed an inner sanctum where he could engineer his ingenious devices, conduct his nefarious research and plan to conquer the world. Forry called them "Mad Labs." The most eye-catching devices populating their domains were designed and built by one inventive technician, Kenneth Strickfaden.

In the early 1920s, Strickfaden's deep fascination with everything electrical led him to assorted jobs working at the pier in Venice, California. By 1925 he was an on-set electrician at Universal, Famous Players-Lasky, Fox, and Paramount Pictures, on productions such as *Wings* (1927). He was also a pioneering sound engineer on films such as *Words and Music* (1929).

The laboratories of *Frankenstein* (1931) and *Bride of Frankenstein* (1935) were alive with pseudo-scientific personality thanks to the awe-inspiring snap, crackle and pop of Strickfaden's high voltage "aurora generator cyclotron," "nebularium," "plasmatron," "neutron analyzer," "pyrogeyser" and "cosmic ray diffuser"—whatever *those* were! His proudest achievement was a huge Tesla coil he dubbed "the megavolt senior." The concave mirrored reflector of the nebularium was also used to bounce light that produced the imposing shadows of the Frankenstein monster.

Strickfaden's unique props premiered in the futuristic musical **Just Imagine** (1930), and soon helped equip Boris Karloff to execute his heinous schemes in MGM's **The Mask of Fu Manchu** (1932). One scene called for the dastardly villain to be struck by intense voltage but Karloff recalled his unpleasant experience in **Frankenstein**, being showered by sparks, so he asked Strickfaden to double him. Dressed and made up accordingly, Strickfaden came in direct contact with 1,000,000 volts of electricity which knocked him off his feet!

The Undersea Kingdom (1936) was full of his devices and similarly, **Flash Gordon** (1936), would never have looked so other-worldly without his help. He even appeared briefly with one of his control panels in **The Lost City** (1935) and his constructs were invaluable for helping set the mood decades later for **The Munsters** (1964-1966) TV series. He offered his home-made contraptions as rentals over several decades and also utilized them in his traveling science shows.

Shifting gears from full scale effects, he was also responsible for generating the "rays" supporting the first Martian war machine seen in George Pal's **War of the Worlds** (1954), created by sending high voltage down wires—a technique that was ultimately abandoned. He also helped produce the green skeleton rays using a high-powered fan to propel a discharge down a horizontal rig.

Strickfaden's last film was **Young Frankenstein** (1974), for which he helped Mel Brooks duplicate the style of Universal's mad labs by providing the same props he had rented to Universal for the original films.

Never known outside of the film industry, the Academy of Motion Picture Arts and Sciences acknowledged Strickfaden's contributions with an evening event in 1981 called "The Magic Machines of Ken Strickfaden," which the 85-year-old electrical wizard attended.

The Mask of Fu Manchu (1932).

Kenneth Strickfaden, 1930s.

Above: *Frankenstein* (1931).
Below: *Frankenstein Meets the Wolf Man* (1943).

Special Effects	HENRY MILLAR JR.
	HAL MILLAR
Construction Coordinator	HANK WYNANDS
Camera Operator	TIM VANIK
Script Supervisor	RAY QUIROZ
Production Mixer	GENE CANTAMESSA
Production Rerecording	RICHARD PORTMAN
Sound Editor	DON HALL
Assistant Editors	STANFORD C. ALLEN
	WILLIAM D. GORDEAN

Special Thanks to KENNETH STRICKFADEN for original Frankenstein laboratory equipment.

Above, left: Kenneth Strickfaden receives his one and only on-screen credit—in Mel Brooks' *Young Franknkenstein*
Above right: Fred Gwynne enjoys the razzle dazzle of the Strickfaden gear in an episode of TV's *The Munsters*.

THE TERMINATOR

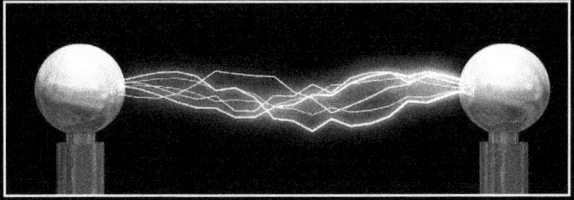

In 1984 Ernest Farino was hired to provide the main title sequence, laser beam animation, and other effects for James Cameron's *The Terminator*, including the electrical effects for the arrival from the future of the Terminator and Reese. He discovered that the original Kenneth Strickfaden equipment was being maintained by Ed Angell of Los Angeles. Arrangements were made and the basic Tesla coil equipment was set up at Fantasy II Film Effects in Burbank (Gene Warren Jr.'s company was providing the miniatures for *The Terminator*).

Farino rotoscoped the primary "contact points" onto clear animation cels, such as the garbage truck *(left)*. These guides didn't need to be precise; final positioning would be made on the optical printer during compositing. Each guide cel was hung from a C-stand in front of the camera and the Tesla coil electrodes positioned accordingly. With Cameron in attendance, a 1,000-foot library of electrical arcs against a black background was compiled, including generic lighting displays and individual arcs *(left)*. All of this was composited on the optical printer by Farino himself, in some cases layering three or four lighting elements onto a single shot.

A couple of years later word came from Cameron and producer Gale Anne Hurd while completing *Aliens* in England: conventional animation of electrical arcing was proving to be inadequate—could a print of the Tesla coil library be provided to production? The answer was yes, and the climax of *Aliens* in which the "Atmosphere Processor" implodes features *Terminator*'s electricity.

Other films for which Farino provided opticals made use of the electricity elements, including Mark Goldblatt's *Dead Heat* (1988) in which dead cop Treat Williams is revived to a zombified state.

Welcome to Altair 4
—and a Galaxy Far, Far Away

In the last chapter I examined robots created for films using specially-made suits. However, while the following "mechanical beings" also incorporated humans inside, they had internal and external mechanisms and power sources that qualify them as special props.

C3PO from the first three **Star Wars** films was covered in the previous chapter. But let's not forget about his companion, R2D2. Six prop versions of R2D2 were made at the EMI/Elstree Studios outside London under the supervision of John Stears. Norank, a company employing aerospace technicians, provided aluminum the components.

For stationary shots diminutive actor Kenny Baker—3' 8" tall—conveyed nuances that endowed R2D2 with character. Baker sat on a stool with his legs inside the robot's limbs, activating lights, turning the head, and rocking the body. Scenes requiring the robot to be mobile utilized a three-legged version with radio controlled servos. But radio technology was still primitive and unreliable, so the bulk of the scenes were done by pulling the props with wires.

Having a little person inside a robot had been done previously in Douglas Trumbull's directorial debut, **Silent Running** (1972). Lone astronaut Bruce Dern is accompanied by small robotic drones, Huey, Dewey and Louie, who handle dangerous chores outside the ship and even perform surgery on Dern.

The secret to these unique designs was using bilateral amputees. While working on **2001: A Space Odyssey** Trumbull saw Tod Browning's **Freaks** (1932) in which sideshow performer Johnny Eck, born without legs, displayed remarkable agility. Trumbull saw that bilateral amputees offered him options to design believably functional robots that were light years beyond past cinematic creations. The studio wanted him to use midgets, but his persistence paid off.

Mark Persons played Dewey and Larry Whisenhunt played Louie in twenty-pound props built to fit them. Cheryl Sparks and Steven Brown were physically similar enough to each perform inside Huey. The antithesis of HAL 9000, audiences responded to their humanizing moments, such as tapping a "foot."

Saturn 3 (1980) features an eight foot tall prop called "Hector" that was a cooperative effort of production designers Stuart Craig and John Barry, with additional input from Oscar®-winning mechanical effects expert Colin Chilvers. They drew inspiration from DaVinci's anatomical drawings and the prop took two years to perfect at a cost north of $1,000,000.

As producer/director Stanley Donen revealed to journalist Alan Brender: "It was enormously expensive because of the number of man-hours that went into building the robot. We had three teams working offstage—each with a set of radio controls. We had a crew of 20 working with this one robot. The robot was generally radio-controlled. Occasionally there was somebody inside of it." (4)

*Right: The lovely Farah Fawcett and the lovely Hector in **Saturn 3**.*

*Below: Mark Persons peers out from inside "Dewey," custom-made specifically to fit him in Doug Trumbull's **Silent Running**.*

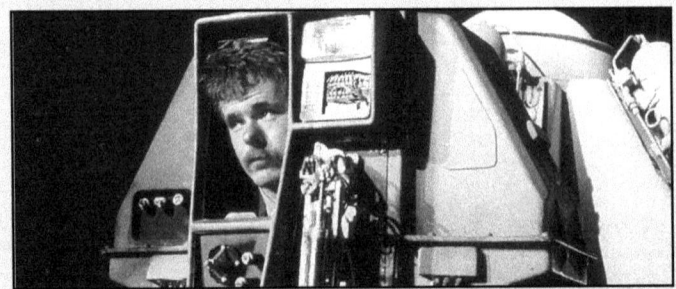

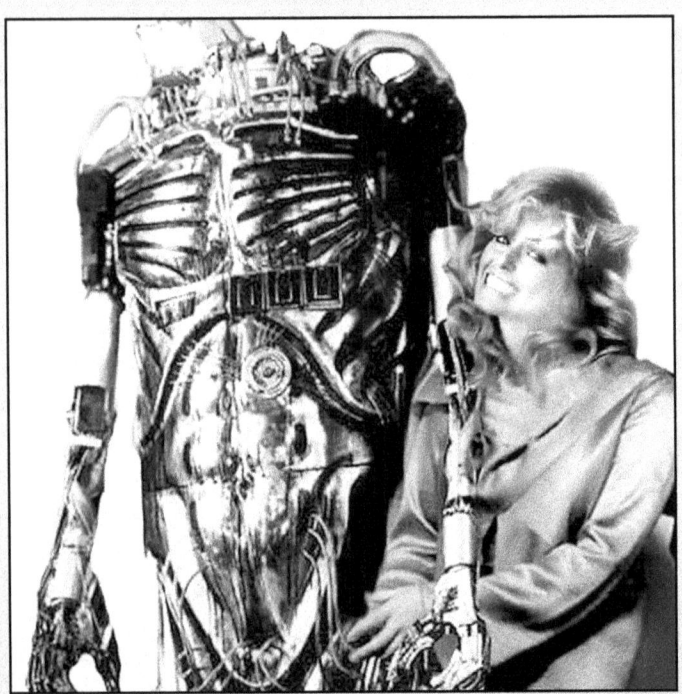

You've seen the rest—now it's time to meet the best. That is, what I consider the most iconic robot ever put on film, Robby the Robot, created for MGM's classic science fiction film, **Forbidden Planet** (1956).

My introduction to Robby wasn't sitting in a theatre, however; one evening, **MGM Parade** #28 was on TV and I was barely aware of it when actor/host Walter Pidgeon segued from an obvious set trying to pass as a passenger ship deck to an imaginatively futuristic interior that was drenched in shadows. As a young sci-fi fan only exposed to 1950s low-budget television like **Tom Corbett, Space Cadet** (1950-1955) or **Rocky Jones, Space Ranger** (1954), the sheer excellence of this got my attention immediately.

Dressed as Dr. Morbius, Pidgeon introduced his audience to what he called "The Robot," which was barely seen until it lit up and responded to him. I was gobsmacked—Robby was 100% real to me!

While the MGM prop department had all the resources of a major studio, they were also tasked with building the full-sized land car, disintegrator cannons, raygun rifles, hand blasters, a force field fence, a multi-purpose tractor, the C57-D saucer exterior, alien Krell machinery and most impressive of all, Robby the Robot. An incredibly daunting workload!

Robby was the result of substantial collaboration. A. Arnold Gillespie, head of special effects at the studio and Arthur Lonergan, the film's art director, settled on a pot-bellied stove as the inspiration for the body and Robert Kinoshita made additional refinements, having previously designed **Tobor the Great** (1954) and would later do the same for "B9" in Irwin Allen's **Lost in Space** (1965). Incidentally, some people think Robby's design was a reflection on Kinoshita's industrial art background designing, of all things, washing machines.

Irving Block, who wrote the original story and was active in special effects in the 1950s as a partner with Jack Rabin and Louis deWitt, also gave his input as did acclaimed concept artist Mentor Huebner.

The hands-on manufacturing was carried out in the MGM prop department by Cliff Grant, Andy Thatcher and Jack McMasters using the then-new vacuum forming process to draw heated Royalite ABS plastic over wooden masters to produce the head, feet, and upper/lower torso. The spherical arm gimbals, legs, and dome were made of Lumarith (acetate). Metal, rubber, wood and Perspex were also used in Robby's construction. An internal backpack-like harness made of metal with back padding and leather-padded shoulder straps, akin to those worn by the flying monkeys in **The Wizard of Oz** (1939), allowed the 120 pounds of the suit to be supported by whoever was inside. The first performer was Dead End Kid Frankie Darro but he was later replaced by stuntman Frankie Carpenter. Robby's interior was roughly textured from the Royalite, which had been developed to simulate crocodile skin for luggage.

Robby's dome was crammed with three "rotating gyroscopic stabilizers," a pair of pivoting arms in a "V" shape, flashing lights, numerous moving levers and two conical mounts facing forward on either side of the head. Additional life was provided by two rotating chrome rings on either side of the head, the one on his left being vertical while the one on his right was horizontal. These functions were powered by five WWII military surplus 12 volt DC motors operated from a control panel on wheels. Sharp-eyed viewers will spot the power cable in the scene inside The Residence when Robby warns, "Something is approaching from the west..."

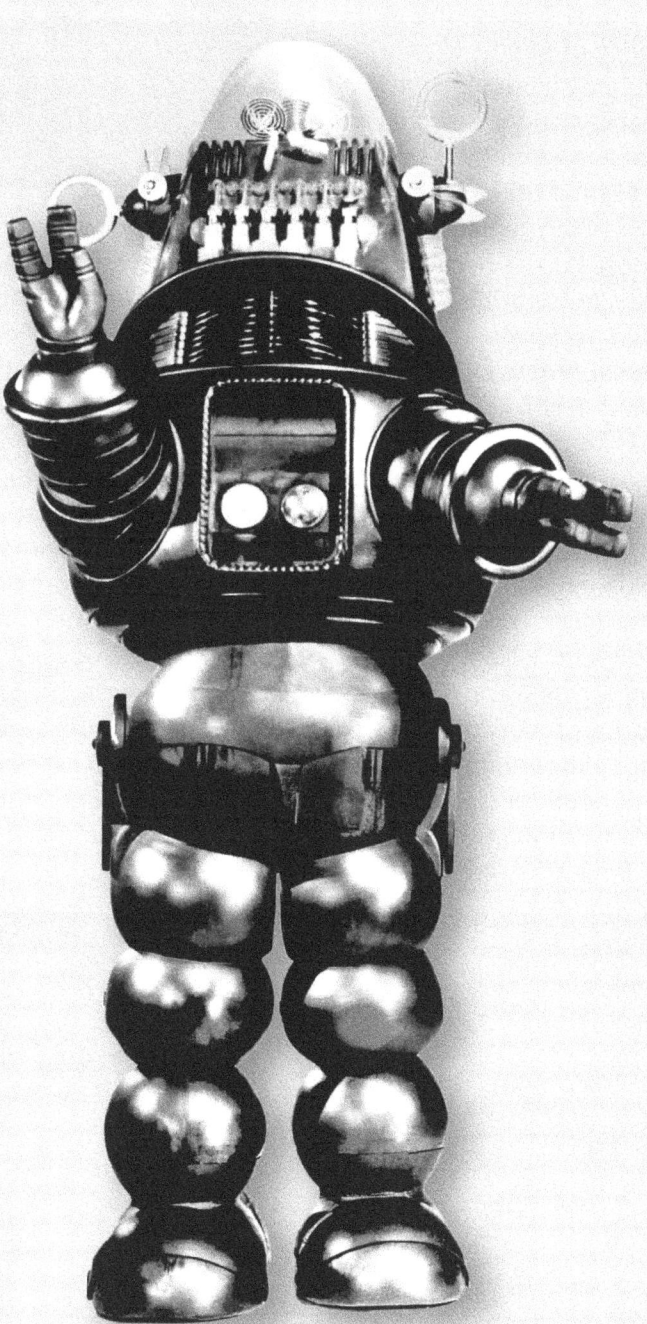

The front grille has horizontal rows of thin blue neon tubes which could flash when desired. During production, an uncredited actor spoke lines into a microphone and caused the tubes to blink in sync with the dialogue. Fortunately for whoever was inside Robby, the grille also admitted some air...

Marvin Miller recorded the dialogue in post production and his wonderful delivery helped sell the illusion that Robby was real. I met Mr. Miller at a special event in 1979 at the NuArt Theatre in L.A. where he appeared with a replica of Robby. Even though many years had passed he still did a very credible Robby voice and remarked about how he enjoyed interpreting the character without the usual "mechanical man" inflections used in other films.

Being inside Robby was physically exhausting, necessitating an inclined support for the performer to rest against between takes (a "slant board"), similar to those used by women performers wearing ballgowns or hoop skirts. The support accidentally appears on-screen briefly during **The Invisible Boy** (1957), Robby's second film.

MGM claimed Robby cost $100,000.00, comparable to $904,239 in current dollars, though some reports suggest he cost more. Whatever the final tally, it was an astronomical sum in an era when entire feature films could be made for less.

Robby was purchased by director Bill Malone from then-owner Jim Brucker of Movie World/Cars of Stars, and restored to his former robotic glory. I will always be grateful to Bill for allowing me to visit his home and shake hands with Robby, a true cinematic icon. After caring for Robby for many years, the unique prop was sold at a Bonham's Auction in September, 2017 where he fetched a staggering $5.3 million, a record price for a motion picture collectible.

After his last theatrical role in **The Invisible Boy** (1957), as the most believable robot prop available for rent, Robby was kept busy making appearances on TV series including **The Thin Man** (*Robot Client*, 1957), **The Gale Storm Show: Oh! Susanna** (*Robot From Inner Space*, 1958), **Mork & Mindy** (*Dr. Morkenstein*, 1979), **The Addams Family** (*Lurch's Little Helper*, 1966), and **Columbo** (*Mind Over Mayhem*, 1974). A modified version of Robby appeared on **Space Academy** (1977) and **Project U.F.O.** (1978). He appeared in episodes of **Lost in Space** (most notably *War of the Robots*, 1966, guest-starring with another Bob Kinoshita robot, B9), as well as Rod Serling's landmark series **The Twilight Zone** (*Uncle Simon*, 1963 and *The Brain Center at Whipples,* 1964).

Someday, a better movie robot will be made. Someday...

The principle fabricators of Robby: L-R Cliff Grant, Andy Thatcher and Jack McMasters.

Fan favorite Anne Francis as "Altaira" with her pal Robby.

Andy Thatcher and Cliff Grant prepare Frankie Darrow. Eye makeup prevented his face from showing.

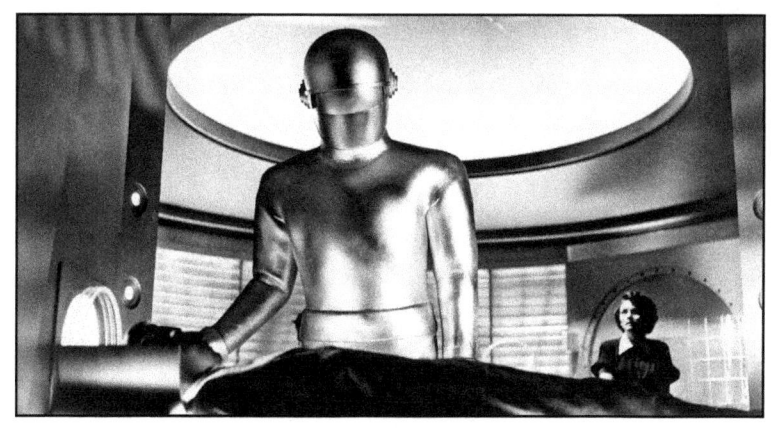

Fly Me to the Moon

In Chapter 3 I described the suit made for Gort, the awesome robot seen in *The Day The Earth Stood Still* (1951). But what about the spaceship that brought Gort and Klaatu to Earth? Their flying saucer is first seen as a miniature that lands in Washington D.C., but for most of the film, the production used a life-sized hollow prop made of wood, wire and plaster—which the crew had to scramble to hold down with weights and stakes when winds threatened to launch the lightweight saucer back into space.

Director Robert Wise wanted the entrance to open seamlessly; to accomplish that illusion, the cracks in the construction were filled with clay and painted to match the ship, so when they were manually activated opening, the results would match Wise's vision. The opening was optically duplicated in reverse, thus simulating closing and flawlessly blending together.

Klaatu's flying saucer was one of the few attempts by filmmakers that dared to show alien technology when the audience gets to go inside the spaceship. The interior is brilliantly minimalist in its design, using shapes and forms combined with careful lighting to make an atmospheric interior awash in shadows, with streaks of light emitted by and spilling across the mysterious equipment, as well as reflecting across Gort's metallic surface.

Inspired by their sci-fi hits, *It Came from Outer Space* (1953) and *The Creature from the Black Lagoon* (1954), Universal went "whole hog" with their prestigious Technicolor production of *This Island Earth* (1955), an effort at keeping up with their competitors, especially the color box-office smashes being made by George Pal.

Other than a matte of the landing bay, the movie resists showing much alien technology inside the huge spacecraft, a puzzling and disappointing decision. The bridge is so devoid of eye-candy that it resembles a ballroom. Worse, the kidnapped scientists meet the ruler of Metaluna while he busily wages war with another planet—from inside an empty room? Considering they had a real budget, it is inexcusable that the studio cheaped-out by re-cycling the boring, empty bridge of the saucer. After traveling so far, that must have been quite a let down for the earth scientists.

Top three photos: **The Day the Earth Stood Still**.
Below: **This Island Earth**.

Prop It Up • 167

I Married A Monster from Outer Space (1958) suffers from minimalism taken to the extreme without any imaginative compensation, as Wise's film had done a few years earlier. The tight budget was undoubtedly stressed creating the alien costumes (by Charles Gemora) and a few opticals (supervised by John P. Fulton), but imagination doesn't cost any more. There is also no effort whatsoever to show the exterior of their spaceship beyond an entrance with trees that conveniently hide the rest of the ship. One wonders how the ship landed among those trees...

Forbidden Planet (1956), on the other hand, rejects any notion of less-is-more, sparing no expense to dazzle the audience with the technology of the 23rd Century. The interior of the United Planets C57-D is lavishly dressed with props that collectively project a sense of being on a naval vessel, with its navigation dome housing a representation of the saucer, and the various workstations where the crew monitors the ship.

Gene Roddenberry's ***Star Trek*** (1966-1969) took us boldly into the space frontier—inspired in no small part by ***Forbidden Planet***—and the command deck of the USS *Enterprise*, especially, looked functional; it was easy to believe Spock, Kirk, Sulu and the other intrepid members of the crew were in a real place. The bridge was altered by degrees for the following incarnations like ***Star Trek—The Next Generation*** (1987-1994), but the concept was retained as a unifying component of all Star Fleet vessels and also remained a distinctive part of the USS *Enterprise* in its feature film outings. The location has the distinction of being the only ***Star Trek*** spaceship deck memorialized as a plastic model kit, the AMT *U.S.S. Enterprise Command Bridge*, which was first released in the 1970s but has been upgraded and reissued a few times since then.

Forbidden Planet: Crew quarters set looking out onto the bridge.

The crew of the U.S.S. *Enterprise* prepares to once again "boldly go where no man has gone before" in ***Star Trek*** (the original series).

Fantastic Voyage: Communications/laser station set.

2001: A SPACE ODYSSEY

Stanley Kubrick's *2001: A Space Odyssey* (1968, Oscar®-winning) truly set the bar for spaceship interiors. For many, it still represents the most plausible spacecraft interiors ever put on film, avoiding being "futuristic" but rather, near-term practical. Everything looked like NASA-on-steroids but were also calculated to be cinematic. Arthur C. Clarke had convinced Kubrick to hire Frederick Ordway, NASA's former chief of space information systems (who had helped develop the *Saturn V* rocket with Wernher Von Braun) and Harry Lange, former head of NASA's future projects section, as technical advisors. They were prescient about such things as astronauts jogging in their spacecraft to preserve muscle tone and in-flight communications, and they also convinced aerospace companies to participate in the production. After seeing the pre-production art and completed sets, senior NASA Apollo administrator George Mueller and astronaut Deke Slayton reportedly referred to the studio as "NASA East."

Touring MGM (England) during pre-production of **2001**. *(L-R): Science consultant Frederick I. Ordway III, Apollo astronaut Deke Slayton, Arthur C. Clarke, MGM assistant, Stanley Kubrick, and George C. Mueller, NASA Administrator for Manned Space Flight (Project Apollo).*

The vast quantity of props is utterly mind-boggling in volume and quality, as seen in the following photos.

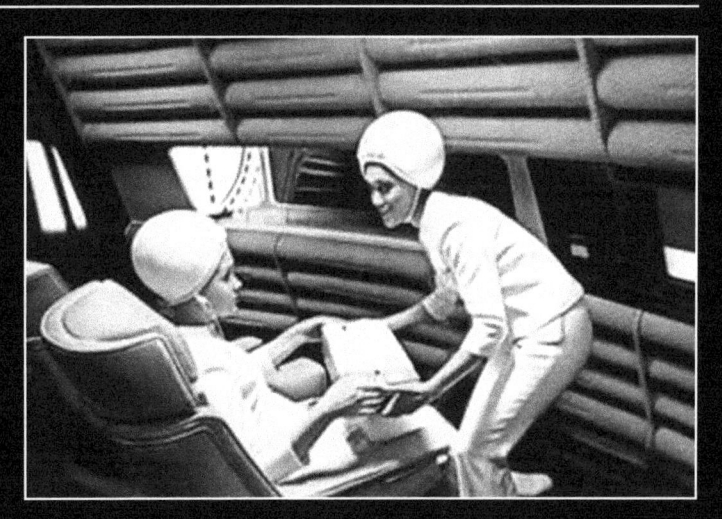

Above, left: The cockpit of the *Pan Am Space Clipper* that transported Dr. Floyd to the space station included colorful display panels created by rear-projecting 16mm animation.

Above: The *Aires* spacecraft that continues to the moon was staffed by Flight Attendants (*L-R:* Penny Brahms, Edwina Carroll) with food tray props. This sequence contains the film's sole intentional "joke"—a very serious Dr. Floyd studies the lengthy instructions for using the Zero Gravity Toilet.

Left: Later, aboard a "moon bus" filled with gear, Dr. Floyd and his associates are taken to the Tycho Crater excavation pit TMA-1 (Tycho Magnetic Anomaly-1) where a four million year old prop...er, Monolith, has been unearthed.

Prop It Up

Kubrick initially envisioned the Monolith as a pyramid, inspired by the Arthur C. Clarke story **The Sentinel** which Clarke and Kubrick used as the basis of their **2001** novel and film. Kubrick commissioned Stanley Plastics, a local British firm, to cast the monolith as a twelve foot transparent pyramid. Unfortunately, this was beyond their technical capability and they recommended a flat rectangular shape. Kubrick approved but became disenchanted with the way the clear prop looked on film. Art Director Tony Masters (Oscar® nominated for **2001**) suggested that the Monolith be made of wood and painted black. High-gloss paint polished with graphite produced an ultra smooth surface. There have been stories that the Monolith was made from black volcanic basalt imported from Scandinavia, but that is a myth (a "monomyth"…?).

Above: The Attendant at "Voice Print Identification" (Ann Barrass) greets Dr. Floyd (William Sylvester) on the space station.

Above: Numerous areas of the ship are loaded with props, including the AE-35 unit and the HAL 9000 "eyes," but perhaps the most memorable is the Pod Bay with its three one-man service crafts with mechanical arms.

Below: Audiences were delighted to see the Flight Attendant (Edwina Carroll) walk up the side of a circular ship corridor until she was inverted. This was accomplished by securely mounting the camera to the floor of a rotating set that gently revolved while the actress walked normally, in reality always remaining at the bottom. Fred Astaire used this same kind of setup to mystify audiences as he danced across the walls and ceiling of his hotel room in **Royal Wedding** (1951).

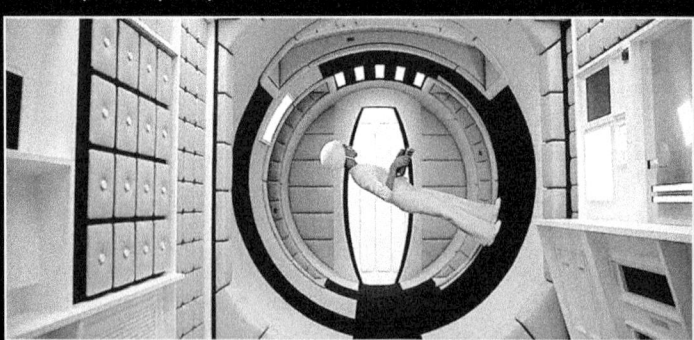

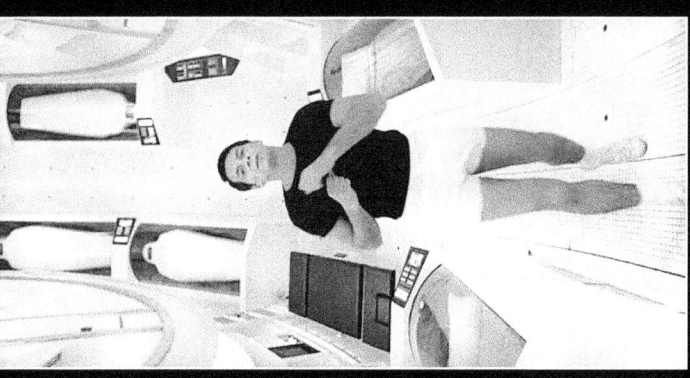

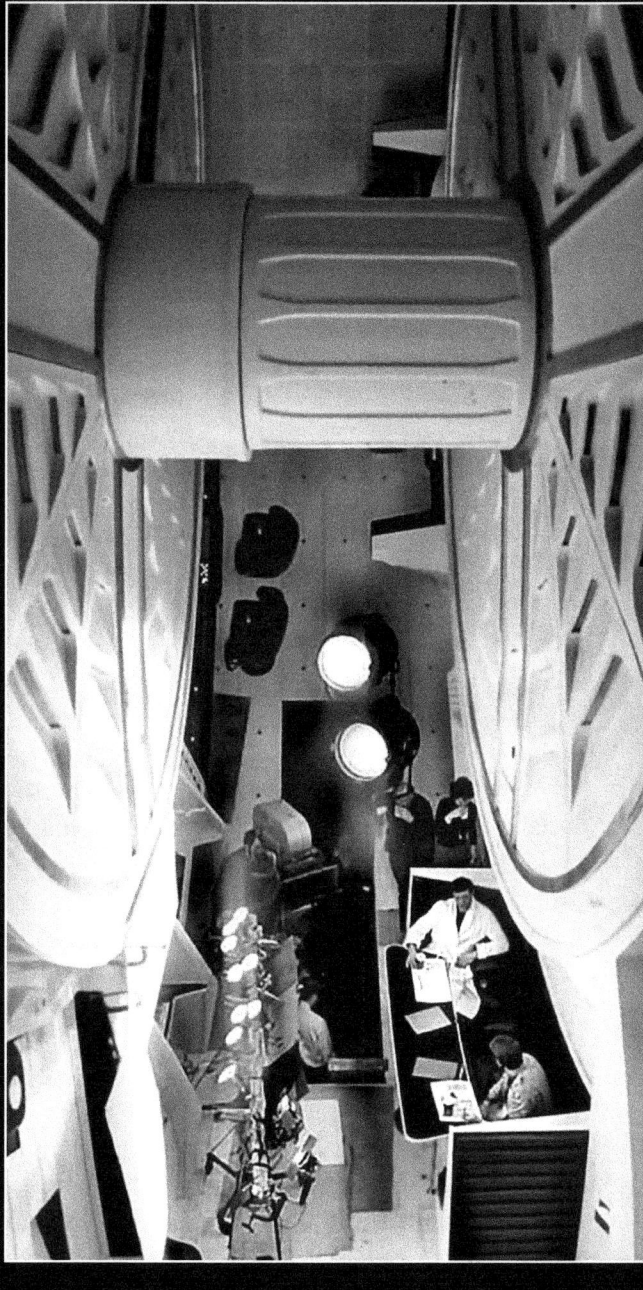

This page: The immense spacecraft *Discovery* is sent on a mission to find out why the Monolith beamed a signal towards Jupiter. The *Discovery* interior features one of the most complex sets ever built up to that time, fabricated around a "ferris wheel" that could spin, which enabled Kubrick to capture tour de force scenes of astronaut Poole (Gary Lockwood) jogging through the circular environment. The thirty ton, vertically-mounted set, thirty-eight feet in diameter and ten feet wide, was built at a cost of $750,000 by the engineering firm Vickers-Armstrong and could rotate at three miles per hour. A thin slot in the center of the floor allowed for a camera mount. Every workstation, hibernation unit and chair had to be bolted to the floor while the actors performed at the *bottom* as the set revolved, *a la* the stewardess in the *Aires*.

The whole film is a feast for the eyes, but perhaps the most fascinating compliment is the bizarre conspiracy theory that Kubrick had assisted in faking the Apollo 11 moon landing!

Prop It Up • 171

A Big Hand For the Little Lady

Special props activated via internal mechanisms were often called "mechanicals," and were used in dozens of movies to facilitate the demands of the story. For his masterpiece, *King Kong* (1933), Willis O'Brien turned to RKO's mechanical effects expert, Fred Reese (not "Reefe," as incorrectly reported over the years as a result of lazy research) to engineer a snarling life-sized close-up head of producer Merian C. Cooper's ferocious "star."

Technician Orville Goldner and author George Turner described the monstrous mechanical in their extensive overview about the production of the film, *The Making of King Kong*:

"Technicians constructed the frame of wood, wire, cloth and metal and covered it with rubber and pruned bearskin. As many as three men could huddle inside and by means of ingeniously designed levers and a compressed air device operate the mouth, lips, nose, eyes, eyelids and brows so that they moved in an astonishingly lifelike manner. It was capable of achieving a wider range of expression than can be summoned by many a professional actor.

"The balsa-and-plaster eyes of this behemoth were about twelve inches in diameter. The balsa wood eye-teeth were ten inches long and the molars were four inches high and fourteen inches in circumference. The ears were one foot long. The mouth was capable of stretching to a six-foot smile or grimace and could accommodate the bodies of actors who portrayed victims of Kong. The nose, which dilated and twitched with the stress of various passions, was two feet across. The heavy brows which could be wagged in the Barrymore manner were more than four feet across. The contraption was mounted on a heavy, rubber-wheeled flatcar so that it could be moved about

"[Marcel] Delgado tried to convince Cooper that the full-scale head would not be worth the effort for the limited use it would receive. Forty years later, at a screening of the film at the Motion Picture Hall of Fame in Anaheim, Cooper gleefully pointed out to Delgado each scene in which the big head appeared. Delgado had to admit that the scenes were tremendously effective." (5)

From Marcel Delgado's scrapbook: work on the life-sized mechanical head of Kong. Marcel is at the upper left and he identified the person in the mouth as E. B. "Buzz" Gibson, OBie's assistant animator.

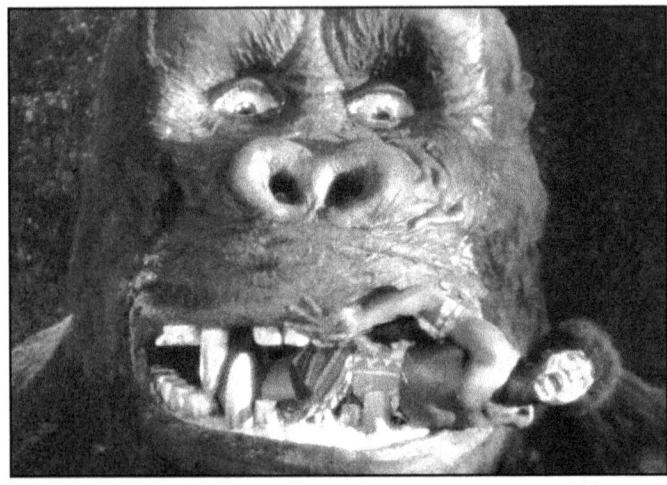

The full-sized head chomps on an unfortunate native. Bear hides were used to cover the prop and the face was capable of a broad spectrum of actions that gave it "life."

Smoke and Mirrors – Special Visual Effects Before Computers

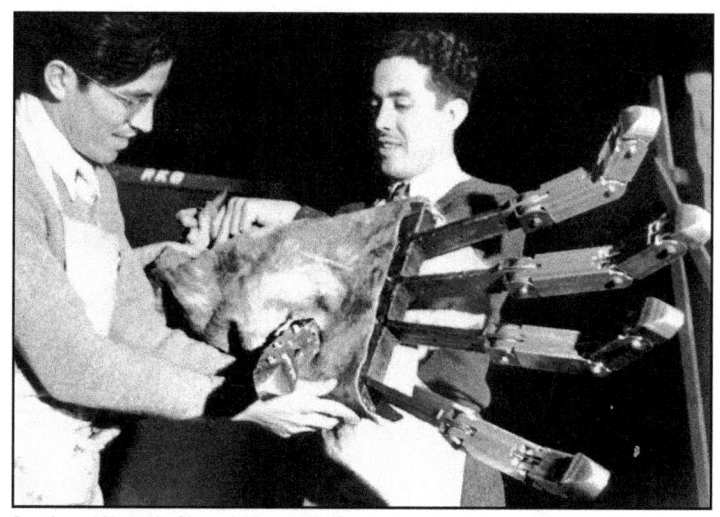

Brothers Victor (left) and Marcel Delgado fine-tune the mechanical hand.

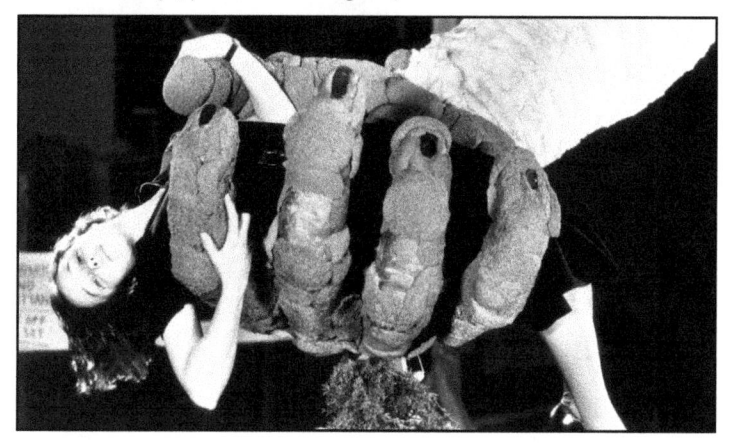

Above: Zoe Porter, producer Merian C. Cooper's personal secretary and assistant for 30 years, helped test the mechanical hand. As she wrote in **Recollections of My Early Days with Merian C. Cooper** *in 1971, "The giant hand and arm of Kong were mounted in place high above the floor of the sound stage. It didn't have the fur covering on it yet, but otherwise it was complete, with the fingers able to open and close and the arm able to raise and lower. Mr. Cooper said, 'Zoe, climb up and sit in Kong's hand.' It never occurred to him that I would refuse, and to tell the truth, it never occurred to me, either. So I scrambled into the huge hand and peered down about 20 feet. Suddenly the fingers closed around me and the hand raised high in the air. I was petrified. Mr. Cooper shouted instructions to me, telling me to lie across the hand as though unconscious, and to LOOK SCARED!!! I was frozen with fright. Who knew how tightly those fingers would close, and it was a long, long way to the floor. I have the pictures to prove that I was the first one to be in King Kong's hand. When I finally came down the ladder, Mr. Cooper said, 'You're a lousy actress, Zoe. Why couldn't you look frightened?' Which proves that real emotions don't always come through on the screen!"*

I have also heard reports that the men inside the head activated functions by using bicycle pedals, gears and chains. Other workers on the large prop included Marcel Delgado's brother, Victor, and assistant animator Buzz Gibson. The operating head was by far the largest and most complex of the full-sized props built for the film, but it was not the only one simulating parts of Kong. There was also a foot with an ankle, used for a scene where Kong viciously steps on a native, squashing him like a bug.

Additionally, a single right hand was built, to shoot close angles of Fay Wray in the jungle and New York City. While not as sophisticated as the head—Marcel lamented the design didn't allow a more natural cupping of the hand—it was especially useful for shooting the background plates for the famous scene in which Kong holds his blonde prize and curiously tugs at her clothing. Fay Wray described her experiences in "How Fay Met Kong, or The Scream That Shook the World"—

"Then I saw the figure of Kong. He was in a miniature jungle habitat, and was less than two feet tall! It was only the great furry paw, in which I would spend the next ten months, that was absolutely enormous...

"The hand and arm in which my close-up scenes were made was about eight feet in length. Inside the furry arm, there was a steel bar and the whole contraption (with me in the hand) could be raised or lowered like a crane. The fingers would be pressed around my waist while I was in a standing position. I would then be raised about ten feet into the air to be in line with an elevated camera. As I kicked and squirmed and struggled in the ape's hand, his fingers would gradually loosen and begin to open. My fear was real as I grabbed onto his wrist, his thumb, whatever I could, to keep from slipping out of the paw! When I could sense that the moment of minimum safety had arrived, I would call imploringly to the director and ask to be lowered to the floor of the stage. Happily, this was never denied for a second too long! I would have a few moments to rest, be re-secured in the paw and the ordeal would begin all over again... a kind of pleasurable torment!" (6)

The paw was also used for an over-the-shoulder shot looking down onto Fay Wray, which also utilized one of the Kong puppets in the foreground. By positioning it nearer to the camera, OBie cleverly created a mixed-scale composite that maintained the illusion the gorilla was holding her. This shot may be the only time a stop-motion puppet appears in a finished effects shot where it is not actually animated.

The 1976 remake of **King Kong** utilized two full-sized paws used in shots with Jessica Lange, that took four months to engineer from duraluminum (with bolts in the knuckle joints to prevent closing too tightly) and were covered with rubber into which Argentinian horsetails were sewn. They could be lifted forty feet in the air on a crane, weighed 1,650 pounds each and were six feet wide so they could comfortably cradle the actress. Reportedly, when producer Dino De Laurentiis visited the set to examine them, the crew demonstrated their dexterity by having one extend its middle finger toward De Laurentiis, who took it in stride. But even though they benefited from technological advances, the digit froze in the upright position for around five days. It's unclear if the same mechanical hands were used for the 1986 sequel, **King Kong Lives**.

Carlo Rambaldi, whose mechanical creations for Italian films like **Hercules and the Princess of Troy** (1965) were seldom convincing, also provided internal mechanisms over which Rick Baker fit his gorilla heads. Baker played Kong in a suit he designed and fabricated in every scene in the movie where Kong does anything.

Rambaldi also built an absurdly conceived and executed forty-foot tall Kong for $1.7 million, more than double the cost of the original RKO film. The prop was based on a 3.5 ton aluminum frame, with 3,100 feet of hydraulic hose and 4,500 feet of electrical wiring inside and required 20 operators; the exterior had foam latex skin and 1,012 pounds of Argentinian horse tails. The huge prop got the lion's share of publicity for the movie and was promoted as having been used all the time for scenes, when in fact the pathetic thing could barely turn its head. However, the utterly useless prop was an ideal candidate for marketing salesmanship! Rambaldi won an Oscar® for his work, which still boggles my mind.

Hercules and the Princess of Troy (1965).

174 · *Smoke and Mirrors – Special Visual Effects Before Computers*

Over the years, large scale mechanical hands became something of a stock-in-trade element for many movies and TV series. **King Kong** (1933) got the ball rolling but before long there was the genie's colossal hand in **Thief of Bagdad** (1940), the evil scientist's huge hand in **Dr. Cyclops** (1940), and in **Attack of the 50 Foot Woman** (1958) the grasping hand of a giant alien and the title star (using the same re-dressed prop). The stars of Irwin Allen's TV series, **Land of the Giants** (1968) found themselves stranded on a world where everything was twelve times larger and were regularly menaced by the immense hands of giant people. The show also featured a plethora of up-scaled props that dwarfed the human cast.

Famous Monsters editor Forry Ackerman on the set of Bert I. Gordon's ***Village of the Giants*** in 1965 (with the new issue #25 of Harvey Kurtzman's **Help!** magazine) and contemplates a "bust" of actress Joy Harmon.

The giant genie lends a hand to Sabu in Alexander Korda's ***Thief of Bagdad*** (1940)

Janice Logan in the clutches of evil Dr. Thorkel, aka ***Dr. Cyclops*** (1940).

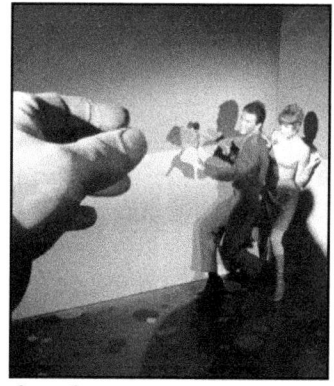

Gary Conway and Diana Lund in ***Land of the Giants*** (1968).

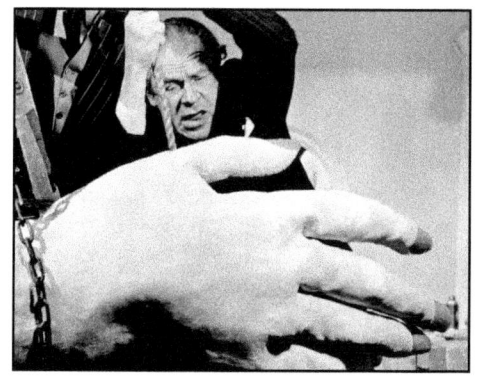

Allison Hayes finds she's giant-sized and commences the ***Attack of the 50 Foot Woman***.

Joe Viskocil slates the shot of Suzanne Fields in the clutches of the God Porno in ***Flesh Gordon*** (1974).

Like **King Kong**, the live action hand is projected behind the stop motion model.

Raquel Welch is baby pterodactyl food in Ray Harryhausen's ***One Million Years BC*** (1966). In the full frame image above, the prop legs extend up beyond the top edge of the background image in this blue screen composite.

Prop It Up • 175

Is That a Giant Pencil In Your Pocket?
(or are you just glad to see me...?

Filmmakers have long been fascinated by situations where human beings are reduced in size. Hal Roach was one of the first producers to explore the possibilities by placing Laurel and Hardy among colossal, upsized furniture to make them look like their own small children in **Brats** (1930).

In MGM's **The Devil-Doll** (1936), as spelled in the opening titles, Lionel Barrymore makes a daring escape from the vicious penal colony Devil's Island with a scientist who reveals his research into shrinking living things to one sixth their normal size. This provides the former financier with the ideal means of exacting revenge on the enemies who led to his false imprisonment. Dressing in drag to conceal himself from the authorities, he exploits scientifically-shrunken people to steal and even murder. The production used superbly constructed up-scaled props and brilliantly designed opticals to achieve the illusions.

For Ernest B. Scoedsack's Technicolor science-fiction film **Dr. Cyclops** (1940) they incorporated outsized props, from furniture to a huge shotgun, to help show what happens when mad scientist Dr. Thorkel (Albert Dekker) shrinks the scientists he has asked to consult with him because of his failing eyesight. The film also makes use of rear projection and split screens to show him interacting with his small victims.

Undoubtedly, the most thoughtful of all the Jack Arnold/William Alland films, **The Incredible Shrinking Man** (1957), takes audiences on a fantastic journey with one poor soul who is exposed to a radioactive cloud and begins shrinking... and continues shrinking. In the early stages, various enlarged pieces of furniture are useful to make the normal-sized actor, Grant Williams, seem progressively smaller. The filmmakers also used mixed-scale in some of those shots to add his unchanged wife in the foreground. By the end of the movie, props such as a ball of yarn, a pencil, a scissors and a chunk of cheese are staggeringly huge to him. They are brilliantly-made and absolutely convincing state-of-the-art studio constructions. Opticals are also used to show him in his ultra-small state, inserted into settings with a dinosaur-sized cat, for instance.

Stan Laurel and Oliver Hardy in **Brats** (1930).

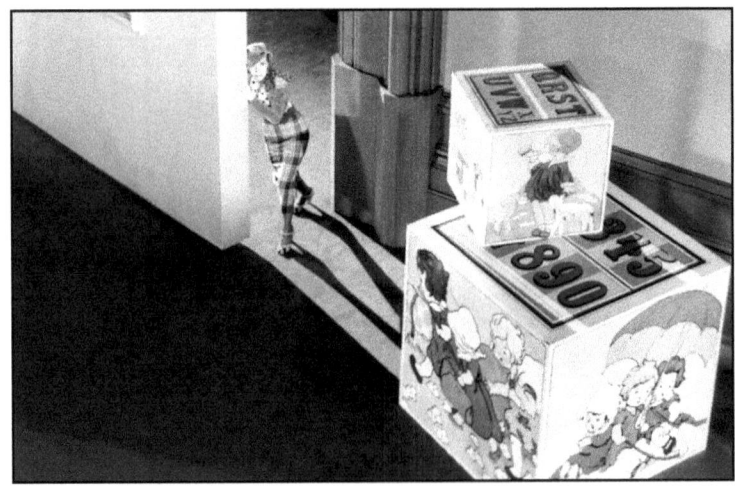

Enlarged props effectively shrink Grace Ford in **The Devil Doll** (1936).

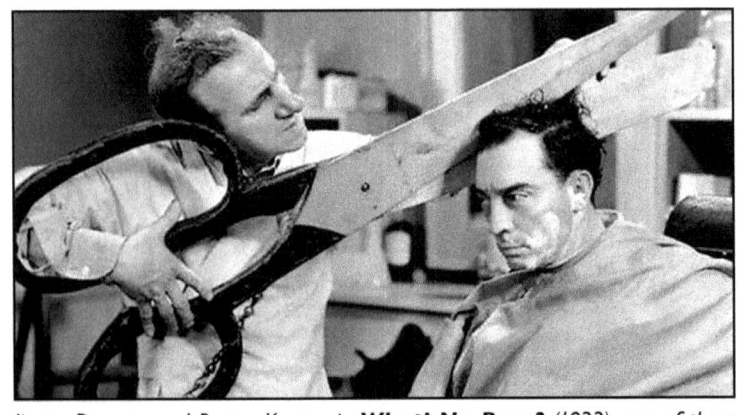

Jimmy Durante and Buster Keaton in **What! No Beer?** (1933), one of three films Durante and Keaton made together for MGM in the 1930s.

The Incredible Shrinking Man

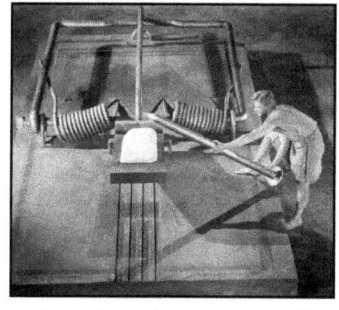

Land of the Giants

Inspired by the huge financial success of **The Incredible Shrinking Man**, opportunistic producer Bert I. Gordon decided to explore the shrinking component of the earlier film with **Attack of the Puppet People** (1958), starring the perennial hero John Agar. Paul and Jackie Blaisdell made a number of up-scaled props for the film as well as the miniature humans seen in canisters. Elgen B. "Buzz" Gibson, assistant animator on **King Kong** (1933), was the Key Grip while Bert Gordon supervised the split screens, himself.

World of Giants (1959) was produced by prolific early TV syndicator ZIV, the company behind **Science Fiction Theater** (1955-1957), **Highway Patrol** (1955-1959), **Sea Hunt** (1958-1961), **Men into Space** (1959-1960), **Bat Masterson** (1958-1961) and many others. Because it lasted for only thirteen episodes before falling into obscurity, it is essentially a "lost" program today. The series followed the adventures of six-inch tall special agent, Mel Hunter (Marshall Thompson), and several episodes were directed by people who knew how to handle projects with special effects: Byron Haskin, Nathan Juran, Jack Arnold and Eugene Lourié. The few episodes I have seen relied heavily on outsized props and rear projection.

For awhile in the 1960s, Irwin Allen was the king of science fiction on television, with **Voyage to the Bottom of the Sea** (1964-1968), **Lost in Space** (1965-1968), and **The Time Tunnel** (1966-1967). The latter was expressly designed to be made economically by exploiting stock shots—and props and costumes—from assorted 20th Century-Fox productions.

At the opposite end of the budgetary scale, **Land of the Giants** (1968-1970) was one of the most expensive series on the air at that time— $250,000 per episode—which was necessary to show what happens to a crew of people who crash land on an alien world where everything is twelve times bigger than on earth. The episodes required an inordinate amount of custom props, including a full-sized mock-up of their futuristic spaceship, the *Spindrift*, and a host of up-scaled props for the actors to interact with. Because of the time required to manufacture such items, the production team found it to be most effective to schedule filming two episodes back-to-back that utilized the same special props. There were also assorted optical effects supervised by L. B. Abbott to composite small humans into settings with giants.

Shut Up, You Dummy!

Actors during the silent era were known for performing their own risky stunts, the pinnacle of which has to be the greatest stunt film ever made, **Play Safe** (1927) starring Monty Banks (who later directed Laurel and Hardy in **Great Guns** (1941). However, there were rare occasions where a shot was deemed too risky to be completed by a living, breathing person and stand-in dummies were substituted to endure mayhem on behalf of their human counterparts.

While the majority of the early prop humans were essentially loose-jointed, stuffed mannequins, perhaps the earliest efforts to make a convincing dummy was for a high fall in D. W. Griffith's epic **Intolerance** (1916). Their first attempt was unsatisfactory for the demanding director, so a more elaborate version with a wooden "skeleton" was built with limbs that could only bend naturally and also used springs to help control their movement; the costumed "extra" looked quite believable on-screen as he fell realistically to his demise.

Silent productions became quite adept at staging live action of, for instance, a dummy smashing into the ground which was expertly edited with matching action by the real actor to create one continuous shot; the deft assuredness successfully matching real to artificial came from experience and can be seen in a number of comedy shorts and continued into the sound era. In Laurel and Hardy's **Busy Bodies** (1933), a life-sized stunt figure of Oliver Hardy endures painfully funny abuse, and at the climax both it and a version of Stan ride a ladder as it falls backwards a couple of stories onto a shed, demolishing it.

The Three Stooges frequently used dummies for potentially fatal stunts such as in **Dizzy Pilots** (1934), where Moe falls into a bath tub of cooking rubber and ends up as a human balloon; he floats out of the Stooges' aircraft workshop, only to be "exploded" by a shotgun blast from Curly that drops poor Moe—a costumed dummy—into a well.

In some scenes, corpses littering the battlefield in Kubrick's **Spartacus** (1960) were manufactured by Project Unlimited so the production wouldn't have to pay for extras to lay around on the ground.

Sculptor-fabricator Stephen Czerkas made a sophisticated life-sized naked girl to stand-in for a high fall in the Dirty Harry film **Magnum Force** (1973).

Dummies in films haven't been the exclusive province of ventriloquists!

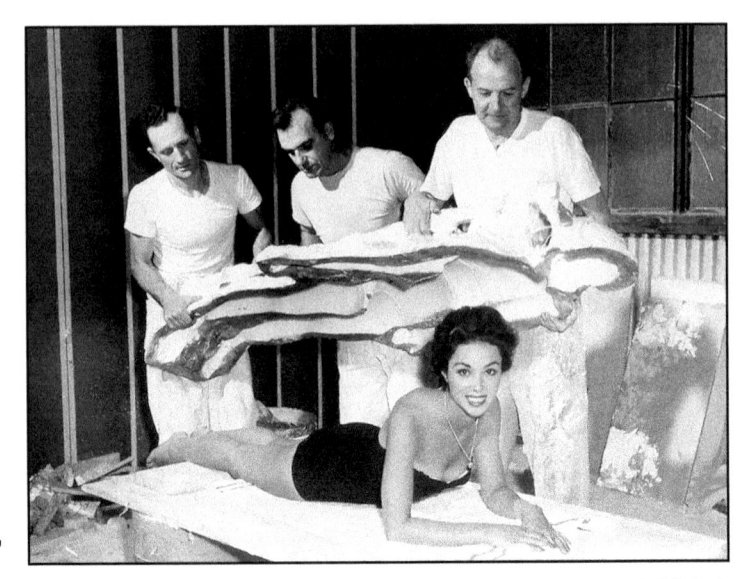

*Above: In case you still need a reason to become a prop maker... A full body mold is made of Dana Wynter to create her alien "substitute" in Don Siegel's **Invasion of the Body Snatchers** (1956). Don Post (right) supervises.*

Below: The Three Stooges in **Dizzy Pilots** (1934).

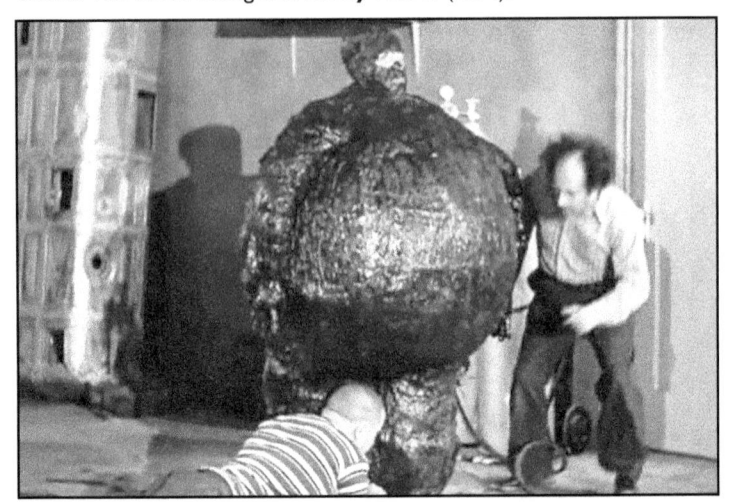

*The alien in Ray Harryhausen's **Earth vs. the Flying Saucers** (1956), above, was sculpted by Columbia Pictures' resident makeup artist Clay Campbell (at right, in his makeup room with Marilyn Monroe). Campbell was a collector of lip imprints of famous female movie stars and amassed over 1,000 lip prints (seen on the wall in the photo), including Marlene Dietrich, Donna Reed and Rita Hayworth.*

It's All Done With Wires (and Smoke and Mirrors)

Stage effects, that is those effects done on stage during photography with live actors, cover a variety of hydraulic, pneumatic, mechanical and hand-operated techniques that simulate inclement weather, send Peter Pan soaring or dress a creepy haunted house with cobwebs.

Some problems were simple. How do you film an ice cream cone under hot lights? It was quickly realized that using the real thing would never work, so necessity being the mother of invention, prop masters learned to use mashed potatoes as a photogenic stand-in that wouldn't melt. Ice on water was simulated with melted parafin wax poured onto the surface. Piles of snowdrifts in *It's A Wonderful Life* (1946) and *The Lemon Drop Kid* (1951) were actually crushed lime, while falling snow often consisted of bleached corn flakes.

In other cases, more elaborate methods were devised. From the shadowy abode of Count Dracula in *Dracula* (1931) to the dank crypts of Roger Corman's *The Fall of the House of Usher* (1960) and *The Pit and the Pendulum* (1961), numerous horror and adventure films made use of the Mole-Richardson Company's Coweb Spinner Kit. It was part of their Moleffect line that also included pedestal-mounted wind machines and two types of fog makers. The device was a modified drill with a 5-bladed fan that blew strands of rubber cement from a reservoir out five to ten feet, where the desired configuration and density of "spider silk" could be achieved.

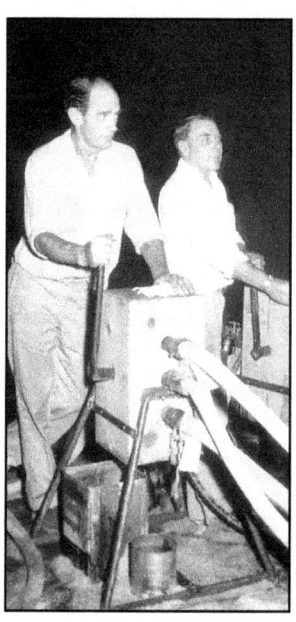

Above: It's snowing in Bedford Falls: ***It's a Wonderful Life*** *(1946).*
Below: Cobwebs aplenty in ***Mark of the Vampire*** *(1935).*

The "arctic" for Ray Harryhausen's first solo feture film, ***The Beast From 20,000 Fathoms*** *(1953), was created on a soundtrage.*

Prop It Up • 179

They recommended "enhancing" the webs by lightly dusting with their Cobweb Dust—at one time made from Fuller's Earth—applied by a pump device similar to an insect sprayer. This was actually necessary because the webs were otherwise annoyingly sticky for performers and crew members. The new M-R WebMaker units use an air compressor, heating gun and hot glue sticks to attain the same results while avoiding being sticky.

Some props were mass-produced, such as lightweight artificial trees and boulders. In the early days they were made from papier-mâché pulp but in the 1960s self-skinning polyfoam was used extensively.

When the movies were young, props were mostly made from wood, plaster, paper and metal. By the time of Fox's **Journey to the Center of the Earth** (1959), studio technicians were experimenting with the first major use of fiberglass in making the remnants of Atlantis, the mushroom forest, cavern walls and more. These modern approaches offered many advantages and became the new standard for prop-making, to such an extent that many years later **Bram Stoker's Dracula** (1992) had a major problem: director Francis Ford Coppola wanted to create props and sets in the old-fashioned studio style, so the call went out to find craftsmen who could still work with older techniques such as lathes and patterns. The search proved to be quite a challenge.

Speaking of the modern materials, I am dismayed that many friends and associates have lost their lives to cancer and other illnesses contracted after being exposed for long periods to resins, catalysts, self-curing polyurethanes and other chemicals that promised better results, faster. No one should pay such a cost merely to make movies.

For years, actors and their stunt dummies had been flown from wires in comedies, however, the most sophisticated prop stand-in was devised and supervised by the Lydecker brothers for the Republic serial **The Adventures of Captain Marvel** (1941). For long shots they utilized a slightly-larger than life, seven foot tall dummy made from papier-mâché and flown from wires by different methods depending on the shots. For closer angles, the Lydeckers suspended star Tom Tyler on a wire rig in front of a process screen where he was photographed by Bud Thackery, Republic's rear projection expert.

George Pal's Oscar®-winning film **Destination Moon** (1950), tried to realistically show what it would be like to blast-off into space on the first trip to the moon. The story required scenes of astronauts drifting outside their spacecraft. This meant puppeteering the actors or stunt men from special rigs. His later film **Conquest of Space** (1955) used the same methods.

*Pat Boone stands amidst prop mushrooms in **Journey to the Center of the Earth** (1959).*

Bram Stoker's Dracula (1992) used old school techniques.*

*A prop version of Tom Tyler flies on wires in **The Adventures of Captain Marvel** (1941).*

*George Pal's **Destination Moon** (1950). John Archer rides on a seat attached to the camera crane while another performer must endure being in the special harness held up by wires.*

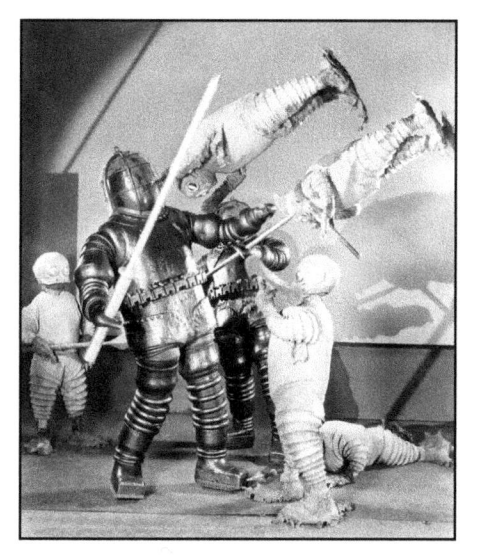

The magical flying carpet in **The Thief of Bagdad** (1924 and 1940) was flown from wires, with the actors precariously balancing themselves as best they could. In **Fantastic Voyage** (1966) the crew ventured outside the *Proteus*—an elaborate prop submarine—by being suspended from wires like living marionettes. Perhaps the largest number of people flown on wires at one time, to simulate being underwater, were for the MGM production of **Mysterious Island** (1927).

Other than movies, flying rigs were used to fly Mary Martin in her 1954 Broadway portrayal of the forever-young Peter Pan, and then later when the production was brought to TV in 1955.

The Adventures of Superman (1952) TV series followed the feature film **Superman and the Mole Men** (1951), which itself became a two-part episode (re-titled **The Unknown People**). The film used wires for the lift-off and flight of George Reeves as Superman until the wires unexpectedly snapped and dropped him to the stage floor. That was that; stunt men took his place from that point on for any wire gags. By the end of the first season, wires were replaced by a springboard designed by new effects supervisor, Thol "Si" Simonson, that enabled Reeves to launch himself as if he was taking flight; the actor ran into frame and used the springboard, hidden by careful camera framing, to seemingly defy gravity—and avoid wires. In other instances, Reeves was shot in front of a rear projection screen or a traveling matte background while laying on a special 35" x 16" fiberglass and steel flying pan rig concealed by his costume. A hydraulic system moved him up, down and side-to-side. Landings were accomplished by Reeves simply jumping down from a ladder or grabbing a horizontal bar which he used to drop into frame.

George Reeves spring(boards) into action in **The Adventures of Superman** *(1952).*

Look! Up in the sky! It's—a process shot!

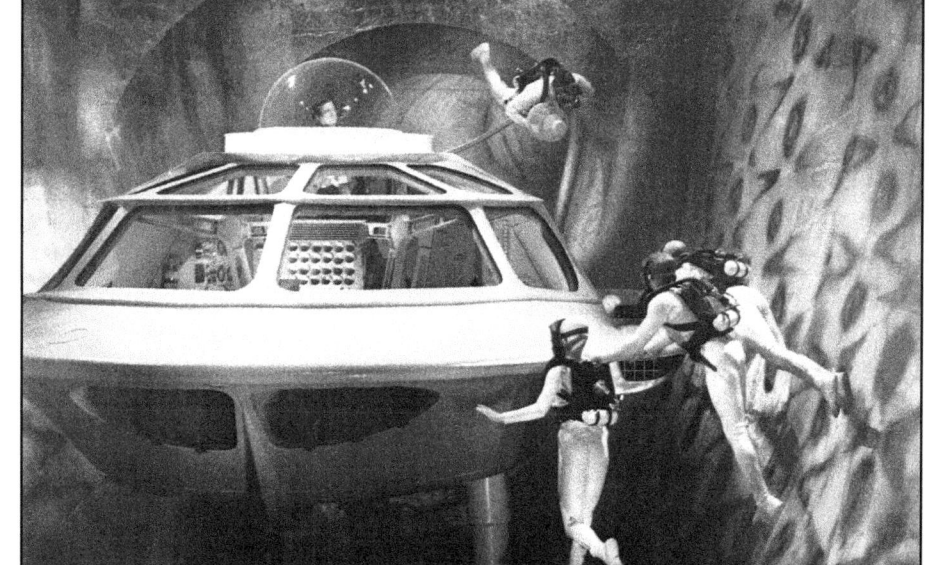

Above: Perhaps the most inventive use of wire-supported spacemen was in Stanley Kubrick's masterpiece **2001: A Space Odyssey** (1968). In some shots they filmed straight up at the dangling space-suited performer, whose body hid the wires.

Left: During their Oscar®-winning **Fantastic Voyage** (1966), miniaturized adventurers inside the human body make an extra-vehicular stop to siphon oxygen from the lungs of their patient.

Even low-budget Italian space operas like ***Assignment: Outer Space*** (1960) and ***War Between the Planets*** (1966) flew spacemen on wires—though not very well. The ZIV TV series ***Men into Space*** (1959-1960) made extensive use of wire supports, supervised by "Si" Simonson, to fly astronauts outside their spacecraft and to simulate low gravity on the moon.

While the Lydecker Brothers were most well known as "The Kings of Miniatures," they were uniquely responsible for all assorted stage effects as well, including everything from flaming lances and rainstorms for westerns, to explosions and bullet hits for Republic's war movies!

Howard Lydecker gave me a set of Xeroxes of his notes that are filled with charts documenting the flow of water through pipes, voltage regulation and more, all related to the physics of stage effects work. He also had formulas for colored smoke, burning torches, fizzing champagne, quicksand, fog, and how to make windows that could be harmlessly shattered in a saloon brawl (in the old days it was not uncommon to see crew people munching on broken "candy glass" after a take, so-called because it had been made from sugar).

The Lydeckers could stage earthquakes on-demand, rigging buildings that could collapse and then be re-assembled for additional takes. Bullet hits ripping into doorways and hand-grenades exploding were simulated by using electrically fired black gun powder charges placed in pre-drilled holes that could be controlled from a detonation board and fired in sequence or individually. The dirt and debris from an artillery impact consisted of flour and cork blasted into the air by carefully-manufactured black powder bombs or, in some cases, compressed air depending on how close they were to actors and stunt people.

What about a bullet striking a rock John Wayne was using for cover? That was a piece of chalk fired from a sling shot. Over time, they started using a compressed-air rifle that fired gelatin capsules filled with talcum powder. For those bullets that had to hit a windshield near a performer? They fired capsules filled with vaseline that would look like a bullet had fractured the windshield. In instances where they needed to see a violent shattering of glass, they launched a ball bearing from *inside* the vehicle to punch through an actual windshield. Last but not least, they used stale beer mixed with a little epsom salts to simulate frost on windows.

In England, John Stears engineered James Bond's DB5 in ***Goldfinger*** (1964) from Production Designer Ken Adam's concept, and later won an Oscar® for his work in ***Thunderball*** (1965). He went on to create effects for ***Star Wars: Episode IV—A New Hope*** (1977), which earned him another Oscar®.

Above: **Men into Space** *(1959). The astronaut floats from several piano wires. Howard Lydecker discovered he could prevent kinking and breaking by baking the music wire overnight at a low temperature.*

Elizabeth Montgomery and Dick York wait patiently for the crew to "smoke it up" for an episode of the series **Bewitched** *(1964-1972).*

Below: Gil Parrondo Art Director on the location shoot in Spain for **The 7th Voyage of Sinbad** *(1958) told David Garcia in 2010, "Everything was done very primitively, which led to a funny episode. When the Princess is sleeping, we had to have a bedside candle with green smoke coming out. Inside the candle was an aluminum tube with a paste to make the smoke. Behind the candle were gold satin curtains, where special effects man Manolo Baquero hid. I am not sure what happened, but as the camera focused on the candle I launched the green smoke—there was an explosion and thick black smoke came out. I laughed so hard as Manolo pulled the curtain back and his face was all black. All he said was, 'It didn't work…'"*

*Above and below: Spoiler alert—it's all done with wires. (And you thought the flying carpet in **The Thief of Bagdad** (1940) was really magic…). Closeup shots elsewhere in the film were blue screen composites to accomodate dialog.*

*Above: Multiple stunt performers float on individual wire rigs for Walt Disney's **Mary Poppins** in 1964. Moreso than most other Disney live action films, this film relied on many effects techniques, including animatronic props.*

In the U.S. Lee Zavitz was a go-to expert in stage effects, helping to unleash a *Hurricane* (1937) for John Ford, burned down Atlanta for *Gone With The Wind* (1939), helped fly the spacemen in *Destination Moon* (1950), staged the impressive ocean plane crash for Alfred Hitchcock's *Foreign Correspondent* (1940), and burned down Manderley in *Rebecca* (1940). For his last production, *Castle Keep* (1966), he staged immense pyrotechnics; on the other end of the scale, he once carved a goldfish from a carrot so an actor allergic to fish could eat the prop…

A.D. Flowers (no one knows his full name) became one of the most respected powder men in Hollywood. "He blowed up things real good." He started his career in props at MGM as a youngster and eventually became the head of mechanical effects at 20th Century-Fox. He won Oscars® for *Tora! Tora! Tora!* (1970), for which he re-created the attack on Pearl Harbor, and Irwin Allen's disaster film *The Poseidon Adventure* (1972), which involved hydraulic, mechanical, and fire effects. He was also nominated for *1941* (1979) for which he toppled a house off a cliff. For that production's extensive miniature flying scenes, he devised a special rig, "the guillotine," with Logan R. Frazee that could make scale model aircraft bank and roll. It was so effective that it earned them a technical achievement Oscar®. On TV, he worked on the long-running western *Gunsmoke* (1955-1975) and the dramatic World War II series *Combat!* (1962-1967). For *The Godfather* (1972) he created a special jacket that was custom-rigged to properly simulate blood spurting from poor Sonny Corleone. For Irwin Allen's star-studded *The Towering Inferno* (1974) he executed countless fire gags without scorching any of the famous stars like Steve McQueen or Paul Newman and also engineered a new type of dump-tank, four of which dropped more than 3,000 gallons of water onto the set—and stunt people—at the end of the movie. For *Apocalypse Now* (1979) he created the most immense explosions and fireballs ever seen before CGI.

In the 21st century, "props" remain an integral part of productions and defy this era of CG-for-everything. New processes like 3-D printing helped make set dressings and other items for *Memoirs of a Geisha* (2005), *World Trade Center* (2006) and, for fantasies like the Marvel superhero films, components of costumes, too.

One thing is certain: regardless of subject matter or budgets, props will forever be a vital part of entertaining audiences!

Anne Francis Was a Real Honey (West)

As a teenager I spent summers in Los Angeles where, thanks to relatives working in the film industry, I was exposed to filmmaking at the studios. I visited the back lot at 20th Century-Fox, which was way better than Disneyland to me, but my fondest memories were visiting Four Star Studios in the San Fernando Valley (formerly Republic Studios). In those days it was quite unusual for a teenager to be so keenly interested in production and it amused the old-timers to let me hang out. A camera crew taught me how to load a Mitchell BNC, some painters taught me the basics of painting large backdrops, and prop makers showed me their tricks. I absorbed it all like a sponge!

Other shows filmed on the lot included *Gunsmoke*, *Gilligan's Island*, *Wild, Wild West*, and *It's About Time*, all of which I saw in production. *Gunsmoke* was the only "closed-set" so I never got to ask Glenn Strange ("Sam the Bartender") about playing Frankenstein's Monster.

I was a six-foot tall robust farm boy full of raging hormones and was utterly gaa-gaa over Dawn Wells and Linda Evans. I did a lot of favors for them, like getting drinks from craft service, which sparked much ribbing from the old-timers.

But my most memorable moment was when my cousin, who worked on the lot, told the crew of *Honey West* that I was head-over-heels in love with star Anne Francis. They were highly entertained at how tongue-tied I was when they arranged for me to meet her! I could barely stammer out how nice it was to meet her. She was just *wonderful* to me—so nice and patient! I told her I hoped I could work on her show someday.

The next thing I knew she asked the prop guy to show me how to pull open the "super-scientific sliding door" to her secret lair. On cue, while the camera rolled, I pulled the 2x4 at the top of the door to slide it open for her to enter the set. *Wow!* Now, every time I see a *Star Trek* door glide open I think back to *Honey West*.

No, it wasn't like hanging out with her and Robby on Altair IV, but let me assure you, this midwesterner was truly star-struck!

SCRAPBOOK

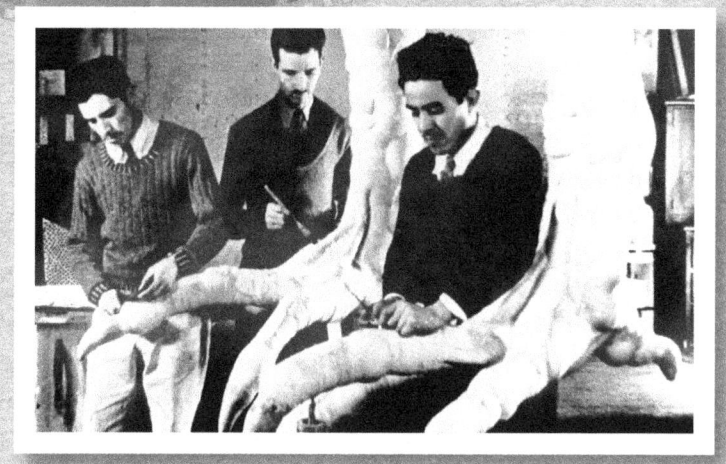

Victor Delgado, Zack Hoag, and Marcel Delgado working on the full-sized pterodactyl claws that will menace Fay Wray in **King Kong** (1933).

In **Son of Kong** (1933, Robert Armstrong gets his turn with the giant paw that had originally tormented Fay Wray in **King Kong**.

Marcel Delgado applies a textured latex skin to the tree miniature for **Mighty Joe Young** (1949).

This spider was built by Wah Chang and became a rental item in several films, including **Mesa of Lost Women** (1953, above). Poor Jackie Coogan is doing his best to look afraid. Provocative stills with actress Tandra Quinn (right) hint at rape, pre-dating Corman's tastelessly lurid poster for **The Nest** (1988).

Prop It Up • 185

Above: **Tarantula** (1955), primarily features superb traveling matte shots of a live spider. This prop was used for close-ups of it leering at Mara Corday.

Right: **The Deadly Mantis** (1957) was limited to a single shot of a live insect on the Washington Monument. The bulk of its scenes were done with a mechanical mantis, while shots of it flying used yet another model.

For **Attack of the Crab Monsters** (1957) this prop was reportedly built by actor Ed Nelson, who "performed" in it along with Beech Dickerson. The styrofoam crab had to be weighted down to sink for underwater scenes.

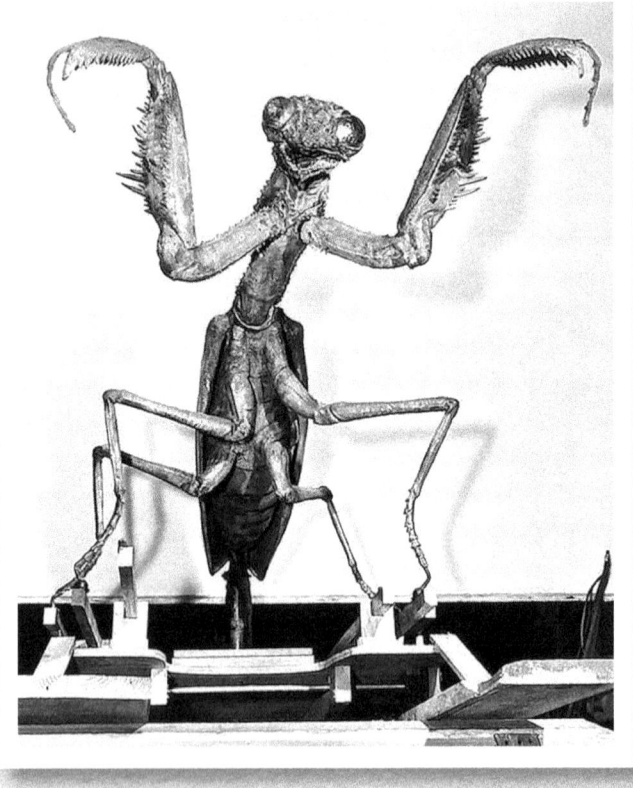

For **The Valley of Gwangi** (1969) Ray Harryhausen explains how to wrestle with a pterodactyl. This life-sized prop was made by Francisco Prosper and his Spanish crew.

George Blackwell examines the mechanical close-up head for **Curse of the Demon** (1957; UK: **Night of the Demon**). Several approaches, including a man in a suit, were used to visualize the hellish creature.

The monstrous close-up head in action. While some reviewers debate the wisdom of showing the supernatural beast, I feel it was essential to the story. What do you think?

In spite of its low budget, **The Man From Planet X** (1951) featured a full-size alien spaceship on a soundstage simulating the Scottish moors.

The aft section of the Luna spaceship for George Pal's Oscar®-winning **Destination Moon** (1950) was used for live action filming.

Three of the "Mole Men" from the 2-part TV episode of **The Adventures of Superman** with their very impressive, dangerous-looking… vacuum cleaner. Phyllis Coates (Lois Lane) told Ernest Farino she thought this was hilarious, as she had one of these at home herself.

A technician adjusts the wire rigging to float an intrepid spaceman to his **Destination Moon**.

A crane positions the full-scale "Moon Sphere" built for **First Men "In" the Moon** (1964) on the lunar landscape set in the huge Stage H at Shepperton Studios in England.

The Robinson family's chariot in **Lost in Space** (1965-1968), based on the chassis of a working 1965 Thiokol Snow Cat modified with "futuristic" additions. A radio-controlled miniature was used in long shots.

Prop It Up • 187

Filming the recreation of the Normandy landing for **The Longest Day** (1962). Organized like a military operation itself, extras were grouped into units commanded by Assistant Directors and other production staff who were also dressed as soldiers to blend into the action. All scenes are "real" (no optical effects, and CGI didn't exist then), winning an Oscar® for special effects.

One of the movies' most charming props was built for George Pal's Oscar®-winning **The Time Machine** (1960). The "timely" intervention of historian Bob Burns saved it.

Left: Actor Rod Taylor is about to embark into the unimaginably distant future.

Above: Science fiction author Ray Bradbury sits in the restored Time Machine at Bob Burns' museum.

188 · *Smoke and Mirrors – Special Visual Effects Before Computers*

George Reeves in **The Adventures of Superman** ("The Gentle Monster," 1958). The robot first appeared in **The Bowery Boys Meet the Monsters** (1954).

Constance Dowling in a publicity photo for Ivan Tors' **Gog** (1954), the only color 3-D release to star two robots. Little people inside the props make the robots work. Following production, Miss Dowling married producer Ivan Tors, and this photo was taken at their home.

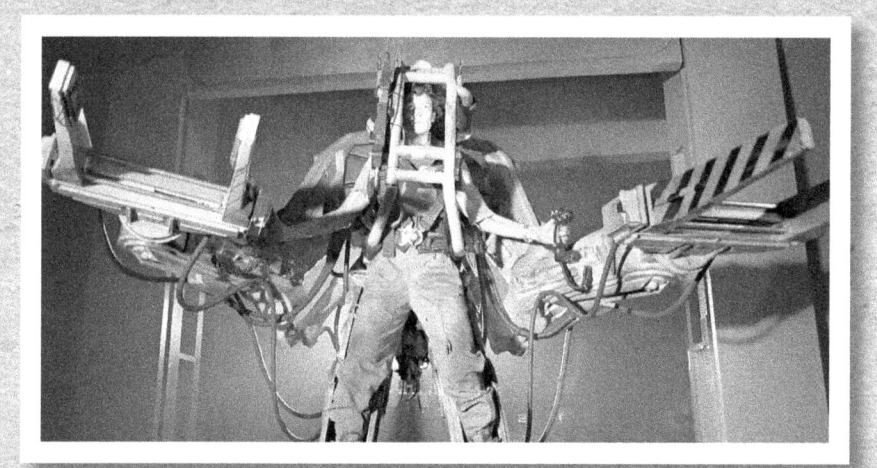

The power-loader, a brilliantly designed and fabricated prop for **Aliens** (1986), had a person hidden inside to help Sigourney Weaver maneuver it.

Tobor the Great (1954) was designed by Robert Kinoshita, who later developed Robby the Robot for **Forbidden Planet** and B-9 for TV's **Lost in Space**.

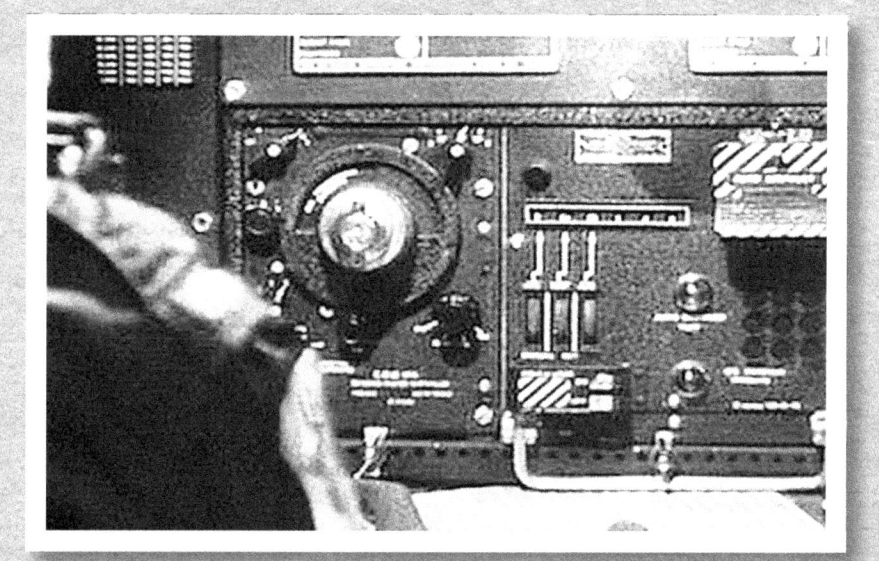

Left: Aboard the B-52s in Stanley Kubrick's **Dr. Strangelove** (1964) is a device called CRM 114 (CRM = **C**argo **R**adio **M**aintenance, and 114 is a series number). This discriminator ensures that the enemy cannot plant false transmissions or fake orders without a daily-assigned, three letter prefix. Setting the dials of the CRM 114 will block any transmission not preceded by the three letter prefix.

While preparing the film in 1963, Kubrick corresponded with Peter George, author of the novel **Red Alert** on which the film was based, to make sure that the failure of the CRM-114 device could credibly interfere with the recall of an aircraft. George replied, "Based on experts' opinions, there is, in fact, no practical way of demonstrating inability to recall the bombers other than by the introduction of a device such as the CRM-114."

Prop It Up • 189

Top: Producer Irwin Allen (in white shirt) joins the crew filming the mechanical Triceratops for **The Animal World** (1956). Willis O'Brien supervised the stop motion sequences and Ray Harryhausen did the animation.

Top, right: Raquel Welch, an American skydiver recruited by Western intelligence agents to recover a lost atomic bomb detonator from hostile foreign agents (yes, Raquel Welch, and no, we're not making this up), takes no bull from a special prop in the film **Fathom** (1967).

Above: During **The Day of the Triffids** (1963) Janette Scott has her hands full with a man-eating, ambulatory plant. The mechanical prop could flail its "arms."

Above, right: Dozens of unmechanized triffids created an army of predators.

Right: Wah Chang designed the "sand shark" and Project Unlimited built and filmed it for "The Invisible Enemy" episode of **The Outer Limits** (S2/Ep7, October 21, 1964). The hand puppet was operated in a small water tank by a scuba diver beneath a surface covered with cork and vermiculite.

190 · *Smoke and Mirrors – Special Visual Effects Before Computers*

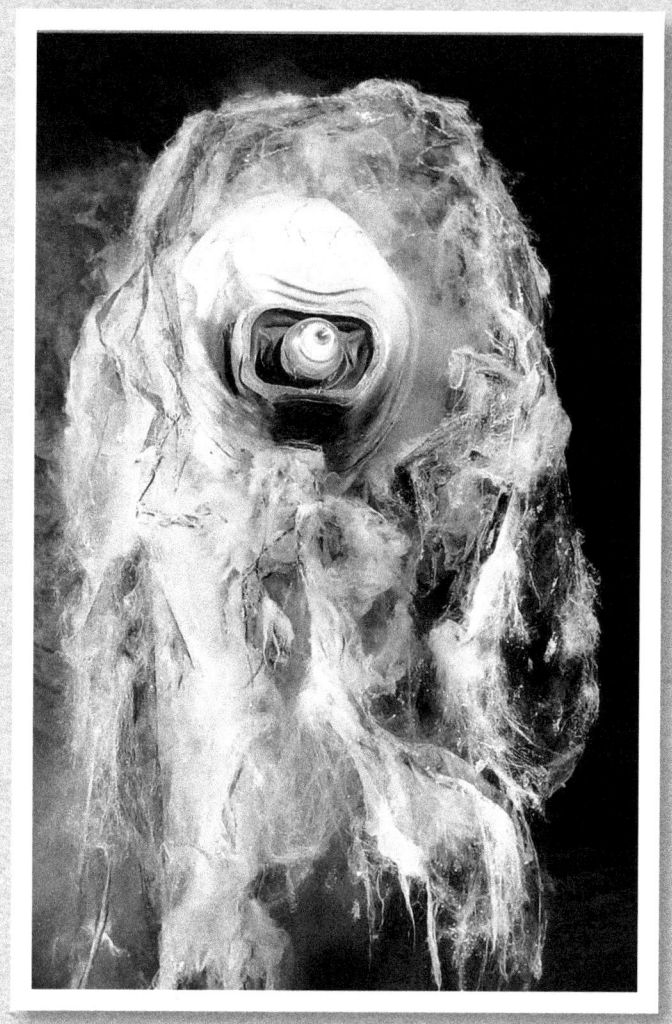

Ray Bradbury's cerebral script for **It Came From Outer Space** (1953) required a nonhuman alien. However, the prop hardly has any screen time, barely justifying the expense.

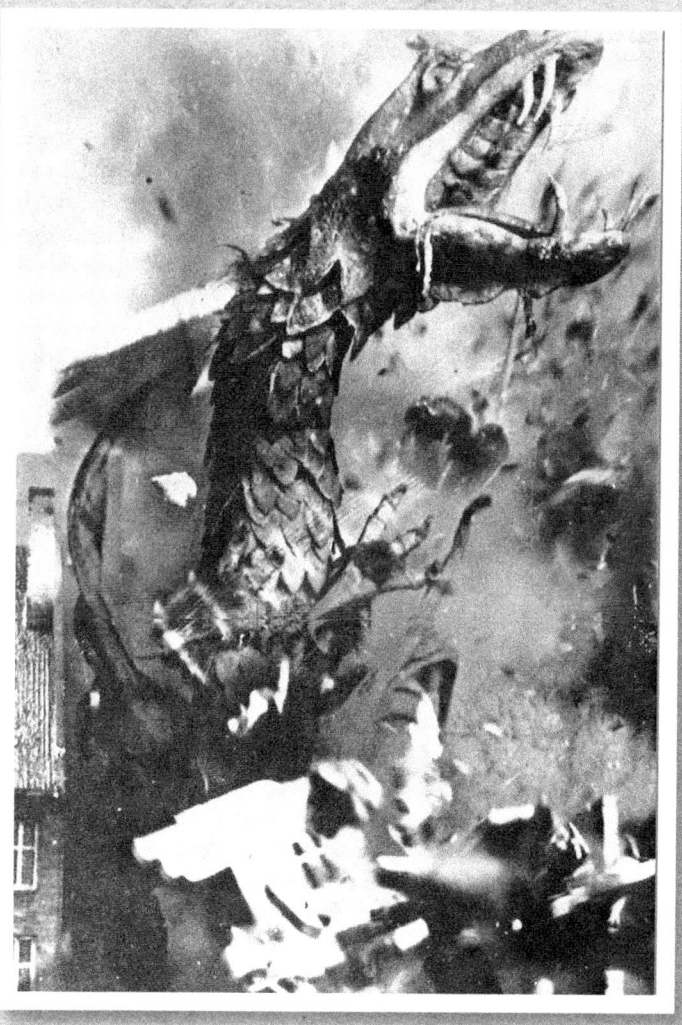

Danish monster **Reptilicus** (1961) demolishes a miniature thanks to a careful assist from photo retouching.

For **First Men 'In' The Moon** (1965) several artificial selenites—in this case, full-sized props—were used in scenes with the actors. L-R: Animator Ray Harryhausen, producer Charles H. Schneer, and Frank Wells (son of author H.G. Wells) study the cobwebbed aliens.

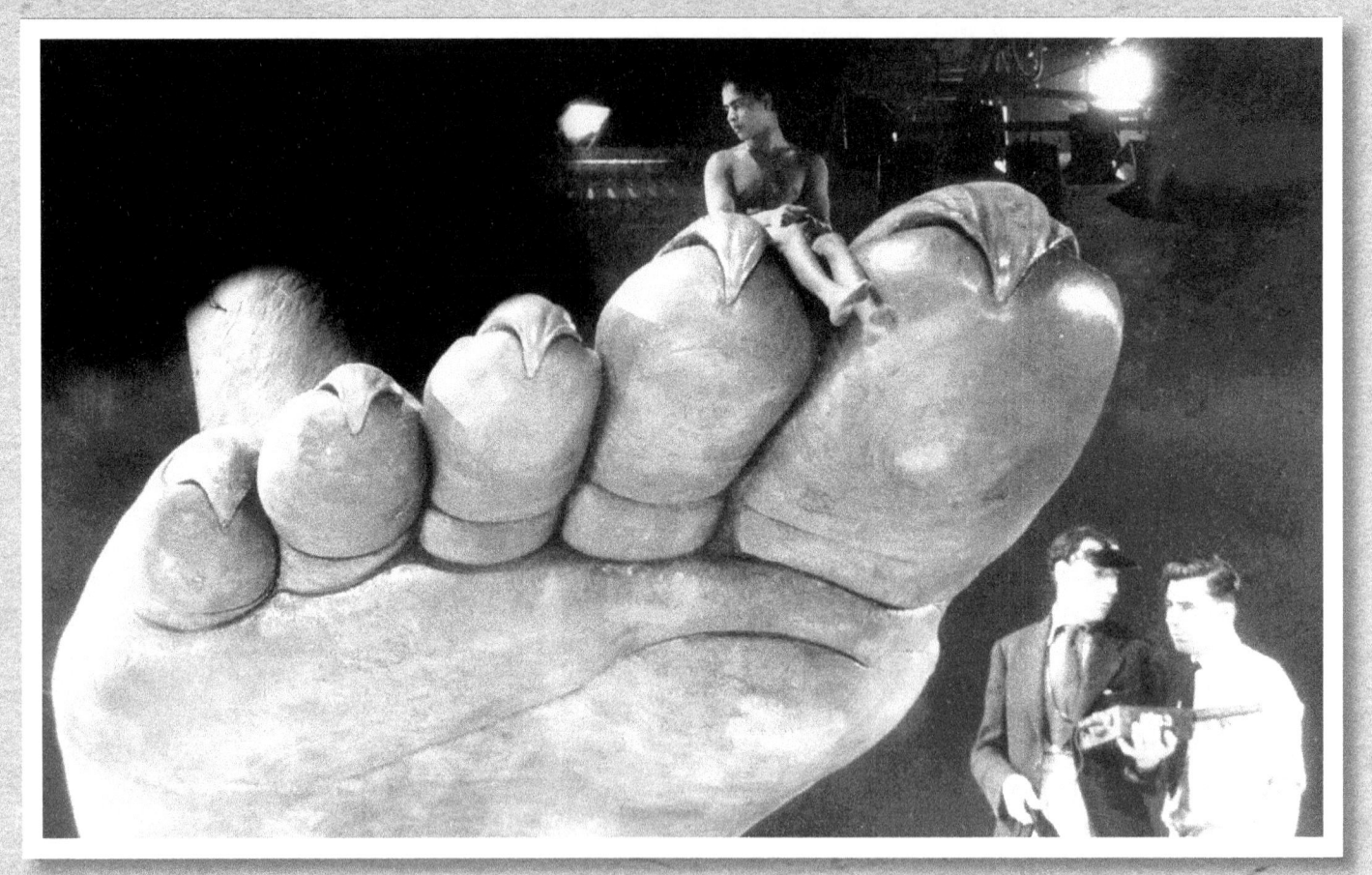

The Thief of Bagdad (1940) had to contend with potentially being squashed by the immense Genie. Sabu rests on an over-sized prop foot.

Above: Ray Harryhausen holds the marvelous Medusa's head made by Colin Arthur for **Clash of the Titans** (1981).

Below: **The Thing from Another World** (1951) starts by growing an army to conquer Earth. The "babies" were built by Marcel Delgado, and some could pulsate with a bulb syringe from off camera.

Dr. Cyclops (1940) threatens to boot Janice Logan from the scene.

192 · *Smoke and Mirrors – Special Visual Effects Before Computers*

For **The 7th Voyage of Sinbad** (1958) a full-sized prop wheel was filmed on location with the actor in front of it. That footage was used as a rear projected "Dynamation" shot by Ray Harryhausen that combined the live action background—and wheel—with his miniature crossbow.

Paul Balisdell's "cucumber monster" for **It Conquered the World** (1956), with glowing eyes (flashlights) and controls for the claws and face.

Mark Wolf operated the primary moves while cables moved the eyes and smile of a creature in **Saturday the 14th Strikes Back** (1988).

The bridge of the U.S.S. **Enterprise** was filled with an array of props, from earbuds to console controls, helping Gene Roddenberry's **Star Trek** (1966-1969) go where no man had gone before.

Frank Oz contemplates his upcoming performance puppeteering Yoda, a prop fabricated by Stuart Freeborn for **Star Wars: Episode V–The Empire Strikes Back** (1980).

Prop It Up • 193

Bruce, the mechanical shark in **Jaws** (1975), was engineered by Robert Mattey, who had worked on the squid for **20,000 Leagues Under the Sea** (1954) and mechanical animals for Disneyland. Many of the problems encountered stemmed from trying to shoot with the complex device in the ocean.

Roger Dicken built an ant prop for **When Dinosaurs Ruled the Earth** (1970). L-R: effects man Alan Bryce, assistant director Miguel Gil, cinematographer Dick Bush and director Val Guest.

In spite of a minimal budget, producer/fabricator Stephen Czerkas built a complete full-scale dinosaur—a polacanthus—for his indie classic, **Planet of Dinosaurs** (1977).

Stan and Ollie have run afoul—yet again—of tough guy Walter Long in **Going Bye-Bye** (1934).

Actor Giuseppe Tosi in makeup as a Cyclops in **The Titans** (1964; aka **My Son the Hero**).

194 · *Smoke and Mirrors – Special Visual Effects Before Computers*

Two of the fleet of vintage aircraft made for **Those Magnificent Men in Their Flying Machines** (1965) take flight.

The Killer Shrews (1959), directed by Ray Kellogg, former matte painter and head of the 20th Century-Fox Special Effects. A hand puppet was used in close-ups while dogs in costumes were used in long shots.

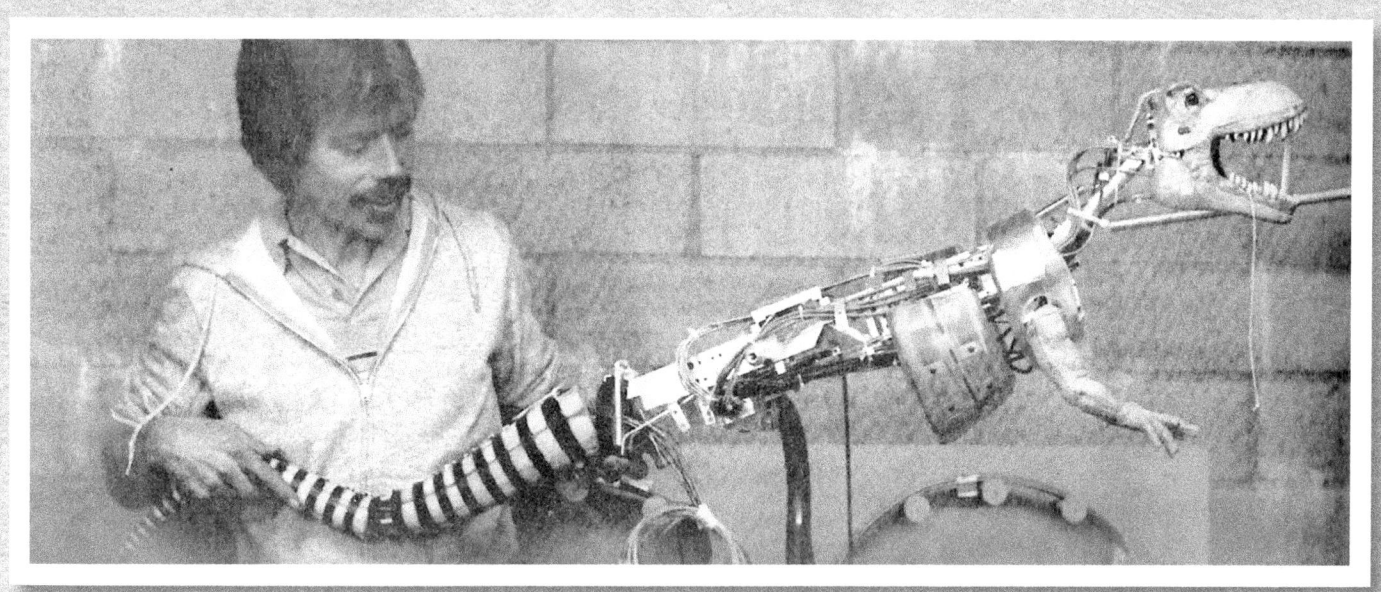

Doug Beswick poses beside his superbly engineered mechanical T-rex made for **My Science Project** (1985).

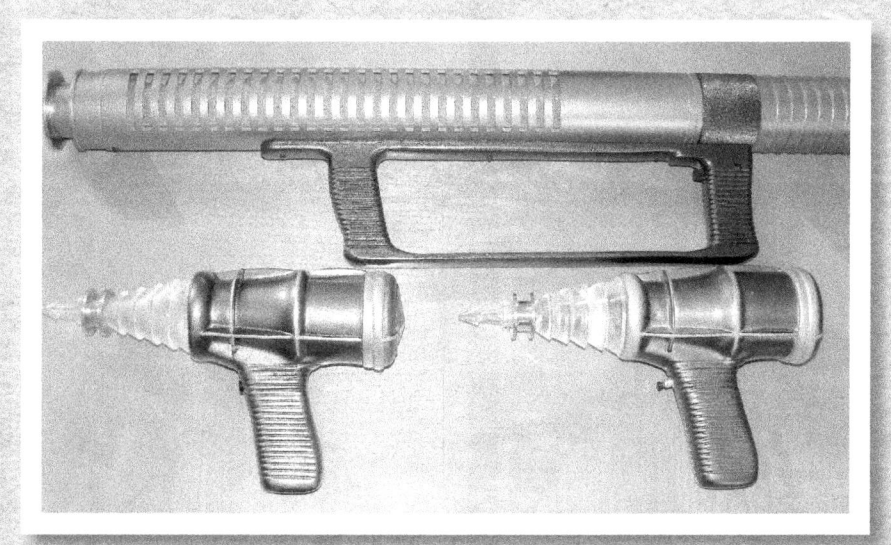

The kind of futuristic arsenal needed on **Forbidden Planet** (1956).

James Whitmore aims his bazooka at **Them!** (1954).

Prop It Up • 195

007 The Incredible (Prop) World of James Bond

The Bond films are one of the most prop-heavy series in movie history. Here's a sampling from two of the best, early Bond films when "gadgets" took center stage.

JAMES BOND IS BACK IN ACTION! "GOLDFINGER"

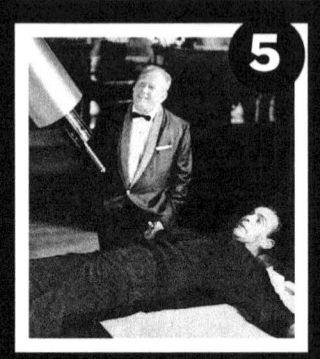

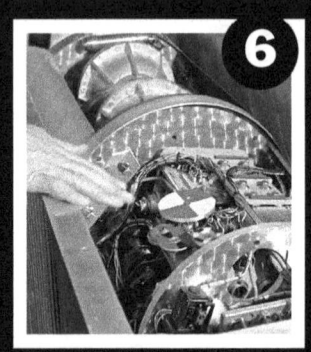

1. Oddjob (Harold Sakata) and his razor-brimmed bowler hat.

2. Goldfinger's golf ball: Slazenger 7.

3. Tilly Masterson (Tania Mallet) and her Armalite AR-7 Sniper Rifle.

4. During their golf game Bond bribes Goldfinger with a bar of gold recovered from the Nazi hoard at the bottom of Lake Toplitz in the Salzkammergut valued at £5000 (about $55,600.00 today).

5. "You are looking at an industrial laser, which emits an extraordinary light, not to be found in nature."

6. The bomb! "It's small, but particularly dirty."

HERE COMES THE BIGGEST BOND OF ALL! "THUNDERBALL"

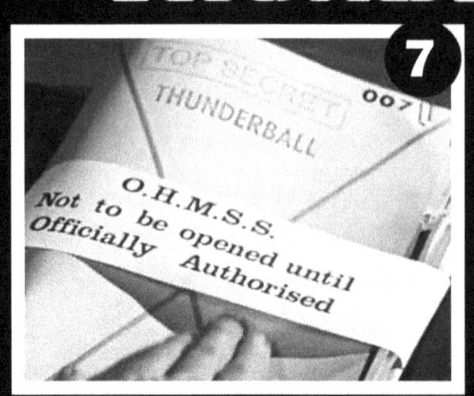

7. Printed documents and signs are prepared by the Prop Department.

8. To escape, Bond straps on a Bell Aerosystems Rocketbelt, developed in 1959. "It was very dangerous, said Production Designer Ken Adam. "You could only fly for 20 seconds. Then you ran out of fuel. You had better land before you ran out of fuel." Shot on February 19, 1965 at Chateau d'Anet, west of Paris. Close-ups of Sean Connery were intercut with long shots of stuntman Bill Suiter piloting the Rocketbelt.

9. A "re-breather" provided oxygen for several minutes. The scene was so convincing that one of the Royal Engineers called chief draftsman Peter Lamont and asked him how long it actually worked. Lamont replied, "As long as you can hold your breath." The engineer hung up.

10. SPECTRE's Fiona (Luciana Paluzzi) on a BSA A65 Lightning motorcycle. Filmed at the Silverstone racetrack in the UK. Motorcycle champion Bill Ivy (wearing a wig) fires two rockets from a working launching system fitted to the motorcycle, but the explosion was detonated remotely by stunt coordinator Bob Simmons (driving the pursuing car).

CHAPTER 5
REEL SCENES WITH REAL PEOPLE

These days it seems like everyone has heard the term "green screen" thanks to Blu-ray or DVD documentaries showing Earth's mightiest defenders, The Avengers, performing in front of large green backings. In fact, the use of colored screens, usually blue, had been a tool of special visual effects production for decades.

In the silent era, photochemical laboratory steps were devised to produce traveling matte composites; i.e., scenes combining live action added over separately filmed background scenes. Over time, such shots became lumped with simpler actions like dissolves and wipes, under the generic term "opticals," and were completed in post-production. Finishing such shots could take weeks for the most demanding scenes.

A different technique that appealed to directors and producers because they could see the finished composite the next day, was "process photography," also known as rear-projection ("RP"), which projected a large format transparency or a 35mm motion picture background onto a translucent screen. That was the key: the projected scene was visible through the screen! Actors could stand in front of the screen without throwing a shadow because they were not standing in the projector beam.

A skilled DP could balance the live action foreground with a rear-projected image and produce believable scenes. The desire to conveniently add actors to imaginary, distant or dangerous locales dates back to the beginning of cinema and many pioneers tinkered with rear projection. Norman Dawn experimented with rear projection but abandoned the process due to the limitations of filmstocks and equipment at the time.

Made possible by rear projection (and a giant prop hand), Albert Dekker as Dr. Thorkel, aka **Dr. Cyclops** *(1940), gets a grip on Dr. Bullfinch (Charles Halton), one of five people he has miniaturized in his experiments in the jungles of Peru. Directed by* **King Kong**'s *Ernest B. Schoedsack, this was the first science fiction film to be shot in three-strip Technicolor.*

Projection Composites • 197

Alfred Hitchcock staged numerous rear projection scenes on a sound stage. Right: Cary Grant takes cover from the attacking crop duster in **North by Northwest** (1959).

Sean Connery and "Tippi" Hedren in **Marnie** (1964). The projected image outside their train window was turned off during rehearsal.

Janet Leigh in **Psycho** (1960). The traffic out her rear window was a back projection plate.

In time, the limitations of rear-projection were overcome and the technique emerged as a standard production tool in the 1930s. As sound recording became the norm, studios were forced to use sound stages. Rear-projection provided all kinds of backgrounds free from the intrusion of real-world noise that plagued location shoots—no more airplanes flying overhead, wind or train whistles.

Producers could see composites at dailies the next day and make quick decisions about re-shoots. They appreciated RP's utility in saving the cost of taking "stars" on exotic locations or risking them in dangerous sequences, and a few gifted technicians like Farciot Eduart made process work a career speciality, producing some astonishingly convincing, award-winning composites.

Some small scale RP was used in Fritz Lang's **Metropolis** (1927) to simulate futuristic telephones with viewscreens.

198 · *Smoke and Mirrors – Special Visual Effects Before Computers*

Lucy, Ricky, Fred and Ethel head to California, courtesy of a background projected behind them. **I Love Lucy** *would use RP from time to time in other episodes.*

Jennifer Jones on a process stage for **Love Is a Many-Splendored Thing** *(1955), clearly demonstrating of a full scale rear projection setup.*

Fay Wray watches a clash of the titans, as **King Kong** *(1933) battles his nemesis, a snarling, hissing T-rex; the animation was shot first and then rear-projected.*

By their very nature RP set-ups relied on the transmission of light through the screen, meaning it necessarily lost some of its brilliance. The early screens were unsatisfactory because they didn't reproduce rich blacks and tended to have "hot spots" in the center of the screen while the edges had "fall-off" (vignetting around the edges). Trying to control these effects with filters further reduced the amount of light being transmitted through the screens, washing out the background.

The first rear projection done at RKO was for *King Kong* (1933), when Fay Wray was perched in a tree and watching helplessly as the monstrous Tyrannosaurus rex comes for her. The scenes were also a first for another reason; prior to this, RP screens had been made of sandblasted glass, which wasn't a great solution as they were susceptible to hot spots. Worse, this type of large glass was fragile and could easily shatter; in fact, such breakage caused serious injuries at other studios.

The industry was aware of the potential hazard to crew and performers, so technical and safety issues relating to a better type of screen material drove invention.

Fortunately for Willis O'Brien ("OBie") and producer Merian C. Cooper and company, the head of the RKO paint department, Sidney Saunders, developed an innovative, unbreakable, cellulose-acetate screen that eliminated the risks of glass. The acetate screens could also be several feet larger than the glass screens. Even better, from a photographic viewpoint, the notorious hot-spots were reduced by half while overall light transmission was bumped up, producing a brighter, more realistic image with a broader tonal range. A higher-quality background made it easier for a skilled cinematographer to better match the foreground set lighting to the background image.

It took OBie three days to work out the specifics and shoot the required takes, but the footage of Fay Wray cowering was good enough to use in the demo that sold "The 8th Wonder of the World" to RKO executives in New York—and, in fact, the shots were good enough to be included in the finished film.

At the 6th Academy Awards, March 16, 1934, Saunders would share a special award with Fox Film Company technicians and Fred Jackman at Warner Brothers for contributing to "the development and effective use of the translucent cellulose screen in composite photography."

King Kong *(1933): The stegosaurus was animated on tabletops with a painted backing and glass mattes of jungle foliage, then that footage was composited with smoke elements of the gas bombs and a foreground painting, which was necessary to simulate the appropriate distance from the sailors. The final composite was rear projected behind the actors. However, on the first take of the sailors firing at the charging dinosaur, blanks from their guns emitted sufficient debris to shred parts of the screen! Needless to say, the powder loads were changed before the next take.*

A basic RP set-up utilized a special 35mm background projector using a 220 volt, 3 phase AC (alternating current) interlock motor. It had no "flicker blade" shutter (as did movie theater projectors) that would interrupt the projected image and decrease the dark interval between frames. Process projectors have camera-type shutters and pin-registered movements that project individual frames; both the projector and camera are electrically-synced so that both sets of shutters are open or closed at the same time. This can look like flickering to the naked eye but in actuality, each frame is projected for the duration the camera shutter is open, providing maximum exposure.

The actual background footage (the "plate"), filmed for the specific production or derived from a stock footage library, was specially prepared on print stock with Bell and Howell perforations.

A "stationary" plate must be perfectly registered to eliminate the unsteadiness that would be evident when filmed with the live action. On the other hand, such precision was unnecessary for "traveling" plates because motion was built-into the scene. Stationary plates would be produced using a pin-registered, camera-style movement, step-printer while a standard continuous printer could be used to generate the traveling plates. Traveling plates, such as a location highway background, could often have naturally-occurring bumps that would draw attention to the artificiality of the scene if the camera remained static; such camera motion required a keen eye and light touch to sell the integration of foreground and background.

The projector and camera lenses were aligned along a single axis to guarantee the brightest image possible for the background; off-center deviation would result in uneven illumination. A formula I used to calculate the throw distance for the projector: Lens Focal Length x Screen Width = Distance (for the projector to fill the screen). Thus, a 5-inch lens to fill a 20-foot screen would need 100 feet of throw distance. If there wasn't sufficient room, a mirror could bounce the beam onto the screen, though this caused 10% loss in light intensity. The camera was positioned to record the live action component usually about one-half the projection distance from the screen.

Filming process set-ups became a blend of art and science, and best results were achieved when camera angles, scene lighting, perspective, spatial relationships and tonal values were consistent. Every cinematographer kept camera reports detailing the time of day, direction of sun, the angle of camera tilt, lens height, focal length, f/stop, and type of weather on location.

The live lizard is a rear projected background in front of which the cave people react to the known actions of the reptile. **One Million B.C.** *(1940) was the proverbial gift that kept on giving as its prehistoric scenes were licensed again and again.*

Longer focal length lenses were preferred, with a 6-inch lens on the projector and a 3-inch lens on the camera a common combination (using shorter focal length lenses would produce more noticeable hot-spots when the camera was moved closer to the screen). If the plate perspective was off, the camera could be pulled further back from the screen.

The quality of process shots was advanced when Kodak introduced a super-sensitive panchromatic film stock in 1928 (and won an Academy Science-Technical Award of Merit in 1931). This stock allowed cinematographers to slightly over-expose the background plates by one f/stop, creating a broader spectrum of tones than the earlier orthochromatic stocks, which tended to produce washed-out images. Additionally, more powerful projection lamps increased the illumination levels across the screen, somewhat compensating for the loss of light as it passed through the screen.

The live action would be staged as close to the screen as reasonable given the needs of the scene so the depth of field would keep both planes—"reel" and real—in focus. So-called "spill" light (accidental light falling on the screen and washing it out), would be controlled by flags on the set and barndoors and scrims on the lights.

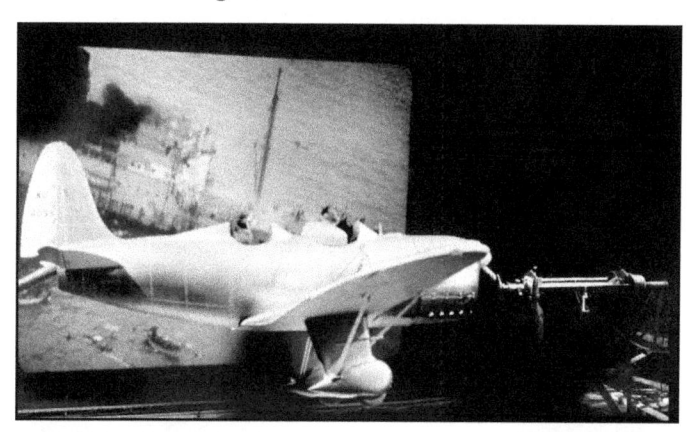

Clockwise, from upper left:

*The climax of **Casablanca** (1942) features a stationary plate, of a plane—a miniature supervised by Larry Butler—taking off.*

*Newsreel cameraman Clark Gable in **Too Hot to Handle** (1938).*

*A specially posed photo—no such scene appears in the movie itself—from **The Beast From 20,000 Fathoms** (1953). Ray Harryhausen had animated the beast in advance to provide this scene as an RP background.*

*Farciot Edouart (pronounced FAR-see-oh ED-oo-art), whom Leonard Maltin described as "The master of process-screen photography." Edouart worked on approximately 350 films, the last being **Rosemary's Baby** (1968).*

*A volcano, threatens to erupt in **Two Lost Worlds** (1950), thanks to a stock shot from **One Million B.C.** (1940). Directed by film pioneer Norman Dawn, oddly, his production has no matte paintings by him.*

Projection Composites • 201

*Above: George Reeves wears a hidden harness that suspends him in front of an RP screen for **Superman and the Mole Men** (1951), which was turned into two-episodes for **The Adventures of Superman** (1951), **The Unknown People**.*

Left: In the 1960s, Batman and Robin race in the bat boat prop in front of a rear-projected traveling background, shot from a speedboat. A little water spray from the floor effects technician helped the illusion.

*Below: In **Way Out West** (1937) Oliver Hardy and Stan Laurel perform in front of a rear-projected background plate of a wild west town.*

*Sarah Connor (Linda Hamilton) runs from the back-projected exploding tanker truck driven by **The Terminator** (1984). Miniatures supervised by Gene Warren, Jr., pyrotechnics by Joe Viskocil, and process projection handled by Austin McKinney.*

*Stuntmen in dinosaur suits built by Ellis Burman for **Unknown Island** (1948) do their best but come off like Toho's lesser efforts.*

202 · *Smoke and Mirrors – Special Visual Effects Before Computers*

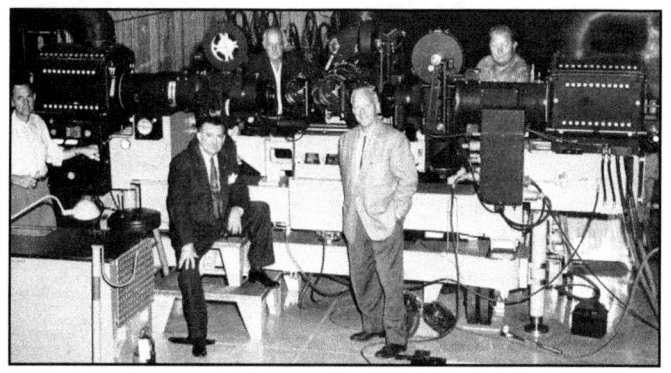

Farciot Edouart, second from left, with the Paramount triple-head background projector.

A. Arnold "Buddy" Gillespie (left) and director Mervyn LeRoy in front of MGM's unique straight ahead triple-head Process Projector.

*RP provides the view through the train windows for **My Little Chickadee** (1940). Spanky McFarland is befuddled as W.C. Fields commandeers the youngster's slingshot.*

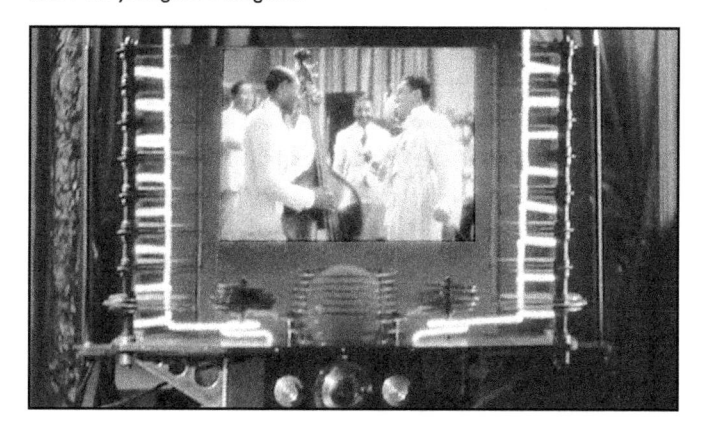

*RP wasn't always about making a large presence in a shot. For **International House** (1933), RP was used to simulate a TV broadcast starring Cab Calloway singing about "That Funny Reefer Man."*

Both ***Liliom*** (1930) and the futuristic musical ***Just Imagine*** (1930), for which Ralph Hammeras received an Oscar® nomination for Art Direction, were honored with the first Class II Academy Scientific and Technical Award on November 10, 1931 "for effective use of synchro-projection composite photography."

The master of process screen composites was Farciot Edouart, ASC, who spent most of his career at Paramount—until they closed his department and unceremoniously ordered him off the lot. [1] He won a 'Special Award' Oscar® for visual effects for ***Spawn of the North*** (1939), the first time for such an award. He eventually had eight Oscar®-nominations for films including ***Dr. Cyclops*** (1940). In 1939, referring to Farciot's noteworthy work at Paramount, *The Journal of the Society of Motion Picture Engineers* proclaimed:

"During the past year a special triple-head projection mechanism has been in use at the Paramount Studio for transparency process work. It involved projection of three separate background positives, through three separate projection heads, superimposing the images upon a single screen to form a single registered image of greater size and brightness than would otherwise be possible." [2]

Byron Haskin became head of the special-effects department at Warners in 1937. Faced with the same needs as Edouart at Paramount, he, too, developed a triple-head background projector which earned him a Technical Achievement Award at the 1939 Academy Awards. Haskin received Oscar® nominations for his special effects for ***The Private Lives of Elizabeth and Essex*** (1939), ***The Sea Hawk*** (1940), ***The Sea Wolf*** (1941), and ***Desperate Journey*** (1942) but is probably best-remembered today as the director of George Pal's ***War of the Worlds*** (1953).

*RP provides the background for one of the best "entrances" of a hero in any movie, as the camera pushes in to introduce the Ringo Kid in John Ford's **Stagecoach** (1939). This shot is slightly controversial: as the camera moves in, the focus lags behind and the shot is briefly out-of-focus, only to sharpen up again as the camera comes to a stop. A goof by the focus puller? Or an intentional stylistic choice by director John Ford to further emphasize the first major appearance of soon-to-be superstar John Wayne? You decide...*

Projection Composites • 203

Rear Screen Projection...

Basil Rathbone as Sherlock Holmes and Nigel Bruce as Dr. Watson.

Above, top to bottom:

Anne Francis as **Honey West** (TV series, 1965).
Burt Lancaster and Barbara Stanwyck, **Sorry, Wrong Number** (1948).
Charles McGraw in **The Bridges at Toko-Ri** (1954).
Clint Eastwood in **Tarantula** (1955).

L-R: Milton Berle, Ethel Merman, Jonthan Winters, Dorothy Provine, Terry-Thomas, Dick Shawn, and Eddie "Rochester" Anderson in Stanley Kramer's **It's a Mad, Mad, Mad, Mad World** (1963).

...Right Outside the Window

Sean Connery in **Dr. No** (1962).

Sean Connery, Daniela Bianchi, and Robert Shaw in **From Russia With Love** (1963).

Rik Van Nutter and Sean Connery in **Thunderball** (1965).

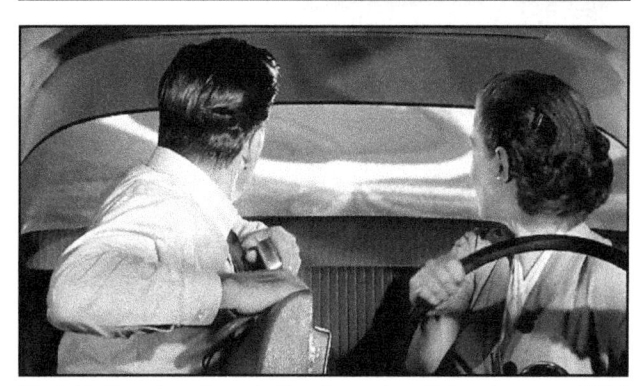

Hugh Marlowe, Joan Taylor in **Earth vs. the Flying Saucers** (1956).

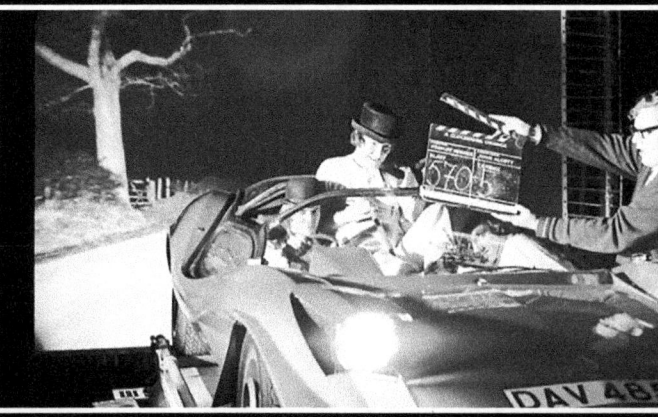

For **A Clockwork Orange** (1971), perfectionist Stanley Kubrick knew when to use RP.

Projection Composites • 205

Front Projection

Another person who carved out a niche with process projection was William Hansard, Sr., starting in the 1930s, later joined by his son, William "Bill" Hansard, Jr., who also specialized in composite photography. Bill Hansard was at the forefront of an advancement in process composites known as "Front Axial Projection," or more commonly as Front Projection.

This technique made use of a highly-reflective screen manufactured by the 3M Corporation, "Scotchlite," which was originally developed to provide improved nighttime visibility of traffic signs and on clothing of people in hazardous conditions—construction workers, firefighters, miners, and oil and gas workers.

The screen was covered with thousands of glass beads that returned a beam of light projected onto them directly back at the light source with no discernible light loss.

A projector positioned at a 45° angle to the camera projected the background through a beam-splitter (a front-silvered, optically clear mirror) and the composite image could be seen through the camera. Because of the unique intensity of the illumination being bounced back to the camera, the background was extremely bright, which gave the cinematographer greater latitude in lighting the live action and set without unduly fearing he would wash out the screen.

Front projection was invented by Philip V. Palmquist while working at the 3M Corporation and he received a patent on the technology. In 1968, the Academy recognized him and his associates with a Scientific or Technical Award (Class I) that read, "To PHILIP V. PALMQUIST of Minnesota Mining and Manufacturing Co., to DR. HERBERT MEYER of the Motion Picture and Television Research Center, and to CHARLES D. STAFFELL of the Rank Organization for the development of a successful embodiment of the reflex background projection system for composite cinematography." (3)

Legendary aviation manufacturer/inventor/investor Sherman Fairchild bought up front projection patents filed by other experimenters and a 1964 *New York Times* article called "Lighting Systems: Front Projection Unit For Backgrounds" described what he was bringing to the market:

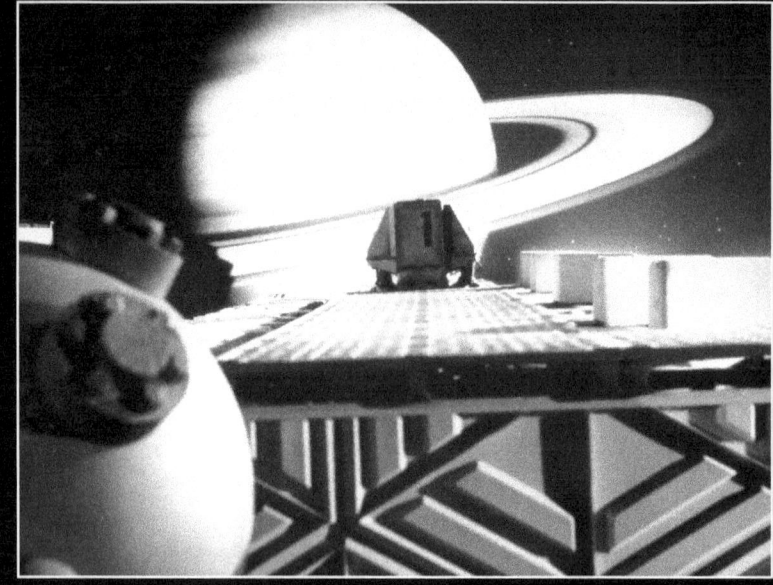

*Douglas Trumbull's **Silent Running** (1972) makes good use of front projection's strengths and also showed boldness in how he approached the robotic drones, hiring physically-challenged performers to work inside the props.*

*Roger Dicken's dinosaur props enliven the prehistoric plate for **The Land That Time Forgot** (1975) made by Amicus Productions in the UK. A large screen area, a strength of front projection, helps give the scene scope.*

*Another film from Amicus, **At the Earth's Core** (1976), used front projection to depict the "Iron Mole" drilling machine—a miniature—starting its journey to the center of the earth.*

"A portrait lighting system that included a background scene projected from a slide at the camera position was demonstrated at the recent photographic product show of the seventy-third annual convention of the Professional Photographers of America.

"Hitherto, the usual practice has been to project the background from the rear on a translucent screen. Named the Front Projection Background System, it was introduced by the Front Projection Corporation, a company recently founded by Sherman Fairchild, the aerial camera pioneer.

"The design embraces a combination camera and projector, and includes a new tungsten-strobe light source and a background screen with a new reflective surface. In the demonstrations, which were among the most popular at the show, subject and projected background were photographed simultaneously on Polacolor film by means of a 45° mirror beam splitter.

"Although the image of the projected background also appeared unavoidably on the subject, it could not be seen because the so-called RetroReflex Screen was 900 times more directional and reflective than the brightest parts of the subject.

"Since the camera exposure is determined by the screen brightness, any image on the subject would be vastly underexposed, hence eliminated." (3)

Forbidden Planet (1956) was the first to use front projection— the stars were Scotchlite dots painted on a masonite cyclorama. The Toho film *Matango: Attack of the Mushroom People* (1963) used painted surfaces for the yacht scenes because beaded screens weren't yet available.

A few years later, Dennis Muren—who would eventually win eight Oscars® for Visual Effects— cleverly adapted Scotchlite made for street signs, to provide front-projected backgrounds for stop-motion set-ups in his indie classic *Equinox* (1970).

The technique was used in several British productions including *The Battle of Britain* (1969), *On Her Majesty's Secret Service* (1969), *The Assassination Bureau* (1969), *The Land that Time Forgot* (1975) and *Warlords of Atlantis* (1978). In the U.S., Doug Trumbull innovated by using front-projection for his cautionary science fiction classic, *Silent Running* (1972).

In 1969 Sherman Fairchild announced he was "looking for the best special effects man in the movie industry to head the West Coast operations *[of his company]*, Front Projection." (4) However, nothing ever seemed to develop further from his lofty goals.

A Different Type of Front Projection *in*
THE BEAST FROM 20,000 FATHOMS

The diagram below shows the basic front projection setup for the lighthouse sequence. Close inspection reveals the "freeze-frame" nature of the distant water that is part of the static photo backdrop. In April, 1995 Ray Harryhausen told Mike Hankin, author of *Ray Harryhausen-Master of the Majicks*, "We used front projection for the lion in the cage in *Mighty Joe Young*. Sometimes you can't get a big enough picture with rear projection because you need a great deal of space behind the screen to get a proper throw. With the limited space I had, I decided to put white cardboard at the front of the set and project onto it. It was really more of an economical reason, rather than any technical innovation. I would have needed such a large projected background because of the size of the animation model, and necessity is the mother of invention. Plus, one of the great advantages of front projection is that the definition is much sharper since the projected image doesn't pass through a translucent screen."

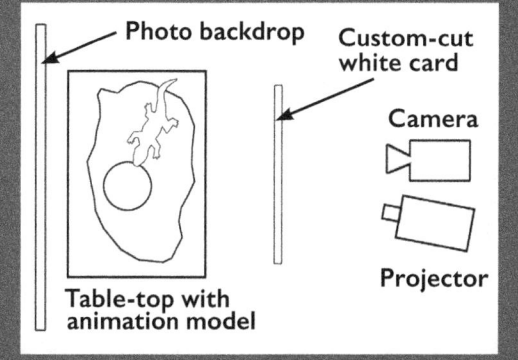

Undoubtedly, the most acclaimed use of front projection was in Stanley Kubrick's *2001: A Space Odyssey* (1968) which remains a spectacular testimony to the advantages of the technique. Kubrick was a demanding taskmaster who expected the best results possible, so he realized the epic scope that he wanted could never be accomplished with the limitations of rear projection. Additionally, a blue screen traveling matte process would be problematic given the complexity of successfully compositing the ape men with location backgrounds. However, no one had ever done front projection on the scale he was contemplating.

Undaunted, Kubrick wisely turned to M-G-M Special Effects Supervisor Tom Howard, a well-regarded optical expert, to design and construct a huge, one-of-its-kind 8x10 transparency projector system based around the most powerful water-cooled arc available, for the brightest light source possible. Heat-resistant glasses prevented the magenta layer of emulsion from peeling off a transparency. When running, the heat was so intense that the rear condensers cracked several times when someone opened the door of the sound stage and incoming cooler air hit the system.

As was often the case with ordinary rear projection, the projector was only turned on during a take to limit possible damage to the primary transparency. During light-balancing on the set, a spare transparency from the location filming was used rather than risk a selected image. They had to take special precautions to avoid dust or dirt on the transparency, which would become noticeable when magnified on the Scotchlite screen. The operator wore clean editing gloves and loaded the backgrounds under NASA-like "Clean Room" protocols, and to avoid fogging the mirror, he wore a surgical mask. In the 1970s and 1980s, when doing mirror shot composites, I used a special cleaner from Kiem Optical to eliminate dust, hairs and fingerprints.

The basic configuration was a heavy steel rig with micrometer adjustments to perfectly align the projector at a right angle to the camera. The projected image was bounced off an optically perfect 36-inch-wide front-silvered mirror positioned about eight inches in front of the camera lens. The camera photographed through the mirror, which bounced the transparency background onto the distant Scotchlite screen and the special beading on it directed the light directly back to the camera. Usually, the camera was fitted with a

208 · *Smoke and Mirrors – Special Visual Effects Before Computers*

75mm lens while the projector had a 14-inch lens. Wider shots typically used a 50mm lens on the camera and to fill in the scene, foreground elements such as boulders were placed to hide the screen cut-off. A nodal head made it possible for the camera to pan across the mirror (although there are no such panning shots in the sequence).

Stanley Kubrick described the shooting of the distant African locations and the way they matched the lighting on the sound stages in England: "The ["*Dawn of Man*"] sequence was especially well-suited to the use of front-projection because all of the backgrounds were desert scenes in which nothing had to move," said Kubrick. "Our location still photographers were able to wait for just the right moment and shoot a scene in light that would remain exactly that way for perhaps only five minutes out of a whole day. But on the stage we could shoot the sequence at our own pace in constant light of the type you could never maintain on location, no matter how much money you might spend.

"An enormous amount of basic light was needed to produce the 'cloudy bright' simulated daylight illumination for the foreground areas in 'The Dawn of Man' sequence, and this was provided by covering almost the entire ceiling of the sound stage with a total of 1500 RFL-2 lamps.

"Each of these lamps had its own individual switch so that we could maintain very delicate control of the foreground lighting," Kubrick pointed out. "This was necessary not only in order to match it with the background lighting, but also because the height of the set varied. The individual switches made it possible to turn off any one light all by itself and to literally shape the light to the contours of the set. We could do this very, very quickly and with the greatest flexibility."

While Brute arcs with straw-colored gels in front of them were used to provide a hint of modeling and relieve the basically flat effect, no attempt was made to create a strong point source suggesting direct sunlight. "There's simply no really effective way to realistically simulate a single light source when you're shooting such a huge area in a high lighting key," Kubrick explained, "but if you're shooting for an effect of cloudy weather or spotty sunlight, you can match it perfectly to the background. And

Projection Composites • 209

that kind of lighting looks better anyway, in my opinion, than full, direct, sunlight." (5)

Because of the brilliant illumination afforded by the high-reflectance of the screen, the night sequences were photographed as standard day-for-night exteriors; that is, they were shot two stops under-exposed and filmed through a light blue filter.

The front projection light source gave an unexpected bonus to a scene with a big cat. When the animal looks into the camera, its eyes glow eerily! Anyone driving down a country lane and encountering an animal at night has seen the same effect as the retinas in their eyes bounce back light from the car's headlights.

210 · *Smoke and Mirrors – Special Visual Effects Before Computers*

*After **2001**, Tom Howard built a projector to run 65mm horizontally, like VistaVision. The system premiered with **Where Eagles Dare** (1969), notably in the fight atop an Austrian cable-car.*

*Robert Shaw dangles from the Goodyear blimp before Bill Hansard's front projection screen in John Frankenheimer's film **Black Sunday** (1977).*

Superman-The Movie (1978) opens on the doomed planet Krypton, where Jor-el (Marlon Brando) and Lara (Susannah York) are dressed in costumes made of Scotchlite. Projecting white light instead of a film image caused the fabric to glow.

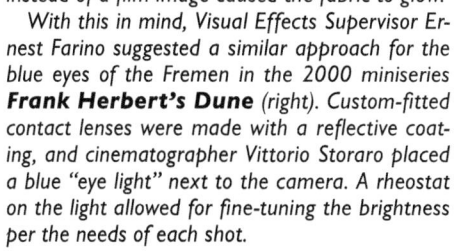

With this in mind, Visual Effects Supervisor Ernest Farino suggested a similar approach for the blue eyes of the Fremen in the 2000 miniseries **Frank Herbert's Dune** (right). Custom-fitted contact lenses were made with a reflective coating, and cinematographer Vittorio Storaro placed a blue "eye light" next to the camera. A rheostat on the light allowed for fine-tuning the brightness per the needs of each shot.

*Christopher Reeve and Margot Kidder aboard the Zoptic platform for **Superman-The Movie** (1978).*

*Harrowing action atop a train trestle for **Stand by Me** (1986), staged safely on the Introvision stages in Hollywood.*

Back in the U.S., William Hansard did front projection for the action thriller **Black Sunday** (1977): "Under the direction of art director Walter Tyler, who did most of Cecil B. DeMille's movies, and myself, one unit was responsible for getting aerial plates and shots of police helicopters and the [Goodyear] blimp. Guided by the logic and reasoning of [producer] Bob Rosen, we got the job done. The stuntmen were brilliant, hanging from helicopters and walking on the blimp over Miami as they doubled for Robert Shaw. We returned to Hollywood and put the real Robert Shaw, one of the most cooperative actors I've worked with, on a 50-foot mock-up blimp built by Walter Tyler. The most brilliant but still economical way of filming Robert Shaw was the front projection system. Blue screen could not be used because the blue in the blimp's tail would make it show up transparent. But there is virtually no limit to what you can do with front projection. If a film calls for big screen work, highlighting, thrift and sharpness, then front projection is the answer." (6)

At about that same time Zoran Perisic devised a new system he dubbed "Zoptic," which was used to simulate the Man of Steel flying for **Superman-The Movie** (1978). The system slaved matching zoom lenses on a camera and projector to zoom in and out simultaneously; as the projection lens zoomed in, a smaller image was projected onto the screen but because the camera was proportionately matching the zoom, the background plate appeared unchanged. However, to the camera it looked like Christopher Reeve was 'flying' towards camera!

The process was also used in **Superman 2** (1980), **Superman 3** (1983), **Deal of the Century** (1983), **Return to Oz** (1985), and the TV series **The Greatest American Hero** (1981). Perisic received an Oscar® and a BAFTA Award (shared with Les Bowie, Colin Chilvers, Denys Coop, Roy Field, Derek Meddings and Wally Veevers) for his work on **Superman-The Movie**, as well as a Scientific and Engineering Award in 1988 from the Academy for "the Zoptic dual-zoom front projection system for visual effects photography.

Projection Composites • 211

In an era when the major studios had divested themselves of their in-house process operations, a company called Introvision set-up shop in Hollywood to provide front-projection process shots. Starting with **Outland** (1981), they provided composites for **Stand by Me** (1986), **Driving Miss Daisy** (1989), **Under Siege** (1992), **Army of Darkness** (1992), **The Fugitive** (1993) and many others.

In the *Los Angeles Times* in 1991, John Milius, director of **Flight of the Intruder**, explained Introvision: "'Basically, the technique lets you create a foreground and a middle ground in front of a background that you've already shot. You can shoot miniature explosions and then put real people in front.'

"'Introvision is best used for shots that would otherwise put the actors in a lot of jeopardy,' said film director John Avildsen, who used the process to make Ralph Macchio appear to scale down a precarious cliff in **Karate Kid III**. 'I think they've built the best mousetrap. Imagination is the only limitation.'

"One of the staunchest supporters of Introvision is production designer Bill Kenny, who used the process on the big-budget Sylvester Stallone films **Rambo III** and **Lock Up**. 'At first, I had a hard time convincing Stallone to use Introvision because he doesn't like opticals,' Kenny said. 'But I told him, 'Listen, we can do these exotic action films and you'll never have to leave Hollywood again.' Director Sam Raimi placed Liam Neeson and Colin Friels nearly 1,000 feet up a steel skyscraper for the climactic fight sequence in **Darkman**. In truth, Raimi's scarred hero and the villain were battling it out among steel girders on the sound stage, with a miniature skyscraper serving as the background shot.

"'I look at it as putting actors in a front projection sandwich,' Raimi said, 'which is different than the normal front projection system where the actor is always in the foreground of the background (shot). Introvision creates a world that allows the actors to seemingly interact with their artificial surroundings.'

"Introvision's owner *[Tom Naud]* flatly rejected an Academy Award presented to his company for technical achievement in 1988 because he said the Academy of Motion Picture Arts and Sciences failed to grasp his unique system and its potential. He bristled at their definition of his work as 'a refined application of front projection to film.'

"'When we started out we had to prove ourselves over and over again,' visual-effects director William Mesa said. "And they were ready to jump on us for any little mistake. Nobody wanted to take a chance on us because nobody wanted to take the fall if it didn't work.'" (7)

As the film industry matured, so did its use of projection composites until they were ubiquitous across all genres. The latest advance can be seen in **The Mandalorian**, which utilized ILM's "Stagecraft," a 20' high by 180' LED video wall that provided virtual backgrounds and lighting. As time marches on we can be sure of one thing: filmmakers will embrace some form of real-time compositing!

Introvision visual effects director Bill Mesa.

Harrison Ford leaps to saftey in **The Fugitive** *(1993)]*

Bill Mesa with the miniatire train for **The Fugitive**.

Jeff Bridges and the ledge added to the scene in **Fearless** *(1993).*

SCRAPBOOK

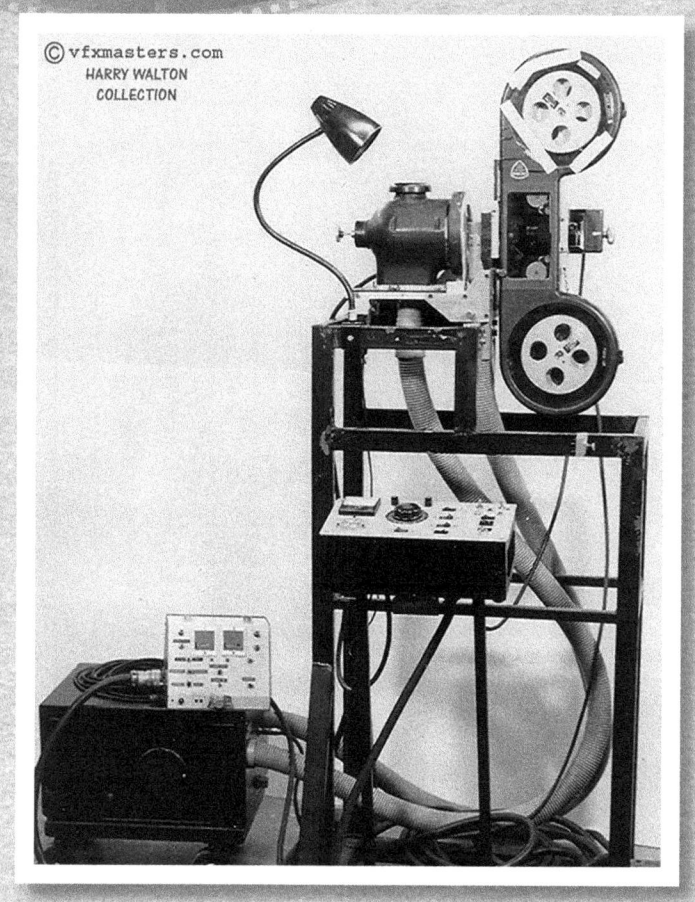

Process projector used for the stop-motion effects in **Caveman** (1980).

20 Million Miles to Earth (1957) used RP when Pepe (Bart Bradley) retrieved a container from a crashed spaceship.

Taking a ride in the underground Krell tunnel on Altair IV, othewrise known as **Forbidden Planet** (1956).

Chico, Groucho and Harpo Marx enjoy **A Day at the Races** (1937) without having to leave the studio.

Projection Composites • 213

If **The Incredible Shrinking Man** did it well, some shots in **Earth vs. the Flying Saucers** (1956) show how **not** to do RP. Donald Curtis, Hugh Marlowe and Joan Taylor try to make running on a treadmill look convincing.

The rat-bat-spider-crab for **The Angry Red Planet** (1959) was designed and filmed by Norman Mauer. The marionette footage was rear projected while a full-sized prop claw enhanced the interaction.

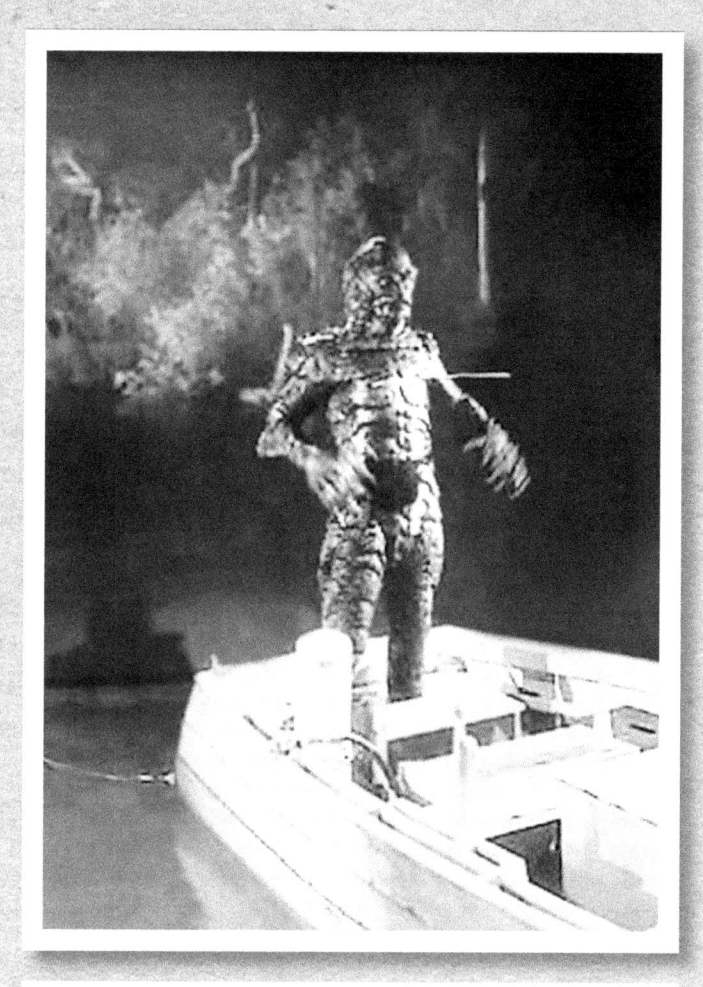

Top, left: In T**he Creature Walks Among Us** (1956), close angles of the Gill Man being struck by tranquilizing spears were conveniently filmed against an RP background.

Top, right: A double-RP scene for **Earth vs the Flying Saucers** (1956). The saucer had an RP background for the animation and that footage was used as an RP plate with the live action plane mock-up.

Right, middle and bottom: Bert I. Gordon occasionally abandoned split screens and traveling mattes in favor of RP. For **The Beginning of the End** (1957) footage of marauding locusts was used to menace soldiers.

Above: The Holland Tunnel miniature for **The Deadly Mantis** (1957) provided several angles for RP backgrounds.

Projection Composites • 215

Edwin Hammeras, Ralph's brother, filmed the water tank/rear projection composites for Hitchcock's **Lifeboat** (1944) but did not receive credit.

In preparation for another scene in **Lifeboat**, Talulah Bankhead seems startled to be wetted down.

RP spares the cast from a vortex in **Saga of the Viking Women and their Voyage to the Waters of the Great Sea Serpent** (1958).

A stage hand helps rock the boat in **Son of Kong** (1933).

216 · *Smoke and Mirrors - Special Visual Effects Before Computers*

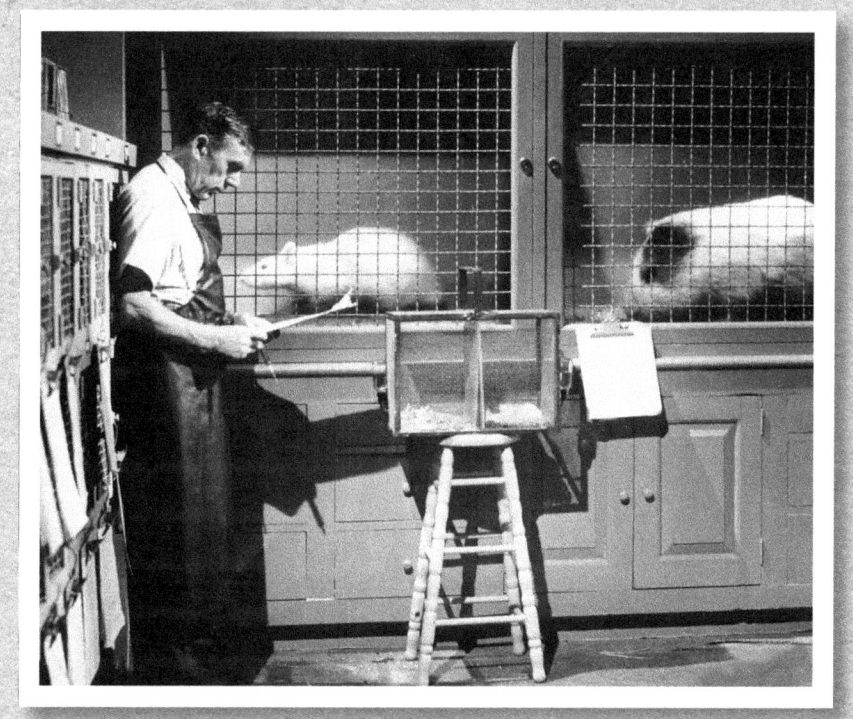

In **Tarantula** (1955), semi-mad scientist Leo G. Carroll's growth serum produces huge experimental specimens—courtesy of rear projection.

The RP is on, the foreground is dressed and lit. Once the talent arrives, **Tarzan Finds a Son** (1939) will roll.

When rear projection couldn't provide a background of sufficient dimensions for **Tarzan Finds a Son** (1939), a painted backdrop was prepared.

During **Tarzan Finds a Son** (1939) young John Sheffield patiently holds the slate in front of an RP screen with the projector turned off.

For **Things to Come** (1936), some scenes used RP backgrounds of futuristic miniatures to chronicle the reconstruction of civilization.

A scene from one of the last Republic serials, **Trader Tom of the China Seas** (1954).

Projection Composites • 217

Voyage to the Bottom of the Sea (1961) introduced Irwin Allen's **Seaview** submarine. Thanks to unique viewports in the bow—and RP—the crew sees a minefield in their path.

RP continued to provide backgrounds for the **Voyage to the Bottom of the Sea** TV series (1964-1968).

The Drop Ship's flaming wreckage sends Hicks (Michael Biehn) running for cover in James Cameron's **Aliens** (1986).

A process shot setup for Gary Cooper's **Real Glory** (1939), set in the Philippines.

Brand new **Foreign Correspondent** (1940) Joel McCrea turns in pursuit of an interview—just as director Alfred Hitchcock strolls past.

218 · *Smoke and Mirrors - Special Visual Effects Before Computers*

In **The Three Stooges Meet Hercules** (1962), Moe Howard dangles in front of a background plate of two stuntmen made up as a Siamese cyclops.

Rigging Moe in a wire harness to hold him aloft.

A deleted scene from **Aliens** (1986). The forest retreat was revealed as a phony background, utilizing its unreality in the story.

Doug Beswick used front projection to visualize the scorching hot alien in **The Cremators** (1973).

Shot down in **Foreign Correspondent** (1940), the survivors struggle in front of an RP background with additional stage effects.

Buck Benny Rides Again (1940) thanks to a prop horse and RP.

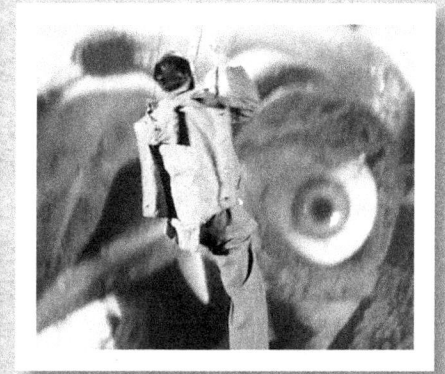

Bail out! A bird as big as a battleship is after you! RP for **The Giant Claw** (1957).

Our heroes look upon **Kronos** (1957), amazed at the (rear projected) alien machine.

Projection Composites • 219

Deluge (1933), the first disaster movie. As buildings collapsed on the background plate—supervised by Ned Mann—debris dropped on stuntmen.

The Amazing Colossal Man (1957)—a back projection—is confronted by soldiers "on top of Hoover Dam."

Ray Harryhausen animated the Ymir in advance of live action photography to provide this RP plate for **20 Million Miles to Earth** (1957).

Ray Harryhausen was an expert in matching the lighting of his foreground stop-motion model to the background plate.

For **Boom Town** (1940) RP provided a raging inferno behind Clark Gable, Spencer Tracy and Frank Morgan, keeping them safe.

All Through the Night (1941): Nazi Conrad Veidt (right) forces Humphrey Bogart to aim a speedboat laden with explosives at a U.S. ship!

220 · *Smoke and Mirrors – Special Visual Effects Before Computers*

Gene Warren, Jr. and John Huneck work on a front projection Purina Chuck Wagon dog food commercial at Excelsior!

A front projection composite for a Chuck Wagon spot. In 1976, these were the most expensive ads on the air.

Willis O'Brien created this famous scene for **King Kong** (1933) which was cut in the 1938 re-release. The live action is rear projected into a miniature set, a technique OBie perfected.

Harry Walton animates the scorpion for **Honey I Shrunk the Kids** (1989) at Phil Tippett's studio. Harry's dynamic animation made the bullying scorpion a serious threat.

A highlight of **One Million Years B.C.** (1966), Ray Harryhausen's stop-motion allosaurus stands on a section of miniature terrain.

At Project Unlimited, Jim Danforth looks through the Mitchell eyepiece at Cormoran for a scene in **Jack the Giant Killer** (1962).

Projection Composites • 221

The climax of **Mighty Joe Young** (1949) used RP backgrounds of a burning orphanage—a five-foot-tall high-speed miniature. The tree and the puppets are in front of a rear screen.

Jim Aupperle, a master of cinematography and lighting, takes a meter reading on a twin-front screen composite for **Planet of Dinosaurs** (1977). The puppets were built by Executive Producer Stephen Czerkas.

In this instance, Willis O'Brien's concept art for **King Kon**g (1933) required modification to make filming practical.

Kong peers in through the window via RP. When he moved away, the mechanical hand entered from a different window to grab Fay Wray.

For **Dinosaurs the Terrible Lizards** (1970) Wah Chang built a menagerie of dinosaur puppets and used front projection for the composites.

Mark Wolf produced and animated a sequel, **The Age of Mammals** (1979), written by Jim Aupperle and Gail Hickman. Models by Tony McVey, John Holmes and Wolf.

CHAPTER 6
OPTICALS: MOVING MATTES AND ANIMATED VISUAL EFFECTS

Norman Dawn and the other early matte artists, foreground miniaturists and mirror-shot specialists understood the limitations to their systems. For instance, they all required a nodal point head in order to move the camera without losing alignment between the live action and element, but even more critically, characters could not cross the matte lines that defined the area of the live action.

The demand for greater creative freedom led to the development of a new photographic process—the traveling matte—which, as the name suggests, permitted actors to move without restrictions across the background image.

Frank Williams became a camera operator at Mack Sennett's Keystone Studios in 1912. By 1914 he was chief cinematographer and responsible for filming several Charlie Chaplin pictures, including ***Kid Auto Races at Venice*** (1914). A few years later, Roscoe "Fatty" Arbuckle hired Williams as his cinematographer for Buster Keaton's first film, ***The Butcher Boy*** (1917). The demands of these productions brought to light the need for a system that would combine foreground action with separately-filmed backgrounds, and he gradually refined concepts he had dating back to 1910 at the Essanay Studios. He filed a patent in May, 1916 (U.S. patent No. 1273435) for "The Williams Process," which was granted in July, 1918.

In his patent application he described the ease with which his process could, for example, allow an actor to appear in a dual role opposite himself in a scene, or, as applied to a typical heroine's dilemma of the era, how an actress tied to the railroad tracks could be rescued from the approaching train—filmed in complete safety in the studio.

*Ernest Thesiger as Dr. Pretorious in James Whale's **Bride of Frankenstein** (1935) contemplates his miniature creations in a sequence of remarkable optical effects by John P. Fulton.*

THE WILLIAMS PROCESS

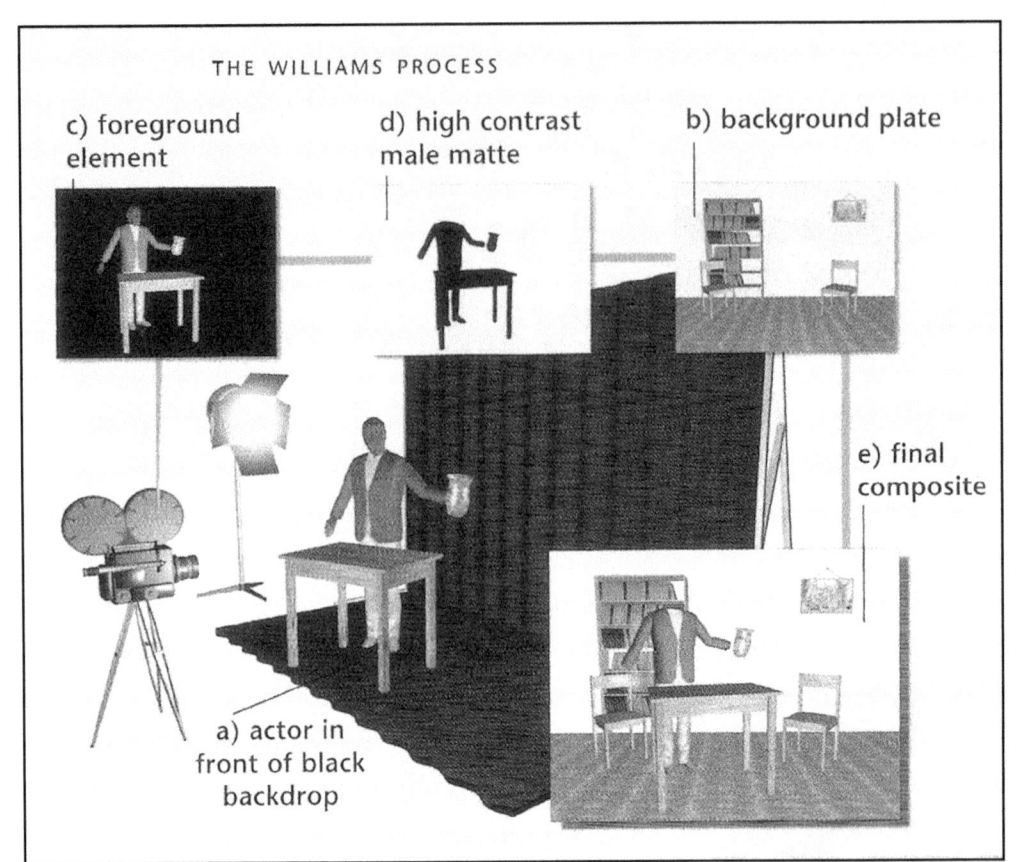

- c) foreground element
- d) high contrast male matte
- b) background plate
- e) final composite
- a) actor in front of black backdrop

Above, left: A simplified diagram of The Williams Process.

*Right, top: Professor Challenger's brontosaurus has escaped and is running amok in **The Lost World** (1925)—thanks to a Williams traveling matte.*

*Right, middle: Claude Rains peels away bandages to reveal his invisibility to shocked onlookers—and an astonished audience—in James Whale's **The Invisible Man** (1933). The actor was filmed against a black background while wearing a black body suit with other clothing and bandages over it. John P. Fulton then produced this composite with a Williams traveling matte.*

*Right: The palace of Pontius Pilate collapses onto horrified onlookers in this scene from the 1925 **Ben-Hur**. A Williams traveling matte added the unfortunate victims and hand-drawn mattes overlapped the miniature stonework atop the people.*

The Williams Process involved filming subjects against a black background, and that film was printed in a succession of high contrast negatives, resulting in a pure black and white silhouette, a "traveling matte." These elements were combined with the background in a bi-pack camera and actors could finally move through the frame without limitations.

The Williams Process had drawbacks, such as image loss because of the duping, and shadow areas on the subject allowed the background to print through.

The process was first used in **Wild Honey** (1922), then in Cecil B. De Mille's **Manslaughter** (1922) and in the 1925 **Ben-Hur** to crush extras beneath a collapsing miniature of the Palace of Pontius Pilate. In F. W. Murnau's **Sunset** (1927), the process made possible a continuous take of actors walking from a city to a tranquil setting.

Willis O'Brien used the new process to send his brontosaurus rampaging through London streets in **The Lost World** (1925), a technological leap beyond the split-screens used previously to add actors to his jungle tabletops. Traveling mattes were also used in Cecil B. DeMille's **The 10 Commandments** (1923) to add crowds to the parting of the Red Sea.

John P. Fulton used the process in **The Invisible Man** (1933) when Claude Rains removed his bandages to reveal—*nothing!* The illusion was accomplished by photographing the actor performing in front of a black screen while wearing a black suit over which he had the bandages and false nose. As he discarded the external trappings it looked like an invisible person was removing his clothing. The process was used for the assorted sequels, even though more sophisticated methods had come about by then.

THE DUNNING-POMEROY SELF-MATTING PROCESS

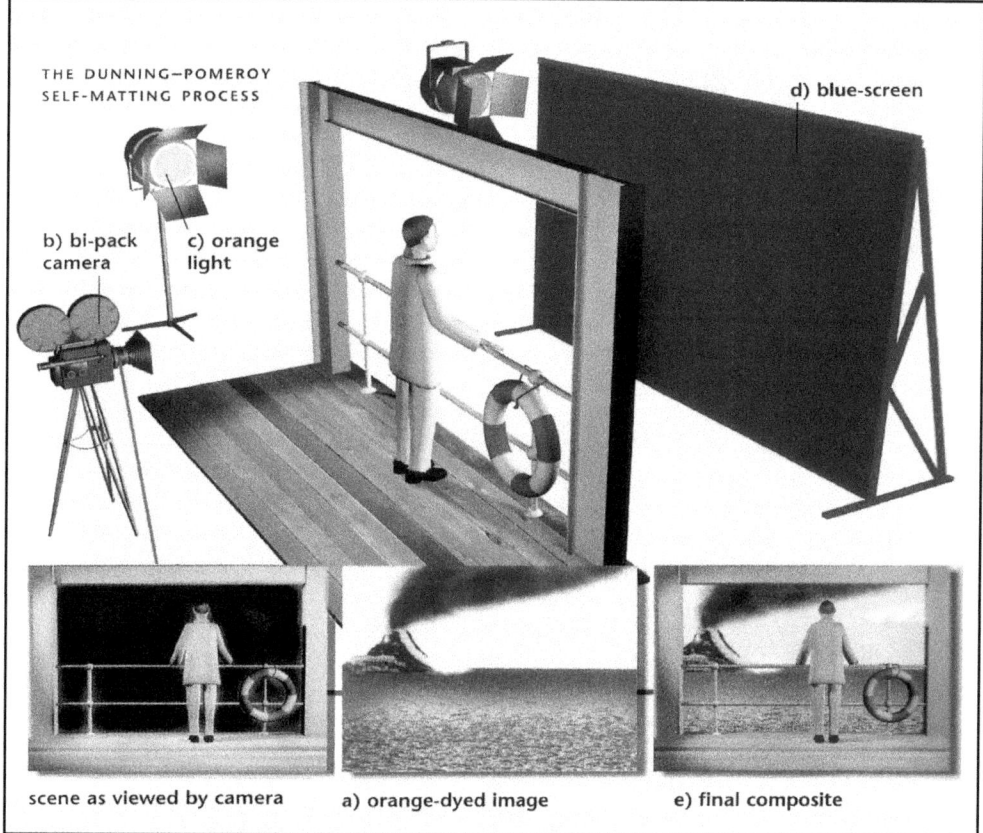

b) bi-pack camera
c) orange light
d) blue-screen

scene as viewed by camera | a) orange-dyed image | e) final composite

Above: A simplified diagram for how a Dunning shot was filmed.

Above, left: A Dunning shot revealed. The performers are in front of a blue screen lit by amber light. A bi-pack camera runs an orange-dyed film of the location. The composite of the couple riding in a foreign city is watched at dailies the next day.

Left: A Williams traveling matte was used in **King Kong** (1933), for the scene of Kong smashing through the great doors as the natives flee in terror.

An alternative process was invented by teenager C. Dodge Dunning in 1925. The Dunning Process did away with the black background and contrast mattes, instead employing a blue background and a foreground illuminated by yellow light. The blue and yellow were separated by filters to create traveling mattes. The Dunning Process used a new panchromatic film stock in its debut in **King Kong** (1933), such as compositing the sailors on their raft with the approaching brontosaurus.

Visual effects artist Jim Danforth described the log-rolling scene in his **Dinosaurs, Dragons, and Drama: The Odyssey of a Trickfilmaker** (Vol.1): "**King Kong** began production with a test sequence designed to convince the RKO management to fund the film, and the Dunning process was used to create full-size live-action composites. Orville Becket, a gaffer on **King Kong**, once showed me frame blow-ups from the live-action foreground for one of the spider pit scenes—stating that it was a Dunning shot.

"My understanding is that the shot of Kong shaking the men off the log was accomplished with a Dunning shot. The log was raised with a cable sling and was rocked a predetermined number of degrees back and forth, derived from the animation of Kong which had been done first. The yellow-dyed film of Kong was bipacked in the live-action camera, as was the norm for a Dunning shot, and the camera was connected to a motor which also drove a Moviola running a print of the Kong animation, thereby enabling the foreground action to be verbally cued or directed as the shot was filmed. This was the methodology I gleaned from conversations with Phil Kellison." [1]

Opticals: Moving Mattes and Animated Visual Effects • 225

Above: Frank Van Der Veer at his optical printer. Van Der Veer operated one of the principal optical houses in Hollywood for many years.

Linwood G. Dunn *(above, right)*, widely regarded as the Father of American Optical Effects, expanded the concept of the optical printer while employed at RKO under Vernon O. Walker *(above, left)*, head of the camera effects department. Dunn engineered the device with an eye to creating complex special visual effects and worked with machinist Cecil Love, who had built the metal armatures in **King Kong**.

The RKO printer was used extensively on **Flying Down to Rio** (1933) and was a workhorse on countless others, providing standard film transitions (fades and dissolves, slow motion, fast motion, binocular mattes), and salvage work such as re-positioning frames to crop out intruding microphone booms.

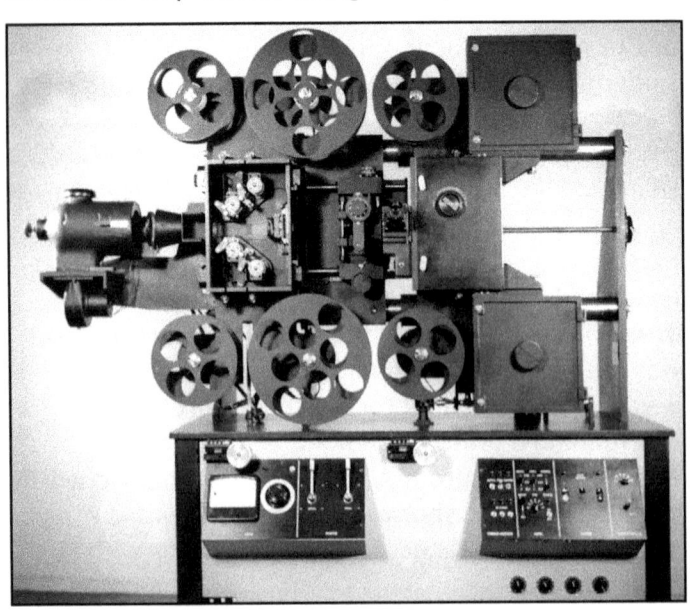

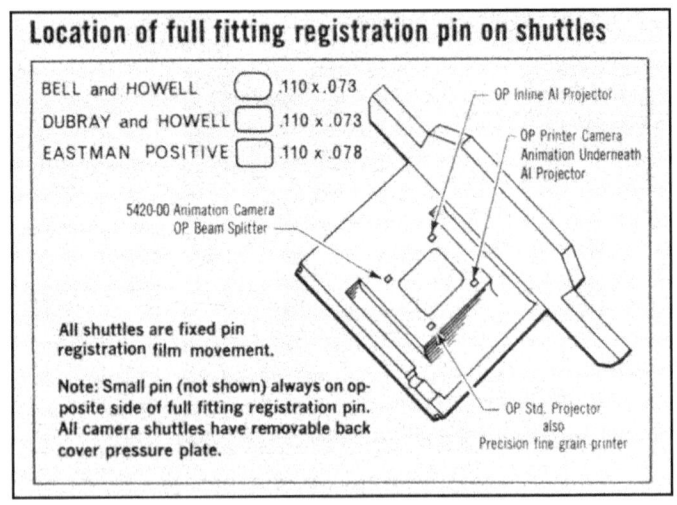

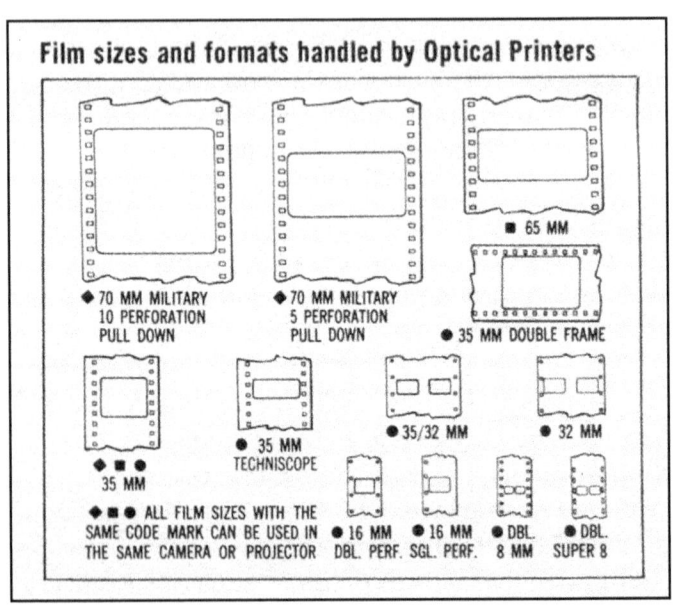

Location of full fitting registration pin on shuttles

BELL and HOWELL	.110 x .073
DUBRAY and HOWELL	.110 x .073
EASTMAN POSITIVE	.110 x .078

5420-00 Animation Camera
OP Beam Splitter

OP Inline AI Projector
OP Printer Camera Animation Underneath AI Projector
OP Std. Projector also Precision fine grain printer

All shuttles are fixed pin registration film movement.

Note: Small pin (not shown) always on opposite side of full fitting registration pin. All camera shuttles have removable back cover pressure plate.

Film sizes and formats handled by Optical Printers

- ◆ 70 MM MILITARY 10 PERFORATION PULL DOWN
- ◆ 70 MM MILITARY 5 PERFORATION PULL DOWN
- ■ 65 MM
- ● 35 MM DOUBLE FRAME
- ◆■■ 35 MM
- ● 35 MM TECHNISCOPE
- ● 35/32 MM
- ● 32 MM
- ◆■■ ALL FILM SIZES WITH THE SAME CODE MARK CAN BE USED IN THE SAME CAMERA OR PROJECTOR
- ● 16 MM DBL. PERF.
- ● 16 MM SGL. PERF.
- ● DBL. 8 MM
- ● DBL. SUPER 8

226 · **Smoke and Mirrors – Special Visual Effects Before Computers**

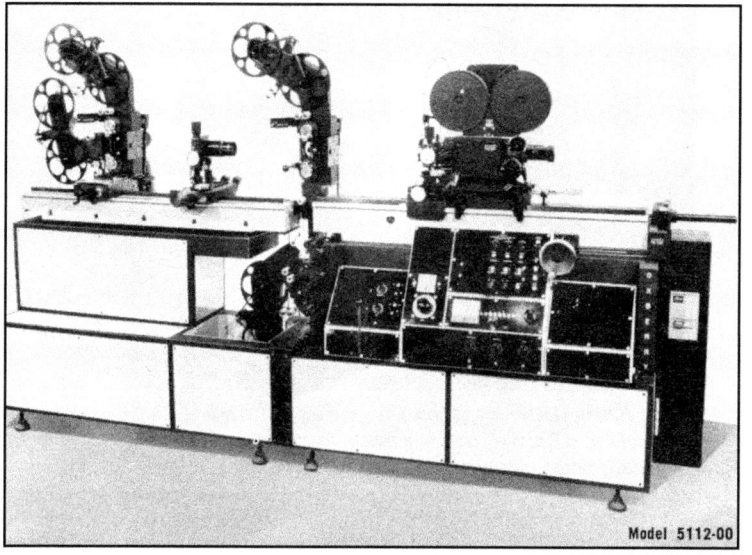

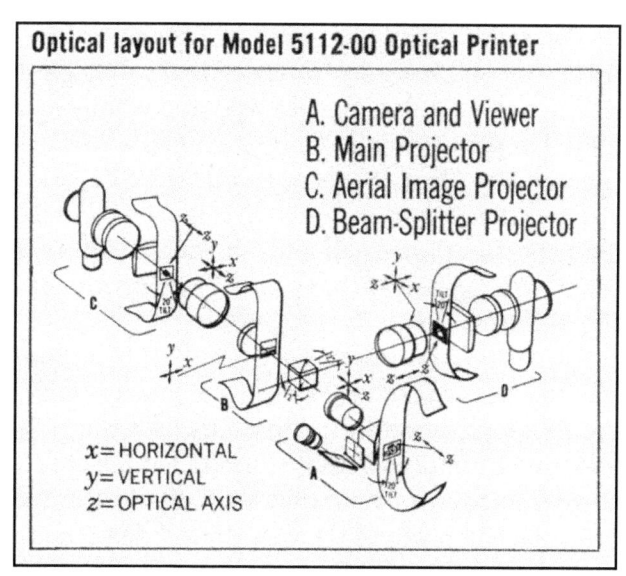

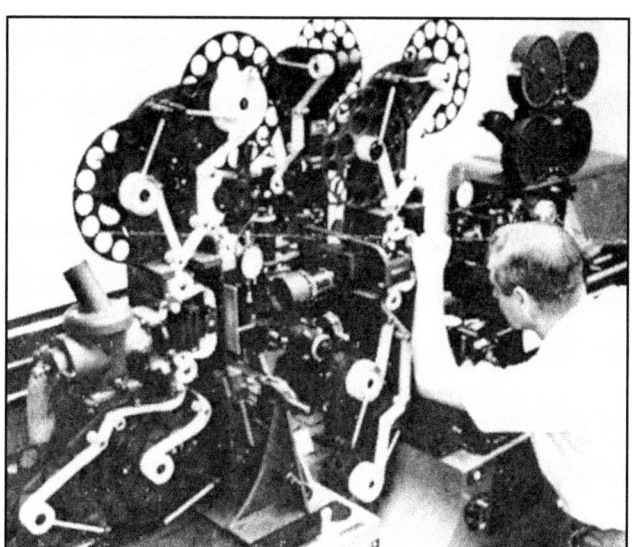

Optical layout for Model 5112-00 Optical Printer

A. Camera and Viewer
B. Main Projector
C. Aerial Image Projector
D. Beam-Splitter Projector

x = HORIZONTAL
y = VERTICAL
z = OPTICAL AXIS

Above: Harry Walton with his aerial image printer, which started out as a Producers Service Company single head bench printer. John Monceaux modified it for VistaVision and Harry later added the aerial image conversion making it even more versatile: it could run six strips of film at one time and could do all 35mm combinations: standard 4-perf, 8-perf (VistaVision), 2-perf (Techniscope), and even 16mm.

In *Cinemagic of the Optical Printer* for the Sixth Edition of **The American Cinematographer Manual**, Linwood Dunn described how the commercial optical printer evolved: "The earliest optical printers were custom built by the major studio and film laboratories, and were usually designed and made in their own shops to fit their particular requirements. Modern standardized optical printing equipment, capable of creating the innumerable effects heretofore possible only in the major studios, became available to the entire motion picture industry in 1943, with the introduction of the Acme-Dunn Optical Printer, designed and built for the United States Armed Forces Photographic Units. Later, the Oxberry, Producers Service, Research Products and other optical printers appeared on the market. Commercial availability of this type of equipment greatly stimulated and widened the scope of the Special Effects field. Even the smallest film producers now could make motion pictures with special effects, limited only by their imagination and budget, utilizing the services of growing numbers of independent Special Effects laboratories which could now operate competitively using equipment available to all.

"More recently, computer technology applied to the optical printer has basically simplified the control and accuracy of some of its important functions, thus making it much easier to produce complex visual effects at less cost while expanding its creative scope. Programming and repeating movement with great accuracy made complex traveling matte composites previously thought impractical now possible. One can truly say that the creative capability of the modern visual effects optical printer is only limited by the talent and skills of the operator. In recent years such major film productions as **Star Wars**, **The Black Hole**, **The Empire Strikes Back** and **Cocoon** have all utilized the full capabilities of the modern optical printer to create a whole new world by extensive use of very sophisticated motion picture visual effects." (2)

Opticals: Moving Mattes and Animated Visual Effects

Dunning shots were used in *Trader Horn* (1931) to combine performers filmed safely on a Hollywood soundstage with wild and woolly action filmed in Africa. The Dunning technique was also used in *The Most Dangerous Game* (1932) and *Tarzan the Ape Man* (1932). Europeans used Dunning shots in films such as Fritz Lang's *Das Testament das Doktor Mabuse* (aka *The Testament of Dr. Mabuse*, 1934).

In *Mutiny on the Bounty* (1934), H.M.S. *Bounty* was to crash against rocks while a smaller boat, the *Pandora*, hung from moorings over the side. Shooting during an actual storm failed miserably, and some sources state that a life was lost in the process. The production then shifted gears and a recreation of the *Bounty* was rigged at the studio to rock on gimbals. The live action area was lit by amber light while a background screen was illuminated with a blue light. As a testimony to the mattes' quality, star Charles Laughton said that he couldn't spot which scenes were Dunning shots.

The problem with the Dunning Process was it only worked in black and white. Color film would require a new methodology, which Larry Butler brought to fruition in Alexander Korda's *The Thief of Bagdad* (1940). After experimenting with yellow and blue backings, Butler chose to shoot performers against a blue background, not only because there is very little blue in flesh tones but he could also count on the fine grain of the blue record to produce quality mattes.

This technique became known as the "blue backing traveling matte process" and was made possible by using an optical printer, which consisted of one or more film projectors mechanically linked to a movie camera that allowed the re-photography of one or more images onto a single negative.

Using a three-strip Technicolor camera, three black and white negatives were exposed by Red, Blue and Green lights. In the Techniclor lab, the negatives were used in the printing process to produce complementary colors which were controlled by the density of dyes to produce a full spectrum of color. Then, using an optical printer, Butler would remove the blue background from the foreground and, using the negative of the traveling matte, remove the foreground space from the background, finally combining foreground and background.

This new process enabled the Sultan to fly on his clockwork horse, for tiny Sabu to appear next to the gigantic Genie, and other fantastic moments that earned Larry Butler an Oscar® for Best Special Effects for *The Thief of Bagdad* in 1940.

King Kong (1933) shakes his pursuers off a log bridge. The bravura execution utilized a Dunning traveling matte to composite Kong's tabletop animation and painted matte glasses with the live actors.

Prior to *King Kong*, Willis O'Brien produced this *Creation* test footage of an armed hunter and a baby triceratops. Ray Harryhausen thought it was a Williams matte; however, it seems that the smoke from the gun would not have been successful, and the background doesn't look duped.

In *The Most Dangerous Game* (1932), the live action foreground and a matte painting are composited via a Dunning matte.

This Dunning shot in *Mutiny on the Bounty* (1934) provides some welcome scope, opening the film up after extensive rear projection—typically limited to closer angles—had made the film feel constrained.

228 · *Smoke and Mirrors – Special Visual Effects Before Computers*

*In **King Kong** (1933), a Dunning traveling matte composited the high-speed mechanical brontosaurus background with the live action foreground.*

*In **The Thief of Bagdad** (1940) the Sultan rides his magical toy thanks to a blue screen.*

*For Hammer's **The Evil of Frankenstein** (1964), mad scientist Peter Cushing whips up his horses without ever setting foot outside the studio—his close-ups are shot against a blue screen.*

*At the end of **The Golden Voyage of Sinbad** (1974), Sinbad (John Phillip Law) duels with nasty sorcerer Prince Koura (Tom Baker). They are matted via blue screen against the Fountain of Destiny miniature. Koura faded away a section at a time thanks to cutout shapes of blue held in front of him (like a shield), through which the background would be seen as he "turns invisible."*

Blue-backing shots, however, also had limitations. The process was extremely time consuming as it involved several steps with an optical printer, which also made it costly. From an aesthetic standpoint, the traveling mattes often had edge issues where a thin blue line was visible around the performers (poor matte fit, showing the actual blue screen through a gap in the mattes). Furthermore, it couldn't handle fine details like hair, smoke or motion blur, and costuming had to avoid blue to prevent the background from printing through the costume. Ray Harryhausen capitalized on this in **The Golden Voyage of Sinbad** in 1974: to show the villain Koura fading away, actor Tom Baker held a blue shield in front of himself into which the background was printed, thus giving the illusion of progressive invisibility.

Despite the limitations, blue screen has been used extensively in such well-known films as **The Ten Commandments** (1956), **Star Wars** (1977), **Dragonslayer** (1981), **Robocop** (1987), **Who Framed Roger Rabbit?** (1988), and **The Addams Family** (1991).

Opticals: Moving Mattes and Animated Visual Effects

For years, legend had it that Linwood Dunn (right) had tried to convince Willis O'Brien to use optical printing in **King Kong** to avoid doing complex shots in-camera (and risking time-consuming re-dos if something went wrong). In his book, Jim Danforth recalled, "Lin Dunn told me [that] story twice. The first time, it was about **Mighty Joe Young** (1949); later it was about **King Kong** (1933). For **Mighty Joe Young** it seems credible; for **King Kong**, it does not. **Mighty Joe Young**, upon examination, shows a large amount of optical duping (to the film's detriment); **King Kong** does not.

"For the record: O'Brien told optical cameraman Phil Kellison that the master shot of Kong on the stage *(above)* was accomplished as an in-camera latent-image-composite split screen. Phil worried about the risk involved in working this way and asked O'Brien what would have happened if O'Brien had made a mistake in the animation, O'Brien replied, '*Then* we would have duped the shot.'" (3)

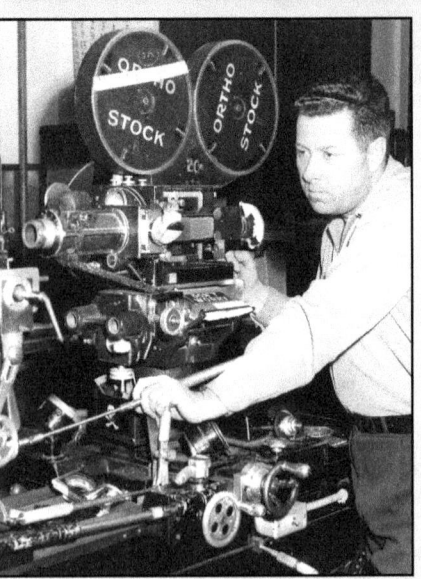

Ray Harryhausen's **One Million Years B.C.** (1967) Note that in this full frame image, the live action element extends off the left edge of the background image (masked in projection).

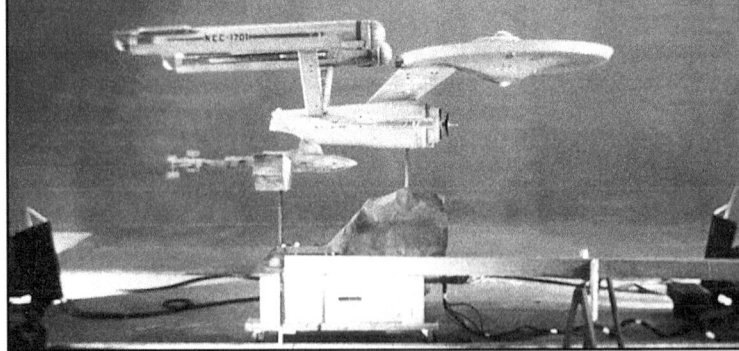

The two spaceship models for the **Star Trek** episode **Space Seed** (1967) are filmed in front of a blue screen at Linwood Dunn's facility, Film Effects of Hollywood. The optical printer will composite the ships with a starfield.

Journey to the Center of the Earth (1959) is full of matte art, props and the best use of live reptiles as stand-ins for dinosaurs. Blue screens composited live actors with the "prehistoric monsters."

Stephen Boyd steadies Raquel Welch as their miniaturized submarine takes a **Fantastic Voyage** (1966) through a man's body. The Blu-ray is a digital restoration with cleaned-up mattes.

230 · *Smoke and Mirrors – Special Visual Effects Before Computers*

Must See (Blue Screen) TV

I Dream of Jeannie (1965-1970)

Land of the Lost (1974-1977)

Land of the Lost (1991-1992)

Charlie's Angels (1976-1981)

The Avengers (1965-1968)

While early video compositing made use of electronic "chroma key," many TV shows through the years were produced on film and used the same blue screen optical compositing methodology as feature films. A few examples, shown above, include **I Dream of Jeannie** for scenes in which star Barabara Eden was "miniaturized," and adventure series such as **Charlie's Angels** and **The Avengers**. Dramatic series relied on blue screen outside the windows of boats and cars in order to speed up costly live action production as well as provide the flexibility of adding exotic locations.

There was an interesting reversal of approach between the original series **Land of the Lost** in the 1970s and the re-boot in the 1990s: the original series elected to add the live action to miniature landscapes and dinosaurs *(above middle, left)*, while the re-boot took a more traditional approach by adding the stop motion dinosaurs to the live action settings, filmed largely in natural environments on exterior locations or on studio sets *(above middle, right)*.

In a presentation to a technical conference in Hollywood on October 18, 1943, Linwood Dunn described his new device as "... an optical printer of radically new design and construction. Besides doing all of the conventional optical printing effects, the Acme-Dunn optical printer can make automatically driven dolly or 'zoom' shots at any practical speed, make horizontal or vertical frame slide-off effects, wipe off in any direction at any speed, do frame-combination printing within a 12-frame cycle, and enlarge from 16mm, including successful 3-frame separation negatives." (4)

Built by Acme Tool Company of Burbank, the Acme-Dunn optical printer differed from the many contraptions turned out by studio workshops by being constructed as a single, complete unit with a cast-iron base and housing. The Bell & Howell camera was fully integrated, and all threading and operational controls were accessible from one side of the device.

Describing his invention as a "dream printer," Dunn said, "[It is] a machine which can do anything that has been done on any all-purpose optical printer, with special emphasis on ease and flexibility of operation. When an imaginative optical printing specialist is not hampered by the limitations of his equipment, his value to his studio can be tremendous." (5)

"On March 15, 1945, the Academy Research Council bestowed a Class 3 Award on Linwood Dunn, Cecil Love and Edward Furer for the design and construction of their new optical printer, commenting, 'This machine exemplifies technical advancement necessary to keep pace with the ever increasing scope of the motion picture art.'

"Nearly forty years later, in 1981, the Academy recognized the same three men for the same achievement, awarding them a special Oscar® for technical merit." (6)

Bond, Barbarella, and Blue Screen Opticals in Main Title Sequences

Maurice Binder *(pronounced BINN-der)* was most famous for creating the title sequences to many of the James Bond films, starting with ***Dr. No*** (1962). Famously, he was pressed for time and in a last-minute effort stuck a line of white dots—file folder labels—onto black paper to illustrate his idea for the "gun barrrel" logo that became the signature image of the Bond series. After ***Dr. No*** Robert Brownjohn took over for ***From Russia With Love*** (1963) and ***Goldfinger*** (1964). Binder returned for ***Thunderball*** (1965) which introduced his iconic use of naked girls in silhouette, either swimming or jumping on trampolines in slow motion. All of this was achieved by the use of blue screen traveling mattes and other optical techniques.

In 1981 popular singer Sheena Easton became the first soloist of a James Bond theme song to appear onscreen in the main title sequence.

Thanks to blue screen, Jane Fonda can perform a "weightless" striptease for the title sequence in Barbarella (1968).

Above: Jane prepares to float weightless once again.

Far right: A bank of lights illuminates a blue screen (oh, yes—Jane is in the photo, too).

232 · *Smoke and Mirrors – Special Visual Effects Before Computers*

Petro Vlahos with the massive 3-strip Technicolor camera adapted for the sodium light traveling matte process.

Above: Dick Van Dyke and Julie Andrews are wired in flying harnesses for **Mary Poppins** *(1964), an Oscar®-winner for its special visual effects. They will be composited with the backgrounds—and animated penguins—by sodium light traveling mattes.*

The Sodium Light Traveling Matte Process

Vic Margutti, a highly respected British effects cameraman, joined Rank Laboratories at Pinewood in October, 1956, specifically to help develop the sodium light traveling matte process with Robert Holt, who had conceived the system. At its heart, the process relied on a customized Technicolor 3-strip camera with a beam-splitter that simultaneously exposed two 35mm motion picture negatives: one was the normal color foreground action, while the second was a perfect matte of the foreground subject. The better-fitting mattes prevented the notorious halo or fringe around live action foregrounds, a common artifact in the blue backing process. The sodium light process also expanded the color palette because there were no longer restrictions on using blue in foreground costumes, sets and props.

Ub Iwerks, who had animated much of the early Mickey Mouse and **Silly Symphony** shorts before departing to form his own studio, had returned to Disney in 1940. He now specialized in technical effects, including optical printing techniques on films like **Song of the South** (1946). He contacted the Rank Organization through the Motion Picture Research Council, a rare organization fostered by the studios to share technical research and development. Through its auspices, he was able to acquire one of the three solium light pelicules and fitted it to a modified Technicolor 3-strip camera. The first production employing sodium light mattes was **Darby O'Gill and the Little People** (1959), followed by **The Parent Trap** (1961), **The Love Bug** (1969), and the Oscar®-winning **Bedknobs and Broomsticks** (1971). Working on a loan-out to Universal, Iwerks received an Oscar®-nomination for Alfred Hitchcock's **The Birds** (1963).

The studio used sodium light traveling mattes to excellent advantage on **Mary Poppins** (1964), which won an Oscar® for Best Visual Effects for Peter Ellenshaw, Hamilton Luske and Eustace Lycett. Matte expert Petro Vlahos had been brought in by the studio to help refine the process, especially for a sixteeen-minute sequence where a live-action Julie Andrews and Dick Van Dyke dance with animated penguins, and Iwerks and Vlahos shared a special Academy Award of Merit for "The Conception and Perfection of Techniques for Color Traveling Matte Composite Cinematography."

RAY HARRYHAUSEN
CREATOR OF SPECIAL VISUAL EFFECTS

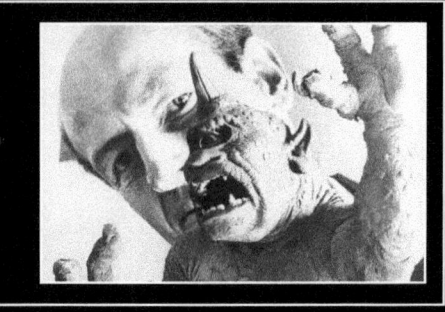

While stop motion animator and visual effects maestro Ray Harryhausen primarily used rear projection in his black and white films throughout the 1950s, vibrant Technicolor for *The 7th Voyage of Sinbad* in 1958 required a switch to blue screen traveling mattes. However, his next film, *The 3 Worlds of Gulliver* (1960), called for yet another approach. Faced with more than 380 traveling matte shots, Ray realized that the time-consuming blue screen process could never complete the sheer volume of composites for *Gulliver* in a timely, affordable manner. Thus, one of the main reasons Ray and producer Charles Schneer relocated to London was to take advantage of the Rank Organization's sodium light traveling matte process (in the U.S. Disney had the only other system and was keeping it proprietary). These two pages offer a sample of the marvelous visual effects designed and supervised by Ray Harryhausen over his remarkable career.

Top: Kerwin Mathews and Kathryn Grant carefully make their way past the dragon—actually, a blue screen in London—in *The 7th Voyage of Sinbad* (1958).

Above: The composite, one of only nine separate blue screen setups in the film.

Below: Despite diligence, the occasional "oops" can end up in a film. In this shot from *Sinbad and the Eye of the Tiger* (1977), Jane Seymour's left hand is "cut off," her flailing motion having extended beyond the edge of the screen. (And we don't like to think of **any** part of Jane Seymour being cut off...)

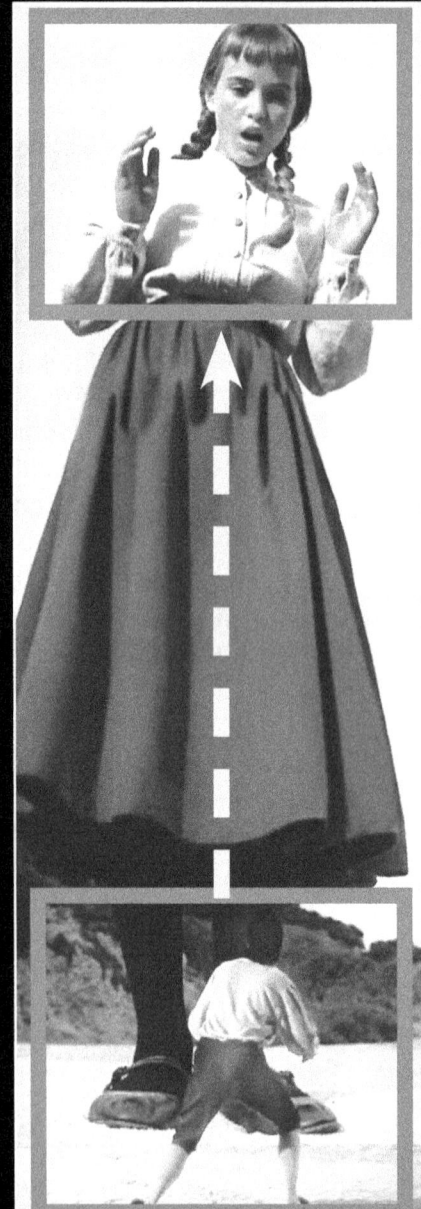

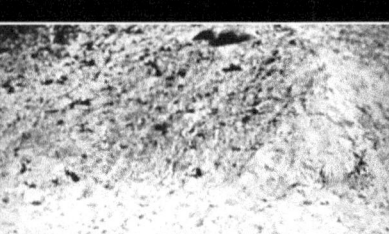

Above: From **One Million Years B.C.** (1967): a) Background plate; b) Stop motion turtle against rear projected background; c) Actors against blue screen; d) Composite.

Left: From **The 3 Worlds of Gulliver** (1960): a tilt-up from Gulliver to the startled Glumdalclitch. The tilt up of both elements had to be carefully scaled and timed.

Top, left and right: The live action portions of the balloon sequence in **Mysterious Island** (1961) were filmed in front of a yellow sodium light screen.

Left, 2nd photo: **Jason and the Argonauts** (1963) used the sodium light process but the dialog scene between Jason and Medea aboard the **Argo** was filmed blue screen to avoid the cost of bringing the actors onto the stage in post production (or conversely, importing he sodium light screen and equipment to location in Italy).

Left, photo 3: One of many sodium composites when Jason visits Mount Olympus.

Left, photo 4: A double blue screen composite from **First Men "In" the Moon** (1964). Ray used blue screen since this film was shot in Panavision (i.e., widescreen 2.35:1) and the longer barrels of the anamorphic lenses wouldn't fit into the 3-strip camera used for the sodium process.

Left: Ray animated the hornet in **Sinbad and the Eye of the Tiger** (1977) in front of a blue screen, tracking the camera in to "grow" it to giant size.

Above, middle: Castaways confront a giant crab in **Mysterious Island**.

Above: Actors in front of a blue screen come face-to-face with the Temple of Many Faces in **The Golden Voyage of Sinbad** (1974).

2001: A SPACE ODYSSEY

There are no conventional opticals in *2001: A Space Odyssey*. Rather, this film is noteworthy for (among other things) combining images on original negative as "held takes." Multiple takes of spaceships would yield one processed print for hand-roroscoping mattes, frame-by frame. This allowed starfields and other elements to be exposed onto another, as yet unprocessed, take, thus keeping all elements as first generation original images. In many cases, high-resolution photographs of a spaceship, such as the Moonbus above, and the backgrounds would be filmed on the animation stand with live action in the windows either projected or doubled-in.

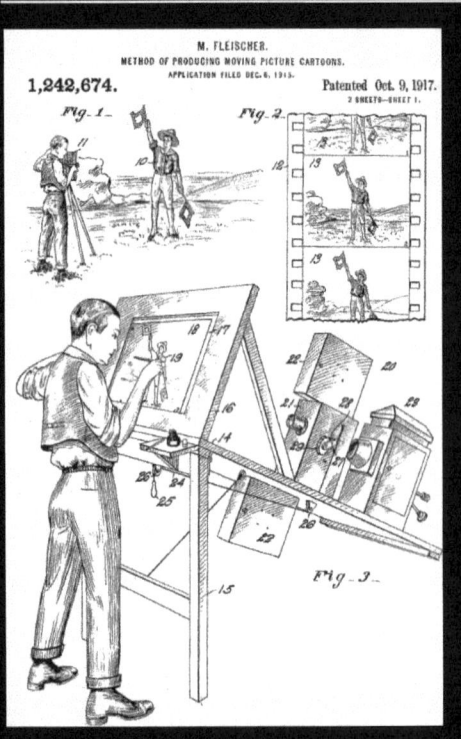

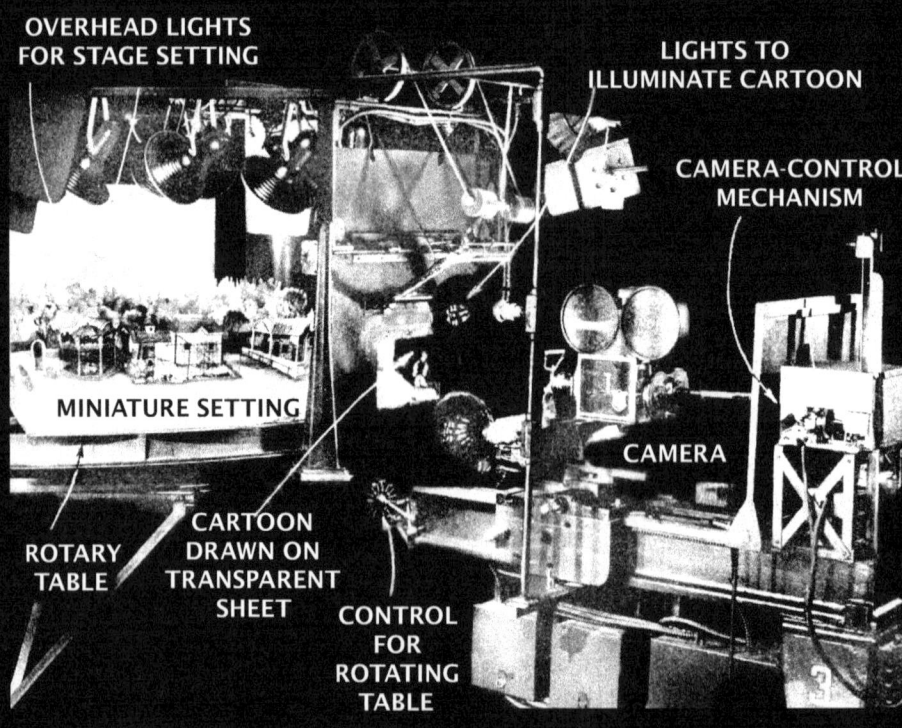

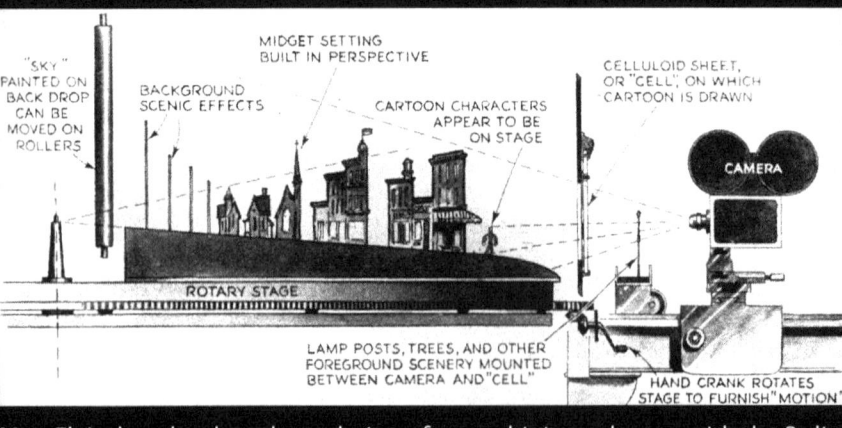

Max Fleischer developed a technique for combining cel animation and miniature backgrounds for several of his Popeye cartoons and some of his feature film work. Instead of relying on an optical printer to combine the animated cels with the 3-dimensional backgrounds, his team engineered a setup, as shown above, that photographed the cels *with* the miniature sets in-camera. The result was a fascinating combination of 2D and 3D, which gave his films a unique look.

236 · *Smoke and Mirrors – Special Visual Effects Before Computers*

*The only significant sequence animated by Ray Harryhausen using the frontlight/backlight matting process was the squirrel scene for **The 3 Worlds of Gulliver** (1960).*

*David Allen animated some of his earliest scenes of the "Lizard Men" for his project **The Primevals** using the frontlight/backlight method.*

*Ernest Farino turned Jeffrey Tambor into a stop motion vampire bat in the Richard Benjamin/Paula Prentiss comedy **Saturday the 14th** (1981).*

The Frontlight/ Backlight Process

The Frontlight/Backlight matting process was a method uniquely suited to stop motion model animation. As Ray Harryhausen told *Ray Harryhausen–Master of the Majicks* author Mike Hankin in 1990, "The basic principle involves shooting two frames of everything. First, the *[miniature]* set is lit to match the background. But the background will not be filmed, so you drop a black card or black velvet behind the model. You shoot that frame all against black. Then, without touching anything, you turn off the foreground lights and shoot the next frame against white which creates a silhouette of the foreground *[the "matte"]*. The model is the same size and in the same position as the previous frame because you haven't touched anything; you've only switched the background from black to white.

"In the laboratory, they skip-print the two *[foreground]* frames onto one strip for the color foreground and the other strip for the 'silhouette' image, thus creating an automatic traveling matte. It saves having to go through the various steps of blue-backing, where you have to make a positive and negative and have to allow for shrinkage of the image, which is the reason you sometimes get the 'halo' around the figure. With blue backing the image goes through the developer so many times it shrinks, and when they're superimposed over one another you're left with a blue line around the figure, which is actually the original blue screen on the set showing through the gap between the mattes. The *[frontlight/backlight]* process is very time-consuming. A lot can go wrong. You can forget that you just shot the black frame and shoot it a second time. Unless you have an automatic setup, it can get rather tedious." (7)

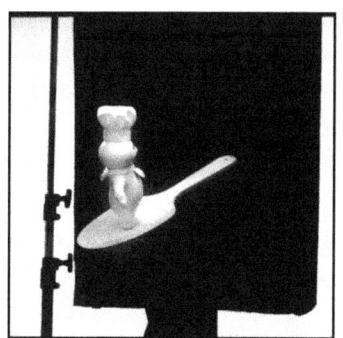

The stop motion Pillsbury Doughboy in a frontlight/backlight setup at Coast Productions in 1979, animated by Ernest Farino. The card for the frontlight pass is covered in black velvet to absorb all light, as is the platform and pylon supporting the Doughboy (positioned on a wooden spatula per the design of the commercial). The black card is hanging from a rudimentary hinge attached to a horizontal bar supported by two C-stands and is easily lifted up to reveal the front-lit white foam core (the silhouettes of the C-stands are removed by garbage mattes). When composited in an optical printer, the matte pass is used with the background image to "hold out" the animation, and a separate pass then lays in the color foreground element.

Opticals: Moving Mattes and Animated Visual Effects

Rotoscope

1. *Noun:* A device which projects and enlarges individual frames of filmed live action to permit them to be used to create cartoon animation or composite film sequences.
2. *Verb:* To transfer an image from a live action film onto another film using a rotoscope.

—*Oxford English Dictionary*

Rotoscoping is a method for creating cel animation or articulate mattes for combination with filmed backgrounds, or to create mattes or other elements for use in optical composites. Some examples of effects animated to match background plates include Claude Rains returning to visibility at the end of **The Invisible Man** (1933), the tracer rounds from B-17s in **Bombardier** (1943), Gene Kelly dancing with Jerry the mouse in **Anchors Aweigh** (1944), the "monkey money" tossed at Joe in **Mighty Joe Young** (1949), the conversion tubes in **This Island Earth** (1955), assorted ray beams in **Star Trek** (TV and movies), the glowing light sabres in **Star Wars** (1977), and the electrical discharges in **Big Trouble in Little China** (1986).

As with optical printers, in the early days the studios devised their own contraptions. Roy Seawright at the Hal Roach Studio came up with his own version that was a horizontal machine. Over time new equipment standardized the processes in a vertical orientation. Oxberry intended their animation stands for cartoon animation but they were also ideal for rotoscoping. In some cases traveling mattes were drawn by hand on the animation stand. In most cases the composites were finished in an optical printer, but some compositing could be done on the animation stand in a bi-pack configuration.

A movie that set the bar for the technique was **Forbidden Planet** (1956), which has breathtaking animation effects throughout the picture. The C57-D saucer (an 8'4" miniature) hovers over the alien landscape of Altair-4 riding on "repulsor beams" that ensure that the ship can gently touch down. The beams are the first of many hand-animated art effects created by Joshua Meador, on loan from Disney. Meador created effects animation for **20,000 Leagues Under the Sea** in 1954—the electrical charge used against the attacking squid, for instance—and is featured in the 1958 Disney short, **Four Artists Paint One Tree**.

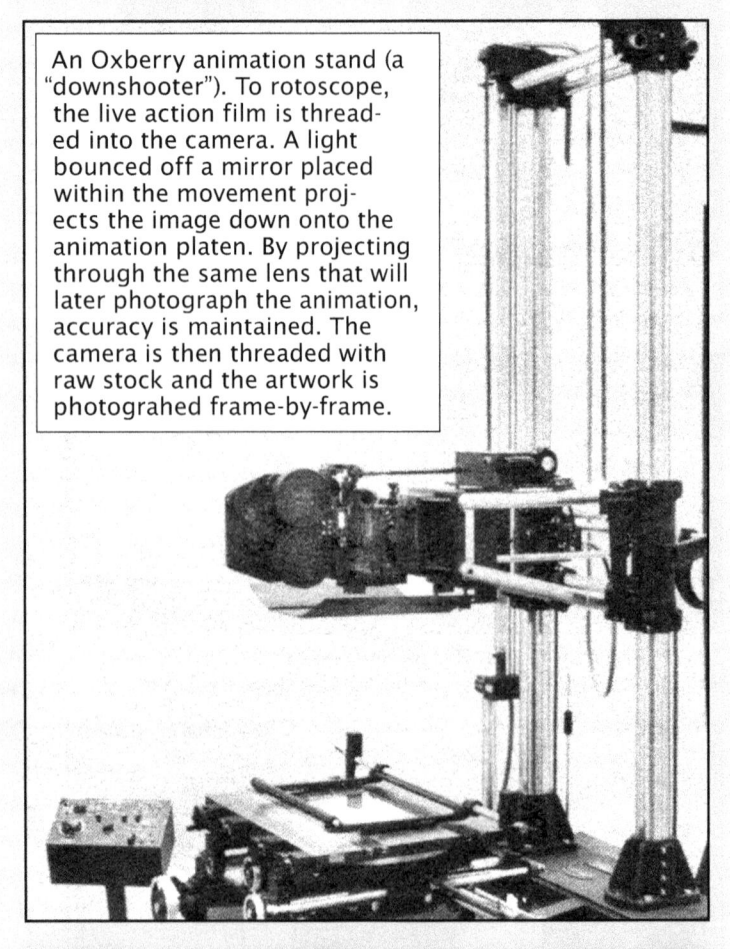

An Oxberry animation stand (a "downshooter"). To rotoscope, the live action film is threaded into the camera. A light bounced off a mirror placed within the movement projects the image down onto the animation platen. By projecting through the same lens that will later photograph the animation, accuracy is maintained. The camera is then threaded with raw stock and the artwork is photograhed frame-by-frame.

Rotoscope effects brought the Monster from the Id to life in **Forbidden Planet** (1956). Live action footage was rotoscoped onto animation paper and Disney artist Joshua Meador animated it to match the live action. Left: An actual animation sheet. Using a Conté crayon helped with the "electrical" look.

*Ray Harryhausen's **Earth vs. the Flying Saucers** (1956) relied on frame-by-frame rotoscope mattes for a few shots of the saucer traveling an extreme distance from far away right up to camera. Follow focus and depth-of-field issues prevented Ray from using his standard rear projection setup. Evidence of the hand-rotoscoped mattes can be seen slightly outside the edge of the saucer in the frame above.*

*Stock footage was rotoscoped to convey Roman columns falling on army soldiers in **20 Million Miles to Earth** (1957). The limitations of the process are evident here, as blurred edges are almost impossible to draw successfully.*

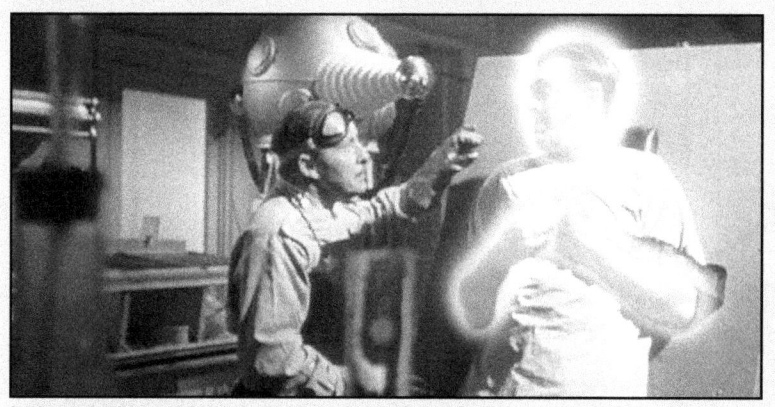

*Lionel Atwill wonders "How did they do that?" as he observes Lon Chaney, Jr., exude that warm (rotoscoped) glow in **Man-Made Monster** (1941).*

*The laser beams seen throughout **Goldfinger** (1964) were created by rotoscope animation. (Turns out it's not that hard to break into Fort Knox after all...)*

Meador brought the 35mm live action footage back from MGM and the visuals were produced in his specialized department at Disney. Meador supplied the ray cannons' blaster effects, the massive sizzling electrical arcs in the miniature Krell shaft, the C57-D's landing beams, the colorful disintegration of the leaping tiger into a gaseous cloud, and Robby's rays and near-meltdown. However, his most startling creation was unquestionably the monstrous, roaring "Monster from the Id," perhaps the most bizarre character to ever appear in a science fiction film. Nothing like it had ever been seen before!

While the Id had been pitched as an invisible monster, the laws of drama meant that the audience would demand to "see it in the flesh." Dr. Morbius' monster went through numerous concepts by writer Irving Block, illustrator Mentor Huebner and art director Arthur Lonergan, alternately looking like a slug, an insect and assorted bipedal shapes, the most horrific of which sported Walter Pidgeon's face. Meador hired animator Ken Hultgren to refine the approach, and some suggest that it's based on MGM's "Leo the Lion" mascot.

Meador did the key animation frames on animation paper with a Conté crayon, helping to give it an indistinct form. Others did the in-betweens, including 18-year-old Joe Alves, who would later be production designer on ***Close Encounters of the Third Kind*** (1977). Alves has remarked the animation was done on cels with color added, but I believe that approach was rejected. Rather, it looks like the animation was shot on black and white film from which a hi-contrast matte was generated. The matte/counter mattes were used in the optical printer and colorized by filters.

Traveling mattes and rotoscoped effects continue being used today, with digital refinements. I have been flabbergasted at the compositing for ***Thor: Ragnarok*** (2017), for instance. If they had to use the old optical processes they'd still be working!

Optical houses were among the first to feel the transition to CG and while I am sorry to see them go, the advantages of CG are too numerous to stop the adoption of better technology—which has been on-going since the earliest days and will continue in the future.

How long before we have holographic interactive event films?

The "Trench" sequence in **Star Wars IV: A New Hope** (1977). To handle the crushing optical workload on the next film, **Star Wars V: The Empire Strikes Back** (1980), Industrial Light and Magic ("ILM") visual effects director Richard Edlund supervised the engineering of a new aerial image optical printer with four VistaVision projector heads. Dubbed "The Quad," the operator could now composite complex shots in a single pass. However, when ILM confronted the even more demanding **Star Wars VI: Return of the Jedi** (1983), The Quad was re-configured into two units, one of which was nostalgically called The Quad while the other was called The Workhorse.

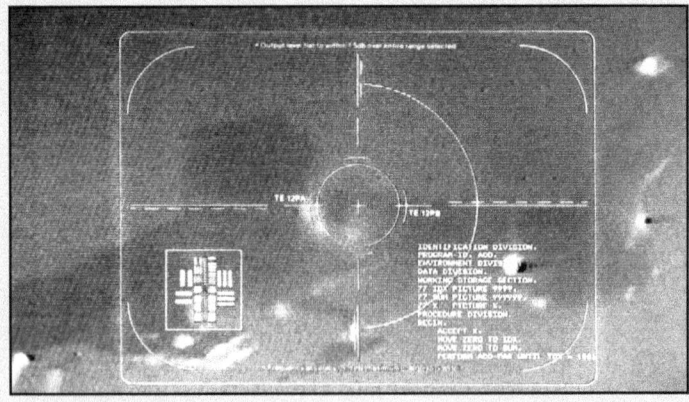

The laser beams and computer readout animations for **The Terminator** (1984) were rotoscoped, animated and composited by Ernest Farino and Bret Mixon at Gene Warren, Jr.'s Fantasy II Film Effects facility in Burbank, California. Lacking motion control equipment, the first appearance of the Hunter-Killer in the pre-title sequence (left) was animated stop-motion style by Gene Warren and crew using an elaborate overhead "aerial brace" rig.

Rotoscoped animation added the magical bolts striking Vermithrax in **Dragonslayer** (1981). The walking go-motion dragon also required hand rotoscoping to optically remove support rods.

The Robot displays its awesome powers in Irwin Allen's **Lost in Space** (1965-1968). L. B. Abbott's team at 20th Century-Fox added the animated electrical discharges.

For Roger Corman's **Galaxy of Terror** (1981) Ernest Farino and Mark Sawicki developed an etheral "glow" effect on the roto camera using ripple glass, fog filters and multiple passes in-camera to obscure the identity of Ray Walston's "Planet Master."

The "Finger of God inscribes the tablets of **The Ten Commandments** in Cecil B. DeMille's 1956 epic courtesy of Disney effects animator Joshua Meador. The visual effects animation team consisted of Ann Lord (supervisor), animators Roberta Johnson, Marlene Kempffer, Ed Parks, Pauline Rosenthal, and George Rowley, and assistant animators Edward Faigin, Marion Green, Angel Jimenez, and Bill Manhood.

The Tingler

Often debated in fan circles, and almost always described incorrectly, is the scene in **The Tingler** (1959) in which Judith Evelyn confronts a bathtub full of blood—from which a hand reaches up. The movie is black and white but the blood in this shot and one or two others, is in color. How can that be...?

An IMDb post claims that the set was painted in gray tones and filmed in color. The shot *was* filmed in color, but the set wasn't repainted (and there's no evidence of "gray" makeup on the actress). Nor was there any hand rotoscoping involved to isolate the blood area; this would have been betrayed by jittery edge irregularities (known as "chatter"). Rather—

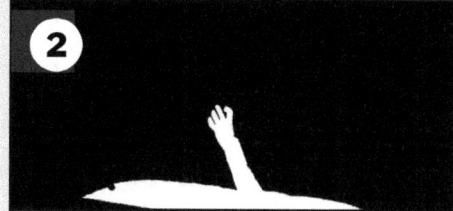

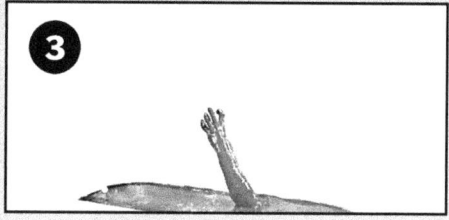

As with graphic arts, red photographs as black on hi-contrast black-and-white film. So the scene *was* filmed in color. Then, on the optical printer, the scene was printed onto hi-con film. The "blood" turned black. Roto animation filled in "holes" from glints or gray tones until a solid black silhouette was achieved (1). A reverse (negative) print yielded a clear center matte (2). A fine grain B&W print of the shot was made and, again on the optical printer, the matte and counter mattes were used to print the color image of the red blood (3) and the fine grain B&W background onto color film.

WITNESS FOR THE PROSECUTION

Optical Effects Tip the Scales of Justice

During the end credits an announcer says, "*The management suggests that you not divulge the secret of the ending of Witness for the Prosecution.*"

Okay, so we'll try not to give it away. But a bit of the action plays out as follows: Sir Wilfred (Charles Laughton) used his monocle earlier to reflect light to test his clients' sincerity. After the end of the trial he uses the monocle to "signal" Christine (Marlene Dietrich) and draw her attention to the knife on the table. The subtle spot of light ("reflected" by his monocle) onto the knife is an animated, rotoscoped optical effect in 2-3 cuts.

```
                VOLE
           (to the girl)
      Come on Diana, let's go.

Miss Plimsoll and Sir Wilfrid are watching the scene.
Sir Wilfrid is spinning his monocle on the ribbon,
the light flashing from it.

Vole and the girl have taken a few steps and are near
the exhibit table when Christine steps forward quickly,
holding Vole by the arm.

              CHRISTINE
      Don't, Leonard -- don't leave me.

                VOLE
      Now pull yourself together.  They'll
      have you up here for perjury -- don't
      make it worse or they'll try you as
      an accessory, and you know what that
      means.

              CHRISTINE
           (holding on to him)
      Let them.  Let them try me for
      perjury, or an accessory --
              (he shakes himself
              loose from her.  Her
              eyes fall on the flickering
              light from Wilfrid's monocle,
              flashing on the blade of
              the knife on the exhibit
              table)
      -- or better yet, let them try me
      for murder!

She grabs the knife, lurches after him, and with one
wild swoop plunges the knife into him.  He looks at
her as if almost in surprise, then crumples instantly.
Diana shrieks piercingly.
```

Opticals: Moving Mattes and Animated Visual Effects

"Well, boys, I reckon this is it—nuclear combat toe-to-toe with the Ruskies."

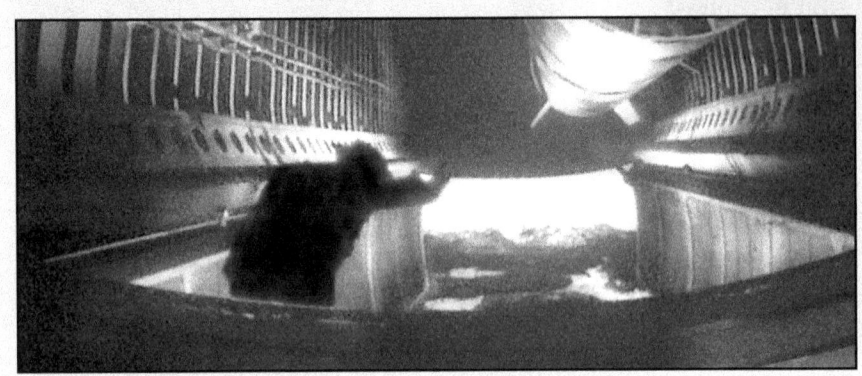

In his book *Calling Dr. Strangelove—The Anatomy and Influence of the Kubrick Masterpiece*, George Case wrote: "[Visual Effects Supervisor] Wally Veevers' main innovation was enabling [director Stanley] Kubrick and [Production Designer] Ken Adam to complete the climactic bomb-bay scene, where Major Kong (Slim Pickens) falls out of the aircraft while straddling a hydrogen bomb.

"Just [two seconds] in duration, the [first shot] of Major Kong dropping from the plane's cavernous interior *(above)* posed a serious problem for Adam. It was not in the shooting script, and the B-52 set was not equipped with working bomb-bay doors. 'So now I arrive at Shepperton and I'm having kittens because I knew it was a fantastic idea but physically, mechanically, we couldn't get it done,' Adam recalled. He brought the issue to Veevers, who returned the next day with a solution of using an 8x10 still photo of the set and placing a moving shot of Slim Pickens astride the bomb against the static picture—with a snipped out section where open bomb-bay doors would have been—as a matte.

"'For the overhead angle on Pickens riding the bomb down to earth *(duration: 11 seconds)*, the actor simply sat on the warhead as the camera was pulled up and away from him, to simulate a perspective of falling. 'We suspended the bomb on the stage at Shepperton [in front of a blue screen], and then craned back and optically reduced the last bit,' said Adam. 'Ground Zero' was a matte painting by Alan Maley." (8)

242 · *Smoke and Mirrors – Special Visual Effects Before Computers*

SCRAPBOOK

Thanks to blue screen, Laurence Olivier observes Roman troops composited with a Peter Ellenshaw matte painting in Stanley Kubrick's **Spartacus** (1960).

Vincent Price wages a battle with Boris Karloff in Roger Corman's **The Raven** (1963). Animation effects by the Butler-Glouner Company.

Willis O'Brien's effects in **The Last Days of Pompeii** (1935). Live action is matted over real water, a matte painting, and a smoking volcano.

Gene Kelly in **Anchors Aweigh** (1945) dances and interacts with Jerry, the mouse. Kelly was filmed first and that footage was rotoscoped frame by frame to plot the animation. Then, the footage was composited optically. Note the "reflection" of Jerry on the polished floor.

Opticals: Moving Mattes and Animated Visual Effects • 243

In **Conquest of Space** (1955), the space station was shot against blue then composited with the Earth and starfield, to provide a background for the spacemen, who were suspended from wires in front of a blue screen.

Shooting of blue screen scenes of the Stay Puft Marshmallow Man for **Ghostbusters** (1984) at Boss Film. The suit was sculpted by Linda Frobos and performed by Billy Bryan.

Peter Lorre watches **The Beast With Five Fingers** (1947) play the piano. The "Beast" performer wore black, and when matted onto the background everything in black disappeared, the same way Claude Rains had in **The Invisible Man** (1933).

In **Dunkirk** (1958), the British troops being rescued cower from a nearby violent explosion. Fortunately, they are matted over mayhem on a miniature.

Jack Gilford avoids the tail of a T-Rex in this blue screen composite from **Caveman** (1981). The film's comical character animation was by Randall William Cook, Pete Kleinow and Dave Allen.

In **The Rains Came** (1939) weather-gone-berserk earned an Oscar® for Fred Sersen, including the above high speed miniature of a building collapsing onto people via rotoscoped mattes.

244 · *Smoke and Mirrors – Special Visual Effects Before Computers*

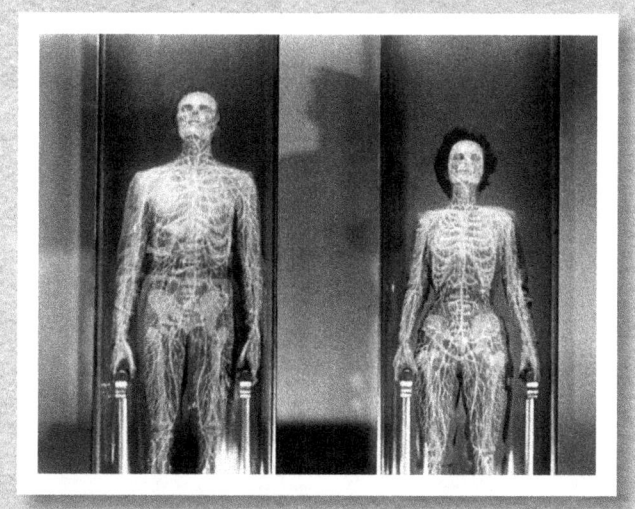

In **This Island Earth** (1955) Earthlings aboard a flying saucer go through "conversion"—that is, be covered with cel animation effects! Roswell A. Hoffmann, Universal's long time opticals expert, ran the printer while Frank Tipper handled the animation effects.

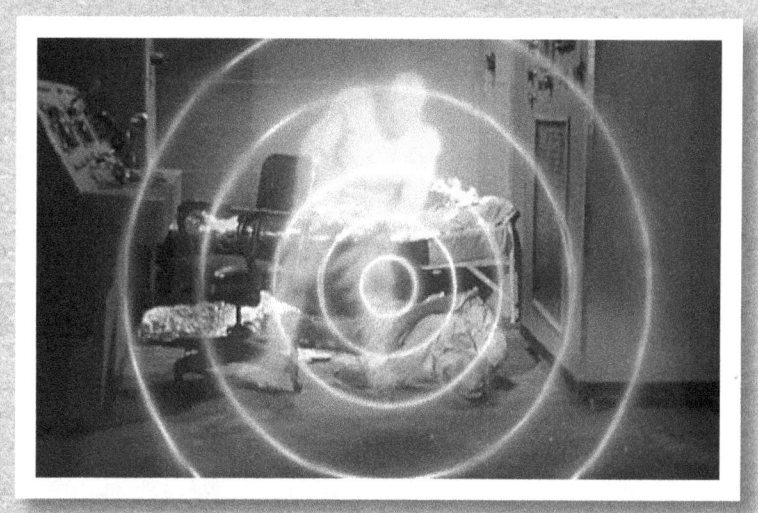

In **Invisible Invaders** (1959), which some feel inspired George Romero's **Night of the Living Dead** (1968), scientists use sound to make an alien visible. The performer is added optically, along with an animated series of concentric circles representing sound waves.

Michael Callan and Beth Rogan confront Ray Harryhausen's energetic bee in **Mysterious Island** (1961) via sodium light traveling mattes. Harryhausen started with the hive walled up by wax and then bit-by-bit enlarged the opening. The action was reverse-printed to give the illusion that the bee was sealing them in.

In another sodium light matte shot, the two young lovers discover Captain Nemo's Nautilus in a hidden grotto. (See Chapter 4 for an unmatted view of the miniature.)

Above: The storyboards for **The 3 Worlds of Gulliver** (1959) were done by a studio artist, the only time in Ray Harryhausen's career that he did not do them himself.

Right: The finished shot—Ray Harryhausen synchronized the crocodile animation to Kerwin Mathews' action, and the two elements were combined via traveling matte.

Opticals: Moving Mattes and Animated Visual Effects • 245

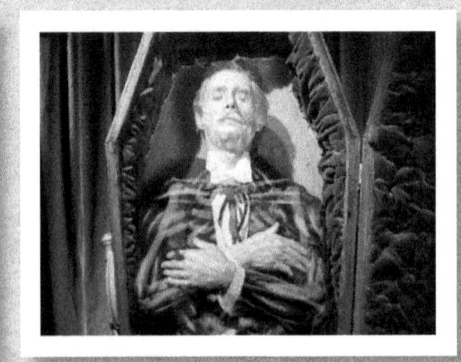

In **House of Frankenstein** (1944), Dr. Gustav Neimann (Boris Karloff) carelessly removes a stake from a skeleton in a coffin and discovers it was truly Count Dracula (John Carradine), who returns to the world of the living—thanks to rotoscoped cel animation.

Charlton Heston leads his people in front of a blue screen at Paramount for **The 10 Commandments** (1956, Oscar®-winner). Numerous elements were composited during the parting of the Red Sea (below, left), thanks to the large format 8-perf VistaVision negative that preserved image quality.

Edwin S. Porter executed this early in-camera matte for Edison's **The Great Train Robbery** (1903) to see a real train passing outside the window. I'm sure he never imagined how sophisticated matting would become by the time of John P. Fulton's work on **The 10 Commandments** (1956).

246 · *Smoke and Mirrors – Special Visual Effects Before Computers*

Above: Talk about irony! Norman Lloyd, a nasty Nazi in Alfred Hitchock's **Saboteur** (1942), plummets from the top of the ultimate symbol of America, the Statue of Liberty. Lloyd is composited over a vertigo-inducing matte painting. A similar live action shot appears in **Ghost Story** (1981), while for **Robocop** (1987) Rocco Gioffre staged the scene with a stop-motion double for Ronny Cox.

Above, right: Preparing to shoot Alan Rickman's climactic fall in **Die Hard** (1988). Because of his cooperation, it was possible to start from a close angle so the audience would have no doubt it was actually him.

Right: Rickman's look of surprise and terror was real; he was dropped earlier than expected to ensure a genuine reaction. Boss Film's composite is outstanding.

Above: A split screen in **The Phantom Planet** (1961), supervised by Louis DeWitt, shows tiny humanoids discovering a "huge" astronaut

Left: Bert I. Gordon's **Attack of the Puppet People** (1958) made use of split screens and upscaled props—many built by Paul Blaisdell—to "shrink" people.

Opticals: Moving Mattes and Animated Visual Effects • 247

When Dinosaurs Ruled the Earth (1970) was Hammer's only Oscar®-nominated film (for visual effects). Caveman Robin Hawdon on a section of land has been matted atop Jim Danforth's stop-motion animation.

The Deadly Mantis (1957) used the mantis and tunnel miniature as a background for matted live action and a claw was matted separately so it could appear to pass in front of the humans.

A split screen between the shoes of a "giant" for Irwin Allen's **Land of the Giants** (1968-1970), supervised by L. B. Abbott. The large scale steps with the actors required careful coordination to ensure they blended properly.

Hammer's **Kiss of the Vampire** (1963) boasts one of their most dramatic effects shots: a flock of cel-animated bats move towards the castle. Effects were supervised by Les Bowie.

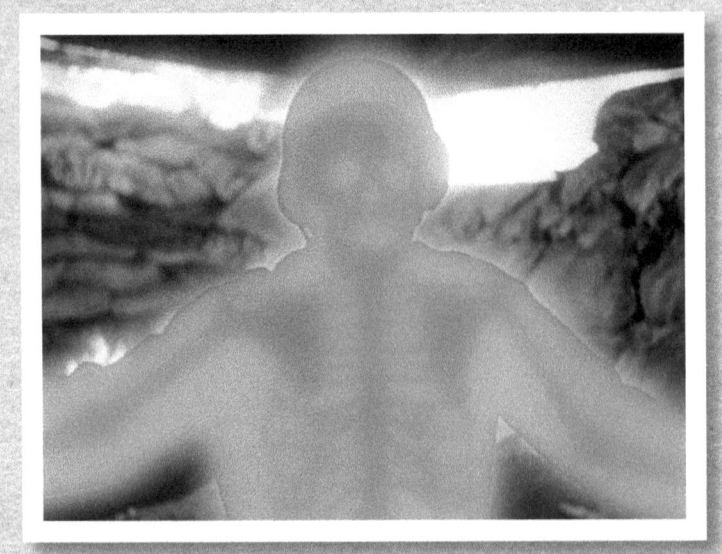

For George Pal's **War of the Worlds** (1953) the Martians' sizzling disintegration of Marine Col. Ralph Heffner (Vernon Rich) took 144 individually-painted cels to accomplish.

Linwood Dunn zapped **The Thing From Another World** (1951) with cel animation. Later, the smaller Billy Curtis replaced James Arness to reinforce the illusion that the Thing was being reduced to ashes.

248 · *Smoke and Mirrors – Special Visual Effects Before Computers*

Clockwise, from top left:

Tarantula (1955) is highlighted by jaw-dropping matte composites of a live spider filmed high-speed by Clifford Stine and David S. Horsely.

The Incredible Shrinking Man (1957) in a one-on-one duel for survival with a tarantula. The actor is optically added to the plate of the spider.

"Help meeee!" The shocking climax of **The Fly** (1958) showed the partially human fly pleading as a monstrous spider advances. Al Hedison was matted into the plate as the arachnid chomps down, courtesy of a hand-drawn matte.

In Bert I. Gordon's **The Cyclops** (1957), humans encounter a giant spider. The transparency on the spider suggests that it was a double-exposure.

One of Bert I. Gordon's trademark split screens added "giant ants" to a location in **Empire of the Ants**, AIP's most successful film of 1977.

The producers of **The Black Scorpion** (1957) saved a few dollars by not paying to print the animation into the mattes, rationalizing that it was, after all, a "black scorpion."

Impressed by the success of **Tarantula**, Bert I. Gordon made **The Spider** (1958). His standard split screens combined the spider and the live action.

Opticals: Moving Mattes and Animated Visual Effects

For **John Carpenter's The Thing** (1981), the reveal of a crashed saucer embedded in the ice is a superb Albert Whitlock matte painting complete with shifting sunlight. The foreground actors have been added via blue screen under Bill Taylor's supervision.

Jim Danforth's animation for **7 Faces of Dr. Lao** (1964) earned his first Oscar®-nomination. Jim shot a rear projection test but Project Unlimited went with frontlight/backlight mattes, composited at MGM under Robert Hoag's supervision.

Cel animation was used in this shot of **Kronos** (1957), a giant robot. Irving Block, Jack Rabin, Louis DeWitt and Gene Warren, Sr., created effective visuals on a slim budget.

The "girl on the swing" in the pre-title sequence of **Terminator 2: Judgment Day** (1991) transitions from normal color to blue-and-white and finally "whites out" to suggest a nuclear blast. The desaturated blue-and-white look had been accidentally created by making several generations of color dupes of the work print (made for sound editors and others). Jim Cameron liked the look and turned to Ernest Farino for the job, suggesting YCM separations, color filters, and so on. Jim said, "So, you want to do that?" Mindful of the release date mere weeks away, Farino said, "No." A room full of editors and producers went deathly silent at the very notion that someone said "No" to James Cameron. But, since they'd worked together on **Galaxy of Terror**, **The Terminator**, and **The Abyss**, Cameron said, "Well, how would you do it...?" Farino pointed to the image frozen on the screen and said, "There it is. Find out how you got that and do it over, clean." So a new color print was made and Frank Holmes Laboratories in Hollywood (which specialized in such color dupes) duped the shot 4 or 5 times until a clean version with the same color scheme was reproduced. A somewhat out-of-the-ordinary "optical" process...

For Ray Harryhausen's **Clash of the Titans** (1981), 5' tall miniatures were pre-cut and rigged to collapse when dump tanks spilled water on them. The flooding was shot high-speed and actors were composited via blue screen.

250 · *Smoke and Mirrors – Special Visual Effects Before Computers*

Klaatu and Gort depart in their saucer at the climax of **The Day the Earth Stood Still** (1951). In the optical printer, under L. B. Abbott's supervision, a first pass added the saucer to the background and a second exposure with a fog filter added the pulsating glow.

In **The Land Unknown** (1957), Jock Mahoney runs back to his helicopter, to hopefully take off before the pursuing man-in-a-suit T-Rex can catch him. The actors and full-sized rotorcraft are matted into the miniature prehistoric setting.

Sherlock Holmes Faces Death (1943) and Basil Rathbone saves Hillary Brooke from rotoscoped cel animation timed to match the on-set pyrotechnics.

Director Eugene Lourié's **The Colossus of New York** (1958) unleashes killer death rays on people at the United Nations. The suit was built by Charles Gemora.

Arnold Bedford (Edward Judd), one of **The First Men 'In' the Moon** (1964), faces many threats, including clinging to a ledge above an immense tunnel—a matte painting by Les Bowie.

Opticals: Moving Mattes and Animated Visual Effects • 251

Above: **Dr. Cyclops** *(1940) falls to his doom. Albert Dekker has been matted onto a painted element of the pit.*

Top, right: Alec Baldwin and Geena Davis dangle precariously above a stop-motion worm monster in **Beetlejuice** *(1988), the work of Jim Aupperle, James Belohovek, Doug Beswick, Spencer Gill, Peter Kuran, and Alan Munro.*

Right: Stuart Whitman and Terry-Thomas fly—via Linwood Dunn's traveling matte work—in **Those Magnificent Men in Their Flying Machines** *(1965).*

Right: Having delivered the Main Title to **The Abyss** *(1989), Ernest Farino took several "simpler" opticals to Pacific Title to lighten the workload at DreamQuest Images. This shot of the* **Benthic Explorer** *originally did not include the approaching helicopters. However, the editors found footage of the two helicopters by themselves, full frame against a plain sky. A "traveling matte" was extracted from the green record of the color negative, which served to place the choppers in the sky. Neither helicopter had its headlight on, so, to match the other shots in the scene, the chopper on the right was tracked frame-by-frame on the animation stand to add a "headlight" effect with animation.*

For **Honey, I Shrunk the Kids** *(1989), young actors and an upscaled bee prop were filmed in front of a blue screen, then a background plate simulating the dizzying trajectory of an insect's flight was composited behind them.*

A Derek Meddings miniature provided a plate for this composite in **Journey to the Far Side of the Sun** *(1969, UK:* **Doppelganger***), Gerry and Sylvia Anderson's first theatrical film. Props were recycled into their live action series* **UFO** *(1970-1971).*

252 · *Smoke and Mirrors – Special Visual Effects Before Computers*

Chapter 7
The Bad and the Ugly

There is an old show Show Biz adage, "Leave 'em laughing!" In that spirit, I present a few films that had the audacity to display some of The Worst Special Effects of All Time, B.C.—Before Computers. These offenders have been culled from a much longer list, and if you are an aficionado of dismal film effects, I hope I haven't left off your favorite. If you are on a quest to catch up with the best of the worst—watch these. I guarantee you will be entertained—admittedly, in a bad way.

It is fair to say that the majority of these shows tended to use classic "bait and switch" posters, borrowing the American International Pictures' (A.I.P.) technique of creating a splashy poster that doesn't deliver on any of its promises. By the way, there are several films from A.I.P., reaping what they sowed!

Many people feel that several of the titles on this list were immeasurably enhanced by appearing on **Mystery Science Theatre 3000** and I can't disagree.

You have been warned!

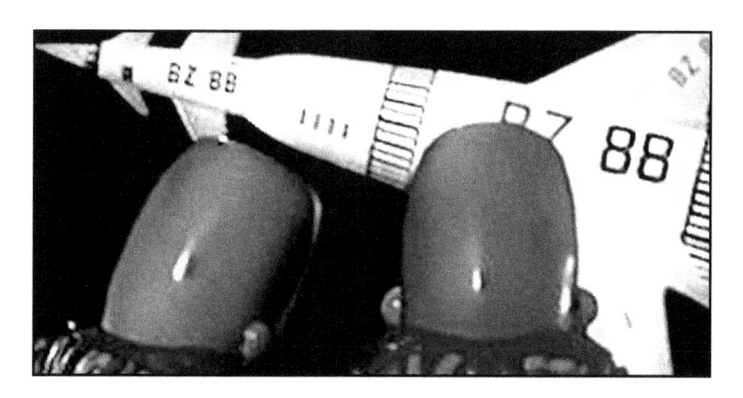

Assignment Outer Space (1960)
—and similar Italian space operas like **Wild, Wild Planet** (1966) are hampered by extremely small models, that are photographed poorly in a vain attempt to hide how shoddy the work is. In some instances, the spacecraft are clearly inspired by Lindberg plastic kits of the era. And, of course, there was never enough money to shoot things high-speed, so spaceships frequently swing from wires like Johnny Weissmuller in the jungle.

At the Earth's Core (1976)
—has some of the worst monster-suits ever designed, built and filmed, period. Someone other than Amicus could have made a terrific adventure film out of this Edgar Rice Burroughs novel. It was a shame the producers didn't turn to Roger Dicken, whose hand-puppets had helped enliven *The Land That Time Forgot* (1975) and *Warlords of Atlantis* (1978). *The People That Time Forgot* (1977) suffers from the same ineptitude that plagues *At the Earth's Core*—and some argue it may even be worse... as impossible as that sounds.

The Brain From Planet Arous (1957)
—gives a three-fer! An alien brain-monster prop laughably wobbling on glinting wires plus two firecracker detonations of airplane model kits. The "Aurora/Revell miniature" shots are made even more mind-numbingly unacceptable when the editor, Irving Schoenberg, couldn't be bothered to cut before sections of the planes' wings came swinging back and spun on their wires. All concerned were embarrassed, I'm sure, and I still feel badly for legendary makeup artist Jack Pierce having his name on this...

The Brainiac (1963)
—is among the rarest of the rare in the realm of z-grade movie-making and dreadful special effects, in that its sheer awfulness is a sales come-on in marketing at least one of its home video releases. Blame entrepreneur K. Gordon Murray, who specialized in importing Mexican productions like *The Robot vs the Aztec Mummy* (1958) and *Santa Claus* (1959), for inflicting the re-titled *El Baron Del Terror* (1962) on us.

Connoisseurs of "gag me with a spoon" films will not be disappointed with an utterly ridiculous storyline featuring a cartoony rubber monster doing silly brain-sucking. The floppy latex head and hands look like rejects from Ernie Kovacs' Nairobi Trio.

The film also has the gall to use a number of the worst rear projection composites since the 1930s. There is not a scintilla of effort expended trying to blend the background and foreground; the most basic matching of the live action camera angles to the backgrounds was an alien concept nor is there minimal effort to light the scenes adequately. These composites hold the audience in contempt.

Believe me when I say that *The Brainiac* is why fast forward was invented.

Captain Sindbad (1963)
—was directed by Byron Haskin, who seems to have sleepwalked through the production. Surprisingly, on such a complex production, there is no credit for production design—which they sorely needed because

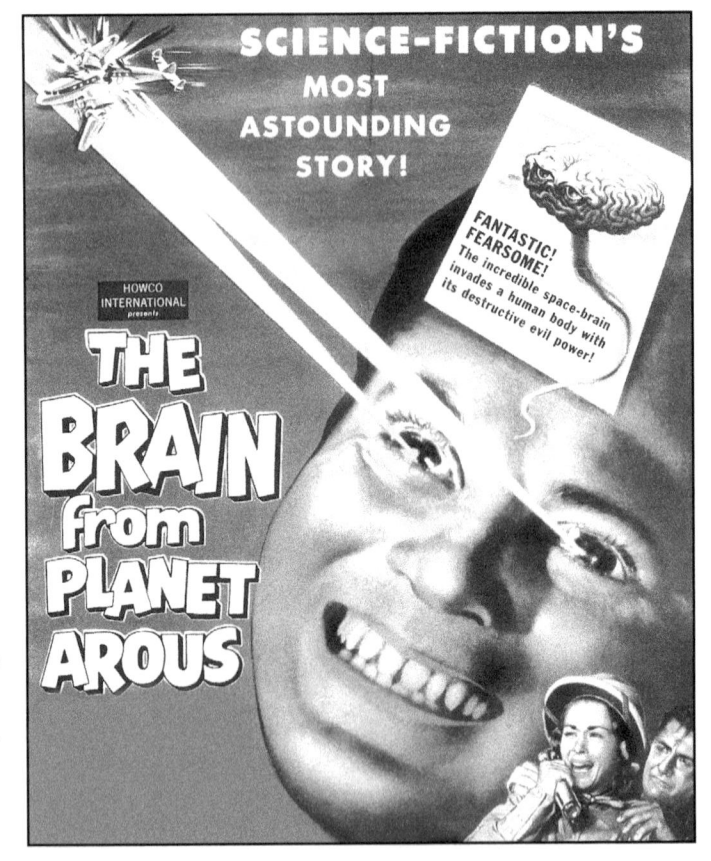

The Brainiac *(1963)*

Captain Sindbad (1963)

the husband and wife team of art directors, Isabella Schlichting and Werner Schlichting, were clearly not up to the task. The film suffers from one of the most embarrassing creatures put on film, a multi-headed dragon that would be better off in the Macy's Thanksgiving Day Parade! The prop does manage to exhale smoke before it is easily dispatched over a cliff, so that's something... Interestingly, a better design with fewer heads dominates the German posters.

There's one full-sized close-up head used for Sindbad to strike with his sword. Augie Lohman and Lee Zavitz, both of whom had extensive effects backgrounds ranging from mechanicals to pyrotechnics, are credited with special effects, but judging by the on-screen results, one has to wonder if they even visited the Bavaria Studios in Munich, Germany.

The film is also cursed with consistently dreadful optical work, from terrible composites of Sindbad (Guy Williams) at sea to the villainous El Kerim (Pedro Armendariz) spinning the head of the sorceror, Galgo (Abraham Soafer). The best opticals are when Sindbad faces an invisible monster who leaves footsteps—a la the Id's tracks in **Forbidden Planet** (1956)—that produce an explosion of green sparks; unfortunately, the timings and positions are not always right. The lackluster opticals are quite surprising because Tom Howard certainly knew what he was doing. The Dell Movie Comic (#309) was considerably more imaginative... and fun.

The Creeping Terror (1964)

—bears the distinction of making Ed Wood's films look like brilliantly crafted masterworks. **The Creeping Terror** had an unsavory production history that is more entertaining than the film itself, having been made by a con man, the notorious A. J. Nelson, who stars in the picture as "Vic Savage." The extent of the technical competence that went into making all aspects of this movie are, to put it generously, subpar.

The monster, designed by John Lackey, is derisively referred to as The Carpet Monster by reviewers because that is exactly what it looks like, with assorted rubber bits and tubing glued onto it. One poor man stands at the front, shaking the head and waddling on flippers while other people inside the body follow along. In spite of its many shortcomings, there are a few unique moments not usually seen in a monster-on-the-loose movie. In one instance, it looks like the monster is having sex with a car. And who could forget the unintentional hilarity of watching a man with a guitar trying to beat the monster senseless—while being very careful not to damage the instrument?

I defy you to stay awake during this meandering display of amateurism.

The Bad and the Ugly • 255

Fire Maidens of Outer Space (1956)
—is a British production also apparently known as *Fire Maidens from Outer Space*. By any title, this is a ponderously tiresome production utterly devoid of craftsmanship on either side of the camera; for instance, why waste money on a miniature spaceship when you can use cheap stock shots of V2 rocket tests? Astronauts land on a moon of Jupiter and discover it is occupied by some descendants of Atlantis, who inexplicably were able to depart the Earth rather than just sail to another continent. Except for one elderly man, the entire population conveniently consists of nubile nymphettes longing for male companionship.

Injected into this hormonal mix is one of the most ridiculous makeups ever, for the menacing "Black God"—a performer wearing a skin tight black leotard with a mask that is awesome in its banality. The most memorable sequence is the Fire Maidens' interpretive dance to the classical music of Borodin, which has to be seen to be believed.

The Giant Gila Monster (1959)
—was produced in Texas by Ken Curtis ("Festus" on the long-running CBS series, *Gunsmoke*), along with *Attack of the Killer Shrews*. Released as a double-bill, what can you say when *Shrews* comes off as being a better film only because of close proximity to *Gila Monster*? Both films were directed by Ray Kellogg, who had been involved with special visual effects on productions like *Rains of Ranchipur* (1955), even heading the department at 20th Century-Fox, which accounts for the passable miniature work. But overall, the tiresome script, unprofessional actors, lame musical interludes and the fact the monster is never in the same frame with the "victims" brings the film down, down, down. It is a safe bet that neither of these gems were on anyone's résumés.

The Giant Spider Invasion (1975)
—deserves some kind of credit for overcoming being shot in Merrill, Wisconsin, by Director/Co-Producer Bill Rebane. Even with that cost-saving maneuver, there was still a limit to how far they could stretch their $250,000 budget. The arachnids seen on film are so inadequate that they could only appear in publicity stills through extensive photo retouching.

Apparently, there were two large "spiders" built with 30' leg spans, constructed over Volkswagen "Beetles" and covered with artificial black fur. Fake legs were operated from inside by crew members while the cars' tail lights provided *eeee-vil*, red-glowing eyes. Stop-motion animator Robert Maine was contacted about designing and creating the spiders but for whatever reason, that job went to effects technician Bob Millay. For the climax, the effects team dusted a spider with gun powder and dropped wooden matches on it, but the prop stubbornly refused to erupt—that is, until immediately after the director called "cut" to stop wasting valuable raw stock. OOOPS...

Godmonster of Indian Flats (1973)
—everyone's favorite mutant sheep film, is like watching a train wreck: you want to look away, but you can't help yourself. The sheer ineptitude at all levels of basic filmmaking guaranteed that the special effects *had* to be equally bad. This movie makes us appreciate the comparatively bravura direction and stellar production values of Ed Wood, Jr.'s **Night of the Ghouls** (1959).

Gojira (1954)
—is much better than the U.S. release, **Godzilla, King of the Monsters** (1956). Inspired by Ray Harryhausen's brilliant—and financially successful—**The Beast from 20,000 Fathoms** (1953), **Gojira** benefits from moody black and white cinematography and an evocative score. However, the visual effects are inconsistent and the creature is ultimately unsatisfying because the technicians were so inexperienced in making a rubber monster suit that the end result allowed little mobility for the performer inside. Haru Nakajima, encased in the heavy suit, stomps stiffly through the miniatures, literally unable to do much else. The most vitality the monster displays is when stop-motion was used for a shot of the tail doing more than flopping about.

Its success fueled a long string of productions that utilized "suitmation," men wearing monster suits and romping around on tabletop settings. While not my cup of tea, I appreciate the affection fans have for the menagerie of creatures from Toho and other Japanese studios. That being said, to me none of them have been as entertaining as the first movie, and while the miniatures themselves have usually been acceptable, they have seldom been photographed in a way to do them justice.

The Great Alligator (1979)
—(original title: **Il Fiume Del Grande Caimano**). This Italian film, shot mostly in Sri Lanka, emphasizes a predatory reptile which is only found in North America and China, even though this film is set on a tropical island complete with stock shots of hippos and elephant sound effects. Maybe it is Africa?

The story is a blend of **Jaws** (1975), Italian films like **Mountain of the Cannibal God** (1978) and disaster films like Irwin Allen's **The Swarm** (1978). A real estate developer played by Mel Ferrar, stokes the ire of a local

The Bad and the Ugly • 257

demon by building a hotel prompting it to exact revenge by manifesting itself as a BIG alligator—that looks suspiciously like a crocodile—which proceeds to masticate both natives and inaugural visitors to the resort.

Carlo De Marchis, who collaborated with Carlo Rambaldi on **Barbarella** (1968), built the full-sized prop of the body, head and jaws that interact with performers. It isn't bad, just limited by budget. On the other hand, underwater miniature shots are so ineptly amateurish they look like they were staged by a child in a bathtub. Clearly, whoever was doing them just didn't know how to get anything usable on a limited budget.

I have read comments that a "baby alligator" was used for the miniature shots but it certainly looks like a rubber toy crocodile to me. The head is peculiar in shape, so it is unlikely to me that they molded an actual specimen, and the use of toy vehicles makes me inclined to believe this was a found item of some sort. They do try to impart a little life by moving the tail slightly, but overall these shots are just dismal.

To their credit, they do burn down a small scale model of the resort, undoubtedly made by De Marchis, who was a trained architectural model maker and had built miniatures for films like **The Bible** (1966).

The alternately titled **Alligator** has a painted poster that features a nude girl in the mouth of the gator, though some versions add a bikini for modesty's sake. Beware of being mislead into thinking this is the superior **Alligator** (1980), written by John Sayles. Other titles include **Alligators**, **Caiman**, **The Big Alligator River**, **The River of the Great Alligator,** and **The Big Caimano River**. Everyone seems to agree that Barbara Bach is the highlight of the film—even if she is dubbed.

***The Great Alligator** (1979)*

The Horror of Party Beach (1964)
—Posters proclaim it is "The First Horror Monster Musical!" however, Ray Denis Steckler's **The Incredibly Strange Creatures Who Stopped Living and Became Mixed-Up Zombies** had been released a few months earlier. **Party Beach** was intended as one-half of a drive-In double-bill, with **Curse of the Living Corpse** made first.

Unusually, the first credit is for the Art Director, Bob Verberkmoes, a theater set designer responsible for the creature concepts. The suits were fabricated at Gutzon Borglum's sculpting studio in Stamford, Connecticut. He is better known for creating Mount Rushmore.

There are two types of creatures, with apparently two of each design being made. One design is featured prominently, covered with flopping vinyl sheets as scales, and a headpiece with immovable pop-eyes and a spiked frill. Worse, they have "sausages" crammed in their mouths! Seriously, what on earth were the filmmakers thinking? Had the monsters attended a Nathan's Coney Island Hot Dog Eating Contest? The better suits

258 · *Smoke and Mirrors – Special Visual Effects Before Computers*

are covered with seaweed and lack the spikey-frill and pop-eyes. Even though these are by far the better costumes, they are inexplicably not used much.

I was optimistic in the first reel when a single stop-motion cut shows an eye roll in the head, but any hopes were quickly dashed. As in many black and white films, chocolate syrup simulated blood, but not even that could sweeten the film.

The best thing about this movie was the one-shot Warren Publishing Company magazine that told the story in stills. saving you from enduring the real thing.

Jaws 3-D (1983)
—had a great idea to use a stop-motion shark *(by Ted Rae, left)* but, oddly, didn't exploit the possibilities. The scariest things are the unrelentingly grainy and murky opticals. The biggest misfire, however, is that they had no clue how to properly shoot for stereo. For instance, some idiot thought to put the 3-D camera *inside the shark's mouth* as it pursues a victim. I nominate this as one of the worst camera angles, *ever...*

Killers from Space (1954)
—features the least intimidating aliens of all-time, thanks to huge eyes rumored to have been made from ping-pong balls. That is, until make-up artist Harry Thomas set the record straight—he used the bottoms of egg cartons. No matter, they sabotage any attempt at serious villains.

Like other movies of the period, it derives much of its production values from stock shots. A-bomb tests provide most of the opening of the film and when the chief alien obligingly fills in nuclear scientist Dr. Doug Martin (Peter Graves) about the invaders' plans, we are treated to a barrage of nature scenes of bubbling lava, tarantulas and horned toads. To represent the alien world of Astron Delta, they used one of the few special effects shots from Monogram's **Flight to Mars** (1951) as well as footage from a World's Fair documentary of futuristic buildings. However, the editor was too lazy to trim an optical wipe that linked two cuts in the World's Fair scenes. Later, nature clips are poorly rear projected as gigantic insects bred by the aliens to unleash on humanity. Graves wisely gives up trying to look frightened.

King Kong Lives (1986)
—simply stinks on ice. I'm glad people made a buck working on it, but that doesn't mean I'll ever watch it again. Even if you're a **King Kong** completist, don't bother.

Konga (1961)
—Saying it makes me shudder—for the wrong reasons. Herman Cohen licensed the use of Kong's name for

The Bad and the Ugly • 259

$20,000 to have something to exploit and A.I.P.'s bait-and-switch posters promise "Not since **King Kong**... Has The Screen Exploded With Such Mighty Fury and Spectacle!" All we got was George Barrows' gorilla suit—rented for the film— shuffling around on "murder missions." The ballyhooed giant ape finally appears in the last reel but a dearth of imagination and lame opticals combine to rob the climax of any impact.

On the other hand, the film does amuse with Michael Gough's array of carnivorous plants, one species of which is large and unapologetically phallic-looking, while another species looks like a pair of, well, testicles. The plants get plenty of screen time, especially when starlet Claire Gordon is assaulted by an aroused Venus flytrap.

But I still want my money back.

Logan's Run (1976)
—is a serious puzzle. My disappointment in the film pertains to the inexcusably small scale miniature city, which is an unfathomable misfire considering L.B. Abbott's credentials. The model wouldn't have been allowed in a World's Fair display. The tabletop further compounds its errors using real running water that kills the illusion by revealing its small scale. And who on earth painted that abysmal backdrop?! On the other hand, Matt Yuricich's paintings are a highlight, and he deserved his Academy Award.

Master of the World (1961)
—is an adaptation of a Jules Verne novel by A.I.P.— your first clue something might go wrong. On the plus side, it features a very intriguing miniature airship, *The Albatross*, built by Project Unlimited. Overall, though, the film is threadbare and never has enough money for the visual effects. Much the same way the Irwin Allen TV series **The Time Tunnel** (1966) relied on past 20th Century-Fox features for stock shots, **Master of the World** could not have been made without stock shots—and generally-poor rear projection.

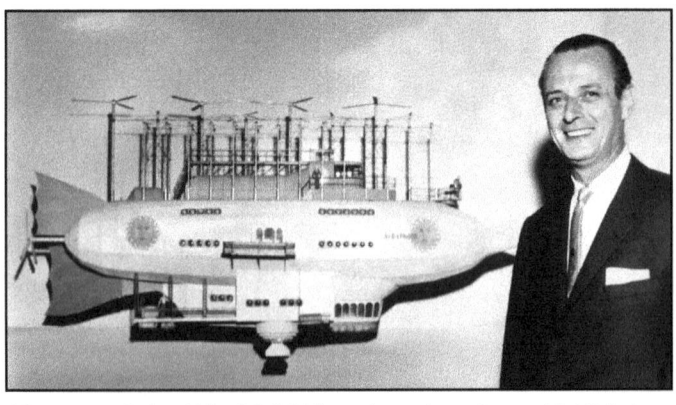

Master of the World *(1961), with producer James H. Nicholson.*

Meteor (1979)
—yet another misfire by A.I.P., co-produced with the Shaw Brothers in Hong Kong. Trying to up their game as a "big" studio, all they succeeded in doing was making the star-studded cast look lost among anemic visual effects—which included recycling disaster footage from **Avalanche** (1978). The menacing meteor was a chunk of volcanic rock from Hawaii.

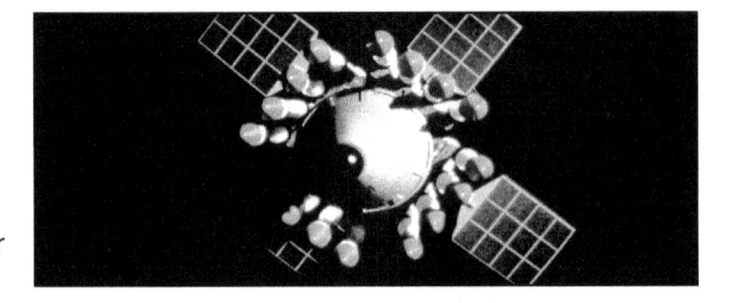

The Mighty Gorga (1969)
—is possibly the most hideously wretched **King Kong** rip-off ever made. Shame on David Hewitt, who certainly knew better. He owes us all an apology.

Night of the Lepus (1972)
—is based upon the science fiction novel *The Year of the Angry Rabbit* (1964) by Russell Braddon. Producer A.C. Lyles, primarily known for westerns, must not have read the script because it is such a radical departure from his bread-and-butter output. Regrettably, his only sci-fi production took a drubbing by the critics and worse, it flopped at the box-office. As a result, Lyles never ventured into the genre again.

How on earth do you make cute widdle wabbits—scary? Having them run around on miniature table-tops is not the answer.

One Million AC/DC (1969)
—is a softcore exploitation film written by Ed Wood, Jr. that shamelessly abuses plastic toys as stand-ins for actual visual effects. It has no respect for the audience, so endure at your own peril.

Plan 9 From Outer Space (1959)
—Any list of the "worst" anything in movies feels incomplete without the presence of Ed Wood, Jr., whom I feel is unfairly branded as the worst filmmaker of all time. Really, there are more deserving candidates (hello **Godmonster of Indian Flats**). I have always respected Wood for trying to rise above his limitations.

People make fun of his use of the Lindberg plastic model kit UFOs, the first injection-molded sci-fi model kits. I applaud Wood's ingenuity, but that doesn't excuse the end result from this list.

Queen Kong (1976)
—A British-German co-production, ostensibly a comedy parodying **King Kong** (1933), is relentlessly unfunny. It was originally kept from distribution after legal action by Dino De Laurentiis to keep them from riding on the coattails of his 1976 re-make. The dreadful gorilla suit—with breasts, no less—is so ghastly, it makes the simian in Toho's **King Kong vs. Godzilla** (1963) look good, a feat I never expected. The only real "asset" is the presence of Hammer starlet Valerie Leon *(far left)*.

Reptilicus (1961)
—The Danes made this and then said "never again." Once was more than enough when it came to making a giant monster movie. There are one or two acceptable publicity stills, enhanced by extensive re-touching, but the film footage of a limp marionette is just "Punch and Judy" bad. The visual effects are an endurance test to watch, including the green acid venom cel animation added by A.I.P. to generate some kind of visual interest. At least the Danish musical interludes were cut for the U.S. release, sparing us *that* indignity.

The Bad and the Ugly

Robot Monster (1953)

—is a 3-D film with no understanding of how to use stereo. But it does have the only screen credit ever for the Automatic Billion Bubble Machine. Unfortunately, Ro-Man the Monster—George Barrows performing in his gorilla suit and replacing his usual head with a prop space helmet—presents us with one of the silliest alien invaders, ever. The best thing about the movie is the unauthorized appearance of the head of Ray Harryhausen's Rhedosaurus from **The Beast from 20,000 Fathoms** (1953) on some of the posters.

The Robot vs. the Aztec Mummy (1958)

—This is the final installment of a trilogy of films shot back to back in 1957 that featured Popoca, the Aztec Mummy. This production was designed to stretch the budget—such as it was—by using clips from the earlier films: La Momia Azteca (1957, U.S.: **Attack of the Mayan Mummy**) and La Maldición de la Momia Azteca (1957, U.S.: **The Curse of the Aztec Mummy**). The less said about this crapper... er, capper to the series, the better. It truly deserved ending up on MST3K.

The Saga of the Viking Women and Their Voyage to the Waters of the Great Sea Serpent (1957)

—(aka **Viking Women and the Sea Serpent**). Special effects artists Irving Block and Jack Rabin brought a presentation to Roger Corman, offering to work for a small fee and profit participation. Roger knew it would cost more than he was willing to spend, but he couldn't resist the "good deal" they were offering.

There are a few acceptable matte paintings by Jack Rabin, but as capable as he, Block and their associate Louis DeWitt were, the sea serpent is proof positive that sometimes you actually need a reasonable budget. Footage of the small sea serpent prop was generated in a minimally-sized tank and rear projected behind the cast with absolutely no interaction during the climax, robbing the audience of a satisfying pay-off.

"Fabulous! Spectacular! Terrifying!" More advertising deceit by A.I.P.? I'm shocked...

Santa Claus Conquers the Martians (1964)

—was conceived by former unit manager of the Howdy Doody marionette series, Paul L. Jacobson, seeking to parlay his experience marketing to kids during the Christmas season. By any metric, it exceeded any realistic expectations and has become a perennial holiday "treat." That being said, do yourself a kindness and just flip through the March, 1966 Dell Comics version.

If you were growing up in the sixties, undoubtedly you were amused to see the Martians' rayguns were

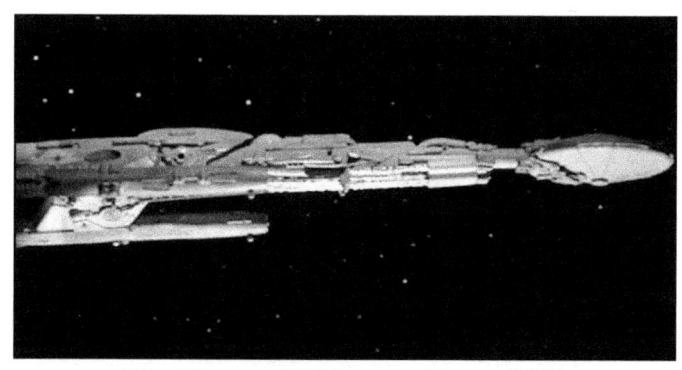

The Shape of Things to Come (1979)

merely Wham-O air blaster toys. The mildly fun toys were perfectly in tune with an abysmal polar bear costume and a robot that looked like a refugee from **The Bowery Boys Meet the Monsters** (1954).

The Shape of Things to Come (1979)
—The best thing to say about this Canadian production is that they didn't even vaguely touch on H.G. Wells' 1933 story **The Shape of Things to Come**. This film seems determined to achieve some kind of record for bad miniatures and worse direction. Poor Jack Palance...

The Ship of Monsters (1960)
—aka **La Nave de los Monstruos** is a Mexican sci-fi musical "comedy" released in the U.S. as **The Ship of Monsters**. I think it could best be described as an Ed Wood fever dream. Two sexy Venusian women, Gamma (Ana Bertha Lepe, Miss Mexico, 1953) and Beta (Lorena Velazquez, Miss Mexico, 1960) are forced to land their rocket ship on Earth, temporarily interrupting their mission of searching alien worlds for mates to help repopulate their planet.

Of course, once they encounter singing cowboy, Lauriano (Eulalio "Piporro" Gonzalez) they quickly fall for him. Also on board their spacecraft is a robot named Tor—left over from the Aztec Mummy series—along with a collection of alien creatures: Uk the cyclops, the many-armed Carasus, Tagual the Prince of Mars, Utirr the spider, and an utterly deranged, off-the-wall concept: a living dinosaur skeleton named Zok. For some reason the Venusians choose monsters as mates. Inasmuch as the (naked) creatures have no visible genitalia, one has to wonder why these specimens were chosen, especially the talking dinosaur bones. Analyzing this could lead to madness...

Collectively, the suits and props are slightly better than homemade Halloween costumes, but not by much. There is a credit for *Effectos Especiales* by Juan Munoz Ravelo, but I have no idea if he made the suits or the spaceship miniature seen in a few shots—which may even be from another Mexican film. From time to time there is a substantial improvement in the visuals thanks to stock shots from a Russian movie, possibly **Road to the Stars** (1957), which are quite well-done.

Fortify yourself before watching this "messterpiece."

Son of Godzilla (1967) *(far left)*
—I am not a fan of suitmation and this is a bottom-of-the-barrel low-point. And that's saying a lot.

Sting of Death (1965) *(left)*
—The monster suit defies description, as it doesn't work on any level. On the other hand, you have to admire the brass it took to release footage of it.

The Bad and the Ugly • 263

Street Trash (1987)
—features a toilet bowl monster. Need I say more?

Star Wars (1977)
—yeah, the original film. While I loved the idea of the storm troopers riding big lizards, the original execution left much to be desired. Just ask George Lucas! The unconvincing props were among the many CG 'fixes' he implemented for his revisionist version of the movie, *Star Wars: Episode IV – A New Hope*.

Superman IV: The Quest for Peace (1987)
—falls flat because of severe budget restrictions and can't be mentioned in the same breath with the first three films. I was part of a team at Cinema Research Corporation that proposed doing the flying scenes with stop-motion, rather like ILM would do in a few years for *The Rocketeer* (1991). Even that approach was too costly for this cut-rate bore trying to make a buck off the earlier films' reputations.

Teenagers From Outer Space (1959)
—was released in the UK as *The Gargon Terror* with an 'X' rating, for people over age 16 (yet again, the UK censors boggle my mind). The UK poster presents a readily-identifiable lobster—er, Gargon—grabbing a human skeleton. Of course, there is no scene in the film even *remotely* like the UK poster. OOPS! I let the cat out of the bag—the Gargon is a lobster.

As cheap as this $14,000 indie was—no sync sound, for instance—the writer-producer-director, Tom Graeff, stretched his budget by grabbing shots around Hollywood. He avoided building an expensive prop by merely double-exposing the ferocious Gargon with his actors. The poor lobster was forced to toil away and then probably ended up as the crew's lunch.

Perhaps Graeff was inspired by Republic's serial **Panther Girl of the Kongo** (1955), which looked like **Citizen Kane** (1941) by comparison, thanks to a rear projected crustacean and full-sized prop claw.

Graeff was confronted with a problem, how to provide actors with prop rayguns that were vital to "blast the flesh off beautiful girls in less than a second," as the publicity campaign promised. Poverty being the mother of invention, he used Hubley Atomic Disintegrator cap-firing toy rayguns, although a different Daisy Buck Rogers disintegrator pistol shows up on the posters. The poster-promised flesh-vaporizing is done via a simple editorial pop-off *ala* Georges Mèliés; a jointed biological supply house skeleton was substituted for the performer—or dog, as the case may be—and then the editor cut from a live specimen to a skeletonized "victim" as a light effect was supered over the scenes.

Troll 2 (1990)
—this Italian film features irredeemably bad facial appliances and hand-puppets that left me embarrassed for those responsible.

The Trollenberg Terror (1958)
—is a British indie based on a six-part TV series directed by Quentin Lawrence with a script by Jimmy Sangster (responsible for many Hammer screenplays like **The Curse of Frankenstein** in 1957). Released in the U.S. as **The Crawling Eye** (1958), it was one of three UK genre films starring American actor Forrest Tucker.

Legendary special effects craftsman Les Bowie was a master at stretching a budget and the visuals include traveling mattes, split screens, custom props and extensive miniature effects but the work is consistently hampered by the woefully limited budget.

He delivered an army of creatures menacing people in an ice-bound observatory. In fact, the picture should have been called **The Trollenberg Terrors** or **The Crawling Eyes**. Sadly, the creature design is so absurd that it produces more laughs than chills—in spite of the snowy setting. I give Bowie and his crew a big tip of the hat for the sheer volume of shots they delivered—they even have a Canberra jet bomber flash through the frame after incinerating the creatures—but, unfortunately, he was forced to take shortcuts, such as making the models very small and the end results suffer.

The Woman Eater (1958)
—was titled **Womaneater** (1958) on its initial UK release. Unfortunately, no mere title change could save this British snooze-fest. During its 1959 U.S. release, the campaign targeted kids, proving once again that marketers seldom knew what to do with genre films.

The chlorophyll creature is rooted in place, forcing the villains to shove a parade of unwilling female victims into its grasp—who obligingly shriek while trying to act like the prop is a menace. Meryl Streep would have found it challenging making this seem "real" because the plant monster is so obviously operated by people inside it. Perhaps I shouldn't be too harsh, as there are reports that just before production commenced, a fire destroyed the original prop and the crew had to concoct what is seen on-screen in just a few days. Having been in similar rush situations on productions, if the story is true, I will concede they made a valiant try, but as Maxwell Smart (Don Adams) said on **Get Smart** (1965-1970), they "missed it by that much." Where, oh, where, is a photo of the original monster?

That's not all, folks – but these were enough!

The Bad and the Ugly

After all of that, here's a breath of fresh air.

Jenny Agutter, as she appears in *Logan's Run*.

One of the very few reasons to watch the movie.

   No.
      Visual.
         Effects.
           Required.

FOOTNOTES

Chapter 1 — Little Things, Big Results

1. Wakeman, John, *World Film Directors*, Vol. 1, 1890-1945, The H. W. Wilson Company, 1987.
2. Ibid.
3. Scorsese, Martin, "*Hugo*, A Very Personal Film, *CBS News Sunday Morning*, April 23, 2012.
4. *LIFE* Magazine, November 22, 1937.
5. Astor, Mary, *My Story: An Autobiography*, Doubleday, 1959.
6. Weaver, Tom, *Interviews With B Science Fiction And Horror Movie Makers: Writers, Producers, Directors, Actors, Moguls and Makeup*, McFarland and Company, 2006.
7. Riley, Philp J. and Welch, Robert A., *The Wizard of MGM*, BearManor Media, 2011.
8. Daynard, Don, "Masters of Miniature Mayhem," *Captain George's Whizzbang*, #16, early 1970s.
9. Trenholm, Richard, "Youth and Ignorance Drove Eye-Popping 'Star Wars' Effects," *C/Net*, May 4, 2017.
   www.cnet.com/news/john-dykstra-star-wars-anniversary-industrial-light-and-magic-special-effects/

Chapter 2 — Spectacle—On Glass

1. Theisen, Earl, *Movie Makers*, November, 1936.
2. Cook, Peter, Interview with Paul Detelfsen.
3. Sersen, Fred W., "Making Matte Shots: Some of the Intricacies of Making Things Seem What They Are Not," *American Cinematographer*, July, 1929.
4. Pal, George, *Astounding Science Fiction*, October, 1953.
5. Haskin, Byron, "Making Modern Matte Shots," *American Cinematographer,* January, 1940.
6. Powell, Michael, *A Life in Movies: An Autobiography*, Mandarin, 1986.
7. MacNab, Geoffrey, "He Made Monsters," *The Independent*, June 20, 2008.
8. Dornisch, Walton and Horowitz, Mark, *Albert Whitlock: A Master of Illusion* (documentary), 1981.
9. Ibid.
10. Kaufman, Helen, "Trickster of the Trade," *Los Angeles Times First Run*, 1978.
11. Ibid.
12. Yuricich, Matthew, "Academy Acceptance Speech," *49th Academy Awards,* 1976.
13. "Discussion with Renowned Matte Painter Syd Dutton and Special FX Supervisor Bill Taylor," New York Film Academy Los Angeles, www.nyfa.edu
14. "A Company Called Matte Effects: The Work of Ken Marschall and Bruce Block," Part 1, May 2, 2015.
    http://nzpetesmatteshot.blogspot.com/2015/05/a-company-called-matte-effects-workof2
15. Damen, Marcel, "David Stipes *Galactica* TV Interview," January 1, 2010.
    www.galactica.tv/battlestar-galactica-1978-interviews/david-stipes-galactica.tv-interview.html.
16. "Interview with Dan Curry," www.startrek.com/startrek/view/community/chat/archive/transcript/1394
17. Shannon, Jody Duncan, "Willow," *Cinefex,* #35, August, 1988.

Chapter 3 — Men In Suits

1. *Movie Weekly*, September, 1923.
2. *Monster Mania* #1, 1966.
3. Ibid.
4. "Jack Pierce Wins the 1932 Makeup Contest," *The Hollywood Filmograph*, January 14, 1933.
5. *Monster Mania* #1, 1966.
6. Smith, Don G., *Lon Chaney Jr.: Horror Film Star 1906-1973*, McFarland and Company, 2004.
7. Eisner, Lotte, *Fritz Lang*, Oxford University Press, 1977.
8. Wells, H.G., *The War of the Worlds*, Harper and Brothers, 1898.
9. Blaisdell, Paul, "The Devil's Workshop," *Fantastic Monsters,* #5, 1962.
10. Cushman, Marc and Osborn, Susan, *These are the Voyages: TOS, Season One,* Jacobs Brown Press, 2013.
11. Gray, Tim, "Planet of the Apes Filmmakers Worried 1968 Original Wouldn't Be Taken Seriously," *Variety*, July 10, 2017.

Chapter 4 — Prop It Up

1. Lizcano, Domingo, e-mail to author, March 19, 2020.
2. Duca, Lauren, "The Hand-Made Magic of 'The NeverEnding Story'," *HuffPost Entertainment*, December 6, 2017.
3. www.starwars.com/news/roger-christian-on-forging-the-lightsaber-hans-blaster-and-more-from-star-wars-a-new-hope
4. *Fantastic Film*s, May, 1980.
5. Goldner, Orville and Turner, George E., *The Making of King Kong*, A.S. Barnes and Co., 1975.
6. Wray, Fay, "How Fay Met Kong or The Scream That Shook The World," *New York Times*, September 21, 1969.

Chapter 5 — Reel Scenes With Real People

1. "After 52 Years With Paramount: Edouart Given 4-1/2 Days Exit Notice," *Variety*, October 13, 1967.
2. *The Journal of the Society of Motion Picture Engineers*, Vol.33, #8, August, 1939.
3. "Lighting Systems: Front Projection Unit For Backgrounds," *New York Times*, August 16, 1964.
4. "Fairchild's Ever-Expanding Universe," *Business Week,* February 22, 1969.
5. Lightman, Herb A., "Front Projection for *2001: A Space Odyssey*," *American Cinematographer*, June, 1968
6. Hansard, Bill, "Creating Front Projection Effects for *Black Sunday*," *American Cinematographer*, August, 1977.
7. Cerone, Daniel, "Movies: Voyage To the Next Dimension: With the Visual Effects Process Introvision," *Los Angeles Times*, January 13, 1991.

Chapter 6 — It's All a Matter of Optics

1. Danforth, Jim, *Dinosaurs, Dragons, and Drama: The Odyssey of a Trickfilmaker*, Vol. 1, 2011.
2. Dunn, Linwood, "Cinemagic of the Optical Printer," *American Cinematographer Manual*, Sixth Edition, 1986.
3. Danforth, Jim, *Dinosaurs, Dragons, and Drama: The Odyssey of a Trickfilmaker*, Vol. 1, 2011.
4. "The New Acme-Dunn Optical Printer," *Journal of the Society of Motion Picture Engineers*, January, 1944.
5. Ibid.
6. Edwards, Graham, "O is for Optical Printer," https://cinefex.com/blog/optical-printer/
7. Hankin, Mike, "Little People Are Shrunken People...," *Ray Harryhausen–Master of the Majicks*, Vol. 3, 2010.
8. Case, George, *Calling Dr. Strangelove—The Anatomy and Influence of the Kubrick Masterpiece*, McFarland and Company, 2014.

Acknowledgements

I extend my sincerest gratitude to the many friends, artists, educators and colleagues whose contributions helped make this an entertaining overview of visual effects B.C. (Before Computers).

Certain visual material and Information appeared previously in *Ray Harryhausen-Master of the Majicks* Vol. 1 (2013), Vol. 2 (2008), and Vol. 3 (2010), by Mike Hankin. Used with permission.

With much gratitude for their help with images from
Lloyd Richards' *Mighty Joe Young* scrapbook and their wonderful exhibition of it:
Dr. Harry Heuser, Exhibition Curator and Art Historian
Neil Holland, Senior Curator
Robert Meyrick, Keeper of Art
Aberystwyth University School of Art Museum and Galleries

Forrest J Ackerman, David Allen, Howard A. Anderson, Jr., Brian Anthony, Colin Arthur, Lee Ashworth, Jim Aupperle, Steven Austin, Dan Baldacchi, Rob Barker, James Belohovek, Jim Bertges, Steven Blasini, Bruce Block, Ted Bohus, David Boston, Tom Brierton, Dave Bryant, Bob Burns, Steve Buscaino, Tom Caldwell, Richard Catizone, Wah Ming Chang, Ken Clark, Webster Colcord, Randall William Cook, Dan Curry, Jim Danforth, Jim Davidson, Al Davis, John Deall, Mervyn J. Dew-Brittain, Roger Dicken, Gavin Doughtie, Jay Duncan, Linwood G. Dunn, Randy Dutra, Jim Earp, Chris Endicott, Ernest Farino, Alan Friswell, Paul Gentry, Rolf Giesen, Wayne Gilbert, Spencer Gill, Rocco Gioffre, Orville Goldner, Mike Hankin, Ray Harryhausen, Bill Hedge, Gail Morgan Hickman, The Higa Brothers, Richard Holliss, Terry Huud, Phil Kellison, Steve Koch, Gregory Kulon, Angus Lamont, Matthew Lamont, Dennis and Sheryl Lancaster, Domingo Lizcano, Ron Lizorty, Howard Lydecker, Ken Marschall, Tony McVey, John Michlig, Terry Michitsch, Darlyne O'Brien (Mrs. Willis O'Brien), Gilles Penso, Neil Pettigrew, Antonio Garcia Jose "Pierrot", Brett Piper, Loren Portillo, Francisco Prósper family, Nick Rashby, Emilio Ruiz del Rio family, Gene Roddenberry, Lee Roop, Douglas Rowan, Ted Rypel, David Sharp, Don Shay, David J. Schow, Pete von Sholly, David Stipes, Mark Sullivan, Bill Taylor, Jeff Taylor, Tom Tomlinson, George Turner, Susan Turner, Joe Viskocil, Gene Warren, Jr., Gene Warren, Sr., Susan Wolf, Norman Yeend, and Kurt Zendler.

I am grateful to the following archives and publications for their generous assistance and contributions:

Peter Cook
   Matte Shot: A Tribute to Golden Era Special FX
   nzpetesmatteshot.blogspot.com

Stephen and Sylvia Czerkas
   The Dinosaur Museum / dinosaur-museum.org

Connor Heaney, Vanessa Harryhausen McKellar, and John Walsh, The Ray and Diana Harryhausen Foundation / rayharryhausen.com

Richard Klemensen
   Little Shoppe of Horrors magazine
   littleshoppeofhorrors.com

Dennis Lynch
   Dennis Lynch's Fantasy Film Archive

Jack Polito
   Jackpolitocollectibles.com

Jeff Sillifant
   Still Things
   stillthings.com

Joey, Diane, Jess and Sonny Vento
   The Haunted Barn Movie Museum
   Movies to Go

Harry Walton
   The Harry Walton Collection
   vfxmasters.com

Stephen C. Wathen
   The Stephen C. Wathen Archives

BIBLIOGRAPHY

"A Company Called Matte Effects: The Work of Ken Marschall and Bruce Block," Part 1, May 2, 2015.
   http://nzpetesmatteshot.blogspot.com/2015/05/a-company-called-matte-effects-workof2.html
"After 52 Years With Paramount: Edouart Given 4-1/2 Days Exit Notice," *Variety*, October 13, 1967.
Astor, Mary, *My Story: An Autobiography*, Doubleday, 1959.
Berry, Mark, *The Dinosaur Filmography*, McFarland and Company, 2005.
Blaisdell, Paul, "The Devil's Workshop," *Fantastic Monsters,* #5, 1962.
Calvin, Sam, "The Comparison Test," *Special Visual Effects Created by Ray Harryhausen ("FXRH")*, #4, Summer, 1974.
Cerone, Daniel, Movies: "Voyage to the Next Dimension With the Visual Effects Process Introvision," *Los Angeles Times*, January 13, 1991.
Clarke, Frank P., *Special Effects in Motion Pictures*, Society of Motion Picture and Television Engineers, 1966.
"Creating Front Projection Effects for 'Black Sunday,'" *American Cinematographer*, August, 1977.
Croydon, John, "Flying Brains", *Fangoria*, August, 1985.
Cushman, Marc and Osborn, Susan, *These Are the Voyages: TOS, Season One*, Jacobs Brown Press, 2013.
Czerkas, Sylvia, *Major Herbert M. Dawley—An Artist's Life, Dinosaurs, Movies, Show-Biz, & Pierce-Arrow Automobiles*, The Dinosaur Museum, 2018.
Czerkas, Sylvia, *Silent Roar—The Dinosaur Films of Herbert M. Dawley* (DVD), The Dinosaur Museum, 2018.
Daynard, Don, "Masters of Miniature Mayhem," *Captain George's Whizzbang,* #16 (early 1970s).
Damen, Marcel David Stipes, *Galactica*, TV Interview, January 1, 2010.
   www.galactica.tv/battlestar-galactica-1978-interviews/david-stipes-galactica.tv-interview.html

Danforth, Jim, ***Dinosaurs, Dragons, and Drama: They Odyssey of a Trickfilmaker,*** Vol. 1, 2011.
"Discussion with Renowned Matte Painter Syd Dutton and Special FX Supervisor Bill Taylor," New York Film Academy/Los Angeles, www.nyfa.edu, October 7, 2014.
Dornisch, Walton and Horowitz, Mark, ***Albert Whitlock: A Master of Illusion*** (documentary), 1981.
Duca, Lauren, "The Hand-Made Magic of 'The NeverEnding Story,'" *HuffPost Entertainment*, December 6, 2017.
Dunn, Linwood, "Cinemagic of the Optical Printer," ***American Cinematographer Manual***, Sixth Edition, 1986.
Dyke, Robert and Skotak, Robert, "Jim Danforth Interview," ***Fantascene***, June, 1976.
Eisner, Lotte, ***Fritz Lang***, Oxford University Press, 1977.
"Fairchild's Ever-Expanding Universe," ***Business Week***, February 22, 1969.
Goldner, Orville and Turner, George E., ***The Making of King Kong***, A.S. Barnes and Co., 1975.
Gray, Tim, "Planet of the Apes Filmmakers Worried 1968 Original Wouldn't Be Taken Seriously," ***Variety***, July 10, 2017.
Guinness World Records online, https://www.guinnessworldrecords.com/world-records/first-animated-film/
Haskin, Byron, ***American Cinematographer***, January, 1940.
Haskin, Byron, ***Cinema Papers***, Australia, March/April 1975.
"How Fay Met Kong, or The Scream That Shook The World," ***New York Times***, September 21, 1969.
"Interview with Dan Curry," http://www.startrek.com/startrek/view/community/chat/archive/transcript/1394
"Interview with Jack Pierce," ***Monster Mania,*** #1, 1966.
"Interview with Val Guest," ***Hammer Horror,*** #7, September, 1995.
"Jack Pierce Wins the 1932 Makeup Contest," ***The Hollywood Filmograph***, January 14, 1933.
Kaufman, Helen, "Trickster of the Trade," ***Los Angeles Times First Run*** (undated).
Kuhn, Annette and Westwell, Guy, ***A Dictionary of Film Studies***, Oxford University Press, 2012.
"Lighting Systems: Front Projection Unit For Backgrounds," ***New York Times***, August 16, 1964.
Lightman, Herb A., "Front Projection for '2001: A Space Odyssey,'" ***American Cinematographer***, June, 1968.
Mandell, Paul, "The Films of Eugene Lourie," ***Fantastic Films***
    — Part 1 (#14, February, 1980)
    — Part 2 (#15, March, 1980)
    — Part 3 (#16, May, 1980)
    — Part 4 (#17, June, 1980)
Movie Weekly, September, 1923.
Pal, George, ***Astounding Science Fiction***, October, 1953.
Pal, George, "Honorary Academy Award for his Puppetoons," www.imdb.com/name/nm0657162/awards
Pettigrew, Neil, ***The Stop-Motion Filmography***, McFarland and Company, 2007.
Powell, Michael, ***A Life in Movies: An Autobiography***, Mandarin, 1986.
Riley, Philp J. and Welch, Robert A., ***The Wizard of MGM***, BearManor Media, 2011.
Scorsese, Martin, "Hugo, A Very Personal Film," ***CBS News Sunday Morning***, April 23, 2012.
Sersen, Fred W., "Making Matte Shots: Some of the Intricacies of Making Things Seem What They Are Not," ***American Cinematographer***, July, 1929.
Shannon, Jody Duncan, "Willow," ***Cinefex***, August, 1988.
Silver, Alain J. and Ursini, James, "Mario Bava–The Illusion of Reality," ***Photon***, #26, 1975.
Smith, Don G., ***Lon Chaney Jr.: Horror Film Star 1906-1973***, McFarland and Company, 2004.
The Film Daily, March 16, 1945.
Theisen, Earl, ***Movie Makers***, November, 1936.
The Journal of the Society of Motion Picture Engineers, Vol. 33, #8, August, 1939.
"The New Acme-Dunn Optical Printer," ***Journal of the Society of Motion Picture Engineers***, January, 1944.
Trenholm, Richard, "Youth and Ignorance Drove Eye-popping 'Star Wars' Effects," C/Net, May 4, 2017. www.cnet.com/news/ john-dykstra-star-wars-anniversary-industrial-light-and-magic-special-effects/
Wakeman, John, ***World Film Directors 1890-1945***, Vol. 1, The H. W. Wilson Company, 1987.
Warren, Bill, ***Keep Watching the Skies***, Vol. 1, McFarland and Company, 1986.
Warren, Bill, ***Keep Watching the Skies***, Vol. 2, McFarland and Company, 1982.
Weaver, Tom, ***Interviews With B Science Fiction And Horror Movie Makers: Writers, Producers, Directors, Actors, Moguls and Makeup***, McFarland and Company, 2006.
Wells, H. G., ***The War of the Worlds***, Harper and Brothers, 1898.
Yuricich, Matthew, "Academy Acceptance Speech," ***49th Academy Awards***, 1976.

Milton Keynes UK
Ingram Content Group UK Ltd.
UKHW050855071123
432124UK00015B/597

9 781629 336534